CANTONESI

Cantonese Colloquial Expressions

廣州話口語詞彙

Compiled and translated by
Lo Tam Fee-yin

盧譚飛燕 編譯

The Chinese University Press

Cantonese Colloquial Expressions（廣州話口語詞彙）
  Compiled and translated by Lo Tam Fee-yin（盧譚飛燕　編譯）

© **The Chinese University of Hong Kong**, 2007

ISBN-10: 962–996–181–4
ISBN-13: 978–962–996–181–7

THE CHINESE UNIVERSITY PRESS
The Chinese University of Hong Kong
SHA TIN, N.T., HONG KONG
Fax: +852 2603 6692
      +852 2603 7355
E-mail: cup@cuhk.edu.hk
Web-site: www.chineseupress.com

Printed in Hong Kong

In memory of my mother

溫碧華女士
Wan Pik Wah

Table of Contents

Preface

The book is a collection of Cantonese colloquialisms emphasizing the metaphorical use of words. Some of them have both a literal and an idiomatic meaning. Take 'faahnwún' as an example, literally, it means 'rice bowl', however, in certain contexts, it means 'job'. Such expressions are originally an appellation of an object, but later acquire the status of idioms when people gradually use them idiomatically to stand for something else. One can also see that the metaphorical use of language involves the interaction of two conceptual contents. People tend to name A in terms of B by mapping the semantic content of B onto that of A.* Both A and B bear a degree of resemblance in certain aspects. Just as 'faahnwún' is a container for the rice that feeds the Chinese, in much the same way, jobs provide the rice that feeds the people. However, for a certain amount of these two-tiered meaning idioms, their idiomatic meanings have become so established that their literal meanings have become more or less obsolete. For example, 'lātsíng máhlāu' originally describes a monkey that is freed from the string that ties it, but now the animal has come to symbolize those naughty children who break away from adults applying disciplinary restraints on them.

Since metaphorical use of language is prevalent in spoken Cantonese in Hong Kong, the knowledge of the idiomatic meaning of a term/phrase can help learners of the dialect have a more effective communication with the Cantonese people and have a better understanding of the messages circulated in the

---

* George Lakoff and Mark Johnson. *Metaphors We Live by* (Chicago: University of Chicago Press, 1980), pp. 85, 108–9.

ix

mass media. Actually, idiomatic expressions should be learned alongside standard Cantonese that expatriate students learn in textbooks. Although a portion of Cantonese idiomatic sayings are deemed as near slang, or even as socially stigmatized vulgarisms, many have decent or even poetic origins.

As with any other language, Cantonese idioms comprise a separate list of vocabulary that is most difficult to learn because an idiom is viewed as a fixed combination of words. However, the overall meaning of an idiom is not the mere sum of its parts. The meanings of idioms are transparent to native speakers, but they are opaque to foreigners who are unfamiliar with the connotations embedded in the new language that they are learning. In order to facilitate efficient and effective learning, literal meanings of most of the idioms discussed in the book are given in English. English equivalents of the idioms are used when the English meaning is relatively transparent since users of this book are of many different nationalities.

It is hoped that users of this book should recognize that it is not an exhaustive presentation of the kind of Cantonese idioms assembled here. Metaphorical use of language is constantly at work, and so any term or phrase can be adopted metaphorically in the spontaneous verbal exchange between interlocutors of Cantonese. There are many people whom I wish to thank, especially Mr. Lo Wood Wai, who answered the many many queries I raised during the preparation of the book. But all errors are my own responsibility. I also thank the two student helpers at The Chinese University of Hong Kong. They are Polly Siu Man-hin, who first helped me with typing the draft, and Fiona Lau Ka-yee, who did the same work for most parts of the book. I would also like to thank Nicole Newendorp, a doctoral candidate at the Department of Anthropology of Harvard University, for reading through and offering some suggestions on the English translations of the text. My colleague Aponte Kwan Choi-wah encouraged me to use the draft version of my work for the course materials of Cantonese Colloquial Expressions when she was Deputy Head of Cantonese Division at the Yale-in-China Chinese Language Center of The Chinese University of Hong Kong. Chang Kwun-hung, also my colleague, and Rev. Fr. James Donovan, C. S. P. have both lent me a helping hand, which I urgently needed in the final stages of the publication of the book. But the book would still have been impossible without the help and effort of Dr. Steven K. Luk, Director of The Chinese University Press, and the editors of the press. Last of all, I am most indebted to the late Mr. Liu Ming, former Director of the Yale-in-China Chinese Language Center, The Chinese University of Hong Kong, who imparted to me the methodology of teaching Chinese as a second language many years ago. Without him, this work would not have been possible.

Lo Tam Fee-yin
(F. Y. Lo)
October, 2006

Explanatory Notes

I. About the framework of the book
1. The entries are divided into nine main areas (see the table of contents), which are put in alphabetical order, but not their sub-divisions.
2. Groups of entries are headed by different keywords.

II. About the keywords
1. A keyword is the word out of which an expression or a group of expressions is generated.
2. The keywords in bold type are listed in alphabetical order.

III. About the entries
1. Groups of entries are listed under a keyword from which they originate, and are put in alphabetical order. For entries made up of two or more keywords, the first keyword is used as the basis for classification.
2. A tick '✓' is attached to the number of any entry if the literal meaning (see 4 below) and the idiomatic meaning (see 5 below) of the entry are both in use.
3. An entry is first introduced in Yale Romanization, followed by Chinese characters, and sometimes by the vernacular form of writing. For a syllable that has no written form in Chinese, a ☐ is used for indication.
4. The literal meaning, preceded by (lit.), of most expressions has become obsolete. However, it contributes to the meaning of an expression when used idiomatically. No parts of speech are given here except that the literal meaning is still in use.

5. The idiomatic meaning, preceded by (idi.), of an expression is intended to be the most crucial part of an entry since it has taken the place of the literal meaning of the expression, and is widely recognized by Cantonese speakers. Parts of speech of the expression are given here. For some expressions, there may be different parts of speech.

6. Different meanings are specified by numbers (1), (2) or (3).

7. A colon in bold type (:) is used to show that what follows is an example sentence. If there is more than one example sentence, the letter ⓐ, ⓑ or ⓒ is used.

8. Example sentences are printed in italics, followed by their translation in English inside the brackets.

9. A '~' is used to stand for the entry in the example sentence, and the idiomatic meaning, or sometimes the literal meaning in its English translation. However, changes in grammatical forms are supposed to be made by the readers where necessary.

10. Cultural notes are given if necessary and are marked by an asterisk (*).

Abbreviations of Parts of Speech

A	adverb
Adj.	adjective
Adj. PH	adjectival phrase
A. PH	adverbial phrase
ATT	attributive (a noun used as modifier of another noun)
BF	bound form
CV	co-verb, which functions like a preposition in English
HIT	Hithauhyúh: enigmatic parallelism or tail-less pun. It is an idiomatic saying made up of two parts where an '→' is inserted in between the parts to mean 'lead to (the real meaning of the saying)'
M	measure, classifiers of nouns
N	noun
NU	number
P	particle, used as an interjection or a suffix to a word
PH	phrase
PN	pronoun
PW	place word
RV	resultative verb, which tells the result of one's doing something
RVE	resultative verb ending (a verb ending indicating the result of one's doing something. It goes with a verb to form a resultative verb [RV])
TS	time spent (the period of time spent in doing something)
TW	time word
V	verb
VO	verb-object compound, which functions like a verb in English and can be split by the modifier(s) of the object, verb suffix(es) or verb ending(s)

Measures and Their Meanings
Used in This Book

bá	:	for something with a handle, human voice or a torch of fire
bāau	:	a packet of
bāt	:	a sum of money
bīn	:	one side
bohng	:	pound
bōu	:	a kettle/ pot of
bouh	:	for a book or a machine
būi	:	a cup/ glass of
bún	:	for a book
chāan	:	for a meal
chàhng	:	a layer/ storey of
chāu	:	a bunch of keys/ fruit
chek	:	(length) foot
chi	:	one time/ occurrence, one count of
chìhng	:	a jar/ jug of
dā	:	dozen
daahm	:	a mouthful of
dāu	:	a bowl of
dáu	:	a Chinese peck of
déng	:	for a hat/ cap
déu/ dó	:	for a flower
dēui	:	a pile/ heap/ crowd of
deui	:	a pair of
dī	:	for plural things
dihk	:	a drop of
dihp	:	a dish/ plate of
doih	:	a bag of

dūk	:	for excrement
faai	:	a thin/ flat piece of, a slice of
fō	:	for an academic subject
fu	:	a set of, a pair of (eye-glasses)
gā	:	for a family/ shop
ga	:	for a car
gāléun	:	gallon
gān	:	(weight) Chinese catty
gauh	:	a (thick) piece/ lump of
geuk	:	one kick
gihn	:	a piece of
go	:	one unit of
gun	:	a can/ tin of
gūngsīng	:	litre
gwan	:	a lash with a rod
gyún	:	a roll of
háu	:	for a nail/ needle
hòhng	:	a row of
hyūn	:	one round of game
jáan	:	for a lamp
jaat	:	a bunch of (flowers)
jah	:	a pinch/ handful of
jahn/ jahm	:	a gust of wind
jek	:	a piece of, for an animal/ insect or a limb/ ghost/ color
jī	:	for something narrow, long and hard/ stiff
jēun	:	a bottle of
jēung	:	a sheet of, a piece of (furniture)
jūng	:	a cup of (with a lid)
júng	:	a kind of
kyùhn	:	a punch of a fist
lāp	:	a tiny piece of
léung	:	(weight) Chinese tael

lūk	:	for something like a thick rod
meih	:	a dish of
ōnsí	:	ounce
ngáahn	:	a glance
ngáan	:	for a nail/ needle/ light
pàahng	:	for teeth
pàaih	:	a bar/ packet of
pāt	:	a bolt of (cloth)
pō	:	a stalk of
pōu	:	a game of, for temper
pùhn	:	a game/ basin of
sān	:	the whole body
sáu	:	for a song/ poem/ transaction
sēung	:	a pair of
tìuh	:	for something narrow, long and soft or for a person one despises
tòhng	:	for an eyebrow/ a ladder
tòih	:	a table of
tou	:	a set of
tóuh	:	a bellyful of
tùhng	:	a roll of (film for a camera)
waahk	:	a stroke of (a Chinese character)
wái	:	a polite measure for people
wohk	:	a pan of
wún	:	a rice-bowl of

A Brief Introduction to Cantonese Pronunciation

A Cantonese syllable is composed of three parts: an initial, a final and a tone.

Initials

An initial is the starting-off sound of a syllable. There are 19 initials.

1. Aspirated stops:	p	t	k	ch	kw
2. Non-aspirated stops:	b	d	g	j	gw
3. Nasals:	m	n	ng		
4. Fricative and Continuants:	f	l*	h	s	
5. Semi-vowels:	y	w			

* 'l' is in free variation with 'n'. To replace 'n' with 'l' does not involve differentiation between meanings.

Finals

A final is the key part of a syllable. There are 51 finals. The main vowel is the most essential part of a final. The vowels may be either long or short. L. is for a long vowel whereas S. is for a short one.

*L.	S.	L.	S.	L.	S.	L.	S.	L.	S.	L.	S.	L.
a		e		eu		i		o		u		yu
aai	ai	eng	ei	eung	eui	iu	ing	oi	ou	ui	ung	yun
aau	au	ek		euk	eun	im	ik	on		un	uk	yut
aam	am			eut		in		ong		ut		
aan	an					ip		ot				
aang	ang					it		ok				
aap	ap											
aat	at											
aak	ak											

Besides, there are two syllabic nasals: 'm' and 'ng'.

Tones

Six tones are used in this book.

Tones are distinguished by a tone mark which is put on the top of the vowel or the first vowel. The letter 'h' is used to signify the lower tones. It should be placed after the vowel(s) and go before the consonant(s). For example:

fā	high level	yùhn	low falling
hóu	high rising	ngáahn	low rising
taai	mid-level	louh	low level

For some people, they would have a high falling tone (53) for the high level one.

Comparative Chart of Yale Romanization and IPA

Yale	IPA
p	p'
b	p
t	t'
d	t
k	k'
g	k
ch	ts
j	dz
kw	k'w
gw	kw
m	m
n	n
ng	ŋ
f	f

Yale	IPA
l	l
h	h
s	s
y	j
w	w
a	a:
aai	a:i
aau	a:u
aam	a:m
aan	a:n
aang	a:ŋ
aap	a:p
aat	a:t
aak	a:k
ai	ai
au	au
am	am
an	an
ang	aŋ
ap	ap
at	at
ak	ak
e	ɛ:
eng	ɛ:ŋ
ek	ɛ:k
ei	ei
eu	œ:
eung	œ:ŋ
euk	œ:k
eui	œi
eun	œn
eut	œt
i	i:
iu	i:u

Yale	IPA
im	iːm
in	iːn
ing	iŋ
ip	iːp
it	iːt
ik	ik
o	o
oi	oːi
on	oːn
ong	oːŋ
ot	oːt
ok	oːk
ou	ou
u	u
ui	uːi
un	uːn
ung	uːŋ
ut	uːt
uk	uːk
yu	yː
yun	yːn
yut	yːt
m	
ng	

Further References

Crystal, David. *The Cambridge Encyclopedia of Language*. 2nd ed. New York: Cambridge University Press, 1997.

Fernando, Chitra. *Idioms and Idiomaticity*. Oxford: Oxford University Press, 1996.

Gibbs, Raymond W. "Why Idioms Are Not Dead Metaphors." In *Idioms: Processing, Structure and Interpretation*, edited by C. Cacciari and Patrizia Tabossi. Hillsdale, NJ: L. Erlbaum Associates, 1993.

Glucksberg, Sam. "Idiom Meanings and Allusional Content." In *Idioms: Processing, Structure and Interpretation*, edited by C. Cacciari and Patrizia Tabossi. Hillsdale, NJ: L. Erlbaum Associates, 1993.

Kwan, Kit-choi. *A Dictionary of Cantonese Colloquialisms in English*. Hong Kong: Commercial Press, 1991.

Lakoff, George, and Johnson, Mark. *Metaphors We Live by*. Chicago: University of Chicago Press, 1980.

Liang, Shiqiu. *Far East Chinese-English Dictionary*. Taipei: The Far East Book Company, 1995.

Lo, Wood Wai, and Tam, Fee Yin. *Interesting Cantonese Colloquial Expressions*. Hong Kong: The Chinese University Press, 1996.

Tam, Fee Yin. "A Cognitive Study on Metaphor in Cantonese." MA dissertation, Hong Kong Polytechnic University, 1997.

White, Geoffrey M. "Proverbs and Cultural Models." In *Cultural Models in Language and Thought*, edited by Dorothy Holland and Naomi Quinn. Cambridge, MA: Cambridge University Press, 1987.

1. Animals

I. Chùhng (insects, worms, and reptiles)

baakjūk 百足 N centipede 蜈蚣 M tìuh

0001

➔baakjūk gam dō jáau 百足咁多爪 (lit.) have as many legs as a centipede 像蜈蚣那樣多爪
(idi.) PH a person who likes to go everywhere (and so others cannot easily get in touch with him) 到處走動的人, (別人很難找到他)：*Kéuih nīgo yàhn, ~, ngóh tái néih dōu géi nàahn wándóu kéuih.* (I think you can hardly find him because he is ~.) (*Nowadays, the expression can also refer to a person having many ways of grabbing money or benefits.)

chùhng 蟲 N insects, worms, bugs 蟲子 M tìuh

0002

➔beihtaichùhng 鼻涕蟲 (lit.) running nose worm 流鼻涕的蟲兒
(idi.) N (1) a small child who has a runny nose 流鼻涕的小孩童 M tìuh/go：*Faaidī maatjó dī beihtai lā, ~.* (Little boy, hurry up and wipe your [runny] nose.) (2) stupid, cowardly and useless person 窩囊/ 愚懦沒用的人 M tìuh：*Gau dáam jauh dá ngóh ā, ~.* (I dare you to beat me! You coward!)

0003

➔chàahmchúng sīyèh 蠶蟲師爺 (lit.) silkworm confidential secretary 像蠶蟲作繭自縛的師爺

(idi.) N a person whose solutions to problems are bad or useless 只能想到壞的或沒有用的辦法的人 M go：*Kéuih jíngyāt haih ~, námmàaih dī síkfu, néih m̀hóu tēng kéuih dím a.* (He always gives others solutions that don't work. Don't rely on his advice that much.)

0004

➔deihtàuhchùhng 地頭蟲 (lit.) bug of a place 專在某一地區出現的蟲子
(idi.) N (1) thug of a place 專在一地方出沒的壞人 M go：*Kéuih haih nīdouh ge ~, ngóhdeih m̀hóu dākjeuih kéuih a.* (He is a bad guy in this place. We'd better not offend him.) (2) (jokingly) a person who knows a place very well (說笑地) 很熟悉一個地方的人 M go：*Kéuih hái nīdouh jyuhjó géi sahp nìhn, haih nīdouh ge ~ .* (He has been living here for decades. He is ~.)

0005

➔(dihnlóuh)chīn nìhn chùhng (電腦)千年蟲 (lit.) N: millennium (computer) bug 電腦千年蟲：*~ haih hóu sāileih ge dihnlóuh behngduhk. Hóu dō dihnlóuh jyūngā séungjeuhn baahnfaat heui deuifuh kéuih.* (~ is a very terrible computer virus. Many computer specialists are exhausting their wits to tackle the problem.)

0006

➔gāi sihk fonggwōng chúng→ sām jī tóuh mìhng 雞食放光蟲

→ 心知肚明 (lit.) chicken eats luminous worms (i.e. firefly)→its heart and stomach will become bright 雞吃了會發光的蟲子,身體內臟都光起來 (idi.) HIT one completely knows what is all about or what one has done 對事情或自己做過的事很清楚 : *Néih jihgéi jouhgwo māt, néih ~ → ~ lā, juhng sáimāt jadai a?* (You ~. Why should you still pretend that you don't know?)

0007

→ hàahmchùhng 鹹蟲 (lit.) salty worm
(idi.) N dirty old man 色迷迷的男人 M tiuh/ go: *Ngóhdeihge gīngléih, jìngyāt ~ làih ga. Néuih tùhngsih yiu síusām dī.* (Our manager is certainly a ~. The lady colleagues need to be cautious.)

0008

→ hàahngwahn yāttiuh lùhng, sātwahn yāttiuh chùhng 行運一條龍,失運一條蟲 (lit.) good luck, a dragon; bad luck, a worm
(idi.) PH everything is great with a person when he is in his heyday, but he'll be like a worm when in adversity 比喻人運氣好及不好時的情形 : *"Kéuih faat gójahnsí, ìnjī géi wāi ; yìhgā móuh dāk lōu, gúpiu yauh cháaulūngjó, móuh lèih sāmgēi gám." "Hàaih, ~, ~ ā ma."* ("He looked gorgeous when he was successful in life. He then lost his job and burned his fingers on the stock market. Now he is in low spirits." "You have learnt about the saying, ~, ~, haven't you?")

0009

→ jáam geukjí beih sāchúng 斬

腳趾避沙蟲 (lit.) cut off the toes to avoid (the bites of) sand worm 為免被沙蟲咬,索性把腳趾斬下來
(idi.) PH make a sacrifice to avoid trouble 為了避免麻煩而作犧牲 : *Waihjó beihmìhn heui gūngchi ge sihhauh béi yàhn tāutái waahkjé tāupaak, gógo ngūkchyūn dī sīnāai, ~, dángdou yáuh yàhn pùih sīnji gám heui.* (To avoid someone peeking at them or taking sneak pictures of them when going to the public toilet, the women residents of that public housing estate ~. They would wait until someone could go with them.) (*There are no private bathroom facilities inside the flats of some old-style public housing estates in Hong Kong. The residents there share a public toilet on each floor.)

0010

→ jūkchùhng 捉蟲 (lit.) (The full form of the expression is 'jūkchùhng yahp sífāt', which means to) catch a worm (and put it into one's anus)捉蟲子(放到自己肛門) (*To avoid vulgarity, some people would just say 'jūkchùhng'.)
(idi.) PH earn oneself trouble 自找麻煩 : *Kéuih jēung kéuih gāan ngūk kèihjūng yātgo fóng chēutjōu, dímjī go jōuhaak sèhngyaht daaimàaih dī ìnsāam ìnsei ge yàhn fāanlàih. Nīchi jānhaih ~ la.* (He rented one of the rooms to a man. But his tenant always brings home with him some triadlike guys. He certainly ~ this time.)

0011

→ jyumáih daaih chùhng 蛀米大蟲 (lit.) weevil, small beetle that feeds on grain 米蟲

2

(idi.) N a good-for-nothing person who only knows how to eat 甚麼也不懂只懂吃的人 M go/ tìuh : *Yáuh dī Hēunggóng yàhn gokdāk Jungwúhn yéuhngláahn yàhn, fáanyih lìhng séhwúi dōjó dī ~.* (Some people in Hong Kong think that the Comprehensive Social Security Assistant Scheme would just make people lazy. The scheme may result in producing more parasites that live on the money of the community.)

0012 ✓
➔jyusyūchùhng 蛀書蟲 (lit.)
bookworm 書蟲 M tìuh
(idi.) N a nerd, one who studies (books) too hard 念書太用功的人 : *Sèhngyaht nēimàaihhái tòuhsyūgún jouh ~, yiu chēutteui wáanháh ji dāk gā ma!* (You always study too hard in the library. You should go out and relax!)

0013
➔(daaih) láahnchùhng (大)懶蟲
(lit.) lazy bug
(idi.) N (very) lazy person (非常)懶惰的人 M go/ tìuh:*Kéuih duhkyùhn syū dōu m̀wán yéh jouh, jìhnghaih sīkdāk mahn bàhbā màhmā lóchín sái, jingyāt ~.* (He had finished his studies, and yet he never looked for a job. He just knew how to get money from his parents. He really was a ~.)

0014
➔laahpsaapchùhng 垃圾蟲 (lit.)
litterbug 製造垃圾的昆蟲
(idi.) N people who throw away rubbish randomly 亂拋垃圾的人 M go/ tìuh : *jūk ~ (catch ~)*

0015✓
➔yāttìuh chùhng 一條蟲 (lit.)
PH a worm, an insect 一條蟲子
(idi.) PH (usually said of babies or very small children) as small and feeble as a worm 嬰孩像一條蟲子那麼弱小 : *hóuchíh ~ gám (~)*

chóumáang 草蜢 N
grasshopper 蚱蜢 M jek

0016
➔fēilòihmáang 飛來蜢 (lit.) a flying in grasshopper 飛來的草蜢
(idi.) N unexpected good fortune (falling on a person suddenly) 突然而來的意外好處 M jek : *Kéuih ngāamngāam sīkjó yāt wái síujé, deui kéuih gwái gam hóu, kéuih yíhwàih haih ~. Dímjī yùhnlòih gówái síujé yáuh oijībehng.* (He just met a lady. She was very nice to him. He took it for an ~. How could he have known that she has Aids.)

mān 蚊 N mosquito 蚊子 M jek

0017
➔mān dōu fan lā蚊都瞓啦(lit.)
even mosquitoes sleep 連蚊子都睡覺了
(idi.) PH it would be too late .... 恐怕太晚了 : *Dáng kéuih làih àh ? ~!* (~ if we wait until he comes.)

0018
➔mānbéi tùhng ngàuhbéi 蚊脾同牛脾 (lit.) the mosquito's legs and the ox's hind legs 蚊子的腿跟牛的腿
(idi.) PH be disparate, so markedly different that comparison is not likely to be made between two things 天淵之別, 無法比較 : *Néih ge sāngā tùhng*

deihcháan daaih wòhng ge sāngā, jānhaih ~ lo. (It's really impossible to make a comparison between your wealth and that of a real estate tycoon.)

0019

➔**mānjī gam saisēng** 蚊蟻咁細聲(lit.) very weak voice like that of a mosquito 像蚊子那樣聲音細小

(idi.) PH very weak voice of a person 比喻人聲音細小：*Kéuih ~, ngóhdeih dím tēngdākgin a?* (How can we hear him talk in such a low voice?)

0020

➔**mānyìhng** 蚊型 (lit.) mosquito style 蚊子的類型

(idi.) ATT (said of area) extremely small (面積)非常細小：*~ láu/ dāanwái* (~ flats)

ngáih 蟻 N ant 螞蟻 M jek

0021

➔**ngáih dō lāuséi jeuhng** 蟻多摟死象(lit.) (even) an elephant would be killed when its body is crawling with ants (連)大象也會被爬滿身上的螞蟻殺死

(idi.) PH union is strength 團結就是力量：*(Láamkàuh choi) géigo kàuhyùhn yúngmàaihheui jaahkjyuh kéuih, jingsówaih ~, kéuih móuh faatjí sehbō.* ([in a rugby match] Some players rushed to him and had him pressed under them. He had no way to shoot then.)

0022

➔**ngáihlāan gám** 蟻闌噉(lit.) crawl like ants 像螞蟻爬行

(idi.) PH walk terribly slowly 比喻人走路太慢：*hàahnglouh ~(~)*

0023

➔**yātsān ngáih** 一身蟻(lit.) with ants crawling all over one's body 滿身是蟻

(idi.) PH be in a troublesome situation 身陷非常麻煩的景況：*Kéuih hái làuhga jeui gōu ge sìhhauh gūngjó yātchàhng láu, hauhlòih kéuih sāangyi sātbaaih, kéuih móuh baahnfaat gūngláu, waahkjé yiu pocháan. Kéuih gúmdou nīchi wúih gáaudou ~.* (He bought a flat with a loan from the bank when flat prices reached a peak. Later he lost money in business and could not afford to pay the instalments. He might go bankrupt too. He had never expected that he would ~.)

sātná 虱嫲 N flea 跳蚤 M lāp/ jek

0024

➔**hóu mèih hóu maauh sāang sāsāt** 好眉好貌生沙虱(lit.) nice looking but having lice (in one's body) 樣貌端好，身上卻有蝨

(idi.) PH (said of a person) be nice in appearance but defective in behaviour 比喻人外表好但行為上有缺點：*Tái kéuih ngoihbíu sīmàhn, daahnhaih yāt hōi háu jauh góng chōuháu, jānhaih ~.* (I find that although he looks gentlemanlike, he starts his speech with bad words. It really is a flaw of him.)

0025

➔**jūk jihsāt** 捉字虱(lit.) catch louse among the (written) words 挑字眼兒

(idi.) VO fool others with (written) words 在文字上愚弄別人：ⓐ *"Gāidáan ditlohk deih m̀laahn." "Dím wúih a?" "Ngóh haih wah 'gāidáan ditlohk, deih m̀laahn' a." "Néih ~ jē."* ("An egg fell on the ground but it did not

4

break." " How come?" "It' refers to 'the ground'." "You just ~.") ⓑ *"Gwónggou seuhngbihn maih wah máaih láu sung gāsī gé, dímgáai móuh a?" ' 'Sung' haih 'sungfo', mhaih 'jahngsung'." "Néih ~ jē."*("Didn't it say in the ad that furniture was given for free to flat buyers? Why didn't you keep your word?" "We meant to 'deliver' the furniture for you, not to 'give it away for free'." "You just ~.")

0026

➔lóuhfú tàuhseuhug dēng sātná 老虎頭上釘虱乸(lit.) kill lice on the tiger's head 在老虎頭上捏死蝨 (idi.) PH beard a lion in his den, dare offend bad or powerful people 太歲頭上動土 : *Dī chaahk yahpheui Gíngmouhchyúh jéung ngūkkéi tāuyéh! Jānhaih ~ lo!* (The thieves got into the Police Commissioner's house and stole! How gutsy they are!)

0027

➔yātmaht jih yātmaht, nohmáih jih muhksāt 一物治一物，糯米治木虱(lit.) there is always something that can control one thing, and so (it is believed that) glutinous rice can kill wood lice 一種東西一定有別的東西可以克制它 (idi.) PH there is always mutual control among things or people in the world 東西或人都有自己的剋星 : *Kéuih hái gūngsī yàhnyàhn dōu pa kéuih, daahnhaih fāandou ngūkkéi, kéuih jauh pa kéuih taaitáai jānhaih, ~, ~ lo.* (Everyone fears him in his company. But when he is at home, he is hen-pecked. His wife certainly controls him/ is his boss.)

sèh 蛇 N snake 蛇 M tìuh

0028

➔dá sèhbéng 打蛇餅(lit.) snake coils itself 蛇把身體盤繞蜷 (idi.) VO a long queue that looks like the coil of a snake 長長的人龍圍成圈 : *Fóchējaahm ngoihbihn yáuh hóu dō yàhn pàaihdéui, ~.* (There are many people outside of the railway station lining up in ~.)

0029

➔dásèh 打蛇(lit.) beat a snake 打蛇 (idi.) VO (1) search for students who have sneaked into a university hostel to stay overnight 搜尋大學走讀生未經許可在宿舍留宿 : *Séhgāam bunyé ~, daahnhaih wātsèh ge hohksāang yáuh kéuihdeih jihgéi ge baahnfaat.* (The hostel warden ~ at midnight, but the students who snake in have their own way [to manage to escape].) (2) search for illegal immigrants 搜尋非法入境者,偷渡客 : *Gíngfōng hái sāanbīn ~, jūkdóu géigo fēifaat yahpgíngjé.* (The police ~ on the hillside and caught several illegal immigrants.) (3) find out lazy employee 捉拿開小差的僱員 : *Nīgo bouhmùhn yáuh hóudō yàhn sèhwòhng, sóyíh seuhngtàuh yiu ~.* (There are many lazy people in this department. So our boss wants to find them out.)

0030

➔dásèh chèuih gwan séuhng 打蛇隨棍上 (lit.) you beat a snake (with a rod) and it just creeps up the rod (用杖)打蛇, 它卻沿著杖爬上來 (idi.) PH take advantage of something at the right moment 乘機, 把握大好機會 : *Ngóh gin lóuhsai jaan ngóhdeih, jauh*

~ *giu kéuih gāsān*. (Seeing that our boss gave good evaluations of our performance, I availed myself of the opportunity to ask him for a payraise.)

0031
➔ **faht háu sèh sām** 佛口蛇心
(lit.) Buddha's mouth but snake's heart 佛口蛇心
(idi.) PH a wolf in sheep's skin 人面獸心 : *Nījek lóuh wùhléi ~, yātmihn wah néih jouhdāk hóu, yātmihn giu seuhngtàuh cháau néih*. (This cunning old fox/ man is ~. He told you that you did a good job, but on the other hand he asked our superior to fire you.)

0032
➔ **fongsèh** 放蛇 (lit.) let the snake go 把蛇放到／進一個地方
(idi.)VO arrest law-breakers by means of undercover police (lurking in the criminals' den) 喬裝了的警察混入歹徒的地方伺機捕捉他們 : *Gíngfōng ~ yahppheui gógāan sīkchìhng kālāōukēi, sihgēi yāt dou, gíngyùhn jauh bíulouh sānfán, jēung dī meih sihngnìhn siunéuih tùhng piuhhaak daaifāan gíngchyúh*. (The policemen, posed as customers, got into the alleged vice karaoke bar. When it was the right time, they identified themselves. They took all the underage girls and the customers to the police station.)

0033
➔ **fútàuh sèhméih** 虎頭蛇尾 (lit.) tiger's head but snake's tail 老虎的頭蛇的尾巴
(idi.) PH start something with a vigorous beginning but fail to see it through 虎頭蛇尾 : ⓐ *Jouhyéh ~ gám, bīndouh wúih sihnggūng ga?* (How can you accomplish

anything if you ~?) ⓑ *Sān bōsí ngāamngāam làih ge sihhauh, yáuh hóu dō daaih gaiwaahk, yìhgā móuh saai sēnghei, ngóh tái dōu haih ~ ge jē*. (When our new boss first came, he appeared to be very constructive. But now everything seems quiet. I think he just ~.)

0034✓
➔ **jūksèh** 捉蛇 (lit.) catch a snake 捉蛇
(idi.) VO see 0029

0035
➔ **léuhngtàuh sèh** 兩頭蛇 (lit.) two-headed snake 有兩個頭的蛇
(idi.)N a Jack on both sides, a person who alternates between two opposing parties 騎牆派 : *Néih mhóu jēung dī gēimaht ge yéh béi kéuih jī a, kéuih jingyāt haih ~ làih ga*. (Please don't let him know the confidential information about our group. He really is ~.)

0036
➔ **sāangsèh** 生蛇 (lit.) have a snake (grown on one's body) 生了一條蛇
(idi.) VO suffer from Herpes Zoster (* It is a kind of skin disease whose symptom is a tape-like rash around the patient's body as if he were entangled by a snake.) 生牛皮癬,患者身上出現帶狀疹環繞身體,如被蛇纏繞 : *Ngóh buijek ~, gwái gam tung*. (I ~ on my back. It's so painful.)

0037 ✓
➔ **sèh** 蛇 (lit.) N snake 蛇 M tìuh
(idi.)V be lazy in one's work, play truant 躲懶,開小差 : *Kéuih yīnggōi háidouh hōigūng ge bo, kéuih ~ jó heui bīn nē?* (He is supposed to be doing his job here.

Where has he sneaked off to?) Adj. (said of employees) lazy 懶惰 (的僱員)：*Kéuih jouhyéh hóu ~.* (He is very ~ in his work.)(* 'Sèh' , when used as an adjective, is the short form of 'sèh wòhng' , see 0043.)

0038
➔sèh dōu séi lā 蛇都死啦 (lit.) even snake would die 連蛇都會死
(idi.) PH it would be too late …., a more emphatic expression than 'mān dōu fan lā' 太晚了,比'蚊都瞓啦'所表示的程度更強：see 0017

0039
➔sèhgwē 蛇□ (lit.) snake arouses fearfulness 蛇令人驚怕
(idi.) Adj. chicken-hearted 膽小及很容易受驚：*Kéuih nīgo yàhn hóu ~ ge, yūkdī jauh heui tái yīsāng.* (He is a ~ person. He will go to see a doctor whenever he is just a little not feeling well .)

0040
➔sèhsyú yātwō 蛇鼠一窩 (lit.) snakes and rats mixed together in the same den 蛇跟老鼠混在一起
(idi.) PH gang up with each other 朋比為奸：*Kéuihdeih léuhnggo, ~, dōu haih séung ngāak néihge chín.* (The two of them conspired to cheat you of your money.)

0041✓
➔sèhtàuh 蛇頭 (lit.) N snake's head 蛇的頭 M go
(idi.) N 'snakehead', illegal immigrant smuggler 偷運人蛇的主腦 M go：*~ jēung dī yàhnsèh chòhnghái syùhnchōng ge ngamgaak léuihbihn, daahnhaih dōu juhng haih béi séuiging faatyihn.* (The smuggler hid the illegal immigrants in the

secret place in the cabin. But they/ the IIs were still found by the water police.)

0042
➔sèhtàuh syúngáahn 蛇頭鼠眼 (lit.) snake's head and rat's eyes 蛇的頭跟老鼠的眼睛
(idi.) PH triad-looking, look wily 樣貌鬼祟, 不似是好人：*Tái kéuih go yéung, ~ gám, dōu m̀fōng haih hóu yàhn lā.* (See what he looks like! He looks like a bad guy. I can hardly believe that he is a good man.)

0043
➔sèh wòhng 蛇王 (lit.) king of the snakes 蛇中之王
(idi.) Adj. lazy (employee) 工作時間開小差：*Kéuih jouhyéh hóu ~.* (He is ~ in his work.) also see 0037 (*In Hong Kong, a snake soup seller would pose a billboard by affixing 'sèhwòhng' to his name. He would also act as a snake catcher for the Agricultural and Fishery Department on the discovery of a snake in public premises.)

0044
➔seingáahn sèh 四眼蛇 (lit.) four-eyed snake 有四隻眼睛的蛇
(idi.) N a nick name for a male teacher/ officer wearing eyeglasses 戴眼鏡的男老師或政府職員 M go/ tiuh：*Yānwaih kéuih daai ngáahngeng, sóyíh dī hohksāang tùhng kéuih héijó go fāméng, giu kéuih jouh ~.* (Because he wears glasses, therefore, the students gave him a nickname and called him ~.)

0045
➔séisèh laahnsíhn 死蛇爛鱔(lit.) dead snake and rotten eel 死了的蛇跟腐了的鱔魚

7

(idi.) PH (1) too lazy to lift a finger 懶得不想動：*Tái kéuih (hóuchíh) ~ gám, tek dōu ṁyūk.* (Look! He is ~. He won't move even when you kick him.) (2) dead tired 疲倦得不想動：*guihdou ~ gám* (be ~) (3) sleep soundly/ like a log 十分熟睡：*fandou ~ gám* (~)

0046

➔séuh 蛇 (lit.) N a transliteration of 'sir' when addressing male teachers or policemen in Hong Kong 是英語 sir 的音譯，用來稱呼男性老師或警察：ⓐ *A- ~, chéng mahn fóchē jaahm dím heui a?* (Hi, ~, would you tell me how to get to the railway station?) ⓑ *A ~ wah gogo dōu kahpgaak.* (Our teacher said that everyone of us passed the exam.)

0047

➔séuisèh chēun gam chèuhng 水蛇春咁長 (lit.) as long as the string of spawns laid by a water snake 好像水蛇下的卵子那樣連綿不斷
(idi.) PH (usually said of word[s]) very long (通常指文字)很長：ⓐ *Yandouh tùhng Dūngnàahma dī yàhn ge sing hóuchíh ~.* (The surnames of the Indians and the people in Southeast Asia are ~.) ⓑ *Kéuihdī hàahmtàuh dōdou hóuchíh ~.* (He has many titles [printed on his name card] which look ~.) ⓒ *Hóudō sāiyeuhk ge méng hóuchíh ~.* (The names of many Western medicines are ~.)

0048

➔wātsèh 屈蛇 (lit.) coil the snake 把蛇盤蜷
(idi.) V (1) immigrate illegally (mostly by hiding in a ship) (坐船)偷渡：ⓐ *~làih/ heui* PW (~ to a place) ⓑ *hái*

fóchē seuhngbihn ~ (~ by train) (2) (said of non-boarding university students) snake in, stay overnight in a hostel without permission 大學走讀生未經許可在宿舍留宿：see 0029 (1)

0049

➔yàhnsām bātjūk sèh tān jeuhng 人心不足蛇吞象 (lit.) a very greedy person is like a snake that wants to swallow even an elephant 人心不足蛇吞象
(idi.) PH be never content 永遠不滿足：*Gāmyaht béi Jungwùhn kéuih, tīngyaht yauh wah yiu yáuh gūngngūk, gódī sān yìhmàhn jānhaih ~.* (This time you give them the Comprehensive Social Security Assistance, next time, they'll ask for a public housing flat. The new immigrants are really ~.)

0050

➔yàhnsèh 人蛇 (lit.) man snake 人蛇
(idi.) N illegal immigrants / IIs 非法入境者，偷渡客 M go：ⓐ see 0041 ⓑ *síu ~* (child ~) ⓒ *néuih ~* (woman ~)

0051

➔yātjīu béi sèh ngáauh, sāamnìhn pa chóusihng 一朝俾蛇咬，三年怕草繩 (lit.) a person bitten by a snake will shy away from ropes for three years 一旦被蛇咬，三年不敢近繩子
(idi.) PH once bitten, twice shy ; a burned child dreads fire 驚弓之鳥：*Jihchùhng seuhng chi cháaulūng gúpiu jīhauh, ngóh ṁgám joi wáan gúpiu la, ~, ~ ā ma.* (Since I got my fingers burned/ lost money on the stock market last

time, I dare not play the market any more. You see, ~.)

0052

➔yùhnpèih sèh 軟皮蛇 (lit.) soft-skinned snake 軟皮的蛇

(idi.) N (1) an inert person 不能振作的人：*Giugihk kéuih dōu m̀yūk, hóuchíh ~ gám.* (No matter how I urge him, he won't move. He is ~.) (2) a person indifferent to blame 對別人的責備沒甚麼反應的人：*Néih laauh kéuih kéuih dōu hóuchíh ~ gám, jānhaih móuh kéuih sāu.* (He did not react to my rebuke. I just can't handle him.)

wōngàuh 蝸牛 N snail 蝸牛 M jek

0053

➔móuh hok wōngàuh 冇殼蝸牛 (lit.) snail without shell 沒有殼的蝸牛

(idi.) N a person having no house to his name 沒擁有房子的人 M jek：ⓐ *Kéuih maaihjó láu wàahnjaai, yihgā binsihng ~.* (He sold his house to pay off the debts, now he is ~.) ⓑ *Ngóh ge sāuyahp sihngyaht dōu jēui m̀séuhng làuhga, sóyíh dou yihgā juhng haih ~.* (My income can never catch up with property prices, so I don't have a house of my own yet.)

wūyīng 烏蠅 N fly 蒼蠅 M jek

0054✓

➔dá wūyīng 打烏蠅 (lit.)VO hit a fly 打蒼蠅

(idi.)VO arrest the petty officals (in a major crime but fail to arrest the high officials involved) 在大宗案件之中捉

拿犯事的小官員 (卻未能捉拿犯事的大官員)：*ICAC/ Lihmchyúh ge háuhouh haih dá lóuhfú, m̀haih ~.* (The slogan of the Independent Commission Against Corruption [in Hong Kong] is to beat the tiger/ arrest the high officials, not to ~.) also see 0249

0055

➔màahngtàuh wūyīng →lyuhn jūng lyuhn johng 盲頭烏蠅→亂椿亂撞 (lit.) a heady/ blind-headed fly flies in every direction to find the right way out 被困的蒼蠅→四處胡亂飛竄

(idi.) HIT a bull in a china shop, run helter-skelter to find one's way out 在陌生的環境中四處尋找出路：*Yānwaih móuh yàhn daaijyuh bāan síu hohksāang chāamgūn bokmahtgún, sóyíh kéuihdeih hóuchíh ~ gám → ~.* (No one showed the primary students around in the museum, so they became ~.)

0056✓

➔paak wūyīng 拍烏蠅 (lit.)VO kill the flies (with a fly swat) (用蒼蠅拍) 打蒼蠅

(idi.) VO (a symbolic way of saying) business is bad 比喻生意不好：*Yihgā gīngjai sēuiteui, hóudō yàhn sātyihp, dī poutáu jauh ~.* (There is [economic] recession here. Many people have lost their jobs and ~ in shops.)(*The expression may have originated from food shops, where the employees can just kill the flies when business is bad.)

0057

➔wūyīng lāu máhméih → yātpaak léuhngsaan 烏蠅摟馬尾→一拍兩散 (lit.) a fly stings the

9

horse's tail→ with one wag (of the horse's tail), the fly is driven away (and there is no more connection between the two creatures) 蒼蠅飛在馬的尾巴上→馬兒把尾巴一搖,蒼蠅飛走了(,二者分開了)

(idi.) HIT smash up an co-operation and each one goes his way 把事情弄糟,然後各走各路 ：*Kéuihdeih yìhchìhn haih yātgāan chàhlàuh ge gúdūng. Daahnhaih sāumēi faatsāng ngaaugiuh, móuh faatjí hahpjok lohkheui, yūsih jauh ~ → ~. Sóyíh gāan chàhlàuh jāpjó lō.* (They were shareholders of a teahouse. But later they had dispute with each other. They found they could not be partners any longer. So they ~, and the teahouse was closed down.)

II. Yùh (aquatic animals and amphibians)

baahkja 白鮓 **N jellyfish** 水母
M jek/ go

0058 ✓
➔baahkja 白鮓 (lit.)N jellyfish 水
母 M go/jek
(idi.) N traffic policeman (who wears a
uniform with long white sleeves) (穿上
有白色長袖制服的)交通警察 M go :
*Kéuih jáchē chūng hùhngdāng, dím jí
béigo ~ táigin, chāau kéuih pàaih.* (He ran
the red light and was caught by a ~ who
then gave him a ticket.)

gaplá 蛤姆 **N toad** 蟾蜍 **M jek**

0059
➔ bīn (douh/ syu) yáuh gam
daaihjek gaplá chèuih gāai tiu ā
邊(度／庶)有咁大隻蛤姆隨街
跳吖 (lit.) how could there be such a
big toad jumping on the street (and let
people catch it for food) 怎會有那麼
大的蟾蜍在街上隨處跳(被人捉來吃)
呢
(idi.) PH there is no free lunch in the world
(either said with incredulity or as a warning)
天下間那會有這麼便宜的事呢 :
*Géichīn mān yáuh yātkā jyunsehk, juhng
yáuh mihnggwai jàhngbán tūm, ~?* (The
diamonds are sold at several thousand
dollars a karat, and the gifts [upon
purchasing the diamonds] are expensive.
That's incredible because usually you can't
get them with that little money.)

gwāi 龜 **N tortoise, turtle** 烏龜
M jek

0060
➔diu gāmgwāi 釣金龜 (lit.)
catch a gold tortoise with a fishing pole
釣金龜
(idi.) VO look for a very rich man and
marry him, hook a rich husband 找一
個很有錢的人嫁 : *Kéuih chāamgā
syúnméih ge muhkdīk, yāthaih séung
yahp yùhlohkhyūn, yāthaih séung
jĕunglòih hóyíh ~.* (Her purpose of
participating in the beauty pageant is
either to enter into showbiz or ~ later.)

0061
➔gāmgwāisai 金龜婿 (lit.) gold
tortoise husband 金龜夫婿
(idi.) N very rich husband 很有錢的丈
夫 M go : *ga go ~ (marry a ~)*

0062 ✓
➔gwāidáan 龜蛋(lit.) N tortoise's
eggs 龜生的蛋 M jek/go
(idi.) N (a term of abuse) son of a bitch
Néih nīgo ~! (You ~!)

0063
➔gwāigūng 龜公 (lit.) male
tortoise/turtle 雄性的龜
(idi.) N (a term of abuse) (1) pimp,
pander 扯皮條的男人 M tiuh/ go (2)
man operator of a brothel 開妓院的男
人 M tiuh/go (3) a man whose wife has
an affair with another man 妻子與別人
有染的男人 M go : *Kéuih jouhjó ~ dōu
m̀jī .* (His wife ~ and yet he doesn't
know.)

0064

➔gwāipó 龜婆 (lit.) N female tortoise/turtle 雌性的龜
(idi.) N (a term of abuse) procuress/woman operator of a brothel 鴇母,淫媒 M go/ tiuh: *Kéuih yíhchìhn haih jouh ~ ge.* (She was a ~.)

0065

➔lóuhsyú lāai gwāi → móuh dehng màaihsáu 老鼠拉龜→冇定(地)埋手 (lit.) a rat wants to drag the tortoise→(but) it does not know where to put its hands
(idi.) HIT not know where or how to start 不知從何入手： *Nīgo sān gēi dōjó hóudō jai, ngóh yíhgā làih yuhng, daahnhaih ~ → ~.* (The new machine has many more switches. I want to use it now but I don't ~.)

0066

➔ sūktàuh gwāi 縮頭龜 (lit.) a tortoise draws back its head (into its shell) 把頭縮進殼裏的龜
(idi.) N coward, a person (usually a man) who cannot face up to difficulty or adversity 懦弱不敢面對困難或逆境的(男)人 M jek: *Yàhndeih hādou néih séi néih dōu ìngám chēutsēng, jíngyāt ~ làih ge.* (You dare not utter a word when being humiliated by them. You are a ~ !)

hā 蝦 N shrimp, prawn 蝦 M jek; gān

0067

➔baahkcheuk hā 白灼蝦 (lit.) N lightly boiled shrimp 放在沸水中煮熟的蝦 M gān; dihp： *Sihk ~ sīnji sihkdóu hā ge sīn meih.* (You can taste the freshness of shrimp only when you eat ~.)

0068

➔cháauhā chaakháaih 炒蝦拆蟹 (lit.) sauté the prawns and tear open the crabs 炒蝦跟拆開螃蟹
(idi.)PH use foul language 說粗言穢語： *Nàahmyán ngaaigāau, yātdihng wúih ~ ge la.* (Men certainly will ~ when quarreling.) (* Both 'hā' and 'háaih' have a pronunciation close to a bad word in Cantonese.)

0069

➔ (hóuchíh) sāang hā gam/ gám tiu (好似)生蝦咁/嗽跳 (lit.) (like) a shrimp floundering up and down on the ground 好像蝦在地上上下跳動
(idi.)PH very furious, dance with rage 非常生氣： *nāudou ~* (~/ be outrageous like ~)

0070

➔ yàuhséui hā 游水蝦 (lit.) swimming shrimp 游泳的蝦
(idi.)N very fresh shrimp (which still can swim before cooking as seafood) 非常新鮮的蝦 (在烹作海鮮之前仍是鮮活的) M gān： *~ jeui hóu yuhnglàih baahkcheuk.* (The best way to cook ~ is by using 'baahkcheuk', which means 'to lightly boil'. Also see 0067)

háaih 蟹 N crab 螃蟹 M jek; gān

0071

➔baahnháaih 扮蟹 (lit.) pose as a crab 裝成蟹的樣子
(idi.) VO be tied up (like a crab that one buys in the market) 像蟹那樣的被綁著： *Yáuh chaahk dágip gógāan gūngsī, sóyáuh ge jíkyùhn dōu yiu ~.* (Some

thieves robbed the company. All the staff were ~.)

0072
➔cháauhā chaakháaih 炒蝦拆蟹 see 0068

0073✓
➔daaihjaahpháaih 大閘蟹 (lit.) N a kind of fresh water hairy crab tied up for sale 大閘蟹 M jek ; gān
(idi.) N one who is losing money on the stock/ property market or in speculative business is like a tied up crab which cannot do anything about the situation 投資正在虧本,資金不能調動,像被綁不能動彈的螃蟹 M go/jek : *Ngóh yìhgā jouh jó ~, m̀jī géisih sīnji hóyíh sūng bóng.* (I have my money locked up in speculation. I don't know when I can get my money back.)

0074
➔daaihsehk jaakséi háaih 大石責死蟹 (lit.) a crab is killed with a rock weighed down on it 大石把螃蟹壓死
(idi.) PH to crush/be crushed by force 持勢強迫別人做事 : *~, gīngléih yātdihng yiu ngóhdeih jouh, ngóhdeih séung m̀jouh dōu m̀dāk lā!* (We cannot but do it since it is imposed on us by our manager.)

0075
➔dóusé lòh háaih 倒瀉籮蟹 (lit.) the bamboo basket is dropped and the crabs inside all come out and crawl everywhere 竹籮傾側,裏面的螃蟹全溜出來
(idi.) PH all in a muddle, a chaotic situation that one can hardly handle 情

況混亂,不知如何收拾 : *Ngóh daihyāt yaht heui sān gūngsī séuhnggūng, māt dōu m̀suhk, hóuchíh ~ gám.* (The first day I went to my new office, I had a hard time handling the details of my job.)

0076
➔yātháaih bātyùh yātháaih 一蟹不如一蟹(lit.) the crab now is not as good as the one before 一蟹不如一蟹
(idi.) PH (said of performance or ability) not as good as one's predecessor/ those going before you 每況愈下, 一批不如一批 : *Yìhgā dī hohksāang, jānhaih ~, Jūng Yīngmán yuht làih yuht chā.* (The students now are worse than those before because their proficiency of Chinese and English are declining.)

0077
➔yùhngeuk háaih 軟腳蟹 (lit.) soft-legged crab 軟腳的螃蟹
(idi.) N slow down in running or racing 跑路或賽跑時慢了下來 M jek : *Dihnsih seuhngbihn yáuh choimáh yìhnchèuhng jihkbo, go máhpìhnggā wah, "Nī jek máh sàhnchōu ge sihhauh johngtaai hóu hóu ge, m̀jī dímgáai yìhgā binsìhng jek ~ (gám)."* (The horse-race is being broadcast live from the race course on TV, and the commentator says, "This horse was in good shape in the morning drill, I don't know why now it ~ like a ~.")

laaihāmōu 癩蛤蟆 **N** toad 癩蛤蟆 **M jek**

0078
➔ laaihāmōu séung sihk

13

tīnngòh yuhk 癩蛤蟆想食天鵝肉 (lit.) a toad wants to eat swan (meat) 癩蛤蟆想吃天鵝肉 (idi.) PH impossible dream 妙想天開，不自量力 ： *Néih nīnjek kùhnggwái séung chéui yàhndeih chīngām síujé! Jānhaih ~ lo.* (You are as poor as a church mouse but you want to marry that lady from a rich family. How dare you have such an ~.)

làihmāang 泥鯭 N rabbit fish
泥鯭 M tìuh

0079 ✓

➔diu làihmāang 釣泥鯭 (lit.) catch rabbit fish (with a fishing pole) 釣泥鯭

(idi.) VO (said of taxi drivers) pick passengers going to the same destination and charge each one of them a fare 的士司機讓的士坐滿想到同一目的地的乘客，然後逐一收費 ： *Jáujóu fàahnmòhng sihgaan, yáuh dīksí hái gāaiháu ~.* (During rush-hours in the morning, you can find at the end of the streets some taxi drivers who ~.) (*When fishing for rabbit fish, people use an 'octopus hook', which has eight fish hooks, so they can catch several fish at a time.)

0080

➔làihmāang dīk 泥鯭的(lit.) N a taxi used by the drivers to pick passengers going to the same destination and charge each of them a fare 釣泥鯭的計程車 see 0079 M ga ： *Yáuh dī yàhn gokdāk chóh ~ fōngbihndī.* (Some people find it more convenient to take ~.)

ngohkyùh 鱷魚 N crocodile
鱷魚 M tìuh

0081

➔daaihngohk 大鱷 (lit.) big crocodile 大的鱷魚 (idi.) Adj. unfriendly and triadlike 樣子不友善又不像好人 ： *Kéuih go yéung hóu ~.* (He looks ~.) N (1) a man who looks unfriendly and triadlike 樣子不友善又像黑社會的人 M tìuh (2) speculative tycoon (on the stock market) 在股市中興波作浪的大戶 M go; dī ： *Nīpáai gúsíh daaih héi daaih dit, haih yānwaih yáuh dī ~ háidouh gáaugáaujan, dī síu gúmàhn yiu síusāmdī sīnji hóu.* (Recently there have been fluctuations on the stock market. It is caused by the ~. Ordinary investors/ shareholders should be cautious.)

síhn 鱔 N eel 鱔魚 M tìuh; gān

0082

➔baahksíhn séuhng sātāan → m̀séi yātsān sàahn 白鱔上沙灘→唔死一身潺 (lit.) a white eel gets on shore→even if it does not die, it gets awfully slimy all over 白鱔走到沙灘上，就算牠不死，也會弄得滿身粘滑泥潯，不好受 (idi.) HIT will be in a very troublesome situation 比喻情況很糟糕，將有大麻煩 ： *Yùhgwó ngóhdeih kwāihūng gūngfún ge sih béi yàhn kitchyūn, ngóhdeih jauh ~ →.* (We ~ if people know we took the money of our company for private use.)

0083

➔séisèh laahnsíhn 死蛇爛鱔 see 0045

Tìhngāi 田雞 **N frog** 青蛙 **M jek**

0084

➔tìhngāi gwohòh → gok yáuh gok yaang 田雞過河→各有各蹺 (lit.) (like) frogs crossing the river →each goes its way 像青蛙各自游走 (idi.) HIT each one goes his way 各人有各人的目標去向 : *Gáuchāt jíchihn, hóudō Hēunggóng yàhn yiu yìhmàhn, hóuchíh ~ gám → ~.* (Many people in Hong Kong emmigrated to foreign countries before 1997. They are like ~ → ~.)

yú 魚 **N fish** 魚 **M tìuh**

0085 ✓

➔baahkfaahnyú 白飯魚 (lit.) N silver fish 銀魚 M tìuh ; gān
(idi.)N cheap old-fashioned tennis shoes (made of rough white cloth) (用白色粗布做的)廉價舊式運動鞋 M jek ; deui : *Hohkhaauh móuh kwāidihng jeuk mātyéh wahnduhng hàaih séuhng táiyuhk tòhng, sóyíh yáuhdī hohksāang jeuk mìhngpàaih wahnduhng hàaih, yáuhdī jauh jeuk ~.* (The school didn't say what kind of tennis shoes the students should put on when having physical education. Some of them wear tennis shoes of well-known brands, and some just put on ~.)

0086

➔ cháau yàuhyú/ yáu 炒魷魚/魷 (lit.) stir-fry squid 炒魷魚
(idi.) VO fire/ dismiss an employee 解僱／開除 : ⓐ*Lóuhsai ~ jó kéuih ~.* (Our boss ~ him.) ⓑ*Kéuih béi gūngsī*

~. (He was ~ by our company.) ⓒ*Ngóh ~ lóuhbáan/ jihgéi ~.* (I resigned/ quit my job.)

0087

➔ dahtngáahn gāmyú 突眼金魚(lit.) gold fish with protruding eyes 眼睛突出來的金魚
(idi.) N a person with protruding eyes 眼睛突出來的人 : *Kéuih sēung ngáahn yáuh dī dahtdátdéi, hóuchíh ~.* (His eyes are a little protruding like those of a gold fish.)

0088 ✓

➔ diuyú 釣魚 (lit.)VO go fishing 釣魚
(idi.) VO doze (while sitting) 坐着打瞌睡 : ⓐ *Léuihhàhng wùihchìhng gójahnsí, hóudō yàhn hái chē seuhngbihn ~.* (Many people ~ on the tour bus when they returned from the trip.) ⓑ*Hahjau séuhngtòhng, hohksāang yáuhsìh wúih ~.* (Sometimes, students will ~ in afternoon classes.)

0089 ✓

➔gāmyùhgōng 金魚缸 (lit.) N aquarium for gold fish 金魚缸 M go
(idi.) PW (a place) the Stock Exchange 進行股票買賣的地方/ 股票交易所 M go : *Kéuih teuiyāu jīhauh, jēung dī teuiyāugām tàuhjī gúpiu, sóyíh yahtyaht dōu làuhyi ~ ge sīusīk.* (After he retired, he invested his pension in stocks and shares. So every day, he wants to hear the news from ~.)

0090 ✓

➔hàahmyú 鹹魚 (lit.) N dried salted fish 鹹的乾魚 M tìuh ; gān
(idi.) N corpse, dead body 死屍 M

tiuh : Go *chaahktáu fānfu dī sáuhah,* "*Jēung tiuh ~ dámlohk hói.*" (The gang leader told his men, "Throw the ~ away into the sea.")

0091

→ hàahmyú fāansāang 鹹魚番生 (lit.) salted fish comes to life again 鹹的乾魚復活
(idi.) PH revive, resume prosperity 恢復生機 : *Gúsíh diṭjó gam noih, nī go yuht ~ la.* (The stock market has been bad for a long time. It ~ this month.)

0092✓

→hàahmyùh chēngchoi 鹹魚青菜 (lit.) PH salted fish and green vegetables
(idi.)PH very simple meal (usually of a poor family) (通常指窮苦人家的)簡單的飯菜 : *Ṁsái chāanchāan dōu daaihyùh daaih yuhk ge, yáuhsìh sihkháh ~ dōu géi hóu ā.* (You don't need to have a rich meal every time. Sometimes a ~ will do you good.)

0093 ✓

→hùhngsāamyú 紅衫魚 (lit.) N red cloth fish (*People can easily buy it in local market. Its proper name is 'golden thread fish'.) M tiuh ; gān
(idi.) N an old way of referring to HK$100 香港面額一百元的紙幣 M jēung

0094

→maaihyùhlóu sáisān → móuhsaai sēnghei 賣魚佬洗身 →冇晒(腥氣→)聲氣 (lit.) the fish monger takes a bath→and the fishy smell on him is all gone 賣魚的人洗澡之後→他身上的腥味全消失了

(idi.) HIT not any news or any sign of hope 全沒有消息／跡象 : *Ngóh séseun heui gógāan gūngsī sānchíng fahn gūng, gam loih dōu móuh wùihyām, ngóh tái dōu haih ~ → ~ ge lo.* (I sent a letter to that company to apply for a job a long time ago, but I haven't gotten any reply yet. I think there would not be ~.) (*A pun is made on 腥氣[fishy smell] and 聲氣 [hopes, news]. Both of them are pronounced 'sēnghei'.)

0095

→mahkyùh chē 墨魚車 (lit.) a car for octopus 載墨魚的車
(idi.) N cars that expel too much exhaust 排出大量廢氣的汽車 M ga : *Ṁgwaaidāk louhbīn wūyíhm jísou gam gōu lā, gam dō ~!* (There are so many ~. That's why the roadside pollution index is so high.)

0096 ✓

→sādīnyú 沙甸魚(lit.) N sardine 沙甸魚 M tiuh ; gun
(idi.) N passengers on a very crowded bus/ train 公共交通工具上擠擁的乘客 : *Hái fāahnmòhng sìhgaan, deihtit/ fóchē/bāsí seuhngbihn ge sìhnghaak bīkdou hóuchíh ~ gám.* (During rush-hours, the passengers on the MTR/ train/ bus are packed like~.)

0097

→sātwàhnyú 失魂魚 (lit.) fish without soul 沒有魂魄的魚
(idi.) N absent-minded person 常忘記東西的人 M go/tiuh : *Kéuih nīgo ~, sìhngyaht ṁgeidāk nīyeuhng ṁgeidāk góyeuhng.* (He is an ~. He always forgets this or that.)

16

0098

→sehkgáugūng → chūng bāan 石九公→充斑 (lit.) a kind of fish that looks like garoupa→so it pretends to be a garoupa 石九公很像石斑魚→所以牠冒充石斑

(idi.) HIT an ordinary man who pretends to be a man of status 普通人冒充高級人士 : *Kéuih chēutyahp dōu jeuk sāi jōng, dátāai, yauh wah jihgéi jouh gīngléih, kèihsaht kéuih haih ~ → ~ jē!* (Whenever he goes out, he puts on a suit and a necktie. He also tells people that he is a manager. In fact, he is only ~.)

0099 ✓

→séuiyú 水魚 (lit.) N terrapin, freshwater turtle (which is killed and cooked as a kind of tonic food) 鱉,用作滋補的食物 M jek

(idi.) N (usually said of customers) be easily taken advantage of by others 容易被人欺騙錢財的人（通常指顧客）M go/ tiuh : *Yùhgwó jēung yàuhhaak dong (jouh) ~, gám jauh wúih yínghéung léuihyàuhyihp ge la.* (If tourists are treated as suckers, there will be a bad influence on tourism.)

0100 ✓

→taatsā撻沙 (lit.) N sole fish, flat fish 鰨目魚 M tiuh

(idi.) N slippers 拖鞋 M jek; deui : *tēt deui ~* (put on a pair of ~)

0101

→ tòhngséui gwán tòhngyùh 塘水滾塘魚 (lit.) fish in a pond can just swim in the same pond 塘裏的魚只能在該個塘中翻滾

(idi.) PH group members grab benefits from one another 同一團體的成員互相尋找利益 : ⓐ *Kéuihdeih géi hīngdaih jímuih dápáai/ dóuchín, maih ~.* (They, the brothers and sisters, are playing mahjong/ gambling together. They win money from people of the same family.) ⓑ *Deihcháansēung yáuh méeh lēk jē, maih ~, jaahnläih jaahnheui dōu haih Hēunggóng yàhn ge chín.* (Who do you think they are? The property developers in Hong Kong just grab money from people in the territory.)

0102

→ yàuhséui yú 游水魚 (lit.) swimming fish 游泳的魚

(idi.) N very fresh fish (which still can swim before cooking as seafood) 非常新鮮的魚（在烹作海鮮之前仍是鮮活的）M tiuh; gān : *~ hóusihkgwo syutchòhng yú.* (~ taste better than frozen fish.)

0103 ✓

→ yú 魚 (lit.) N fish 魚 M tiuh; gān

(idi.) Adj. (a pun is made on it to mean) very embarrassed (跟'瘀'同音) 尷尬,出洋相 : *Ngóh béi yàhn siu, gokdāk hóu ~.* (I feel ~ being teased by others.) V embarrass someone by teasing him 取笑別人令人覺得尷尬 : *béi yàhn ~* (be teased and embarrassed by others)

0104 ✓

→yùhláahm 魚腩 (lit.) N fish belly 魚的腹部 M go

(idi.) N frequent loser in mahjong game 打麻將常輸的人 M go : *Hóudō yàhn jūngyi tùhng kéuih dá màhjeuk, yānwaih kéuih haih ~.* (Many people like to play mahjong with him because he is a ~.)

III. Níuh (birds and poultry)

baahkgap/ gáap 白 鴿 **N pigeon, dove** 白色鴿子 **M jek**

0105

→baahkgap/ gaap ngáahn 白鴿眼 (lit.) white pigeon's eyes 白色鴿子的眼睛 M deui/ sēung

(idi.) Adj. snobbish 勢利: *Kéuih nī go yàhn hóu ~ ge, (táigin) néih jeukdāk gam gwōngsīn/ (jīdou) néih haih daaih lóuhbáan, sīnji deui néih gam hóu jīufū.* (He is a ~ person. He gives you good service just because you are well dressed/ you have business of your own.) N snobbish eyes (of a person) 勢利眼 M deui/ sēung: *Kéuih géisìh sāangjó deui ~ a?* (When has he grown a pair of ~/ become so snobbish?)

0106 ✓

→dá baahkgap/ gaap jyuhn 打白鴿轉 (lit.) (said of a pigeon) hovers around 鴿子在空中盤旋

(idi.) VO roam around and then return to the old place (like a pigeon) 到附近走走再回來: ⓐ*Fēigēi meih gonglohk jīchìhn ~ go ~ sīn.* (Before landing, the plane hovered in the air.) ⓑ*Chan juhng yáuh hóudō sìhgaan sīnji gau jūng, ngóh (heui fuhgahn) ~ go ~ sīnji fāanlàih.* (Since there is still a lot of time [before the appointed time], I'll walk around and then come back.)

gāi 雞 **N chicken** 雞 **M jek**

0107

→baaisàhn m̀gin gāi 拜神唔見

雞 (lit.) lose a chicken (as a sacrifice) when worshipping an idol 拜祭神靈的時候不見了(作祭品)的雞

(idi.) PH murmurous sound of a complaint 低聲埋怨: *Kéuih sìhngyaht ngàhmngàhm chàhmchàhm, hóuchíh ~ gám.* (He is murmuring all the time as if he is complaining about something.) (*A chicken is offered most often when one is paying tribute to an idol. S/he would mumble prayers. But now the chicken is gone, so her/ his prayers turn into a complaint.)

0108

→bōlòhgāi → kaau chī 波羅雞 → 靠黐 (lit.) Bolo Temple's (paper-pasted) hen →(it) all depends on the stickiness 波羅廟裏用紙做的雞→全靠黏糊

(idi.) HIT a grabber of petty benefit (usually a free meal) 喜揩油水, 佔人小便宜的人 (通常指飲食): *Máih gam gūhòhn sìhngyaht jouh ~ (→ ~) dāk gá, wán yātchi chéng yàhndeih sihkfāan chāan lā.* (Don't always be so stingy and get free meals from others. Do treat people to a meal some time.)

0109

→chàahnggāi 俵雞 (lit.) the gamecocks of Làuh Chóng 劉錩的鬥雞 (* Làuh [around A.D. 947] was the king of the Southern Han. It is said that he loved watching cock fight.)

(idi.) Adj. (said of a woman) shrewish and contentious, not ladylike (女人)像

18

潑婦：*Nīgo néuihyán hóu ~ ge.* (This woman is ~.)

0110

➔daaih gāi m̀sihk sai máih 大雞唔食細米 (lit.) a big chicken does not eat small rice 大的雞不吃小的米 (idi.) PH not want to do something of little remuneration (*Usually, the status of the person descriptive of this idiom is not commensurate with what he will earn.)不屑做酬勞少的事：*"Kéuih dá màhjeuk, jí sihk sāamfāan waahkjé baaupàahng." "Kéuih haih màhjeuk jyūngā, gánghaih ~ lā."* ("He only wants royal flush or grand slam when playing mahjong." "Of course! He is an expert at mahjong. He certainly has no interest in winning little money.)

0111

➔daaih gāi sāam méi 大雞三味 (lit.) with a big chicken, you can make three (routine) dishes 一隻大的雞可以做三個菜 (idi.) PH one can only make limited tricks out of something but it's enough to get by 可預料的,有限的種類：*Sāiyī yīmouhsó léuihbihn ge yeuhk dōuhaih ~ jē: gámmouh, sēungfūng, kāt, jītung, haih gam dō jīma.* (What you can find in a Western doctor's clinic are just limited kinds of medicine, say, drugs for healing flu, cold, cough and relieving pain. That's all and that's enough, too.)

0112

➔dīn gāilá 癲雞乸(lit.) crazy hen 瘋了的母雞 (idi.) N furious woman 非常忿怒的女人 M jek：*Kéuih yìhgā hóuchíh jek ~*

gám. (Now she is mad about something like a ~.)

0113

➔faat gāi màahng mè 發雞盲咩 (lit.) as blind as a chicken at night 像夜盲的雞 (idi.) PH a term of abuse at one when bumping into others 撞到別人,給別人罵的說話：*~ ! Johngséi yàhn la!* (Are you blind? It hurts me so much when you bump into me!)

0114

➔ga gāi chèuih gāi, ga gáu chèuih gáu 嫁雞隨雞，嫁狗隨狗(lit.) when you marry a chicken, follow it; or when you marry a dog, follow it 嫁雞隨雞,嫁狗隨狗 (idi.) PH (said of a woman) defers to her husband in whatever he does and follows him wherever he goes (妻子)跟隨丈夫的決定去做：*~, ~, go lóuhgūng yiu yìhmàhn ge, jouh lóuhpòh ge gánghaih yiu gānjyuh heui lā, m̀tūng béi go lóuhgūng jouh taaihūngyàhn mè!* (A woman should ~. If her husband wants to emigrate to foreign places, she should go along with him. Would it be good for the husband to live without his wife?)

0115 ✓

➔gāi 雞 (lit.) N chicken 雞 M jek (idi.) N (1) hooker, prostitute 妓女 M go：ⓐ *jouh* ~ (a woman who prostitutes herself) ⓑ *giu* ~ (visit / call a ~) (2) whistle 哨子 M go：*kàuhjing chēui ~* (the referee blew his ~)

0116

➔gāibéi dáyàhn ngàhgaau yùhn

19

雞脾打人牙較軟 (lit.) a chicken's thigh would beat a person's jaw soft 用雞腿打人，會令人牙關軟

(idi.) PH beat a dog with a bone and it will not howl, convince somebody by means of the benefits you offer him 動人以利：~, néih béi dōdī chín kéuih, táiháh kéuih juhng haih m̀haih m̀háng bōng néih jouh ā. (~. You give him more money and see if he is still not willing to do it for you.)

0117

→ gāichēun gam maht dōu bouhchēut gāijái 雞春咁密都暴出雞仔 (lit.) the chick can still be hatched even though it is sealed in the egg 雞蛋雖是密封的,可是裏面的小雞還是可以孵出來

(idi.) PH the cat will eventually be let out of the bag, the secret will eventually be known 秘密始終會被人知道：Saigaaiseuhng móuh jyuhtdeui ge beimaht ge, ~ ā ma. (There is no absolute secret in the world. Don't you know that ~?)

0118 ✓

→ gāichéung 雞腸 (lit.) N chicken's intestine 雞的腸子 M tiuh

(idi.) N (written) English (which looks snaky) (寫的)英文 (看起來彎彎曲曲) M dī：ⓐ Lóuhyàhngā dōsou m̀sīk ~. (Most elderly people cannot read ~.) ⓑ Hahptùhng seuhngbihn gódī ~, yiu leuhtsī sīnji hóyíh yùhnchyùhn mìhngbaahk. (Only lawyers would completely understand the ~ written on the contract.)

0119

→ gāidau 雞竇 (lit.) coop 雞聚居的地方

(idi.) N/PW brothel, vice den 妓院,色情架步 M go：Yíhchìhn gódouh yáuh hóudō ~. (There were many ~ there.)

0120

→ gāi dēung m̀tyúhn 雞啄唔斷 (lit.) (like) chicken pecking ceaselessly 雞不停地啄食

(idi.) PH/A.PH talk and talk and talk (showing no sign of stopping) 說話不停(多指女性)：Wòhng sīnsāang dánggán kéuih taaitáai, daahnhaih Wòhngtáai juhnghaih ~ gám tùhng pàhngyáuh góng dihnwá. (Mr. Wong is waiting for his wife, but she still ~ to her friend on the phone.)

0121

→ gāi fēi gáu jáu 雞飛狗走 (lit.) chickens fly and dogs flee 雞飛狗走

(idi.) PH (1) people's panicky reaction in order to get away from the scene 人們四處逃跑的慌亂情形：Yáuh go chīsinlóu jáijyuh bá dōu chèuihgāai jáam yàhn, or：Gíngféi hái fàahnmòhng ge gāai seuhngbihn faatsāng chēungjin, gāai seuhngbihn dī yàhn haakdou ~. (A crazy man was wielding his chopper and trying to slay the passers-by at random, or: The police and the bandits were exchanging fire on the busy street, people were terrified and ran away.) (2) said of people who are in disorder and it seems difficult to get control of them 人們四處亂跑,不守秩序：Dī hohksāang móuh sīnsāang daaidéui, sóyíh ~, móuh saai dihtjeuih. (The students had no teacher to lead and oversee them [during the school outing], so they scattered all around. No one knew that they should keep order.)

0122

➔ gāi gám geuk 雞噉腳 (lit.)
have a pair of feet like that of a chicken
像雞那樣的腳
(idi.) A.PH go away hurriedly and
stealthily (like a chicken) (像雞那樣)溜
走 : *Kéuih yāt tēnggin wah yiu kéuih
chéng yámchàh jē jauh ~ jáujó la.* (As
soon as he knew that we wanted him to
treat us to dimsum, he ~.)

0123

➔ gāi hùhng 雞紅 (lit.) chicken red
雞的紅色
(idi.) N chicken blood 雞血 M dī :
Yìhgā dī yàhn hóu síu sihk ~ la. (Now
people seldom eat ~.)

0124

➔ gāijái mùihyán 雞仔媒人
(lit.) chicken as match-maker 小雞做
媒人
(idi.) N go-between (who does a
thankless job for people) 為人們作吃
力不討好的工作 : *Seuhngchi ngóh
bōng kéuihdeih gaaisiuh daaihgā hahpjok,
sāumēi kéuihdeih fáanjó mín. Ngóh
wahgwo mjoi jouhmàaihsaai dī ~.* (That
time I introduced them to each other
and they cooperated. Later, they became
enemies. I swear that I won't be a ~
any more.)

0125

➔ gāijáisēng 雞仔聲 (lit.) voice
of a chick 小雞的聲音
(idi.) N (originally said of a Cantonese
opera actress) voice that is not sonorous
enough 聲線柔弱幼嫩,不夠響亮(多
指粵劇女演員) : *Kéuih bá ~, dím
jouhdāk fādáan ga?* (She has a ~. How
can she play the leading female role in
the opera?)

0126

➔ gāiméih 雞尾 (lit.) chicken's
tail 雞的尾巴
(idi.) ATT cocktail 雞尾 : ⓐ ~ jáu (~,
a kind of drink) ⓑ ~ jáuwúi (~ party)
N chicken's rump 雞的屁股 M go :
Lóuhyàhngā jūngyi sihk ~. (Elderly
people like to eat ~.)

0127

➔ gāimòuh ngaaphyut 雞毛鴨
血 (lit.) chicken feathers and duck
blood 雞的毛鴨的血
(idi.) PH suffer very heavy losses 損失
嚴重 : *Kéuih hái ngóhdeih ngàhnhòhng
jouh gīngléih gójahnsí, kwāihūng
gūngfún, hóudō waaihjeung dōu
sāuṁdóu, yìhgā ngàhnhòhng juhng yiu
syūnbou pocháan. Nīchi jānhaih béi kéuih
leuihdou ~.* (When he worked as
manager in our bank, he stole the bank's
money for his private use. Many bad
debts could not be recovered. Now the
bank has to claim bankruptcy. This time
he really caused us to ~.)

0128

➔ gāiná/ lá gam daaih jek jih 雞
乸咁大隻字 (lit.) written characters
as big as a hen 像母雞那樣大的字
(idi.) PH very large character(s) 寫得
很大的字 : *"~ néih dōu táiṁdóu àh?"
"Yānwaih ngóh hóu sāam gahnsih."*
("You can't see even those ~?" "Because
I have very bad eyes.")

0129 ✓

➔ gāingáahn 雞眼 (lit.) N
chicken's eye(s) 雞的眼睛 M jek; deui
(idi.) N corns grown on a person's foot

長在腳上的肉粒 M lāp : *jek geuk sāang* ~ (have ~)

0130 ✓

➔ gāisáhn 雞腎 (lit.) N chicken's digestive organ 雞的消化器官 M go
(idi.) N little purse for small coins 盛零錢的小錢包 M go : *ṁginjó go* ~ (lost the ~)

0131

➔ gāisāmjóu 雞心棗 (lit.) N chicken-heart shaped dates 像雞心形狀的棗子 M go/ lāp; gān : *yuhng ~ bōutōng* (make soup with ~)

0132

➔ gāi sáu ngaap geuk 雞手鴨腳 (lit.) chicken's hands and duck's feet 雞的手跟鴨子的腳
(idi.) A. PH clumsy in doing menial work 做事笨手笨腳 : *Nàahmyán jyúfaahn dōsou dōu haih* ~ *ge la.* (Most men are clumsy when doing cooking.)

0133

➔ gāiseui gam dō 雞碎咁多 (lit.) as little as chicken-feed 像餵食雞隻的飼料那麼少
(idi.) PH very little (money) 很少(錢) : *"Néih jouh gófahn gīmjīk haih maih hóudō chín a?" "~ jī ma."* ("Can you earn much money from your part-time job?" "No, ~.")

0134

➔ gāiseui gam dō dōu yiu dēung 雞碎咁多都要啄 (lit.) peck even the little feed of a chicken 就算像養雞用的那樣少的飼料也要把它吃掉
(idi.) PH grab as many benefits as possible even though they are petty in nature (because several small streams feed a river) 雖然利益很少,也要奪取 (因爲集少可以成多) : *Hái gāaibīn paakchē dōu yiu yahpchín àh ? Jingfú jānhaih* ~. (People have to feed the parking meters when they park their cars on the street. The government wants to ~.)

0135

➔ gāi sihk fonggwōngchúng →sām jī tóuh mìhng 雞食放光蟲→心知肚明 see 0006

0136

➔ gāi tùhng ngaap góng 雞同鴨講 (lit.) (like) a chicken talking to a duck 雞跟鴨子談話
(idi.) PH people talking in their own languages/ dialects find it difficult to communicate with one another 操不同語言/方言的人很難溝通 : *Kéuih haih Seuhnghóiyàhn. Ngóh haih Gwóngdūngyàhn. Yùhgwó ṁhaih daaihgā dōu sīk Póutūngwá, jauh wúih* ~ *ge la.* (He is from Shanghai and I am Cantonese. We would be like ~ if we didn't know Mandarin.)

0137

➔ jājyuh gāimòuh dong lìhngjin 揸住雞毛當令箭 (lit.) hold a chicken feather and take it for an arrow used as a token of authority (* Such an arrow was usually ornamented with a kind of feather.) 拿著雞的毛就把它當是令箭
(idi.) PH put on airs, assume authority by means of cheap/unreliable device 狐假虎威 : *Kéuih chíhjyuh tùhng gīngléih ge múi paaktō jauh* ~. (Relying on the fact that he is the boyfriend of the manager's sister, he ~ in the office.)

0138

➜ jáugāi 走雞 (lit.) gone the chicken 雞跑了

(idi.) VO miss a chance/ an opportunity 錯失機會 : *Gógo síufáan daaihsēng gám ngaai, "Faaidī máaih la wei, ìmmáaih jauh ~ la!"* (The vendor cried, "Come and buy! Otherwise, you'll suffer loss.")

0139

➜ jihng gāi gāi/ jihngjíng gāi 靜雞雞／靜靜雞 (lit.) as quiet as a chicken (walking) 像雞（走路時）那樣靜

(idi.) A.PH quietly and stealthily 一聲不響地 : *~ jáujó* (sneaked away)

0140

➜ jūk wòhnggeuk gāi 捉黃腳雞 (lit.) catch a yellowfeet chicken 捉黃色腳的雞

(idi.) VO blackmail a man by catching him when he is committing adultery, and the woman turns out to be a conspirator of the gang 捉姦在床,用來勒索錢財 : *béi yàhn ~* (be blackmailed by a gang when one is caught committing adultery)

0141

➜ jūngwān gāi 椿瘟雞 (lit.) plagued chicken 得了瘟症的雞

(idi.) N a person walking recklessly is likely to bump into others 走路不小心,隨時會碰到別人 : *hàahnglouh hóuchíh jek ~ gám* (walk like a ~)

0142

➜ lohktōng gāi 落湯雞 (lit.) chicken falls into soup 落湯雞

(idi.) N (a person) soaking wet from rain 被雨水濕透身體,很狼狽 : *Kéuih béi yúh dahpdou hóuchíh ~ gám.* (He is ~.)

0143

➜ lùhngléuih gāi jokfáan 籠裏雞作反 (lit.) chickens inside the coop raise a rebellion 籠子裏的雞做反

(idi.) PH internal squabble 內鬨 : *Gógo hāak séhwúi ~, gógo daaihlóu ge máhjái fānsihng sāampaai.* (That triad society is having an ~. The gang leader's men have split into three groups.)

0144

➜ móuh yím gāilùhng→jihchēut jihyahp 冇掩雞籠→自出自入 (lit.) a coop without a flap→so the chicks can go out and come in freely 沒有掩扉的雞籠,小雞可自由出入

(idi.) HIT a place where people can come and go (and so sometimes there may be theft) 大眾可自由出入的地方（所以或許會有偷竊事情發生）: *Ngóhdeih séjihláuh jingyāt haih ~ làih ga, néih chēutyahp jeui hóu sómùhn.* (Our office is really ~. You'd better lock your door when you go out.)

0145

➜ ngok gāiná/ lá 惡雞乸 (lit.) fierce hen 很兇的母雞

(idi.) N a shrew/ bad-tempered bullying woman 惡婦 M jek/ go: *Kéuih laauh yàhn gójahnsí hóu ngok, hóuchíh jek ~.* (She's like a ~ when she's mad at somebody.)

0146

➜ séigāi chaang faahngoi 死雞

撐飯蓋 (lit.) a dead chicken (still) props up the lid of the rice cooker 死了的雞(還)把炊具的蓋撐起
(idi.) PH (said of a person) being defensive in speech and showing strong reluctance to yield 錯了還強辯：*Mìhngmìhng haih néih ìhngāam la, juhng ~.* (Obviously it is your fault but you still want to go on defending yourself against us.)

0147
→ tàhngāi 騰雞 (lit.) trembling chicken 顫抖的雞
(idi.) Adj. (said of a person) in a flurry and a little frightened 人坐立不安、慌張的樣子：ⓐ *Kéuih nīgo yàhn hóu ~ ge.* (He is a person who is always ~.) ⓑ *Néih ìhsái gam ~, kéuih ìhwúih laauh néih ge.* (You don't have to be ~. He won't blame you.)

0148
→ tāugāi 偷雞 (lit.) steal chicken 偷雞
(idi.) VO (1) avail oneself of a moment of rest (at the expense of the empolyer) 工作時偷閒：*Búnlòih ngóh yīnggōi hái gūngsī jouhyéh ge, ngóh yìhgā ~ chēutheui yám būi gafē sīn.* (I am supposed to be working in the office, but now I have sneaked out to enjoy a cup of coffee.) (2) skimp material 偷工減料：*Dī ginjūk gūngyàhn héiláu ge sihhauh ~ / yuhng síujó chòihlíu, sóyíh héichēutlàih ge láu yáuh mahntàih la.* (The construction site workers ~ / use less than enough of the material needed when building the house. Now it has a lot of problems.)

0149
→ tāugāi ìhdóu siht jā máih 偷雞唔到蝕渣米 (lit.) try to steal a chicken but end up losing a handful of rice (used as a bait to attract the chicken) 偷不到雞時還浪費了一手用來作餌的米
(idi.) PH fail to gain benefits and suffer loss at the same time 得不到預期的好處反而有損失：*Ngóh yíhwàih chéng gīngléih sihk géi chāan faahn, dá màhjéuk yauh dahkdāng syūchín béi kéuih, kéuih jauh wúih sīng ngóh, dímjī kéuih fātyìhngāan chìhjīk, nīchi jānhaih ~ lo!* (I treated our manager to meals, and I deliberately lost money to him in mahjong game, hoping that he would promote me. But suddenly he quit our company. This time I am really a fool because I ~.)

0150
→ titjéui gāi 鐵咀雞 (lit.) iron-mouthed chicken 用鐵做咀巴的雞
(idi.) N quarrelsome woman, a woman with a sharp and bitter tongue 說話厲害喜爭辯的女人 M jek/ go: *Gójek ~, ìhjí nàahmyán ìhjūngyi kéuih, lihn néuihyán dōu pajó kéuih.* (Not only men dislike that ~, but also women are disgusted by her.)

0151
→ yātsìh ìhtāugāi jouh bóujéung 一時唔偷雞做保長 (lit.) a person now acts as a judge / becomes a senior of the village though he used to steal chickens 一次不偷雞就做村裏的長老
(idi.) PH moralize others when one is not doing something bad 一時不做壞事就教訓別人：*Kéuih giu yàhn ìhhóu*

bāau yihnāai, kèihsaht kéuih ~ jī ma, kéuih jihgēi dōu bāaugwo yihnāai lā. (He admonished/ told others not to have a mistress. But he is not qualified to do so because he had one before.)

0152

→ yáuh gāijái m̀gún gún màh/ ngàh yīng 有雞仔唔管管麻／牙鷹 (lit.) not discipline (one's own) chickens but interfere with the eagle (自己的)小雞不管要管鷹
(idi.) PH mind your own business (but not other's) 不管好自己的事，卻管別人的事：*Néih m̀hóu wah yàhndeih dī sáuhah la, néih jihgéi dī sáuhah lē, ~.* (Don't criticize others' subordinates. What about yours? ~.)

hók/ hok 鶴 N crane 鶴 M jek

0153

→ tōng baahkhók 劏白鶴 (lit.) kill a white crane
(idi.) VO vomit after one is drunk 酒醉後嘔吐：*Tàuhsīn kéuih hái jáugā tùhng yàhn déui jáu, yihgā hái gāaidouh ~.* (He has drunk too much with others in the restaurant and now he is vomitting on the street.)

jegū 鷓鴣 N partridge 鷓鴣 M jek

0154

→ gahm jegū 拎鷓鴣 (lit.) press down the partridge (before it escapes and then catch it) 按下鷓鴣不讓牠飛走,然後把牠捉住
(idi.) VO get the evidence of someone's wrongdoing and then blackmail him for money 找到別人錯處然後勒索他：

Kéuih béi yàhn ~. (He was blackmailed to pay money because someone had gotten the evidence of his wrongdoing.)

jeukjái/ jéuk 雀仔／雀 N little bird 鳥兒 M jek

0155

→chóijéuk 彩雀 (lit.) colourful bird 彩色羽毛的小鳥
(idi.)N a woman dressed showily 打扮得花枝招展的女人 M jek：*dabaahndou hóuchíh jek ~ gám* (dressed up like a ~)

0156 ✓

→gāmsījéuk 金絲雀 (lit.) N canary 金絲雀 M jek
(idi.) N a beautiful woman who is finanically well supported by a man but has no freedom (*She is just like a beautiful bird confined in a cage.) 給有錢男人供養但沒有自由的美麗女性 M jek：*Gógo néuih mihngsīng béi go yáuhchínlóu bāauhéi jīhauh, jauh jyuhhái kéuih ngūkkéi, daahnhaih m̀hóyíh chèuihbín chēutgāai, hóuchíh jek ~ gám.* (That movie star was 'taken care of' by a rich man, and lived in his big house but couldn't go out. She's just like a ~.)

0157

→ hōilùhngjéuk 開籠雀 (lit.) the flap of the cage is open and the released bird rejoices in singing 鳥籠打開了,鳥兒高興得放聲唱歌
(idi.) N (a person) bursts into chatter 喜愛不停說話 M jek：ⓐ *Kéuih yāt gindóu yàhn jauh hóuchíh jek ~ gám ge la.* (Whenever he sees his friends, he ~.)
ⓑ *Dī hohksāang séuhngtòhng ge sihhauh m̀jéun góngyéh, daahnhaih yāt lohktòhng*

chēutjó fosāt jauh hóuchíh ~ *gám.* (The students are not allowed to chat in class. But after class, they walk out of their classroom and ~.)

0158 ✓
➔ **màhjéuk** 麻雀 (lit.) N sparrow 麻雀 M jek
(idi.) N mahjong 麻將牌 M jek ; tòih ; pōu ; hyūn ; fu : *dá* ~ (play ~)

0159
➔ **màhjéuk sēui síu, ńgh johng kēui chyùhn** 麻雀雖小，五臟俱全 (lit.) although the sparrow is small, yet it has all the five viscera 麻雀雖小、五臟俱全
(idi.) PH (said of a place) has all the required facilities though small (and so it can function well) 面積雖小但設備齊全 : *Hēunggóng ge ngūk sēuiyihn hóuchíh dauhfuhyéun gam sai, daahnhaih* ~, ~. (The flats in Hong Kong are as small as a bean curd cube, but you can find all the necessary facilities inside them.)

0160
➔ **syuh seuhngbihn ge jeukjái dōu béi kéuih tamlohklàih** 樹上便嘅雀仔都俾佢氹落嚟 (lit.) even birds in the tree would be attracted by him and fly down 就算是樹上的鳥兒也會被他哄下來
(idi.) PH a person having an oily tongue 說話油腔滑調,擅於說服人 : *"Kéuih góngyéh hóu lēk ga,* ~ *a." "Gám, kéuih jeui ngāam jouh gīnggéi la."* ("He can talk very well. He can move people with his honeyed words." "Well, being a broker would be the best job for him.")

līugō 了哥 N mynah 八哥兒 M jek

0161
➔ **chēut līugō** 出了哥 (lit.) let the mynah out 把八哥兒放出來
(idi.) VO cheat by means of tricks 用小詭計騙人 : *Yùhgwó tùhng kéuihdeih jāang, ngóhdeih yātdihng wúih syū ge, ngóhdeih yiu* ~ *yèhng kéuihdeih sīnji dāk.* (We will certainly lose if we compete with them. We'd better use some tricks if we want to win.)

0162
➔ **wòhngpéisyuh līugō→m̀suhk m̀sihk** 黃皮樹了哥→唔熟唔食 (lit.) a mynah in a whampee tree→it does not eat the unripe fruit/ it only eats the ripe fruit 黃皮樹上的八哥,專挑熟的果子吃
(idi.) HIT a person who cheats his friends (out of their money) 欺騙熟悉朋友(的錢財) : *"Kéuih béi pàhngyáuh ngāakjó yātbāt chín bo." "Hōigóng dōu yáuh wah lā,* ~ → ~ *ā ma."* ("His friend cheated him out of a sum of money." "There's a saying, ~ → ~. Don't you know that?")

ngaap/ ngáap 鴨 N duck 鴨子 M jek

0163
➔ **gāimòuh ngaaphyut** 雞毛鴨血 see 0127

0164
➔ **gāisáu ngaapgeuk** 雞手鴨腳 see 0132

0165

➡ gāi tùhng ngaap góng 雞同鴨講 see 0136

0166

➡ gwa laahpngáap 掛臘鴨 (lit.) hang out/ up a preserved duck (to let the north wind dry it) 把醃製好的鴨掛起 (讓北風把牠吹乾)
(idi.) VO hang oneself (to commit suicide) 吊頸自殺：*Gógāan chāantēng ge chisó yíhchìhn yáuh yàhn háidouh ~, sóyíh yáuh dī haak m̀gám yahpheui.* (A man ~ in the toilet of that restaurant some time ago. Some customers are afraid to go in there.)

0167 ✓

➡ ngaap/ ngáap 鴨 (lit.)N duck 鴨子 M jek
(idi.) N gigolo, man prostitute 男妓 M jek/ go： ⓐ *jouh* ~ (a man who prostitutes himself) ⓑ ~ *dim* (a place where ~ would be available)

0168 ✓

➡ ngaapjái 鴨仔 (lit.) N duckling 小鴨 M jek
(idi.) N (1) members of a tour group 旅行團的成員 M bāan/ tyùhn： ⓐ *Jouh douhyàuh ge, yiu sìhsìh daaijyuh dī ~ seiwàih heui.* (As a tourist guide, he has to take the tourists to different places.) ⓑ *chāamgā dī ~ tyùhn* (join a tour group) (2) student passengers on a nanny van 乘坐保姆車的學童 M dī; bāan; deuih： *táijyuh bāan ~ séuhng bóumóuh chē* (take care of the young students when they are getting on the nanny van)

0169

➡ ngaapná/ lá geuk 鴨乸腳
(lit.) female duck's feet 母鴨的腳
(idi.) N flat feet 平足 M deui： *Kéuih deui haih ~, sóyíh m̀jáudāk faai.* (He has a pair of ~, so he cannot run fast.)

0170

➡ séui gwo ngaapbui 水過鴨背
(lit.) (like) water falling on the back of the duck. It does not stay. 水在鴨子的背上流過,但不被鴨毛吸收
(idi.) PH forgetful, do not retain what has been taught 不能記住老師教過的東西： *Sīnsāang gaau ge yéh, yiu wānjaahp dō géichi sīnji dāk, yùhgwó m̀haih jauh ~ ge ja.* (You have to review what your teacher has taught a few more times, otherwise it's like ~.)

ngòh/ ngó 鵝 N goose 鵝 M jek

0171

➡ ngòhgūng hàuh 鵝公喉(lit.) gander's throat 公鵝的喉嚨
(idi.) N low and coarse voice (like that of a gander) 低而暗啞的聲音(像公鵝的那樣) M bá/ fu： *Kéuih go yéung hóu leng, daahnhaih góngyéh jauh ~ gám ge sēng.* (She is pretty but has a masculine voice [when she speaks].)

wūngā 烏鴉 N crow 烏鴉 M jek

0172

➡tīnhah wūngā yātyeuhng hāak 天下烏鴉一樣黑(lit.) all crows are black in the world, in every country dogs bite 天下烏鴉一樣黑
(idi.) PH bad people behave the same everywhere in the world 世界上的壞

27

人都一樣：*Kéuih wah kéuih lóuhbáan m̀sīng kéuih haih yānwaih kéuih m̀sīk tok, kèihsaht, ~, gogo lóuhbáan dōu haih gám ge la.* (He said that his boss did not give him a promotion because he did not flatter him. In fact, ~. Any boss in the world would do the same as his.)

0173✓

➔ **wūngā jéui/ háu** 烏鴉嘴/口 (lit.) N crow's mouth 烏鴉的嘴巴 M go

(idi.) N a person who likes to say things that people don't like 臭嘴巴，專說不好的或別人不愛聽的說話 M go/ bá：*Kéuih bá háu jingyāt ~, móuh hóu yéh góng ge.* (He's gotten a ~. He never says anything that people like.)

yihk 翼 N wing 翼 M jek；deui/ sēung

0174

➔ **yáuh mòuh yáuh yihk** 有毛有翼 (lit.) fully-fledged 鳥兒的羽毛長成了

(idi.) PH (said of one's own children) wanting to be autonomous, and not wanting to rely on their parents any more (兒女)長大,不屑倚賴父母：*"A mā, ngóh séung būnchēutheui jyuh," go jái wah. "Yìhgā ~ la, m̀yiu a mā la, haih m̀haih a?" màhmā wah.* ("Mum, I want to move out and live alone," said the son. "You are now a ~ bird, and you don't want your mother any more. Am I right?" said the mother.) (*The idiom is usually uttered by the parents in a negative sense.)

yūnyēung 鴛鴦 N mandarin ducks 鴛鴦 M deui/ sēung

0175

➔ **sīk jauh yūnyēung, m̀sīk jauh léuhng yeuhng** 識就鴛鴦，唔識就兩樣 (lit.) if you know them, you know they are mandarin ducks. But if you don't know them, you think they are just two different birds. 要是你認識牠們，你知道牠們是鴛鴦，要是你不認識牠們，你覺得牠們只是兩隻不同的鳥兒

(idi.) PH cannot appreciate the wonder of being different 不懂得欣賞事物相異的妙處：*"Hóu dō yàhn yíhwàih ngóh jeukchojó deui yūnyēung hàaih, kèihsaht haih sān fún làih ga." "óh, ~, ~."* ("Many people think I've put on two different shoes. Actually it's a new design." "They just ~ .")

0176✓

➔ **yūnyēung** 鴛鴦 (lit.) N mandarin ducks (which always go in pairs) 鴛鴦 M deui

(idi.) N grande creme, a mixture of coffee and tea 咖啡與紅茶的混合 M būi; bāau ATT (1) unmatching pair 兩個但不成對：~ *maht/tōháai* (an ~ of socks/ slippers) (2) asymmetrical 不對稱的：~ *ngáahn/ mihn/ yíh* (eyes, face [both sides], ears of different sizes or shapes)

0177

➔ **yūnyēung faahn** 鴛鴦飯 (lit.) N (a dish you can order in a Chinese restaurant. It is) rice topped with two sauces, white and red 酒樓的一款食品, 飯上有紅白二汁 M dihp：*Fógei, m̀gōi, yātgo ~.* (Waiter, one order of ~ please.)

IV. Sau (animals, beasts, and quadrupedes)

chūksāang 畜牲 **N animals**
畜牲 **M dī**

0178 ✓

➜chūksāang　畜　牲　(lit.)　N
animals 畜牲 **M dī**
(idi.) N (a term of abuse) you animal
(罵人語) 你這個畜牲: *Néih jek ~,
gēuiyín dá lóuhdauh!* (~, how dare
you beat your father!)

daaihbahnjeuhng 大笨象 **N**
(big and clumsy) elephant 象
M jek

0179 ✓

➜daaihbahnjeuhng geuk 大笨
象腳 (lit.) N big clumsy elephant's
legs 大象的腿 **M jek; deui**
(idi.) N (usually said of babies) plump
and strong legs (通常指嬰兒) 胖而強
的腿 **M jek; deui : *Nīgo bihbī mihnjái
saisai daahnhaih táiṁchēut yáuh deui
~.* (The baby's face is small and you
didn't know that it has a pair of ~.)

0180

➜ngáih dō lāuséi jeuhng 蟻
多摟死象 see 0021

0181

➜yàhnsām bātjūk sèh tān
jeuhng 人心不足蛇吞象 see
0049

gáu 狗 **N dog** 狗 **M jek**

0182

➜dáséi gáu góngga 打死狗講

價 (lit.) beat a dog to death and then
bargain over it 打死了狗之後才講價
(idi.) PH bargain over something that
has been damaged or already
consumed by the customer 待顧客把
貨物弄壞或用過之後才講價 :
ⓐ *Búnlòih dī dáan maaih yātmān
yātjek, daahnhaih ngóh ṁsíusām
dálaahnjó léuhngjek, kéuih jauh yiu
ngóh béi sei mān, móuh baahnfaat lā,
~.* (The eggs were sold at one dollar
each. I broke two unintentionally, but
he wanted me to pay him four dollars.
I could not but give him the money.
You know, one can hardly bargain
over things damaged by oneself.)
ⓑ *Dihnheipóu ge sauhfoyùhn wah,
"Nījúng sān chēutbán gachihn juhng
meih dihng, ngóhdeih sungfo heui néih
ngūkkéi sīn, hóu ma?" "Ṁhóu la,
faisih ~."* (The salesman of the
electrical appliance store said, "We
have not set a price for this new
product yet. We can send it to your
house first, OK?" "No, thanks. I don't
want to bargain with you then.")

0183

➜dīngáu 癲狗(lit.) mad dog 瘋
了的狗
(idi.) N furious man 很忿怒的男人
M jek : *Kéuih nāudou hóuchíh jek ~
gám.* (He is extremely angry like a ~.)

0184

➜ga gāi chèuih gāi, ga gáu
chèuih gáu 嫁雞隨雞，嫁狗隨
狗 see 0114

0185
→gāi fēi gáu jáu 雞飛狗走 see
0121

0186
→gānméih gáu 跟尾狗 (lit.)
(like) a dog always following his
owner 常跟隨主人的狗
(idi.) N a man who always goes after
a woman 常跟在女性後的男人 M
jek : *Dímgáai néih sihngyaht gānjyuh
ngóh hóuchíh jek ~ gám a?* (Why do
you always follow me like a dog?)

0187✓
→gáu 狗 (lit.) N dog 狗 M jek
(idi.) N a man who works very hard
工作非常辛苦的人 M jek : *jouhdou
hóuchíh jek ~ gám* (work like a ~)

0188
→gáudau gam lyuhn 狗竇咁
亂 (lit.) messy like a kennel 像狗窩
那樣亂
(idi.) PH very messy room 房間髒
亂 : *Gāan fóng sihngyaht dōu m̀jāp,
hóuchíh ~.* (You never tidy up your
room. It's like ~.)

0189
→gáujáidéui 狗仔隊 (lit.) N
puppy team, paparazzi 專門跟蹤名人
或明星的記者 M dī: *Mihngsīng
sihsih béi ~ gān.* (Movie stars are
often stalked by ~.)

0190
→gáu nàahmnéuih 狗男女
(lit.) dog and bitch 狗跟母狗
(idi.) N quite an old term of abuse
hurled at a man and a woman in

liaison 通姦的男女 (舊時罵人語)：
Néihdeih nīdeui ~! (You are a ~!)

0191
→gáungáahn hon yàhn dāi 狗
眼看人低 (lit.) dog's eyes look
down on man 狗眼看人低
(idi.) PH snobbish, put on airs and
despise others 勢利，看不起人 :
*Gódī jingfú gūnjái, ~. Yùhgwó néih
haih daaihlāplóu, táiháh kéuihdeih
wúih m̀wúih gam ngokséi ā!* (The
minor staff of the government are ~.
I wonder if they would be that fierce
with you if you were a VIP.)

0192
→gáu ngáauh gáugwāt 狗咬
狗骨 (lit.) dogs eat dog's bone 狗
咬同類的骨頭
(idi.) PH (quite explicitly) not on
good terms (between colleagues or
siblings) (同事或兄弟姊妹之間)不
和 : ⓐ *Kéuihdeih géi hīngdaih
jímuih, pihngsih yíhgīng haih ~ ge la,
lóuhdauh yāt séi jauh jāang sāngā.*
(The brothers and sisters [of that
family] are ~. As soon as their father
died, they started fighting over his
wealth.) ⓑ*Kéuihdeih tùhngsih jīgāan,
bíumihnseuhng hóuchíh géi hóu,
kèihsaht haih ~.* (Superficially, as
colleagues, they get along quite well.
But actually, they are ~.)

0193
→gáu ngáauh Léuih Duhng
Bān, bātsīk hóu yàhn sām 狗咬
呂洞賓，不識好人心 (lit.) a dog
bites one of the eight immortals of
Taoism, it does not know the good
man's heart 狗咬呂洞賓，不識好人心

30

(idi.) PH be ungrateful in not realizing the good intention of others 不明白別人好意,反而錯怪別人 : *Néih bōng kéuih kéuih juhng laauh néih, jānhaih ~, ~.* (You helped him but he blamed you. He really is ~.)

0194

→gáu séuhng ngáhhāang → yáuh tìuh louh 狗上瓦桁→有條路 (lit.) a dog goes up to the tile roof→there must be a road 狗走上用瓦片做的房頂→一定有一條途徑
(idi.) HIT people say this when they are suspicious about others' secret behaviour 懷疑別人有秘密行徑 : *A-Wóng gahnlòih sìhsìh heui A-Chán ūkkéi yauh sìhngyaht wah móuh chín. Kéuih taaitáai sīyìh kéuih ~ → ~. Kéuih gánghaih heui A-Chán douh dóuchín, yānwaih A-Chán haih dóujái.* (Recently Wong often goes to Chan's house, and he is always in need of money. His wife has become suspicious. He must have gone there to gamble because Chan is a gambler.)

0195

→gáusí laahpsaap 狗屎垃圾 (lit.) dog shit and trash 狗的糞便和廢物
(idi.) N rubbish and worthless things 無用的, 一文不值的東西 M dī : *Mātyéh ~ dōu ṁsédāk dám, ṁgwaaidāk gāan fóng hóuchíh laahpsaap gōng gám lā.* (He doesn't throw away even the ~. That's why his room is like a rubbish bin.)

0196

→gón gáu yahp kùhnghohng

趕狗入窮巷 (lit.) drive a dog into a blind alley 把狗趕到前無去路的小巷
(idi.) PH put someone into a desperate situation (but you have to beware of his fighting back) 迫使人無路可逃(但要提防那人反擊) : *Néih yìhgā cháaujó kéuih, yauh giu nīhòhng kèihtā ge lóuhbáan dōu ṁ hóu chéng kéuih, néih gám yéung jouh, jīkhaih ~ jē.* (You have already fired him. Now you tell the bosses in this line of business not to hire him. You really ~ by so doing.)

0197

→gwa yèuhngtàuh maaih gáuyuhk 掛羊頭賣狗肉 (lit.) put up a sheep's head but sell dog meat 掛羊頭賣狗肉
(idi.) PH do legal things superficially but do the opposite secretly 以正當事掩飾, 但暗中作非法勾當 : ⓐ *Gógāan yeuhkfòhng ~, lìhn daaihmàh dōu maaih.* (That drug store ~. They even sell cannabis.) ⓑ *Gógāan léihfaatdim ~, kèihsaht haih sīkchìhng gabouh.* (That barber shop ~. Actually, it is a vice den.)

0198

→hāakgáu dāk sihk, baahkgáu dōng jōi 黑狗得食,白狗當災 (lit.) black dog gets food, but white dog gets trouble 壞的狗得到食物,好的狗要受災殃
(idi.) PH the bad enjoy benefits but the good suffer loss 壞人得到好處, 好人卻受罪 : *Kéuih hái bōsí mihnchìhn góng néih sihfēi, gitgwó, bōsí cháaujó néih, sīngjó kéuih, jānhaih ~, ~.* (He spoke ill of you to our boss. As a

result, you were fired but he was promoted. It's true with the saying, ~, ~.)

0199
→hahji gáu, móuh dehng jáu 夏至狗，無定(地)走 (lit.) PH a dog at summer solstice finds no place to get away from the heat of the weather 盛暑時天氣熱得令狗隻無處可喘息 : " ~, ~ !" "Daahnhaih yàhn hóyíh taan láahnghei." ("~!" "But people can cool themselves in air-conditioned places.")

0200
→jáugáu 走狗 (lit.) running dog 走狗
(idi.) N henchman, lackey, a man who works for a supposedly bad man 替被認爲是壞人的人做事 : ⓐ Kéuih bātgwo haih bósí ge ~ jī ma. (He is merely a ~ of our boss.) ⓑ fuhbaaih jingfú ge ~. ([said of officals] ~ of a corrupt government)

0201
→jyūpàhng gáuyáuh 豬朋狗友 (lit.) pigs and dogs as friends 跟豬、狗做朋友
(idi.) N bad friends 壞朋友 M dī; go : Kéuih sīkmàaihsaai dī ~, gaau kéuih dóuchín sihkyīn. (He makes friends with the bad guys. They teach him to gamble and smoke.)

0202
→lohk gáusí 落狗屎 (lit.) down the dog shit 有狗的糞便落下來
(idi.) VO raining cats and dogs 傾盆大雨 : Ngoihbihn ~, néih juhng

chēutgāai! (It's ~.   Why do you still go out?)

0203
→lòhngsām gáufai 狼心狗肺 (lit.) wolf's heart and dog's lungs 狼心狗肺
(idi.) Adj.PH/ PH wicked minded and relentless 心腸狠壞 : Gógo sēui nàahmyán jānhaih ~. Kéuih wah ngoi kéuih, daahnhaih ngāakjó kéuihdī chín, yauh maaihjó kéuih chàhng láu, gáaudou kéuih yihgā yiu fangāai. (That bad guy really is ~. He said he loved her, but he conned her out of her money and sold her flat. Now she is homeless.)

0204
→lùhngchòhng m̀chíh gáudau 龍床唔似狗竇 (lit.) a dragon's / king's bed is not as good as a kennel 皇帝的床不比狗窩好
(idi.) PH there is no place like home (even if a much better place is offered to one) (雖然有更好的地方,可是)自己的家是最舒服的 : Sēuiyìhn léuihhàhng hóyíh jyuh nghsīngkāp jáudim, daahnhaih ~, dōu haih jihgéi ngūkkéi ge chòhng (fandāk) syūfuhkdī. (Although I can stay in a five-star hotel when going on a tour, yet ~. I like it better sleeping in my own bed.)

0205
→mòuhsīnggáu ngáauhséi yàhn 無聲狗咬死人 (lit.) a silent dog will kill a person with its bite 無聲狗咬死人
(idi.) PH a barking dog never bites 被不露聲色的人所害 : M̀chēutsēng

ge yàhn sīnjì dākyàhngēng a, ~ ā ma.
(Fearful are those who keep silent because ~.)

0206

➔mùhnháugáu 門口狗 (lit.) watchdog, a dog that only barks at the doorway of his owner's house 只會在主人家的門口吠的狗
(idi.) N a person who dares to be fierce in his own place, but not in other places 只敢在自己的勢力範圍內發惡的人,到外邊便不敢張聲 ：
ⓐ *Kéuih hái nīdouh jauh ngok jē, chēutdouheui ngoihbihn jauh m̀gám ngok ge la, jingyāt ~.* (He can be very fierce here in this place. He daren't be so outside. He is really like a ~.)
ⓑ*Néih hái jihgéi ngūkkéi jauh gam daaih sēng laauh kéuih, heuidou kéuih ūkkéi jauh m̀gám chēutsēng, jingyāt ~.* (You scolded him severely in your house, but you're afraid to do so in his house, you are really like a ~.)

0207

➔saahpsuhk gáutàuh 焓熟狗頭 (lit.) cook the dog's head by boiling it thoroughly 用很多水把狗頭烹熟
(idi.) PH a man offers a wide grin to a woman he is fond of 男人向他喜歡的女性獻露笑容 ：*Chán jái jēui Wòhng síujé, kéuih yāt gindóu kéuih jauh ~ gám.* (Young Chan is chasing after Miss Wong. Whenever he sees her, he smiles [quite unnaturally] at her.)

0208

➔séuigwā dá gáu, m̀gin yātgyuht/ jiht 水瓜打狗,唔見一橛／截 (lit.) beat a dog with a water gourd, one part of the gourd is lost/ breaks off 用水瓜打狗,斷了一部分
(idi.) PH a considerable amount is gone after use 不見了相當可觀的一部分 ：*Chēutl̀euhng gāaujó jōu jīhauh jauh ~, ~ la.* (After I pay the rent on my pay day, a certain amount of my salary is gone.)

0209

➔sōng gā gáu 喪家狗 (lit.) homeless dog 喪家犬
(idi.) N a man who looks sad and dull, and is in low spirits 氣色很差,臉帶愁容,精神又不好的男人 M jek ：*Tái néih mihn chēng sèuhn baahk, fúháu fúmihn, hóuchíh jek ~ gám.* (You look so sad and dull. You are like a ~.)

0210

➔wòhngpèihgáu 黃皮狗 (lit.) yellow-skinned dog 黃色皮膚的狗
(idi.) N a term of abuse hurled at a Chinese man by another Chinese 中國人罵另一中國男人的說話 M jek ：*Gáuchāt jīchihn,hái jingfú jouhyéh ge Jūnggwok yàhn wúih béi yàhn laauh haih ~.* (Before 1997, a Chinese man who worked in the British colonial government in Hong Kong would be ridiculed as ~.) (* 'Gáu' here may be viewed as 'jáugáu', see 0200)

jyū 豬 N pig 豬 M jek

0211

➔baahkpèih jyū 白皮豬 (lit.) white-skinned pig 白色皮的豬
(idi.) N a term of abuse hurled at a

white man (罵人語)白種人 jek/ go : *Kongyíh ge wàahngngáak seuhngbihn séijyuh, "Dádóu ~!"*. (It was written on the banner of the protesters, "Down with the ~!".)

0212

➜baahn jyū sihk lóuhfú 扮豬食老虎 (lit.) pose as a pig but eat the tiger 裝扮成豬的模樣卻把老虎吃掉
(idi.) PH take advantage of others by posing as a fool 裝蒜來佔人家便宜 : *Néih máih yíhwàih kéuih hóu chéun, yānjyuh kéuih ~ a.* (Don't think that he is stupid. Keep in mind that he will ~.)

0213

➜béi yàhn maaih jyūjái 俾人賣豬仔 (lit.) be sold like piglets 給人家當小豬般出賣了
(idi.) PH be cheated and taken advantage of by others 被人欺騙及佔便宜 : *Léuihhàhngséh wah kéuihdeih wúih chóh hòuhwàh léuihyàuhbā, jyuh nghsīngkáp jáudim, sihk fūngfu máahnchāan, dímjī yùhnchyùhn mhaih, gāmchi jānhaih ~ lo.* (The tourist agency said that they would go by luxurious coach bus, stay in five-star hotels and have rich dinners. But things turned out to be completely different. This time they were ~.)

0214

➜chéundou hóuchíh jek jyū gám 蠢到好似隻豬咁 (lit.) PH as stupid as a pig 笨得好像豬那樣子: *Ngóh gaaugihk kéuih (kéuih) dōu msīk, ~.* (No matter how I teach him, he won't understand. He is ~.)

0215

➜chéunjyū 蠢豬 (lit.) stupid pig 笨的豬
(idi.) N stupid person 愚蠢的人 M go/jek: *Néih béi yàhn ngāakjó dōu mjī, ~!* (You've been cheated but even now you don't know. You are a ~ !)

0216

➜fáanjyun jyūtóuh yātmihn sí 反轉豬肚一面屎 (lit.) turn a pig's stomach inside out and one finds there is only shit 把豬的肚反過來,只有牠的糞便
(idi.) PH (1) turn friendship into enmity 翻臉成仇 : *Kéuih tùhng ngóh yíhchìhn haih hóu pàhngyáuh, daahnhaih yihgā ~.* (He was a good friend of mine before. But now we are enemies.) (2) a person with bad human nature hiding behind his good appearance 外表好看,內心醜惡的人 : *Kéuih sihngyaht dábaandāk hóu gōugwai, yauh jūngyi yānséung ngaihseuht, dím bātjī haih ~.* (She likes to dress elegantly. She likes arts too. Who would have known that she is ~.)

0217

➜fandou hóuchíh jek séijyū gám 瞓到好似隻死豬噉 (lit.) sleep like a dead pig 酣睡得像死了的豬
(idi.) PH sleep like a log, sleep soundly 非常酣睡: *Kéuih yihgā ~, go laauhjūng géi chòuh, kéuih dōu mséng.* (Now he is ~. No matter how loud the alarm clock is, it won't wake him up.)

0218

➔ fān jyūyuhk 分豬肉 (lit.) divide up the pork (after ancestral or religious worship) (在祭祀後)把豬肉分給大家

(idi.) VO everyone gets a share 人人有份 ： Mātyéh dihnyíng dihnsih gāmjeuhngjéung, jīkhaih ~. (~ in whatever movie or TV awards ceremony.) also see 0238

0219

➔ gwaihdeih wai jyūná/ lá 跪地餵豬嫲 (lit.) bend one's knees to feed the sow 跪在地上給母豬餵食

(idi.) PH suffer disgrace and insults in order to accomplish a task 低聲下氣,忍辱負重 ： Sēuiyihn ngóh hóu jāng kéuih, daahnhaih yihgā yiu kàuh kéuih, wàihyáuh ~ hái lā. (I hate him. However, I have something to beg of him. All I have to do is ~.)

0220

➔ gwánséui luhk jyūchéung 滾水淥豬腸 (lit.) use boiling hot water to lightly boil the pig's intestine (which will shrink then) 用燙的水灼豬的腸子(它便會縮短)

(idi.) PH (usually said of money) becomes less (通常指金錢)少了 ： Tūngjeung sāileih ge sihhauh, dī ngàhnjí hóuchíh ~ gám. (When inflation is severe, money is like boiled pig's intestine.)

0221 ✓

➔ hàahm jyūsáu 鹹豬手 (lit.) salty pig's hand/ salted pig's knuckle 鹹豬手

(idi.) N (said of a man) nasty hands 男人毛手毛腳(有非禮女性之嫌) ：

Yáuh go néuih jīkyùhn béi yàhn fēiláih, yáuh móuh yàhn jīdou bīngo haih ~ a? (A lady staff was molested by a man. Does anyone know who has the ~?)

0222

➔ jyū gam chéun 豬咁蠢 (lit.) as stupid as a pig 像豬那樣蠢 ： Kéuih sihkyéh jauh lēk, jouhyéh jauh (hóuchíh) ~. (He is good at eating but when doing things, he is ~.)

0223

➔ jyūhùhng 豬紅 (lit.) pig red 豬的紅色

(idi.) N pig blood 豬的血 M gauh ： ~ jūk (congee with ~)

0224

➔ jyūjái chìhnngāang 豬仔錢罌 (lit.) N piggy bank 小豬造型的撲滿 M go ： chóuhchín yahp ~ (save money in a ~)

0225

➔ jyūjái tyùhn 豬仔團 (lit.) piglet group 小豬的團隊

(idi.) N a tour group in which the tourists are cheated and are taken advantage of by the travel agency 欺騙遊客的旅行團 ： Mhóu tāam pèhng, yānjyuh chāamgājó dī ~. (Don't join a cheating tour group just because it is cheap.) also see 0213

0226

➔ jyūlùhng yahpséui 豬籠入水 (lit.) water gets into the pig's cage (through the many holes on it when immersed in water) 水從豬籠的多個洞口進入

(idi.) PH money floods in, many sources of getting/ earning money 很多賺錢途徑： ⓐ *Nīpáai jānhaih ~, m̀jí gā yàhngūng, (máaih ge) gúpiu ngoihbaih dōu sīng.* (For him, ~. He has a payraise. The prices of the shares and foreign currencies he buys have also gone up.) ⓑ *Kéuih yahttáu fāanggūng, yehmáahn yauh jouh léuhngfahn gīmjīk, jānhaih ~ la.* (He works by day, and does two part-time jobs by night. He really has ~.)

0227

➜ jyūmāk 豬嘜 (lit.) pig's mark 豬的記號
(idi.) N dumb-bell, stupid person 笨人 M go ： *Kéuih ge yéung yáuhdī chéunchéun déi, dī yàhn giu kéuih ~.* (He looks a little dumb, so people call him ~.)

0228 ✓

➜ jyūná/ lá 豬乸 (lit.) N sow 母豬 M jek
(idi.) N woman who has many children 生養很多孩子的女人 M jek ：*Sāang gam dō (saimānjái), jouh ~ mè!* (She has so many children. Is she going to be a ~!)

0229

➜ jyūtàuh(bíng) 豬頭 (炳) (lit.) pig's head called Bíng 豬的頭叫阿炳
(idi.) N stupid person 蠢人 M go ： *Kéuih tùhng yàhn jouh sāangyi, béi yàhn ngāakjó dī chín, jīngyāt ~ làih ga.* (He did business with someone but was cheated by him. He is really a ~.) (* 'Bíng' is a Chinese name for man. The reason is not

known why it is picked for this expression.)

0230

➜jyūtàuhgwāt 豬頭骨 (lit.) pig's skull 豬的頭骨
(idi.) N a job from which one cannot earn much money 不能賺很多錢的工作 M gauh ： *béimàaihsaai dī ~ ngóh (jouh/ sihk)* ([They] just give me ~)

0231

➜làahmyán kaau dākjyuh, jyūlá dōu wúih séuhngsyuh lā 男人靠得住，豬乸都會爬上樹啦 (lit.) if men are reliable, then sows might climb up trees 要是男人可靠，母豬便會爬上樹
(idi.) PH men are unreliable 男人都是靠不住的 ： *"Néih sáimāt sihngyaht hāujyuh go lóuhgūng a? Néih yiu seuhnyàhm kéuih sīnji dāk ga." "~, ~!"* ("Why should you always keep a watchful eye on your husband? You need to trust him." "~!")

0232

➜laahnfanjyū 爛瞓豬(lit.) heavy sleeper pig 嗜睡的豬
(idi.) N (1) a person who likes to sleep all the time 嗜睡的人 M jek/ go (2) a person who does not want to get out of bed 睡得不願起床的人 M jek/go ： *~, héisān lā!* (Get up, you ~!) (* 'Laahnfan jyū' can be an intimate address to children or even adults.)

0233

➜láahnjyū 懶豬 (lit.) lazy pig 懶的豬

(idi.) N lazy person 懶的人 M jek/ go: *Yātgo yaujihyún lóuhsī mahn dī hohksāang, "Yáuh móuh yàhn séung jouh ~ a?"* (A kindergarten teacher asked her students, "Does anyone want to be a ~?")

0234
→mōkgwōngjyū 剝 光 豬 (lit.) take off all the clothes of a pig 把豬的衣服脫光
(idi.) VO (1) strip off clothes 把衣服脫光 : *Dī cháak jēung kéuih ~, sóyíh kéuih m̀hóyíh jēui kéuihdeih.* (The robbers stripped him of his clothes so that he could not chase them.) (2) a thorough loss (in a Chinese game of chess in which one loses all of his pieces to his opponent) 在中國象棋賽中輸掉所有棋子: *Nī pùhn kéi, kéuih ~.*(In this game of chess, he suffers ~.)

0235 ✓
→sāang jyūyuhk 生 豬 肉 (lit.)N raw pork 生的豬肉 M gauh
(idi.) N false charge 插的贓,嫁的禍 M gauh : *Chāailóu chai ngóh sihk ~, jāi dī baahkfán hái ngóhge dóidouh, wah ngóh chòhngduhk.* (A cop put some heroine into my pocket and then charged me with possession of drugs.)

0236 ✓
→sīujyū 燒豬 (lit.) N roast pig 烤豬 M jek
(idi.) N (said of a person) (1) sunburnt (人)給太陽曬傷 : *Hahtīn taaiyèuhng gam máahng, saai géigo jūngtàuh saaidou bin ~.* (In summer, the sun is very strong. If we stay in the sun for

hours, we'll get ~.) (2) (burned) like roast pig（被火燒得）像烤豬 : *Sīufòhngyùhn jēung dī yàhn hái fóchèuhng léuihbihn tòihchēutlàih, (dī yàhn) hóuchíh ~ gám.* (When the firemen got the victims out from the fire, they were just ~.) PH as in 'sīujyū míhn cháau', which means 'no need to do the same thing to each other'出現在 '燒豬免炒' 中, 意思是 大 家 不 必 做 同 樣 的 事 : *"Ngóhdeih tùhng yāt yaht sāangyaht/ tùhng yātgo yuht gitfān, sóyíh ~, daaihgā dōu m̀sái sungláih,"* yātgo yàhn deui kéuihge pàhngyáuh góng. ("We have the same birthday/ Our wedding days are in the same month, so we need not bother to send a gift to each other," said a person to his friend. (* The literal meaning of the expression is 'a roast pig doesn't need to be fried again'.)

0237
→sòhjyū 傻豬 (lit.) silly pig 愚笨的豬
(idi.) N (a teasing and also an intimate address to children) you silly kid (對小孩親暱的謔稱)小傻子 M go/ jek : *Néih nīgo ~! (~!)*

0238
→taaigūng fān jyūyuhk→ yàhnyàhn yáuh fán 太公分豬肉→人人有份 (lit.) HIT the head of the clan divides up the pork→everyone gets a share 家族的長老分豬肉, 每個人都有份兒 : see 0218 (*It is a Chinese custom that after worshiping the ancestor(s), the head of the clan would chop a roast pig and give a portion to every male of the clan.)

0239 ✓

→tōngjyū 劏 豬 (lit.) VO slaughter a pig 宰豬

(idi.) VO sing very terribly like a pig being slaughtered 唱歌非常難聽,好像豬被宰時的聲音 ： *cheunggō hóuchíh ~ gám* (~)

0240

→yàhn pa chēutméng jyū pa fèih 人怕出名豬怕肥 (lit.) a person is afraid of becoming famous and a pig, fat 人怕出名豬怕肥

(idi.) PH it is so said because one will lose some of his privacy when he becomes a public known figure, and a pig will be killed if it grows fat 人出了名,就會喪失一些私隱,豬肥了就會被人宰 ： *"Yáuh yàhn chéng néih séuhng dihnsih, dímgáai néih m̀heui a?" "~ ā ma!"* ("Someone has invited you to appear on TV. Why don't you go?" "I don't want to become famous. Don't you understand?)

0241

→yūnjyūtàuh dōu yáuh màhng beih pòuhsaat 冤豬頭都有盟鼻菩薩 (lit.) even a foul pig's head has a bad nose goddess (to appreciate it) 臭豬頭有鼻子塞了的菩薩來聞(而不覺它臭)

(idi.) PH love is blind 情人眼裏出西施 ： *"Kéuih yauh kāpduhk yauh dóuchín, juhng yáuh yàhn ga kéuih gé?" "~ ā ma!"* ("He takes drugs and gambles, but still there is someone marrying him." "Haven't you heard of the saying that ~!")

kèihlèuhn/léun 麒 麟 N unicorn 麒麟 M jek

0242

→fókèihléun→jāusān yàhn 火麒麟→周身癮 (lit.) a fiery unicorn → it has fuses all over its body 著火的麒麟→因爲身上滿是火藥引線

(idi.) HIT a slave to many (bad) habits 有很多(不良的)嗜好 ： *Kéuih yauh (sihk) yīn, yauh (yám) jáu yauh dóuchín, jingyāt ~ → ~.* (He likes to smoke, drink and gamble. He is really like ~.)

lèuihjái 騾仔 N mule 騾 M jek

0243

→ngàaih lèuihjái 捱騾仔 (lit.) suffer hardship like a mule 像騾那樣捱苦

(idi.) VO work very hard for a living 辛勞工作,賺錢生活 ： *"Néih yahttáu jouhyéh, yehmáahn yauh jouh gīmjīk, sáimāt gam bokmehng a?" "~ jē, móuh baahnfaat lā."* ("You have a job by day and have a part-time job by night. You don't need to work that hard." "I ~. I have no other way.")

lòhng 狼 N wolf 狼 M jek

0244 ✓

→lòhng 狼 (lit.)N wolf 狼 M jek

(idi.) Adj. (1) cruel, relentless 凶狠 ： *Go cháak lójó kéuih dī chín, yauh dádou kéuih chúhngsēung, jānhaih ~ la.* (The thief took his money and beat him very badly. How ~ the thief was!) (2) too covetous 太貪心 ： *Ngóh punglaahn néih ga chē ge bāmbá jē, néih jauh yiu ngóh pùih gam dō chín, néih jānhaih* ~ *la.* (I just damaged the bumper of your car, but you want me to pay so much compensation. You are really ~.)

0245
➔ **lòhngsām gáufai** 狼心狗肺
see 0203

0246
➔ **lòhngtōi** 狼胎 (lit.) wolf's fetus 狼的胎兒
(idi.)Adj. same as 'lòhng' see 0244

0247
➔ **sīklòhng** 色狼 (lit.) color wolf 有顏色的狼
(idi.) N (said of a man) sex maniac 想非禮女性的男人 M jek/ go : *Ṁgwaaidāk kéuih béi* ~ *fēiláih lā, kéuih jeukdāk gam singgám.* (She should not blame the ~ for having molested her. She puts on too sexy clothes.)

lóuhfú 老虎 N tiger 老虎 M jek

0248
➔ **baahn jyū sihk lóuhfú** 扮豬食老虎 see 0212

0249
➔ **dá lóuhfú** 打老虎(lit.) beat the tiger 打老虎
(idi.)VO apprehend the high ranking officials (for their having broken the law) 捉拿犯法的高官 : *Lihmjing gūngchyúh ge háuhouh haih* ~, *m̀haih dá wūyīng.* (The watchword of the Independent Commission Against Corruption/ ICAC is to ~, not the minor ones.) also see 0054

0250
➔ **fútàuh sèhméih** 虎頭蛇尾
see 0033

0251
➔ **jí lóuhfú** 紙老虎 (lit.) N paper-made tiger 紙做的老虎
(idi.) N a person with imposing features is in fact quite fragile M jek 圖具威名,其實不堪一擊 : *Tái kéuih sàhn gōu sàhn daaih, hóuchíh hóu dádāk gám, kèihsaht haih* ~ *jauh jān.* (He is tall and big, and looks as if he is a good boxer. But actually, he can be very easily defeated.)

0252
➔ **lóuhfú dōu wúih hāp ngáahnfan** 老虎都會瞌眼瞓
(lit.) (sometimes) even a (vigorous) tiger would doze 老虎也會打瞌睡
(idi.) PH although one is on the alert, one is still caught napping 雖然很小心謹慎,仍不免有錯 : "*Kéuih gam síusām dōu wúih tái lauh ngáahn ge mē.*" "*Yáuhsìh* ~ *lā!*" ("He is so cautious and yet errors can escape his eyes." "Sometimes ~.)

0253
➔ **lóuhfúgēi** 老虎機 (lit.) tiger machine 老虎機器
(idi.) N (1) parking meter 停車收費錶 M go : *wai* ~ (feed a ~) (2) slot machine in a casino 賭場的吃角子機 M go : *māng/ lāai/ wáan* ~ (pull/ play a ~)

0254
lóuhfúlá/ ná 老虎乸 (lit.) tigress 雌老虎

(idi.) N shrewish/ fierce wife 惡妻 M jek/ go : *Kéuih jek ~ yiu kéuih múihmáahn sahpyāt dím jīchihn jauh yiu fāandou ngūkkéi ge la.* (His ~ wants him to be back at home before eleven o'clock every night.)

0255
➔lóuhfú m̀faatwāi néih dong behngmāau 老虎唔發威你當病貓 (lit.) a tiger exercising no power is taken for a sick cat 老虎不發惡就被錯認是有病的貓
(idi.) PH take a sleeping wolf for a dead dog 我不作聲，你就把我欺負 : *Wai, hóu la bo, néih joi haih gám ngóh jauh m̀haakhei ge la. ~!* (Alright, that's enough. I can't stand it any more if you go on like this. Don't ~!)

0256
➔lóuhfú tàuhseuhng dēng sātlá 老虎頭上釘虱乸 see 0026

0257
➔lùhng jīng fú máahng 龍精虎猛 (lit.) as vigorous as a dragon and/ or a tiger 像龍跟／或虎那樣威猛
(idi.) PH full of energy, in extremely high spirits 精神很好,充滿活力 : *Búnlòih kéuih hóu ngáahnfan ge, daahnhaih yámjó léuhngbūi gafē jīhauh jauh ~ la.* (He was sleepy. But after he drank two cups of coffee, he became ~.)

0258
➔móuh ngàh lóuhfú 冇牙老虎 (lit.) toothless tiger 沒有牙齒的老虎

(idi.) N (1) an authority unable to exercise its power 不能運用權力的領導層 M jek : *Jauhsyun gūngngūk dyúnjōng, sihngginsēung dōu m̀wúih yáuh yihngsih jaakyahm, jingfú maih binjó jek ~ lō.* (The contractors of public housing developments would not be held responsible even though the piles are found too short. The government is like a ~, isn't it?) (2) big fire (as disaster, which was the original meaning of the expression when used idiomatically. But it is seldom used this way nowadays.)大火

0259
➔sauchòih/chói yuh lóuhfú, yàhmsī dōu yàhm m̀lāt 秀才遇老虎，吟詩都吟唔甩 (lit.) a scholar comes across a tiger, he finds no way to flee even though he recites poems 秀才遇見老虎,就算他吟詩也逃不掉
(idi.) PH have no way but ...... 沒法逃避 : *Seuhngchi néih wah chéng ngóhdeih yámchàh. Yihgā gindóu néih, néih jānhaih ~, ~ la.* (Last time you said you would treat us to dimsum. Now you're here, you ~ keep your promise.)

0260
➔séuhngdāk sāan dō jūng yuhfú 上得山多終遇虎 (lit.) one goes up the mountain so often that eventually one encounters a tiger 常常上山, 終於遇到老虎
(idi.) PH the fish who nibbles at every bait will be caught, too many risks will result in a failure 冒險太多,終有一次失敗 : *Kéuih hái gāaibīn maaih fāanbáan CD, hóu*

hóujaahn. Daahnhaih ~, yáuh yātyaht béi gíngchaat lāaijó. (He had made much money by selling pirated compact discs on the street. But ~. One day he was caught by the police.)

0261

➔sung yèuhng yahp fúháu 送羊入虎口 (lit.) send a sheep to a tiger's mouth 送羊入虎口

(idi.) PH put someone at risk 使人身陷險境 ： *Kéuih heui tùhng daaihyíhlūng góngsou, dímjī béi daaihyíhlūng jūkjyuh, laahksok kéuihge lóuhdauh. Nīchi jānhaih ~.* (He went to talk to the loan shark. How could he have known that the loan shark would catch him and blackmail his father. This time, he fell prey to the loan shark.)

lóuhsyú 老鼠 N rat, mouse 老鼠 M jek

0262

➔dihndāng chaam gwa lóuhsyú sēung 電燈杉掛老鼠箱 (lit.) on the street lamp pole, there hangs a trap-box for mouse (街上的)電燈柱掛著捉耗子的箱

(idi.) PH a big difference of height (between a couple or two lovers) 夫婦或情侶之間的身高差距很大 ： *Kéuihdeih léuhng gūngpó, ~, m̀haih hóu chan.* (There is ~ between the husband and his wife. They don't look like a good match.)

0263

➔gwogāai lóuhsyú, yàhnyàhn haam dá 過街老鼠，人人喊打 (lit.) a rat sneaks across the street, and people all want to beat it 老鼠竄過街,人們都喊著要打他

(idi.) N a person hated by everybody 大家都討厭的人 M jek ： *Yānwaih kéuih hái daaihluhk bāau yihnāai, go lóuhpòh láamjyuh léuhnggo jái tiuláu séijó. Dī gāaifōng yāt gindóu kéuih jauh laauh kéuih. Kéuih yihgā binsihng ~, ~.* (Because he had a mistress in the mainland, his wife, together with their two sons, plunged to their death. Now whenever his neighbours see him, they hurl curses at him. He has become ~.)

0264

➔jīu sihk máahn sái, máahnsihk lóuhsyú sái 朝食晚洗，晚食老鼠洗 (lit.) eat in the morning but wash (the dishes) at night, eat at night and the rats will wash (the dishes) for you 早上吃晚上洗碗,晚上吃老鼠替你洗碗

(idi.) PH leave the dishes unwashed 吃飯後不立刻把碗碟洗乾淨 ： *Néihdeih ~, ~ gám, chyùhfóng gánghaih dō wūyīng gaahtjáat lā.* (You ~. That's why there are flies and cockroaches in your kitchen.)

0265

➔lóuhsyú ditlohk tīnpihng → jihgéi jaan jihgéi 老鼠跌落天秤→自己讚自己 (lit.) a rat falls on the scale→it praises itself 老鼠掉到天秤上→牠稱讚自己

(idi.) HIT sing one's own praises 自己稱讚自己 ： *M̀haih wah ngóh ~ → ~ ā, nīdouh chèuihjó ngóh jīngoih, jauh móuh yàhn jídou jíng daahngōu ge beikyut.* (Please don't think that I

~. Nobody here but me knew the art and craft of making a sponge cake.) (*A rat is supposed to weigh itself on the scale, but the Chinese word for 'to weigh', i.e. 稱 [ching], can also mean 'to praise' when changed into a high level tone. However, a synonym of it, i.e. 讚 [jaan] is used instead.)

0266

➔lóuhsyú fo 老鼠貨 (lit.) rat's goods 老鼠的貨物

(idi.) N stolen goods (for sale) 當貨物賣的賊贓 M dī; gihn : ~ sēuiyihn hóu pèhng, daahnhaih béi gíngchaat táidóu jauh yáuh màhfàahn la. (The ~ are cheap, but you will be in trouble if they are spotted by the police.)

0267 ✓

➔lóuhsyújái 老鼠仔 (lit.) N little mouse 小老鼠 M jek

(idi.) N bulging bicep 手臂上隆起的肌肉 M jek : sáubei seuhngbihn yáuh jek ~ (~ as if there's a ~ on the arm)

0268

➔lóuhsyú lāai gwāi → móuh dehng màaihsáu 老鼠拉龜→冇定埋手 see 0065

0269

➔māau hūk lóuhsyú → gá chíhbēi 貓哭老鼠 → 假慈悲

(lit.) a cat mourns for a (dead) rat→ (it's all) fake sympathy 貓哭老鼠→假慈悲

(idi.) HIT shed crocodile tears 假裝同情敵人 : "A-Chán sauhjó sēung, A-Wóng giu ngóh mahnhauh kéuih wo." "Kéuih ~ → ~ jīma. Kéuih

tùhng A-Chán haih séi deuitàuh làih gé." ("Chan was wounded and Wong asked me to give his regards to him." "He just ~. He is an enemy of Chan.)

0270

➔sātāan lóuhsyú 沙灘老鼠 (lit.) rats on the beach 沙灘上的老鼠

(idi.) N thieves on the beach 沙灘上的小偷 M go/ jek : Hahtīn heui hóitāan yàuhséui, yiu síusām dī ~. (When you go swimming at the beach in the summer, be aware of the ~.)

lùhng 龍 N dragon 龍 M tìuh

0271

➔fagwātlùhng 化骨龍 (lit.) bone-melting dragon 骨會融化的龍

(idi.) N one's own children (who will eat up his money [, and even his bones]) 會耗盡父母金錢去撫養的子女 M tìuh : Kéuih dāk yātfahn yàhngūng, jauh yiu yéuhng lóuh móu, lóuhpòh tùhng géi tìuh ~. (He has only one salary, yet he is the bread winner of his mother, his wife, and ~.) (It is said that 'fagwātlùhng' is a kind of poisonous reptile which looks like a fish. It would melt in the soup after being cooked for hours. People would try to identify it by throwing it hard on the ground many times until it could not move. Its feet would then stretch out because of the pain.)

0272

➔gwahtméih lúng→gáau fūng gáau yúh 掘尾龍→攪風攪雨

(lit.) blunt-tailed dragon→ (it likes to)

stir wind and rain 鈍尾巴的龍→喜愛攪得滿天風雨
(idi.) HIT trouble maker 製造麻煩的人 : *"Bāan sáuhah búnlòih hóu tēngwah ge, daahnhaih gahnlòih diuhjó géigo yàhn gwolàih jīhauh, jauh m̀tùhng la."* *"Gó géigo yàhn maih ~ → háidouh ~ lō."* ("My men were very obedient, but since several new staff members have been transferred to our department, things are different." "Those new comers are ~.")

0273
➔hàahngwahn yāttìuh lùhng, sātwahn yāttìuh chùhng 行運一條龍，失運一條蟲 see 0008

0274 ✓
➔lùhng 龍(lit.)N dragon 龍 M tìuh
(idi.) N queue 隊伍 M tìuh : *Wa! Tiuh ~ gam chèuhng.* (Wow! The ~ is so long!)

0275
➔lùhngchòhng m̀chíh gáudau 龍床唔似狗竇 see 0204

0276
➔lùhng jīng fú máahng 龍精虎猛 see 0257

0277
➔lùhng máh jīngsàhn 龍馬精神 (lit.) PH energetic and vigorous like a dragon and/ or a horse 好像龍和／或馬那樣精力充沛 (*The expression is written on a piece of red paper as a lucky poster and taped on the wall at Chinese New Year.) : *Nī jēung fāichēun seuhngbihn séjyuh ~.* (It is written ~ on this red poster for Chinese New Year.)

0278 ✓
➔lùhngméih 龍尾 (lit.) N dragon's tail 龍的尾巴 M tìuh
(idi.) N end of a queue 人龍末端 M tìuh : *Tiuh lùhng gam chèuhng, dōu mohngm̀gin ~ hái bīn.* (The queue is so long that we can't see the end of it.)

0279 ✓
➔lùhngtàuh 龍頭(lit.)N dragon's head 龍(的)頭 N go
(idi.) N (1) head of a queue 人龍的前端 : *~ yáuh yàhn dájīm.* (Somebody cuts in at the ~.) (2) triad boss/ dragonhead 黑幫首領 M go : *Gógo hāak séwúi ~ sāangyaht, hái jáulàuh báaijáu, gíngchaat jauh heui jáuhlàuh dahtgīk sáuchàh.* (The ~ of that triad gang gave a banquet in a Chinese restaurant on his birthday, but the police raided the restaurant.)

0280
➔lùhng yàuh chínséui jōu hā hei 龍游淺水遭蝦戲 (lit.) (like) a dragon being fooled by shrimps when it is swimming in shallow water 龍在淺水的地方游泳,便被蝦戲弄
(idi.) PH a person would not be honoured once he leaves the place of his dominance 虎落平陽被犬欺,人離開自己的勢力範圍便會被人欺負 : *Kéuih búnlòih haih yātgāan jūnghohk ge haauhjéung, daahnhaih kéuih (beih) diuhlàih nīgāan síuhohk jīhauh, nīdouh ge sīnsāang m̀haih géi háng tùhng kéuih hahpjok, kéuih gokdāk*

43

jihgéi hóuchíh haih ~ gám. (He was the prinicpal of a secondary school. But after he had been transferred to this primary school (also as principal), he found that the teachers here were somewhat uncooperative with him. He felt that he was like ~.)

0281

➔ ṁhaih máahng lùhng ṁgwogōng 唔係猛龍唔過江
(lit.) if it were not a fierce dragon, it would not cross the river 不是猛龍就不過江
(idi.) PH only a very capable person dares to come for the challenge 來者不善,善者不來 : ⓐ "*Kéuih haih júng gūngsī jēung kéuih hái Sāngabō ge fān gūngsī diuhgwolàih ge.*" "~, ngóhdeih yiu síusāmdī.*" ("He was transferred to our company from the Singapore branch by our headquarters." "~. We'd better take care.") ⓑ "*Hēunggóng múih nihn ge Gwokjai Lùhngjāujit dōu yáuh hóudō ngoihgwok lùhngjāudéui làih chāamgā.*" "~, làihchàn ge dōu haih dōngdeih ge gungwán.*" ("Every year, many racing teams from foreign places come to Hong Kong to participate in the International Dragon Boat Race." "~. The teams who come are the champions of their local races.)

0282

➔ tok séui lùhng 托水龍 (lit.) carry on one shoulder a water dragon 用一邊肩膊抬著水龍
(idi.) VO (said of a person) runs away with/ uses the money entrusted to him 拿了別人轉交第三者的錢

跑/用了 : *Ngóh giu kéuih jēung dī chín gāau béi A-Chán, dímjī (béi) kéuih ~ jó ~.* (I gave him the money and asked him to give it to Chan, but he ~/ it was all spent by him.)

0283

➔ wūlúng 烏龍(lit.) black dragon 黑色的龍
(idi.) Adj. muddled 糊塗 : *Kéuih nīgo yàhn hóu ~ ge, sihsìh gáaucho dī yéh.* (He is a very ~ person. He always makes mistakes.) N (1) mistake, blunder 錯誤 M chi : *báai ~* (make a ~) (2) (name of a kind of Chinese tea) oo-lung : *~ chàh (~)*

0284 ✓

➔ yāttìuh lùhng 一條龍(lit.)PH one dragon 一條龍
(idi.) PH (1) one queue 一條隊伍 : *Yìhgā hóudō ngàhnhòhng dōu pàaih ~ ge la.* (Now many banks ask their clients to queue up in one line.) (2) the 'one way through' education system (in which a primary student can go straight to secondary school without sitting for any assessement exams) 教育制度:小學生可直升中學,不需參加任何評核考試 : *Hēunggóng jingfú séung sahthàhng ~ (ge gaauyuhk jaidouh), daahnhaih hóudō gājéung fáandeui, yānwaih kéuihdeih séung bōng jáinéui wán mìhnghaauh.* (The Hong Kong government wants to implement the ~, but the proposal is strongly opposed by the parents because they want to find a prestigious school for their children themselves.) (3) all are included 全包 : *~ fuhkmouh* (one-stop service)

lúk 鹿 N deer 鹿 M jek

0285

➜jūkdóu lúk/ luhk dōu m̀sīk tyutgok 捉到鹿都唔識脫角
(lit.) catch a deer but not know that one should take off its antlers (which can be sold/cooked as a very valuable tonic food) 捉到鹿卻不曉得應該把牠的角脫下
(idi.) PH let an opportunity slip away 不懂把握機會：*Kéuih jūngyi néih sung ge láihmaht, jīkhaih jūngyi néih lā, dímgáai néih m̀jīkhāak heung kéuih kàuhfān, jānhaih ~.* (She liked your gift so much. That meant she loved you. Why didn't you pop the question to her at once? You really ~.)

māau 貓 N cat 貓 M jek

0286

➜ché māauméih 扯貓尾 (lit.) pull a cat's tail 拉貓的尾巴
(idi.) VO conspire to hide the truth from someone 合謀把事情隱瞞別人：*Néih mahn A-Chán, kéuih wah m̀jī. Néih mahn A-Wóng, kéuih yauh wah m̀jī. Kèihsaht kéuihdeih māt dōu jī, kéuihdeih ~ jē.* (You asked Chan, he said he didn't know. You asked Wong, he didn't know either. In fact, they knew everything. They just ~.)

0287

➜chēutmāau 出貓 (lit.) put out cat 放貓出來
(idi.) VO cheat at exams 考試作弊：*háausi ~ (~)*

0288

➜fāmihn māau 花面貓 (lit.) messy face cat 花臉的貓
(idi.) N dirty and stained face 污垢滿臉 M go/ jek：*Màhmā deui sāam seui ge néui wah, "Néih wáan mātyéh wáandou ~ gám a?"* (Mother said to her three-year-old daughter, "You've gotten a ~. What have you been playing with?")

0289

➜laaimāau 賴貓 (lit.) put the blame on the cat 把過錯賴在貓兒身上
(idi.) Adj. not admitting mistakes 不肯認錯：*Néih gam ~, jouhcho yéh yauh m̀yihng.* (You are such an irresponsible person. You did it wrong but you don't admit.) V (1) deny mistakes 否認錯誤：*Néih jouhchojó, séung ~ àh?* (You did it wrong but you are going to ~?) (2) shirk (responsibilities) 推搪責任：*Kéuih séung ~ m̀béichín.* (He intends not to pay [the money].)

0290

➜lóuh māau sīu sōu 老貓燒鬚 (lit.) old cat gets its whiskers burned 老貓的鬚燒掉了
(idi.) PH an expert would unexpectedly fail/ err sometimes 就算是專家,有時也會有失誤：*Daaih chyùhsī jīnlūng dáan, jānhaih ~ la.* (A famous chef fried an egg and scorched it. He did make an unlikely mistake.)

0291

➜māau hūk lóuhsyú→gá chihbēi 貓哭老鼠→假慈悲
see 0269

0292

➔māaují 貓紙 (lit.) cat paper 貓的紙

(idi.) N paper used for doing cheating in an exam (*Clues needed are written on it.) 考試作弊用的紙, 上面寫了考試所需要的資料 M jēung : *Gāamháauyùhn hái kéuih ge dóidouh wándóu jēung ~.* (The examiner found in his pocket a sheet of ~.)

0293

➔sàhntòih māausí→sàhn jāng gwái yim 神檯貓屎→神憎鬼厭 (lit.) cat shit on the altar/shrine → (is) hated by gods and ghosts 祭檯上的貓糞→令鬼神憎惡

(idi.) HIT a person disgusted by everybody 大家都討厭憎惡的人 : *Kéuih sihngyaht tok lóuhsai daaihgeuk, hā dī dāikāp jíkyùhn, sóyíh hái gūngsī léuihbihn, kéuih binsihng ~ → ~.* (He flatters his boss, but bullies the minor staff. He has become ~ in the office.)

0294

➔sihk māaumihn 食貓麵 (lit.) eat the cat's noodles 吃貓的麵

(idi.) VO be scolded 被責罵 : *Gīngléih giu néih heui, néih jauh faaidī heui lā, chihdī jauh wúih ~ ge la.* (Our manager asked you to go, so you'd better hurry up and go. If you go later, you will ~.)

0295

➔sihk séimāau 食死貓 (lit.) eat a dead cat 吃死了的貓

(idi.) VO be a scapegoat, take all the blame 做替死鬼/代罪羔羊 : *Kéuih*

jouhchojó jauh ngāt ngóh ~. (He made all the mistakes, but he put the blame on me.)

0296

➔waihsihkmāau 為食貓 (lit.) greedy cat 貪吃的貓

(idi.) N greedy person 饞嘴的人 M go/ jek : *Néih jek ~, sihkjó gam dō yéh juhng m̀gau, juhng yiu sihk àh?* (You ~! You have eaten a lot and yet you are not enough. You still want to eat more?)

máh 馬 N horse 馬 M jek

0297

➔ báaimìhng gēuimáh 擺明車馬 (lit.) (in Chinese game of chess) move the 'chariot' and the 'horse' to show apparently that one wants to checkmate his opponent's 'general' (下中國象棋時)移動 '車' 及 '馬' 並向對手宣示要吃掉他的 '將軍'

(idi.) PH do something by disclosing one's intention first 公開表示做事的意圖 : *Kéuih ~ haih tùhng jingfú jokdeui ge lā.* (He openly showed /It is very obvious that he would do something against the government.) (*Sometimes people would just say 'báaimihng' or 'báaidoumihng', which is now used as an adverb.)

0298

➔ bāanmáh 班馬 (lit.) round up horses 把馬兒聚集在一起

(idi.) VO call the men of the same triad society to come and help 把同一個幫會的人叫來幫忙 : *Ngóhdeih yáuh léuhnggo hīngdaih béi yàhn hāp.*

Faaidī ~ làih bōng kéuih. (Two of our [gang] members are being bullied by others. Hurry up and call our men to come.)

0299

➔ **chēutmáh** 出馬 (lit.) put out horse (*Originally it is said when a person moves the 'horse' in a Chinese game of chess.) 本是玩中國象棋時說的,意思是讓馬兒出動 (idi.) V face up to and tackle a problem by oneself 挺身而出,應付困難 : *Méihgwok júngtúng làih Hēunggóng fóngmahn. Bóuōnguhk Guhkjéung tùhng Gíngmouhchyùh Chyúhjéung dōu yiu chānjih ~ fuhjaak bóuōn ge mahntàih.* (The president of the United States will visit Hong Kong. The Secretary of the Security Bureau and the Police Commissioner have to shoulder the responsibility for security themselves.)

0300✓

➔ **chīubāanmáh** 超班馬 (lit.) a horse which shows more mettle than those in the same group 比其他馬優勝的馬匹 M jek (idi.) N one who is beyond the level of his fellows 一班人之中水準超乎其他人的人 : *Kéuih hái nībāan hohksāang jījūng haih ~, bātyùh béi kéuih tiubāan lā.* (In this class, he is ~. We'd better let him go to a class of higher level.)

0301✓

➔ **dīngdōng máhtàuh** 叮噹馬頭 (lit.) PH two horses will reach the winning post at the same time, and so it is hard to tell which one will win 兩匹馬將會同時到終點,所以難分勝負 (idi.) PH it is hard to tell which one [of the two competing parallels] will outdo the other 兩個競爭對手難分高下 : *Nī léuhnggāan daaihhohk gihngjāngdāk hóu gányiu, jānhaih ~.* (These two universities are in keen competition with each other and ~.)

0302

➔ **gwáigwái máhmáh** 鬼鬼馬馬 (lit.) ghosts and horses 鬼跟馬 (idi.) PH look mysterious by playing a prank 開玩笑而顯得神神秘秘的 : *Néihdeih háidouh ~ gám, gáau māt gwái yéh a?* (You ~. What the heck are you going to do [with me]?)

0303

➔ **gwái máh** 鬼馬 (lit.) ghost and horse 鬼跟馬 (idi.) Adj. funny, laugh provoking 有趣引人發笑的 : *Kéuih jouhhei hóu ~.* (He is ~ in movies.) (*A sentence pattern is made up of 'gwái' and 'máh' as in 'Vgwái Vmáh mè!' meaning 'how could it be possible for a person to do that?' or even 'it's obviously impossible for a person to do that!')

0304

➔ **gwái ngh máh luhk** 鬼五馬六 (lit.) ghost five and horse six 鬼五個馬六隻 (idi.) PH do something disorderly and untidily 做事做得一塌糊塗 : *dī gūngfo jouhdou ~ gám* (do homework ~)

0305

→hàahngsyùhn páaumáh sāamfān hím 行船跑馬三分險 (lit.) PH there's always a degree of danger in sailing a boat as well as in riding on horseback 船隻航行跟跑馬都有一定程度的危險：*"Gógo kèhsī ditmáh sauhjó sēung bo." "Hōigóng dōu yáuh wah, ~ ā ma."* ("That jockey fell off the horse [in the race] and got hurt." "There's a saying, ~. Don't you know that?")

0306

→hóu máh bāthek wùihtàuh chóu 好馬不吃回頭草 (lit.) a good horse will not come/ go back for the grass it has had before 好的馬兒不會回到從前的地方吃草 (idi.) PH (1) when a capable person quits his job, he won't come back again 有本領的人不會回到從前的地方做事：ⓐ*Ngóh yíhchìhn ge bōsí giu ngóh fāanheui kéuihdouh jouh, daahnhaih ~, dōu haih m̀hóu la.* (My old boss asked me to resume my job in his company. But, ~. I'd better not go.) ⓑ *"Wai, A-Chán fāanheui kéuih yíhchìhn ge gūngsī jouh bo." "Haih mē! ~, yáuh búnsih ge jauh m̀sái fāanheui lā."* ("Hey, Chan is going back to his old company." "Really? But ~. If he is a capable person, he should not go back.") (2) not come/ go back to the old place for more benefits 不回到從前的地方去繼續謀利：*Nī géinihn, hóudō yihmàhn wùihlàuh Hēunggóng, daahnhaih ~, ngóh jauh m̀wúih la.* (In recent years, many Hong Kong emmigrants have come back [for jobs]. But for me, I won't ~.)

0307

→jáu máh hon fā 走馬看花 (lit.) look at flowers while galloping/ riding on horseback/a (running) horse 走馬看花 (idi.) PH go on hasty tours 匆匆瀏覽：*Chāamgā léuihhàhngtyùhn hóu fōngbihn, sihk jyuh dōu m̀sái dāamsām, daahnhaih ~.* (If you join a tour group/guided tour, you will find it very convenient. You won't have to worry about eating or where to stay, only that you will ~.)

0308

→jouhmáh 造馬 (lit.) make horse 製造馬匹 (idi.) V race-fixing (originally and usually in horse-racing) (本來及通常指賽馬) 製造賽果：ⓐ *Gāmyaht baau daaih láahng, haih dī kèhsī ~ jī ma.* (The dark horses won in many races today. The results had all been fixed by the jockeys. Didn't you know that?) ⓑ *Múihchi syúnméih jīhauh, dōu yáuh lohksyún ge yàhn wah haih ~ ge.* (After each beauty pageant, there are always some unsuccessful contestants who complain that the outcome has already been fixed.)

0309

→jouh ngàuh jouh máh 做牛做馬 (lit.) be/work like a cow and/ or a horse 做牛做馬 (idi.) PH do hard work and work very hard 幹粗活幹得很辛苦：*Múihyaht ~, sīnji wándóu léuhng chāan.* (I ~ every day before I can earn enough money to get by/ feed myself.)

0310

➜kèh ngàuh wán máh 騎牛搵馬 (lit.) ride a cow and look for a horse (at the same time) 一面騎牛,一面找尋馬兒

(idi.) PH get on with one's job and at the same time look for a better one 一面做目前的工作,一面找更好的工作 : *Kéuih yìhm yìhgā fahn gūng yàhngūng taai síu, daahnhaih yauh mhóyíh jīkhāak jyungūng, wàihyáuh ~ hái lā!* (He is not satisfied with his job because the salary is too low. Yet he can't find a new job quickly. All he can do is ~.)

0311

➜láahng máh 冷馬 (lit.) cold horse 冷的馬

(idi.) N (in horse-racing) dark horse (賽馬)黑馬,難勝出的馬 M jek : *Nī jek haih ~, yùhgwó páauchēut, paaichói jauh hóu sāileih ge la.* (This is a ~. If it wins, you will win a lot of money.)

0312

➜louhchēut máhgeuk 露出馬腳 (lit.) expose the horse's leg 馬兒的腿露了出來

(idi.) PH incautiously reveal one's secret 不小心的洩露了秘密 : *Kéuih ngāak lóuhpòh wah heui hōiwúi, dímjī kéuih sēutsāam seuhngbihn ge sèuhngōuyan ~.* (He lied to his wife that he had gone to a meeting, but he ~ because there's lipstick on his shirt.)

0313

➜louh yìuh jī máhlihk, yahtgáu gin yàhnsām 路遙知馬力,日

久見人心 (lit.) a horse's mettle is shown in the long run, and over time you can see a man's heart 路遙知馬力,日久見人心

(idi.) PH time can tell what a person has on his mind 時間久了才可以知道一個人的內心怎樣 : *Sówaih ~, ~, néih yiu tùhng kéuih sēungchyú noihdī sīnji hóyíh jīdou kéuih haih hóuyàhn yīkwaahk haih waaihyàhn.* (As the saying goes, ~, ~. You have to spend more time with a person before you know if he is good or bad.)

0314

➜lùhng máh jīngsàhn 龍馬精神 see 0277

0315 ✓

➜máhfū 馬伕 (lit.)N A man who takes care of horses in a stable, a groom 馬伕 M go

(idi.) N mafoo, pimp, pander, a man who escorts a prostitute to a customer's place 帶妓女應召的男人 M go : *Néih yíhwàih kéuihdeih léuhnggo paaktō, kèihsaht gógo nàahmyán haih ~.* (You would think the two of them are taking a lover's walk. Actually the man is a ~.)

0316 ✓

➜máh hauh paau 馬後炮 (lit.) PH (in Chinese game of chess) a 'cannon' placed after a 'horse' 馬後炮

(idi.) PH a prediction or/and criticism voiced as an afterthought 事後才說出預測或／及批評 : *"Ngóh jóu jī nīgo yàhn fáangwāt ge lā!" "Néih yauh mjóudī góng, yìhgā jauh (fong)*

~." ("I already knew that he was rebellious." "Why didn't you tell me earlier rather than just telling me now?")

0317 ✓
➔máhjái 馬仔 (lit.) N pony 小馬兒 M jek
(idi.) N (1) henchman of a triad leader 黑幫首領的下屬 M go; dī : *Gógo hāak séhwúi daaih agō giu kéuih bāan ~ tùhng yàhn hōipín.* (That triad boss sent his men to fight another gang.) (2) (said in a joking way) one's subordinate (開玩笑的性質) 下屬 M dī; go : *Wai, néih dī ~ tēng mtēngwah a?* (Hey, do your ~ obey you?) (3) a kind of crispy egg cake 一種甜品小吃

0318 ✓
➔máhméih 馬尾 (lit.) N horse's tail 馬的尾巴 M tiuh
(idi.) N (a kind of hair style) ponytail 一種像馬的尾巴的髮型 M tiuh : *sō/ jaat ~* (have a hair style like a ~)

0319
➔máhmihn 馬面 (lit.) horse's face 馬的臉
(idi.) N a person with a long face (like that of a horse) 臉很長的人 M faai : *~ ge yàhn jeui hóu sō dyún ge tàuhfaat.* (It would be better for ~ to have his hair cut short.)

0320
➔máh séi lohkdeih hàahng 馬死落地行(lit.) the horse is dead and so one has to get off and walk 馬兒死了,你就要下馬步行

(idi.) PH be flexible in coping with a very difficult situation 要靈活對付困境 : *Kéuih jouh gógāan gūngsī jăpjó. Búnlòih kéuih haih jouh gīngléih ge, daahnhaih yihgā wán gūng gam nàahn, yàhngūng dāidī dōu móuh sówaih ge la, ~ ā ma!* (The company he worked in was closed down. He was the manager of it. But now it's so difficult to find a job, he doesn't care if he could get a job of lower salary. Anyway, one has to ~.)

0321
➔máhseuhng 馬上 (lit.) on horseback 在馬上
(idi.) A right away 立刻 : *Ngóh ~ làih.* (I'll come ~.)

0322
➔ngàuh gāangtìhn, máh sihkgūk, lóuhdauh jaahnchìhn jái héungfūk 牛耕田,馬食穀,老豆賺錢仔享福 (lit.) PH cows plough fields, horses eat grain, and a father earns money for his children to live a good life. 父母辛勤工作,讓子女生活得好 : *~, ~, ~. Sóyíh néih mhóu jíyi jáinéui yéuhngfāan néih a.* (~, ~, ~. So don't expect that your children will support you when you are old.)

0323
➔ngàuh gōu máh daaih 牛高馬大 (lit.) as tall as a cow and as big as a horse 像牛那麼高,馬那麼大
(idi.) PH be tall and big, and of well-built figure (sometimes derogatory) 身材高大(有時是貶義) : *Kéuih sāangdāk ~, daahnnhaih láahndou séi.* (He is ~, but he's very lazy.)

0324

➔ngàuhtàuh máhmihn 牛頭馬面 (lit.) cow's head and horse's face 牛的頭跟馬的臉
(idi.) PH the ox-headed devil and the horse-faced devil (who take the soul of the dead to hell) 鬼差 M dī : Kéuih muhnggin dī ~ làih lāai kéuih jáu. (He dreamt of ~ to take him away.)

0325

➔páaumáh seh mānsōu 跑馬射蚊鬚 (lit.) shoot at a mosquito's antenna while galloping/ riding on horseback 一邊騎著馬兒跑,一邊射蚊子的觸鬚
(idi.) PH an impossible task with zero chance of success 成功機會等於零的事情 : Jung luhkhahpchói tàuhjéung, jīkhaih hóuchíh ~ gám lō. (To win the first prize of Mark Six is the same as to ~.)

0326

➔saaimáh 晒馬 (lit.) display all the horses 把所有的馬都擺放出來
(idi.) V (said of two opposing triad leaders) get all the gang members armed and then go for a negotiation and get ready for a showdown 黑社會首領集中所有手下,帶備武器去談判,必要時一戰 : Kàhmmáahn Jīmdūng yáuh léuhng bōng yàhn ~. Hóuchói gíngfōng kahpsíh jaijí. (Last night, there were two triad bosses who ~ in East Tsimshatsui. Luckily, the police stopped them in time.)

0327

➔séuimáh 水馬(lit.) water horse 水做的馬

(idi.) N (a kind of road-block) water-filled plastic barricades (used to keep off/ back people) 一種充水的路障 M dī : Gíngfōng fongjó hóudō ~, m̀béi sihwāi ge yàhn jìpgahn daaihsigún. (The police put many ~ around the embassy to keep the protesters out.)

0328

➔sih gāp máh hàahng tìhn 士急馬行田 (lit.) (in Chinese game of chess) when the chessman 'sih' is in trouble, the 'máh' would move in the pattern of 田 on the chessboard on behalf of 'sih' 中國象棋中的'士'被困,'馬'便要代'士'走'田'字形的路
(idi.) PH be flexible in coping with a difficult situation 要隨機應變 : Go daaihtóuhpóh jokduhng. Lóuhgūng chē kéuih heui yīyún sāang bìhbī. Dímjī bunlóu daaih sākchē, bìhbī yauh yiu chēutsai, ~, go lóuhgūng wàihyáuh jouh jìpsāng sīn. (The pregnant woman was going into labor and started to have regular contractions. Her husband drove her to hospital for delivery. But there was a bad traffic jam, and the baby was coming. All the husband could do was to act as a midwife.)

0329

➔ tit geuk máh ngáahn sàhnsīn tóuh 鐵腳馬眼神仙肚(lit.) iron feet, horse's eyes and a fairy's stomach 鐵腳馬眼神仙肚
(idi.) PH said of an energetic person who can endure hard work by standing, staying awake and not eating for a very long time 體能很好,可以長時間站著,不睡不吃的辛勞工作的人 : Sahtjaahp yīsāng yiu yáuh ~ ji dāk yānwaih yáuhsih yiu dōngjihk 33

go jūngtàuh. (An intern/A houseman is supposed to have ~ because sometimes s/he is to be on call for 33 hours at a time.)

0330
➔titmáh 鐵馬(lit.) iron horse 鐵做的馬
(idi.) N iron road-block (used to keep off/back people) 放在路上用來隔阻人群的鐵欄 M dī：*Sihwāi jé jeung gíngfōng gahéi ge* ~ *tēuidāi*. (The protesters pulled down the ~ set up by the police.)

0331
➔wūyīng lāu máhméih → yāt paak léuhng saan 烏蠅摟馬尾 →一拍兩散 see 0057

0332
➔yìhsyūn jih yáuh yìhsyūn fūk, mohk waih yìhsyūn jok máh ngàuh 兒孫自有兒孫福，莫爲兒孫作馬牛(lit.) PH one's own children and grandchildren will have their own blessing, and so don't work too hard (to earn so much money) for them 兒孫自然有他們的福氣,不要爲他們那麼辛苦工作(掙錢)：*"Chán baak gam lóuh juhng yiu jouhyéh, wán dōdī chín béi dī jáinéui." "Ngóh wah kéuih yīnggōi teuiyāu lā, ~, ~."*("[Old] Mr. Chan is so old and he still has to work in order to earn more money for his children." "I think he should retire. ~, ~.)

máhlāu 馬騮 N monkey 猴子 M jek

0333
➔hàuhgāp/ kàkm 猴急／擒
(lit.) as impatient as a monkey 像猴子那樣性急
(idi.) Adj. (1) impatient 個性急進：*Kéuih nīgo yàhn hóu ~ ge.* (He is an ~ person.) (2) hurried 急不及待的樣子：*Maahnmáan sihk lā, m̀sái gam ~.* (Take your time. Don't eat so ~ ly.)

0334
➔lātsíng máhlāu 甩繩馬騮
(lit.) a monkey freed from the string that ties it 脫了繩子束縛的猴子
(idi.) N naughty children who break away from adults 脫離大人管束的頑皮小孩 M jek：*Pihngsìh yiu wan kéuihdeih hái ngūkkéi jouh gūngfo, yāt daai kéuihdeih chēutgāai jauh binsìhng ~.* (Usually I have them stay at home to do homework. Once I bring them out, they become like ~.)

0335 ✓
➔máhlāu 馬騮 (lit.) N monkey 猴子 M jek
(idi.) N very active or naughty children/ students 很頑皮的小童／學生 bāan; jek：*Gaau bāan ~ gaaudou ngóh sokhei.* (I am exhausted in teaching those ~.)

ngàuh 牛 N cow, ox 牛 M jek

0336 ✓
➔daaihngàuh 大牛 (lit.)N big cow 大的牛 M jek
(idi.) N a HK $500 bill/note 面額五百元的香港紙幣 M jēung：*yāt jēung ~ (~)* also see 0878

52

0337

→deui ngàuh tàahnkàhm 對牛彈琴(lit.) play a harp to a cow 對牛彈琴
(idi.) PH sing to the wrong audience, cast pearls before swine 找錯了對象 : ⓐ *Néih deui dī síufáan góng gīngjaihohk ge mahntàih maih jīkhaih ~.* (You talk about economics with the vendors. You ~.) ⓑ *Kéuih jíhaih deui wánchín yáuh hingcheui jē, néih tùhng kéuih góng ngaihseuht, maih ~.* (He is only interested in [earning] money. You just ~ when you talk about arts with him.)

0338

→hōifōngngàuh 開荒牛 (lit.)a bull opening up a barren land 開闢荒地的牛
(idi.) N a pioneer 先驅者 go/ jek : *Nīgāan hohkhaauh yāt hōi ngóhdeih jauh làih jouh ~ la.* (We were the first teachers in this school when it just opened.)

0339

→jouh ngàuh jouh máh 做牛做馬 see 0309

0340

→kèh ngàuh wán máh 騎牛搵馬 see 0310

0341

→lāai ngàuh séuhng syuh 拉牛上樹 (lit.) (like) pulling a cow up a tree 把牛拉到樹上
(idi.) PH have great difficulty in teaching somebody 很難教 : *Nībāan hohksāang gam chā, daahnhaih yiu hohk gam sām ge yéh, sīnsāang hóuchíh ~ gám.* (The academic level of these students is low, but we want them to learn such difficult things. The teacher feels like ~.)

0342

→mohk waih yìhsyūn jok máh ngàuh 莫為兒孫作馬牛 see 0332

0343

→ ngàuh gāangtìhn, máh sihk gūk, lóuhdauh jaahnchìhn jái héungfūk 牛耕田，馬食穀，老豆賺錢仔享福 see 0322

0344

→ ngàuhgéng 牛頸 (lit.) cow's neck 牛的脖子
(idi.) Adj. stubborn, stiff-necked, obstinate 倔強固執 : *Kéuih nīgo yàhn hóu ~ ge.* (He is a very ~ person.)

0345

→ ngàuh gōu máh daaih 牛高馬大 see 0323

0346 ✓

→ ngàuhjái 牛仔 (lit.)N calf 小牛 M jek
(idi.) N cowboy 美國西部的牛仔 M go : *Tiu ~ móuh.* (Dance ~ dance.) ATT made of strong cotton cloth for jeans 用牛仔布做的 : ⓐ ~ *fu* (jeans) ⓑ ~ *kwàhn* / ~ *lāu* (a skirt/ jacket ~)

0347

→ngàuh jiuh máauhdāan 牛嚼

53

牡丹 (lit.) (like) a cow chewing peony flower 牛嚼牡丹花
(idi.) PH cannot appreciate good food 不懂欣賞食物好處 : *Néih jyú gam hóu ge yéh béi kéuih sihk dōu móuh yuhng ge. Kéuih ~ gám, jáan sāai sāmgēi jē!* (It's no use [your] making such good dishes for him. He eats like ~. It's just a waste of your time.)

0348

→ ngàuh m̀yámséui m̀gamdāk ngàuhtàuh dāi 牛唔飲水唔拎得牛頭低 (lit.) you can lead a horse to water, but you cannot make it drink 牛要是不想喝水,你是沒有辦法把牠的頭按下去的
(idi.) PH no one can impose on you what you don't want to do 沒有人可以強迫你做你不願意做的事 : *Néih m̀hóu gwaai yàhndeih gaauwaaih néih, ~, néih jihgéi dōu yiu fuhjaak ge.* (Don't blame others for teaching you to do bad things. ~. You are responsible for what you have done.)

0349

→ ngàuhpèih dānglùhng → dímgihk dōu m̀mìhng (牛皮燈籠→點極都唔明) (lit.) a lantern made of hide→no matter how it is lit, it won't be bright 用牛皮做的燈籠,無論你怎樣點火,它都不會光亮照人
(idi.) HIT no matter how you teach/say, one does not understand 無論你怎樣教／說,別人都不明白 : ⓐ *Nī bāan hohksāang, hóuchíh gám → ~.* (These students are like ~

→ ~.) ⓑ *Nīgo douhléih ngóh góngjó hóudō chi la, jouh māt néih juhnghaih ~ → ~ ga?* (I have explained this to you for so many times. Why are you still as dumb as a ~ → ~?)

0350

→ ngàuh pèihhei 牛脾氣 (lit.) cow's temper 牛的脾氣
(idi.) N stubborn (like a cow) 像牛的性格那樣固執 M pōu : *Kéuih nīgo yàhn yáuh pōu ~.* (He is ~.)

0351

→ ngàuhtàuh máhmihn 牛頭馬面 see 0324

0352

→ ngàuhtàuh m̀daap máhjéui 牛頭唔答馬嘴 (lit.) the cow's head does not answer [the questions from] the horse's mouth 牛的頭不答馬的嘴巴(裏的問題)
(idi.) PH give irrelevant response, beside the point 答非所問 : *Néih mahn kéuih nīyeuhng, kéuih jauh daap néih góyeuhng, ~ gám.* (You ask him this and he answers that. He just ~.)

0353

→ ngàuhyāt 牛一 (lit.) cow and one 牛和一
(idi.) N/V birthday (*This is the break down of the Chinese character 生, which means birth, into 牛[cow] and 一[one].) 生日(把 '生' 字拆成 '牛' 及 '一') : *Kéuih gāmyaht ~.* (Today is his ~.)

0354

→ séingàuh yātbihn géng 死

54

牛一便頸 (lit.) as stiff-necked as a dead cow 像死牛的脖子那樣硬 (idi.) PH too stubborn 非常固執倔強 : *Mhóu gam ~ lā, néih yiu tēng yàhn hyun sīn dāk gaak.* (Don't be ~. You should listen to others' advice.)

0355
→ tōng séingàuh 劏死牛 (lit.) kill a dead cow 宰死了的牛 (idi.) VO rob 打劫 : ⓐ *béi yàhn/ cháak ~* (be ~ by somebody/ a thief) ⓑ *Gódouh yehmáahn hóu hāak hóu jihng, yáuh yàhn ~.* (It is very dark and quiet there at night, and sometimes there are robberies.)

0356✓
→ wòhngngàuh 黃牛(lit.) N ox 黃牛 M jek
(idi.) N profiteers (selling tickets on the black market) 炒賣黑市票的人 M go : *Dī ~ cháaugwaisaai dī fēi.* (The ~ got all the tickets and then sold them at a high price.)

0357
→ yātgeuk ngàuhsí 一腳牛屎 (lit.) foot is covered with cow shit 滿腳沾了牛糞 (idi.) PH country folk, farming folk, country cousin 鄉下人, 鄉巴佬: *Kéuih chōchō hái hēunghá chēutlàih ge sihhauh, ~. Géisahp nìhn jīhauh, kéuih sìhngwàih nīdouh seuhnglàuh séhwúi ge jīmìhng yàhnsih la.* (When he first came here from his native place, he was just a ~. After several decades, he has become a celebrity in the upper class here.)

sījí 獅子 N lion 獅子 M jek

0358 ✓
→ sījí beih 獅子鼻 (lit.)N lion's nose 獅子的鼻子 M go (idi.) N pug-nose, snub nose like that of a lion 像獅子那樣大而扁的鼻子 M go : *"Kéuih go yéung dím ga?" "Máh mihn, dahtngáahn gāmyú, ~.".* ("What does he look like?" "He has a long face [like that of a horse], protruding eyes [like those of a gold fish], and a ~.)

0359
→sījí hōi daaih háu 獅子開大口 (lit.) lion opens its mouth wide 獅子張開大的口 (idi.) PH demand as much as possible (in a bargain) 在討價還價之中盡量索取 : ⓐ *Làuhga jeui gōu ge sìhhauh, yùhgwó néih séung máaih yihsáu láu, dī yihpjyú dōu ~.* (If you want to buy a second-hand flat when flat prices are at their peak, the flat owner will ~.) ⓑ *Nàahmgā mahn néuihgā yiu géidō láihgām, néuihgā jauh ~.* (When the bridegroom's family asked the bride's family how much money they wanted for the betrothal, they just ~.)

wùhléi 狐狸 N fox 狐狸 M jek

0360
→lóuh wùhléi 老狐狸 (lit.) old fox 老的狐狸 (idi.) N cunning old person 老奸巨滑 M jek : *Kéuih jingyāt haih ~ làih ga, néih yiu síusām m̀hóu séuhng kéuih dong.* (He is really an ~. Be careful not to fall into his trap.)

0361

→wùhlèihjīng 狐狸精 (lit.) fox demon 狐狸妖精
(idi.) N a woman who seduces other's husband 勾引別人丈夫的女人 M jek/ go : *Néih jek ~, ngāuyáhn ngóh lóuhgūng!* (You ~! You seduced my hushand!)

yèuhng 羊 N sheep, goat 羊 M jek

0362

→gwa yèuhngtàuh maaih gáuyuhk 掛羊頭賣狗肉 see 0197

0363 ✓

→mìhnyéung/ yèuhngjái 綿羊仔 (lit.) N little lamb 小綿羊 M jek
(idi.) N motor-cycle 摩托車 M ga : *Chē, ngóh jauh móuh la, ~ jauh yáuh yātga.* (A car? I don't have one. I just have a ~.)

0364

→m̀sihk yèuhngyuhk yātsān sōu 唔食羊肉一身臊 (lit.) even though you don't eat mutton, people still can smell it's odour on you 雖然你不吃羊肉,人們還是可以從你身上嗅到羊肉的氣味
(idi.) PH get involved in an unexpected and troublesome case 無端惹禍上身 : *Ngóhge tùhngngūk chòhngduhk, gíngchaat làih sáuchàh kéuihge fóng, lihn ngóh dōu yiu séuhng chāaigún hipjoh diuhchàh, nīchi jānhaih ~ la.* (When the police came to search my flatmate's room and found some drugs, they had me

go to the police station to assist in enquiries. This time I certainly ~.)

0365

→sung yèuhng yahp fúháu 送羊入虎口 see 0261

0366

→yèuhnggú 羊牯 (lit.) ram 公羊
(idi.) N a fool (both as a layman and as a dupe/ sucker) 被人欺騙的行外人 M jek/ go : *Sāamchīn mān yáuh yātkā jyunsehk, néih gú ngóh haih ~ mè!* (These diamonds cost $3,000 a karat. Do you think that I am ~?)

0367

→yèuhngmòuh chēutjoih yèuhng sānseuhng 羊毛出在羊身上 (lit.) wool grows on sheep 羊毛在羊身上生出來
(idi.) PH all charges are shifted to customers 所有費用都由顧客承擔 : *Gógāan baakfo gūngsī yauh daaih jahngsung yauh yáuh chāujéung, kèihsaht maih ~ jī ma.* (They offer free items and have lucky draws in that department store. In fact, all the expenses have already been included in the price of the things you buy.)

56

2. Body Parts and Their Functions

beih(gō)鼻(哥)N nose 鼻子 M go

0368

➔beihgōlūng móuh yuhk 鼻哥窿冇肉 (lit.)nasal cavity has no flesh 鼻孔沒有肉
(idi.) PH extremely terrified 非常驚恐：*Ga fēigēi fātyihngāan gāp gong géi chīn chek, haakdou dī sihnghaak/dī sihnghaak haakdou ~.* (The plane suddenly plunged thousands of feet. The passengers were ~.)

0369

➔dūk ngáahn dūk beih 篤眼篤鼻 (lit.) prick the .eyes and the nose 刺眼和刺鼻
(idi.) PH like a thorn in one's eye 如眼中釘：*Ngóh gindóu kéuih jauh ~.* (When[ever] I see him, I feel that he is ~.)

0370

➔lyūnmōu ngāubeih → ngok kaau 鬈毛鈎鼻 → 惡靠 (lit.) (people born with) curly hair and a Roman nose → they are unreliable (天生有)鬈曲的頭髮和鈎曲的鼻子 →(這種人)不可靠
(idi.) HIT Chinese with a face like a Westerner are (considered to be) unreliable 樣貌像西方人的中國人不可靠：*"Ngóh séung tùhng kéuih hahpjok jouh sāangyi." " ~ → ~. Néih yiu síusāmdī."* ("I want to do

business with him." "(He looks like a Westerner and since) ~. You'd better take care.")

0371

➔sījí beih 獅子鼻 see 0358

0372

➔tùhng yātgo beihgōlūng chēuthei 同一個鼻哥窿出氣 (lit.) (people) breathe with the same nose (人們)用同一個鼻子呼吸
(idi.) PH (said of people) have the same opinion when arguing with others 人們在與人爭辯時有同樣意見：*Kéuihdeih léuhnggo haih tùhngsih, yihkhaih lóuhyáuhgei, sóyíh sihsih dōu ~.* (The two of them are fellow workers, and they have become very good friends. They always ~.)

boktàuh 膊頭 N shoulder 肩膊 M go; bīn

0373

➔boktàuh gōugwo yíh 膊頭高過耳 (lit.) shoulders are higher than ears 肩膊比耳朵高
(idi.) PH skinny/ bony person (usually referring to drug addicts) 非常瘦的人(通常指癮君子)：*Kéuih saudou ~.* (He is a ~/ so thin that his ~.)

0374 ✓

➔paak boktàuh 拍膊頭 (lit.) VO pat on the shoulder 拍肩膊

(idi.) VO ask somebody to do something for you out of friendship (and so you don't have to pay him money) 請朋友幫忙（因為彼此的友誼，不用付酬勞）： *Yáuhsih pàhngyáuh ~ giu ngóh bōngsáu, ngóh dōu móuh sāuchín ga.* (Sometimes my friends ~ and I don't ask them to give me any money.)

buijek 背脊 N back 背 M go

0375

➔buijek heung tīn yàhn só sihk 背脊向天人所食 (lit.) all things that (walk/crawl on four legs and) have backs facing the sky can be eaten by man 所有背向天的東西都可被人吃

(idi.) PH all animals can be eaten by man 所有動物都可以吃： *Sāiyàhn gin Jūnggwok yàhn sihk dahkbiht ge duhngmaht jauh gokdāk hóu kèihgwaai, daahnhaih Jūnggwok yàhn jauh wah ~, móuh māt chēutkèih ā.* (Westerners are surprised when they see Chinese people eating unusual animals. But the Chinese would say ~. There's nothing unusual.)

0376

➔dūk buijek 篤背脊 (lit.) prick one's back 刺背

(idi.) VO backbite, speak ill of somebody behind his back 在背後用說話中傷別人： *Kéuih hái bōsí mihnchìhn ~ ngóh ~, ǹgwaaidāk ngóh sīngm̀hdóu kāp lā.* (He ~ me before our boss. No wonder I have not been promoted yet.)

0377

➔tòhbui 駝背 (lit.) camel's hump 駱駝的背

(idi.) N (said of a person) humpback 佝僂，彎背： ⓐ*Kéuih ~ ge.* (He has a ~.) ⓑ *Sānjihk tiuh yīu, yùhgwó m̀haih, jauh wúih ~/ hòhnbui ge la.* (Straighten up. Otherwise you'll have a ~.) ATT hump-backed 佝僂的： ~ *lóu* (a ~ man)

chéung 腸 N intestine 腸子 M tiuh

0378

➔hīn chèuhng gwa tóuh 牽腸掛肚(lit.) pull the intestine and hang the belly 牽腸掛肚

(idi.) PH very anxious (about someone) 很掛念某人： *Néih yātgo néuihjái, yàuh jīu heuidou máahn, yauh m̀dá dihnwá fāan ngūkkéi, dáng néih màhmā ~.* (You are a girl. You go out from morning till night without ringing up your mother at home. You make her ~ about you.)

0379

➔jihk chèuhng jihk tóuh 直腸直肚 (lit.) straight intestine and straight belly 直的腸子和肚

(idi.) Adj.PH/ PH (1) frank and straight forward in one's speech 說話坦白,不轉彎抹角： *Kéuih nīgo yàhn ~, yáuh māt góng māt.* (He is ~. He says whatever he wants to say.) (2) easily let out the secret 容易說出秘密： *Nīgihn sih m̀hóu góngbéi kéuih tēng, ngóh pa kéuih ~, yàhndeih yāt mahn kéuih jauh góngsaai chēutlàih.* (Don't tell him about this. I'm afraid that he will ~ and tell people everything when they ask him about this.)

0380

➔waahk gūngjái waahkchēut chéung 畫公仔畫出腸 (lit.) draw a person, and his intestine too 畫一個人,連他身體內的腸也畫出來

(idi.) PH too explicit in description (, in fact a tacit knowledge is enough) 描述太過露骨 : *Kéuih yìhgā tùhng lóuhbáan ge néui paaktō, wahìndihng jēunglòih wúih jouh ngóhdeih ge gīngléih." "Néih sáimāt ~ jē!"* ("He is now the lover of our employer's daughter. Maybe one day he will be our manager." "Oh, it's not necessary for you to tell us. [We all think so.]")

dáam 膽 N gall bladder 膽囊 M go

0381 ✓

➔dáam 膽 (lit.)N gall bladder 膽囊 M go

(idi.) BF (1) things that look like a gall bladder 像膽囊形狀的東西 : *dāng* ~ (light bulb) (2) inner part (that functions) 在裏面發生作用的部分 : ⓐ*sósih* ~ (~ of a lock) ⓑ*nyúhnséuiwùh* ~ (~ of a thermos bottle)

0382

➔dáam daaih sām sai 膽大心細 (lit.) gall is big and heart is small 膽很大,心很小

(idi.) PH courageous and cautious 膽子大而小心 : *Kéuih nīgo yàhn ~, hóu sīkhahp jouh yīsāng.* (He is a ~ person. Being a doctor suits him.)

0383

➔dáam daaih sām sai mihnpèih háuh 膽大心細面皮厚 (lit.) gall is big, heart is small and the skin of the face is thick 膽很大,心很小,臉皮厚

(idi.) PH be bold, considerate and thick-skinned 膽子大, 無微不至, 及不怕不好意思: *Jēui néuihjái yiu ~.* (When chasing after a girl, one needs to ~.)

0384

➔dáam sāang mòuh 膽生毛 (lit.) hair grows on the gall 膽囊長出毛

(idi.) PH dare to do something incredible 好大的膽子去做不好的事情 : *Dī cháak jānhaih ~, lihn gíngchyúh ge chē dōu gám tāu.* (The thieves ~. They even stole a car from the police station.)

0385

➔sādáam 沙膽 (lit.) sandy gall bladder 有沙的膽囊

(idi.) Adj. see 0384

fai 肺 N lung 肺 M go; bīn

0386

➔chīfai 黐肺 (lit.) glued lungs 黏著的肺

(idi.) VO exhausted 筋疲力盡 : *jouhdou* ~ (work until ~)

0387

➔dám sām dám fai 扰心扰肺 (lit.) beat one's chest (enclosing heart and lungs) with one's fist(s) 用拳捶打自己胸膛

(idi.) PH deeply regret 很後悔 :

59

Kàhmyaht ngóh jek gúpiu sīngdāk gam gōu ngóh móuh maaih, gāmyaht jauh daaihdit, jānhaih ~. (I ~ for not having sold the stocks and shares I bought. Their prices soared yesterday but plunge today.)

0388

➔dou hàuh m̀dou fai 到喉唔到肺 (lit.) reach the throat but not the lungs 只到喉嚨,去不到肺部
(idi.) PH just half satisfied 只滿足了一半 : *Cheung yuhtkūk ge yàhn jūngyi cheung chèuhng ge kūk, nīsáu kūk gam dyún, kéuihdeih wúih gokdāk ~.* (People who sing Cantonese opera like to sing long songs. This song is so short, they would feel ~.)

0389

➔yīu sām yīu fai 扶心扶肺 (lit.) pierce through the heart and lungs 刺透心和肺
(idi.) PH break one's heart 令人傷心 : ⓐ*Kéuih yāt námhéi lóuhgūng go yihnāai jauh (gokdāk) ~.* (She would ~ as soon as she thought of the mistress of her husband.) ⓑ*Kéuih góngyéh (lihng ngóh) ~.* (His words hurt me so much.)

géng 頸 N neck 脖子 M tiuh

0390

➔dínggéng 頂頸 (lit.) prop up the neck 把脖子頂住
(idi.) VO quarrel 吵架 : *M̀hóu sìhngyaht tùhng yàhn ~ lā.* (Don't always ~ with others.)

0391

➔diugéng dōu yiu táuhei 吊

頸都要抖氣 (lit.) take a breath even in the midst of hanging onself 上吊也要鬆一口氣
(idi.) PH avail oneself of an opportunity to relax (even though one is very busy) 就算忙得透不過氣來也要鬆弛一下 : *Gāmyaht sèhngyaht góngūng, daahnhaih ~, yihgā taanfāan būi gafē sīn.* (I've been very busy at work all day today. I need to ~. Let me enjoy a cup of coffee first.)

0392

➔ fógéng 火頸 (lit.) fiery neck 有火的頸
(idi.) Adj. a person who easily flies into a temper, touchy 容易生氣發怒的人 : *Kéuih nīgo yàhn hóu ~ ge.* (He is ~.)

0393

➔ gánggéng sei 梗頸四 (lit.) stiff-neck four 硬脖子四
(idi.) N (in a competition) the third runner-up, be in the fourth place 在比賽中得到殿軍/第四 : *Gó chi béichoi, kéuih jíhaih dākdóu go ~ jē.* (He was only ~ in that contest.)

0394 ✓

➔géng 頸 (lit.) N neck 脖子 M tiuh
(idi.) BF the neck of, having the shape of a human neck 像頸項形狀的 : *jēun ~* (bottle ~)

0395

➔ jā géng jauh mehng 揸頸就命 (lit.) grip one's neck to maintain life 握住脖子生存下去
(idi.) PH suffer humiliation in order to

60

survive in a difficult situation 忍辱偷生,忍氣吞聲 : "Wai, jīngfú yìhgā m̀sìhngyìhng ngóhdeih ge jīgaak bo!" "Wàih yáuh ~ hái lā. Yàhngūng dāi gam dō dōu yiu jouh ge la." ("Hey, our qualifications are no longer recognized by the government." "The only thing we can do is ~. We have to take this job even though the pay is so low.")

0396

➔ láam tàuh láam géng/gai 攬頭攬頸／髻(lit.) embrace heads and necks/ buns (of hair) 抱頭相擁
(idi.) PH behave intimately (usually said of lovers) 舉動親熱 (通常指情侶) : ⓐ Gam dō yàhn háidouh jauh m̀hóu ~ lā. (You shouldn't ~ when there are so many people here.) ⓑ Dī gwáilóu yāt ginmihn jauh ~ ge la. (Foreigners will hug each other when they meet.)

0397

➔ mohng VO/ PH mohngdou géng dōu chèuhng(jó) 望⋯⋯望到頸都長(咗) (lit.)stare at something until one's neck becomes longer 注視東西,連脖子也長了
(idi.) PH anxiously long for something 非常渴望 : ⓐ Dágūngjái, sìhsìh ~ chēutlèuhng ~. (For the salaried class, they always ~ their payday/ pay check) ⓑ Ngóh ~ kéuih làih ~. (I ~ her arrival.)

0398

➔ ngaahnggéng 硬頸 (lit.) stiff neck 硬脖子
(idi.) Adj. stubborn, too strong-willed 固執倔強 : Kéuih nīgo yàhn

hóu ~ ge, wah gám jauh gám, m̀tēng yàhn hyun ge. (He is very ~. He just does what he has decided to do, and won't listen to anybody's advice.)

0399

➔ ngaaugéng 拗頸 (lit.) twist a neck 扭曲脖子
(idi.) VO argue 爭辯 : Kéuih hóu jūngyi tùhng yàhn ~. (He likes to ~ with others very much.)

0400

➔ ngàuhgéng 牛頸 see 0344

0401

➔ paaujéung géng 炮仗頸 (lit.) fire-cracker neck 爆竹造的脖子
(idi.) N a person who flies into a temper very easily, but after that, he won't be angry with you any more 很容易生氣發脾氣的人,但發完脾氣之後便沒事 : Kéuih nīgo yàhn ~. Sēuiyihn kéuih tàuhsīn laauh néih, daahnhaih yātjahngāan jauh wúih móuh sih ge la. (He is ~. Although he has just scolded you, he will forget all about it in a short while.)

0402

➔ sān gwōng géng leng 身光頸靚 (lit.) brilliant body and beautiful neck 身體發光,脖子美麗
(idi.) PH (said of a person) looks smart/ sharp by dressing nicely 衣著光鮮好看, 人也容光煥發 : Nīpáai gin kéuih ~ gám, gánghaih wándóu fahn hóu gūng la. (Recently I have noticed that he ~. He must have found a good job.)

0403

➔sauhsīnggūng diugéng → yihm mehng chèuhng 壽星公吊頸→嫌命長 (lit.) the God of Longevity hangs himself→(because) he dislikes living such a long life 壽星上吊→他不喜歡長命

(idi.) HIT (usually referred to elderly people) put one's life at risk 做對生命有危險的事(通常指上了年紀的人)：*"Gógo a-baak hái nīdouh gwo máhlouh, jānhaih ngàihhím la." "Kéuih gánghaih ~ → ~ díng la."* ("It's really dangerous for the old man to cross the road here." "He certainly ~/ Did he want to kill himself?")

geuk 腳 N foot, leg 腳 M jek; deui/ sēung

0404

➔chāu hauhgeuk 抽後腳 (lit.) draw the hind leg 拉起後腿

(idi.)VO pull one's leg, tease someone by repeating what he says 重覆別人的說話以取笑他：*"Néih maih wah yihmàhn jīkhaih yiu jouh yihdáng gūngmàhn, yihgā néih yauh yihmàhn." "M̀hóu ~ ngóh ~ lā."* ("You criticized those emmigrants that they were going to be second-class citizens (as expatriates). How come you are emigrating now?" "Please don't ~.")

0405

➔chōu sáu chōu geuk 粗手粗腳(lit.) rough hands and feet 粗糙的手跟腳

(idi.) PH too clumsy to do delicate work（用手)做事不夠細心：ⓐ *Nīgihn sī jāt ge sāam m̀hóu béi kéuih sái lo. Kéuih ~ gám, yùhng māt yih sáilaahn ngóh gihn sāam a.* (Don't let him/her wash this silk dress, s/he is ~. S/he might easily damage it when washing it.) ⓑ *Kéuih ~ gám, dím hóyíh saufā a?* (She is ~. How can she do embroidery?)

0406

➔dahmgeuk 扰腳 (lit.) stamp one's feet 頓足

(idi.) VO stamp the floor 把腳大力踏在地上 ： *hōisāmdou/nāudou (háidouh)* ~ (~ in happiness/ anger)

0407

➔dō sáu dō geuk 多手多腳 (lit.) many hands and many feet 很多手很多腳

(idi.) Adj. PH touch anything one likes 亂摸東西：*"A jái, yātjahngāan ngóhdeih heuidou Chàhntáai ngūkkéi, néih m̀hóu gam ~ gáau yàhndeih ge yéh bo,"* màhmā wah. ("My boy, don't be so naughty when we are in Mrs. Chan's house. Don't ~ and meddle with her things," said the mother.)

0408

➔ gaap sáu gaap geuk 夾手夾腳 (lit.) put together everybody's hands and feet 把各人的手和腳放在一起

(idi.) A.PH cooperatively 一起合作 ： *Ngóhdeih daaihgā ~ bouji láihtòhng.* (We are decorating the auditorium ~.)

0409

➔gāi gám geuk 雞噉腳 see 0122

0410 ✓

➔geuk 腳(lit.) N foot, leg 腳 M jek; deui / sēung

(idi.) BF (1) leg of furniture 傢俱的支撐部分 : tói/ dang/ chòhng ~ (~ of table/ chair/ bed) (2) the lower part of 底的部分 : sāan/ syuh ~ (foot of a mountain/ tree) (3) the lower part of clothing 衣物的下方 : sāam/ fu ~ (~ a top garment/ trousers) N player of mahjong 打麻將的搭子 M jek : Ngóhdeih sēung dá màhjeuk, daahnhaih jāang yātjek ~. (We want to play mahjong, but we lack one ~.)

0411

➔ geukjāang ṁdou deih 腳睜唔到地 (lit.) heels not touching the ground 腳跟不踩到地面

(idi.) PH according to Chinese physiognomy, a person walking this way will not live long 中國相術認為不是長壽的人的走路姿態 : Kéuih hàahnglouh ~ gám, néih faaidī giu kéuih hàahngfāanhóu. (He walks with his ~. You hurry up and tell him to walk in a better way.)

0412

➔gōn sáu jehng geuk 乾手淨腳 (lit.) clean hands and feet 乾淨的手跟腳

(idi.) PH it will be more simple 事情會簡單一些: Jyúfaahn hóu faisih, chēutgāai sihk maih ~ lō! (It takes one a lot of time and energy to cook a meal. ~ if we eat out.)

0413

➔gwánséui luhk geuk 滾水淥腳 (lit.) pour boiling hot water on the feet 燙的水倒在腳上

(idi.) A.PH/PH a hasty visitor leaves soon after his arrival 匆匆而來,不能久留的客人 : Kéuih làihjó móuh géinói jauh ~ gám jáujó la. (He left soon after arriving.)

0414

➔ hàahngwahn hàahngdou lohk geukjí mēi 行運行到落腳趾尾(lit.) even one's smallest toe is having good luck 連尾趾也走運

(idi.) PH (1) very lucky indeed 非常僥倖 : Gūngsī géichi chòihyùhn dōu chòih ṁdóu néih, néih jānhaih ~. (Our company has been laying off its staff members for several times, but every time you are ~ for not being made a victim.) (2) have good luck in everything 事事順利: Gāmyaht jungjó géichèuhng máh, yihgā lihn méihchèuhng dōu jungmàaih, jānhaih ~. (I've already won several times in horse-race today. And I just won even the last race, I really ~.)

0415

➔ hēunggāi geuk 香雞腳 (lit.) the leg of an incense stick 香的腳

(idi.) N human legs as thin as incense sticks 人的腳如香的腳那麼瘦 M jek; deui: Kéuih hóu dō sih jeuk chèuhng ge kwàhn, haih ṁséung yàhn táigin kéuih deui ~. (She mostly wears long skirts. It's because she doesn't want her thin legs to be seen by others.)

0416

→hóu geuktàuh 好腳頭 (lit.) good foot front 好腳兒
(idi.) PH one who can bring good luck to one's family or the social group that one belongs to 能給家人或自己所屬社團帶來好運的人 : *Kéuihge néui ~, chēutsai móuh géi noih kéuih jauh faatdaaht la.* (His daughter is ~. Not long after she was born, he made a fortune.)

0417

→ jáam geukjí beih sāchúng 斬腳趾避沙蟲 see 0009

0418

→ jé sáu jé geuk 姐手姐腳 (lit.) maid's hands and feet 姐兒的手和腳
(idi.) PH clumsy in or not accustomed to doing heavy work 很笨拙或不習慣做粗活 : *"Tái kéuih jouhyéh ~ gám." "Gánghaih lā, kéuih gam sīmàhn, kéuih haih chīngām síujé làih gā ma."* ("I can see that she is ~." "Of course. She is so ladylike. She is a daughter of a rich man. Didn't you know that?")

0419

→jí sáu waahk geuk 指手劃腳 (lit.) point with fingers and draw with feet 用手指及用腳畫
(idi.) PH (1) use body language or make gestures by using one's hand 用手指指點點 : *Kéuih hái gódouh ~ gám, m̀jī séung góng mātyéh.* (He is using his hands to make gestures. It seems that he is trying to tell us something.) (2) a gesture of giving an order 發號司令的神態 : *Kéuih*

ngāamngāam sīngjó kāp, jauh sihngyaht ~ gám. (He has just had a promotion but he always puts on airs and gives us orders.)

0420

→jouh sáu geuk 做手腳 (lit.) make hands and feet 製造手和腳
(idi.) VO do some tricks (in order to accomplish a task) 為達到目的而做一些手段 : ⓐ *Gógo hohksāang búnlòih m̀sīngdāk bāan ge, daahnhaih sīnsāang hái kéuihge sihngjīkdouh ~ jó ~, sóyíh sāumēi kéuih sīngdóu bāan la.* (Originally, that student could not be promoted [to a higher level]. But later he could because his teacher ~ in his grade.) ⓑ *Gójek máh ge johngtaai hóu chā ge, daahnhaih máhfū ~ jó ~, sóyíh kéuih páauchēut.* (That horse was not in good shape, but the groom ~, and so it won the race.)

0421

→lāai yàhn kwàhn kám jihgéi geuk 拉人裙冚自己腳 (lit.) draw another's skirt to cover one's feet 拉別人的裙子來把自己的腳蓋著
(idi.) PH put oneself in other's shade of honour 滔別人的光 : *Kéuih sihngyaht tùhng dī mìhnglàuh yātchái, tòihgōu jihgéi ge sānga, kèihsaht haih ~ jē.* (He always associates with the celebrities in order to upgrade his social status. He just ~.)

0422

→làhmsìh／gāp póuh faht geuk 臨時／急抱佛腳 (lit.) embrace Buddha's leg (pleading help) in emergency 事情緊急時抱著佛的腳 (求助)

(idi.) PH make hasty preparations at the last moment 最後關頭才匆匆準備：*Pihngsih m̀wānjaahp, háausi jauh ~, hōi yehchē dōu móuh yuhng lā.* (Usually you don't study or review your lessons. You just ~ . You study till a late hour the night before your exam. That won't help.)

0423

➔ màhjeuk geuk 麻雀腳 (lit.) sparrow's leg 麻雀的腳
(idi.) N see 0410

0424

➔ m̀hóu sáu geuk 唔好手腳 (lit.) not good hands and feet 不好的手跟腳
(idi.) PH one who has a tendency to steal money 有偷錢傾向：ⓐ *Kéuih nīgo yàhn ~.* (He is ~.) ⓑ *M̀hóu jāi gam dō chín hái poutáu, ngóh pa yáuh fógei ~.* (Don't leave so much money in the shop. I'm afraid some of the employees will steal it.)

0425

➔ ngaaplá geuk 鴨姆腳 see 0169

0426

➔ nganngan geuk 印印腳 (lit.) shake one's legs 彈腿
(idi.) PH (1) feel relaxed 覺得輕鬆：*Jouhyùhnsaai yéh, yihgā hóyíh ~ la.* (I have finished all my work. Now I can ~.) (2) enjoy life 生活寫意：*Kéuihdī jáinéui daaihsaai la, wánchín yéuhng kéuih, kéuih yihgā ~.* (His children are all grown up and earn money to support him. Now he can ~.)

0427

➔ sái geuk m̀maat geuk 洗腳唔抹腳 (lit.) wash the feet but not dry them 洗腳後不把腳抹乾
(idi.) PH (said of a big spender) squanders money 揮霍金錢：*Sihngyaht ~, m̀jí yātgo sīn dōu móuh dāk jihng, juhng himlohk hóudō kāatsou tīm.* (He always ~. He is not only penniless, but also has a lot of credit card debts.)

0428

➔ sáu dō geuk dō 手多腳多 see 0407

0429

➔ sáugeuk m̀hóu 手腳唔好 see 0424

0430

➔ sāu máaihlouhchìhn dá geukgwāt 收買路錢打腳骨 (lit.) compel you to give a toll and beat your leg 強索過路者金錢又打他們
(idi.) PH rob (the travelers) 攔途截劫：ⓐ *Hàahngsāan yàhnsih yiu síusām, taai pīnpīk ge deihfōng, wúih yáuh sèhféi ~.* (Hikers need to be on their guard in remote places where they might be ~ by illegal immigrants.) (* In recent years, the expression has not been as commonly used as 'dágip' 打劫.) ⓑ *Sīgēi kongyìh seuihdouh gāga. Kéuihdeih ge wàahngngáak seuhngbihn séjyuh "~."* (Drivers stage a protest against the harbour tunnel toll rise. They write on their banner [to condemn the tunnel operator], "You are a [highway] robber!")

0431

➔ sáu mòhng geuk lyuhn 手忙腳亂 (lit.) hands are busy and feet are in disorder 手忙腳亂 (idi.) PH be in a flurry and not know how to handle things 很慌亂不知如何處理事情才好 : *Ngóhdeih sāang daihyātgo jái gójahnsí, yānwaih móuh gīngyihm, sóyíh chau bihbī jauh ~.* (When we had our first child, we were ~ because we didn't have any experience of taking care of a baby.)

0432

➔ syún sáu laahn geuk 損手爛腳 (lit.) hands hurt and feet are rotton 手有損傷,腳也潰爛 (idi.) PH suffer heavy losses/ get burned in investment or speculation 投資或投機虧損厲害 : *Kéuih tàuhjī hói gūngchóng, dím bātjī gáaudou ~.* (He invested his money in openning a factory. How could he have known that he would ~.)

0433

➔ tàuhtung yī tàuh, geuktung yī geuk 頭痛醫頭，腳痛醫腳 (lit.) have a headache, heal the head ; have a footache, heal the foot (i.e. to undergo local treatment only, which is a typical way of practice in Western medicine.) 頭痛便醫治頭,腳痛便醫治腳 (局部的醫病方法,西醫常用) (idi.) PH not treat the real problem, but just the symptoms 治標不治本 : *Hēunggóng deih síu yàhn dō, làuhga sīnji wúih gam gōu jē, yùhgwó jingfú jíhaih ngaatyīk làuhga, jauh jíhaih ~, ~ jē.* (Hong Kong is a small place but has a large population. Therefore, property prices are so high. If the government only suppresses flat prices, it does ~.)

0434

➔ tit geuk máh ngáahn sàhnsīn tóuh 鐵腳 馬眼 神仙肚 see 0329

0435

➔ tok daaih geuk 托大腳 (lit.) carry on one's shoulder a pair of big feet of someone else's (肩上)抬著別人的一雙大腳 (idi.) VO crawl to the boss, flatter one's boss 拍馬屁,討好上司 : *Kéuih sīngdāk gam faai, kaau ~ jī ma.* (He has had so many promotions [in such a short time] merely because he ~.)

0436

➔ yàhn dō sáugeuk lyuhn 人多手腳亂 (lit.) too many people and so their hands and feet get entangled 人太多做事會亂 (idi.) PH too many cooks spoil the broth 幫倒忙 : *Msái gam dō yàhn lo, ~.* (We don't need that many people. ~.)

0437

➔ yātgeuk daahp léuhng syùhn 一腳踏兩船 (lit.) stand on two boats with one pair of feet 一雙腳分別踏在兩隻船上 (idi.) PH seek benefits from two sides 從雙方之中獲取好處 : ⓐ *Kéuih tùhng Chàhn síujé paaktō, yauh tùhng Léih síujé paaktō, ~, gám dím dāk ga?* (He dates Miss Chan, but he also dates Miss Lee. He shouldn't alternate between two ladies.) ⓑ *Léuhnggāan gūngsī dōu chéng*

66

kéuih jouh dúngsí, kéuih yihgā ~, dōu m̀ jì géi hóu. (Both companies want him to be one of their directors. Now he gets benefits from them. How nice!)

0438

➔ yātgeuk ngàuhsí 一腳牛屎
see 0357

0439

➔ yātgeuk tek 一腳踢 (lit.) kick with one foot 用一隻腳踢
(idi.) PH one-man band, do everything all by oneself 一個人做所有的事 : *"Ngóh sáisāam tongsāam, máaihsung jyúfaahn dásou ~," yātgo gūngyàhn deui kéuihge pàhngyáuh góng.* (A maid servant told her friend, "I do washing, ironing, grocery shopping, cooking, and cleaning all by myself.")

0440

➔ yātsáu yātgeuk 一手一腳
(lit.) one hand and one foot 一隻手跟一隻腳
(idi.) A.PH do the job all by oneself 一個人自己做 : ⓐ *Sihnggāan poutáu, dōu haih ngóh ~ dáléih ge.* (I run the shop all by myself.) ⓑ *Nīgihn sih haih kéuih ~ jouhchēutlàih ge, yīnggōi yàuh kéuih séung baahnfaat gáaikyut sīnji ngāam.* (The whole thing was done by him. So he should be responsible for working it out.)

gwāt 骨 N bone 骨頭 M tiùh; gauh; faai

0441

➔ fáangwāt 反骨 (lit.) the

(inside) bone turns outside 骨頭反了出來
(idi.) Adj. ungrateful and unreliable 忘恩負義又靠不住 : ⓐ *Nīgo yàhn yíh hauh gin sōi, hóu ~ ge.* (You can see from behind that this person has a square jaw which sticks out from under his ears. [According to Chinese physiognomy,] He is ~.) ⓑ ~ *jái* (a man who is ~)

0442

➔ gūnjái gwātgwāt 官仔骨骨
(lit.) PH a young gentleman who looks as if he comes from a rich family 外表斯文，像出身富有家庭的年青人 : *"Kéuih làahm pàhngyáuh ~ gám bo." "Gánghaih lā. Kéuih haih deihcháan daaihwòhng ge jái ā ma."* ("Her boyfriend is ~." "Sure, he is the son of the local property tycoon. Didn't you know that?")

0443 ✓

➔ gwāt 骨 (lit.)N bone 骨頭 M tiùh; gauh; faai
(idi.) N (1) implication [of words] that may hurt others 說話裏有刺 : *Kéuih taùhsīn góng gógeui syutwah yáuh ~ ga.* (What he just said has ~.) (2) crease 衣或褲子上的摺痕 M tiùh : *tongsāam yiu tong ~* (iron the ~) (3) wishbone of an umbrella 雨傘的骨架 M tiuh : *Daaihfūng chēuityúhnjó tiuh jē ~.* (The strong wind blows so violently that it breaks the ~.)

0444

➔gwātbei 骨痺 (lit.) bone is numb 骨麻痺了
(idi.) PH/Adj. feel unnatural 覺得不

67

自然：ⓐ *Yùhgwó Jūnggwok yàhn hóuchíh gwáilóu gám sihngyaht góng 'honey', 'darling' , kèihtā yàhn jauh gokdāk ~.* (If Chinese people always say honey, darling like Westerners, others would ~ [on hearing that].) ⓑ *Kéuih jēung kéuih sébéi Chàhn síujé ge chihngseun béi ngóhdeih tái, ngóhdeih táidou gwāt dōu bei.* (He let us see the love letter(s) he wrote to Miss Chan. We just ~ when we read the letters.)

0445

→gwāttàuh dágú 骨頭打鼓 (lit.) bones hit drum 骨頭打鼓
(idi.) PH (said of a person) already been dead for a long time 人死了很久 ： *Ngóh gam lóuh, ngóhge syūn gam sai, kéuih gitfān gójahnsí ngóh dōu ~ lo.* (I am so old and my grandchildren are so young. By the time they get married, I would have ~.)

0446

→gwātyuhk 骨肉(lit.) bone and flesh 骨肉
(idi.) N one's own children 親生子女 M dī ： *Nīgo bìhbī haih néihge (chānsāang) ~ làih ge bo, dímgáai néih gam yánsām m̀yiu kéuih a?* (This baby is your ~. Why are you so hard-hearted and want to dump it?)

0447

→gwogwāt 過骨 (lit.) pass the bone 通過了骨頭
(idi.) VO manage to get through 蒙混過去，僥倖過關 ： *Kéuihge leuhnmán yáuh hóudō mahntàih, hóuchói sāumēi dōu ~ jó ~.* (There

were quite a lot of problems in his dissertation. Luckily, he ~ in the end.)

0448

→sūkgwāt 縮骨 (lit.) shrink the bone 骨頭縮短了
(idi.) Adj. cunning and selfish 狡猾自私 ： *Kéuih nīgo yàhn hóu ~ ge, néih m̀hóu béi kéuih wánbahn.* (He is a ~ person. Don't let him take advantage of you.)

0449

→ yáuh gwāt lohk deih/ déi 有骨落地 (lit.) there are bones dropped on the ground 有骨頭跌在地上
(idi.) PH a nice meal, not just dimsum (*Here 'gwāt' refers to the more special and expensive cuisine in a Chinese restaurant.) ： *Ngóh bōng néih jouhsìhng nīgihn sih jīhauh, néih yiu chēng ngóh sihk yātchāan, yiu ~ ga.* (You should treat me to ~ after I help you do this.)

hahpàh 下巴 N chin 下巴 M go

0450

→hahpàh hēnghēng 下巴輕輕 (lit.) chin is very light 下巴很輕
(idi.) PH make wild promise, give promise too easily 隨便承諾別人 ： *Kéuih nīgo yàhn ~, māt dōu wah hóyíh bōng néih jouh.* (He always ~. He can promise to do anything for you.)

0451

→jíjaat hahpàh → háu

hēnghēng 紙紮下巴 → 口輕輕
(lit.) paper made chin → (so) the mouth is light 用紙做的下巴→(所以)口很輕
(idi.) HIT give a promise too easily 輕易作出承諾 : *Néih yīngsihngjó yàhn ge yéh yātdihng yiu jouh a, m̀hóu ~ → ~ gám.* (You should keep your promise. Don't ~.)

háu □ N mouth □ M go

0452
➔bānghául yàhn geih bāngháu wún 崩口人忌崩口碗 (lit.) a hare-lipped person avoids using a chipped bowl 嘴唇裂開的人避免用崩裂邊緣的碗
(idi.) PH avoid mentioning something that may hurt others 避免提及令人不快之事 : *Néih hái kéuih mihnchihn m̀hóu joi góng chāailóu m̀hóu ge sih. ~, kéuih bàhbā haih gíngchaat.* (Don't talk about the misconduct of policemen before him. You should ~. His father is a policeman.)

0453
➔chōuháu 粗口 (lit.) rough mouth 粗糙的口
(idi.) N bad (spoken) words, foul language, swear-words 粗言穢語 M geui : *Nàahmyán m̀hóu hái néuihyán mihnchihn góng ~.* (Men should not use ~ in front of ladies.) Adj. foul-mouthed 喜說粗言穢語的 : *Kéuih hóu ~.* (He really likes to use bad words .)

0454
➔dāk bá háu 得把口 (lit.) have

a mouth (only) (只)有一張嘴
(idi.) PH just talk, be all mouth and no action 只說, 不做 : ⓐ *Kéuih wah jihgéi jyúsung géi lēk géi hóusihk, ~, yauh m̀gin kéuih jyúháh béi ngóhdeih sihk.* (He boasted that he was good at cooking and the food he cooked was delicious. He ~. He has never cooked anything for us to eat.)
ⓑ *Kéuih sìhngyaht wah yiu dá yiu faht dī saimānjái, ~ jī ma, kéuih bīn sédāk ā?* (She always says that she would beat or punish her children. She ~. How would she be willing to do so [since she loves them so much]?)

0455
➔fáan háu fūk siht 反口覆舌
(lit.) turn over the mouth and fold up the tongue 把口反過來, 把舌覆蓋著
(idi.) PH fail to keep a promise, be inconsistent with what one says 言而無信 : *Kéuih mihngmihng yīngsihng wah wúih bōng ngóhdeih, yìhgā jauh ~.* (He did promise to help us. But he says 'no' now.)

0456
➔faht háu sèh sām 佛口蛇心
see 0031

0457
➔fúgwāgōn gám ge mihnháu 苦瓜乾咁嘅面口 (lit.) face looks like a dry bitter gourd 臉像乾的苦瓜
(idi.) PH wear a sad look 愁眉苦臉 : *Jouh māt gámyaht ~ a?* (Why do you ~ today?)

0458
➔gūnjih léuhnggo háu 官字

兩個口 (lit.) the Chinese character for officals 官 has two mouths 官這個字有兩個口 (* Nowadays, 'gūn' 官 can refer to 'government'.)
(idi.) PH the government/ official can say what it/ he likes 政府/ 官說甚麼都可以 : *"Jingfú yauh wah dunggit làuhga, daahnhaih yauh wah ìmmaaih deih. Gám làuhga dōu wúih sīng ge bo!" "~. Kéuih wah dím maih dím lō."* ("The government says it would freeze property prices, and it also says it is not going to sell any land. If so, the property prices will still rise." "~. Let it say whatever it likes.")

0459
➔ hāak háu hāak mihn 黑口黑面 (lit.) black mouth and black face 黑色的口和臉
(idi.) PH pull a long face 板起臉 : *Dī jīkyùhn chihdou yāt fānjūng jē gīngléih jauh ~.* (The manager will ~ when the staff is only one minute late.)

0460
➔ hāakmàaih háumihn 黑埋口面 see 0459

0461 ✓
➔ háu 口(lit.) N mouth 口 M go
(idi.) N entrance or exit 入口,出口 M go : *Gógo deihtitjaahm yáuh gam dō chēutháu, ngóhdeih hái bīngo ~ dáng kéuih a?* (There are so many exits in that MTR station. At which one are we going to wait for him?)
BF (1) mouth of a bottle 樽的口 : *jēun ~ (~)* (2) cuff 袖口 : *jauh ~ (~)*

0462
➔háu bāt deui sām 口不對心
(lit.) mouth is not equal to heart 口(說的)跟心(所想的)不一樣
(idi.) PH not say what one means 口是心非 : *Kéuih nīgo yàhn ~, góng yāttou, jouh yāttou.* (He is a person who does ~. He would say one thing and do another.)

0463
➔háufā 口花 (lit.) flower in the mouth 口裏有花
(idi.) Adj. (said of a man) be loose-tongued when flirting with girls 男人對女人說話輕佻 : *Kéuih hóu ~ ge.* (He is ~.)

0464
➔háu fāfā 口花花 (lit.) flowery mouth 嘴裏有很多花
(idi.) PH/A.PH (said of a man) be loose-tongued when flirting with girls 男人對女性說話輕佻 : *Kéuih sihngyaht ~ liuh néuihjái.* (He behaves frivolously in being ~.)

0465
➔háu jahtjaht 口窒窒 (lit.) mouth (is going) with pauses 口不順
(idi.) A.PH (1) stammer/ stutter (habitually) (慣性)口吃 : *Kéuih góngyéh ~ gám.* (He ~.) (2) stammer/ stutter (because of excitement or fear) (因緊張或驚怕而)口吃 : *Gíngchaat pùhnmahn kéuih gójahnsí, gin kéuih góngyéh ~ gám, jauh ganggā sīyih kéuih la.* (The policemen found him more suspicious because he ~ when being questioned by them.)

70

0466

→háuséui dōgwo chàh 口水多過茶 (lit.) (one's) saliva is more than (one's) tea 唾沫比茶多 (idi.) PH be all mouth and no action 說話太多,不注重實際 : *Sihngyaht ~ gám, yiu jānhaih jouh sīnji dāk gā ma.* (You are ~. You should really do it.)

0467

→háu sih sām fēi 口是心非 (lit.) mouth says yes, but heart says no 口不對心 (idi.) see 0462

0468

→háu tùhng beih ngaau 口同鼻拗 (lit.) mouth argues with nose 口跟鼻子爭論 (idi.) PH it's useless to argue 爭論也沒有用 : *Néih yihgā béijó chín, jauh yātdihng yiu kéuih béifāan jēung sāutiuh néih. Faisih daihyihyaht ~.* (Now that you have paid, you'd better ask him to give you a receipt. Otherwise, ~ with him later [whether you have paid].)

0469

→hōiháu 開口 (lit.) open mouth 張開口 (idi.) ATT unsealed 不封口的 : ~ *seun* (~ letter) VO (1) open (a sealed letter) 把封了的信拆開 : *Nīfūng seun ~ jó ~ bo!* (Oh, this letter has already been ~ [by someone].) (2) talk 說話 : *Kéuih nīgo yàhn hóu jihng, géi go jūngtàuh m̀~ dōu dāk.* (He is a very quiet person. He can be silent for several hours.) (3) mention

提及 : *M̀sái yàhndeih ~ néih dōu yīnggōi bōng yàhn lā.* (You should offer help before other people ask for help.)

0470

→hōiháu kahpjeuhk leih 開口及著脷 (lit.) one bites his tongue as soon as one opens his mouth 一開口便咬到舌頭 (idi.) PH irritate others as soon as one talks 一說話便觸怒別人 : *"Dímgáai néih m̀chói kéuih a?" "Faisih la, ~."* ("Why don't you answer him [when he talks to you]?" "I don't want to. He'll/ I'll ~.")

0471

→hōiháu màaihháu 開口埋口 (lit.) open and close the mouth 把嘴巴張開及合上 (idi.) A.PH always talk about 常掛在嘴邊 : *Kéuih ~ jauh wah kéuih lóuhgūng deui kéuih hóu hóu.* (She ~ that her husband is very nice to her.)

0472

→hóu cheung háu 好唱口 (lit.) good singing mouth 唱得很好的嘴巴 (idi.) Adj.PH (1) (said of a bird kept in a cage) always sings (籠中鳥)常唱歌 : *Nījek jeukjái hóu ~.* (This bird ~.) (2) (said of a person) feels happy and sings (指人)覺得快樂而唱歌 : *Dímgáai gāmyaht gam ~ a?* (What makes you ~ today?) (3) utter something to show happiness (at the escape from something undesirable) 慶幸自己沒有發生不愉快的事 : ⓐ*Néih jauh ~ lā, bōsí laauh ngóh m̀laauh néih.* (Well, you can ~. Our boss scolded me, but not you.) ⓑ *Néihdeih jauh ~ lā, chyùhnbāan jihnghaih néihdeih géigo hahpgaak.* (Now you can ~. You are the few ones in our class who passed the exam.)

0473
➔ **hūng háu góng baahkwah/ wá** 空口講白話 (lit.) empty mouth talks blank words 口裏沒有東西,白說
(idi.) PH empty talk, be all mouth and no action 祇是說,不實行: *Ngóhdeih yáuh gam hóu ge gaiwaahk, daahnhaih móuh gīngfai, dōuhaih ~ ge jē!* (We have such a good project, but we don't have any funding. We can just talk.)

0474
➔ **jēng yàhn chēut háu, bahn yàhn chēut sáu** 精人出口,笨人出手 (lit.) a wise person uses his mouth, but a stupid person uses his hand 聰明的人用口,笨的人用手
(idi.) PH a stupid person lured by a wily person to do silly things 愚蠢人被狡猾的人教唆代他出頭做事: *Kéuih deui A-Chán góng lóuhbáan dímyéung dímyéung m̀ngāam, A-Chán jauh jáuheui wah lóuhbáan, jingyāt ~,~. Sāumēi A-Chán maih cháaujó yàuhyú lō.* (He told Chan about the wrongdoings of their boss. Chan then went to criticize the boss. He really was ~. Later, Chan was fired.)

0475
➔ **jíjaat hahpàh** → **háu**

hēnghēng 紙紮下巴→口輕輕 see 0451

0476
➔ **laahnháu** 爛口 (lit.) rotten mouth 潰爛的口
(idi.) Adj. see 0453

0477 ✓
➔ **làuh háuséui** 流口水 (lit.) VO mouth-watering, dribble saliva 垂涎
(idi.) VO show greed for 起貪念: *Kéuih yihgā daai ge bīu gam mihnggwai, dī cháak táigin jauh ~ la.* (The watch he wears is so expensive that thieves would ~ it when they see it.) ATT cheap and of poor quality 價錢便宜品質差: *Nīgo bīu haih ~ yéh làih ge jē.* (This watch is ~.)

0478
➔ **leih háu m̀leih fūk** 利口唔利腹 (lit.) good for the mouth but bad for the stomach 對口好,但對腸胃不好
(idi.) PH (said of food) good to eat but bad for health 食物好吃但對健康不好: *Jīn ja ge yéh, ~, m̀hóu sihk gam dō a.* (Fried and deep fried foods are ~. Don't eat so much of them.)

0479
➔ **lihm háuwóng** 念口簧 (lit.) recite by mouth and tongue 用口背誦
(idi.) PH/ VO say something fluently by rote learning 記熟後很流暢地說出來: *"Néih ge jái lihm Tòhngsī lihmdāk hóu hóu bo!" "Kéuih ~ jē."* ("Oh, your son can recite the poems

of the Tang Dynasty very well."
"Oh, he just ~.")

0480
➔màaihháu 埋口 (lit.) close one's
mouth 合上嘴巴
(idi.) ATT sealed (letter) 封了口的
(信)：~ seun (a ~ letter) VO (wounds)
heal (傷口)癒合：Sáuseuht jīhauh
yātgo láihbaai, sēunghàu sīnji wúih
yùhnchyùhn ~. (The wound would
completely heal one week after the
surgery.)

0481
➔móuh háuchí 冇口齒 (lit.)
have not a mouth or teeth 沒有口跟
牙齒
(idi.) Adj.PH break a promise 不守
諾言：Néih jānhaih ~ la. Néih
yīngsìhnggwo wah m̀tùhng kéuih
hahpjok, yìhgā yauh tùhng kéuih
hahpjok. (You certainly ~. You
promised that you would not cooperate
with him, but you do.)

0482
➔ngám háu fai 揞口費 (lit.)
money to cover the mouth 遮蓋口的
錢
(idi.) N hush money, money to buy
someone's silence 封口費,遮羞錢 M
dī：Yáuh yàhn laahksok gógo
mìhnglàuh, yiu kéuih béi ~, yùhgwó
m̀haih jauh baau kéuih dī sēui yéh
chēutlàih. (Someone black-mailed
that celebrity. If he refused to pay
~, his filthy story would be exposed
to the public.)

0483
➔sām gógeui, háu gógeui 心

嗰句，口嗰句 (lit.) in the heart a
word, in the mouth that same word 心
裏有什麼說話，口裏便說什麼
(idi.) PH one says what one means 說
話坦白：Yáuh dī yàhn góng syutwah
háu bāt deui sām, daahnhaih ngóh jauh
~, ~, móuh ngāak néih ge. (Some
people do not say what they mean.
But I'm different. I ~. I won't cheat
you.)

0484
➔sáu tìhng háu tìhng 手停口
停 (lit.) hands stop, then the mouth
stops too 手一停下來也跟著停
(idi.) PH if you don't work, you'll get
nothing to eat 不做事便沒飯吃：
Dágūngjái jeui pa sātyihp ge la, ~ ā
ma. (The salaried class are most
afraid of losing their jobs. ~, isn't
that right?)

0485
➔séijihng bá háu 死剩把口
(lit.) what one will leave after his
death is his mouth 死後剩下一張嘴
(idi.) PH never yield but insist on
arguing with others or defending
oneself 強辯不服輸：Kéuih nīgo
yàhn, ~, haih dōu yiu ngaaudou yèhng
wàih jí. (He is a person who ~. He
won't give in and won't stop arguing
with you until he convinces you.)

0486
➔sījí hōi daaih háu 獅子開大
口 see 0359

0487
➔tái yàhn háumihn/ mihnháu
睇人口面／面口 (lit.) look at

other people's face and mouth 看人家的嘴臉
(idi.) PH at the mercy of other's pleasure or anger 看人家臉色 : *Ngóh jūngyi jouh síufáan, sēuiyihn yiu hái gāaibīn maaihyéh, daahnhaih wahsaai dōu haih jihgéi jouh lóuhbáan, ṁsái ~.* (I like being a vendor. Although I have to sell things on the street, I am my own boss, so to speak. I don't have to be ~.)

0488
➔yātháu 一口 (lit.) one mouth 一個口
(idi.) ATT fixed 定實了的 : ~ *ga* (one ~ price only) A (1) definitely 肯定地 : *Kéuih ~ ngáauhsaht ngóh haih saatyàhn hūngsáu.* (He said ~ that I was the murderer.) (2) (in giving a promise) at once 立即(答應) : *Ngóh giu kéuih bōng ngóh kéuih jauh ~ yīngsìhng la.* (He promised me as soon as I asked him to help me.)

0489
➔yātháu hei 一口氣 (lit.) a mouthful of air 一口氣
(idi.) A.PH in one breath, in one go 沒停地 : ⓐ*Kéuih ~ yámsaai sèhng jēun bējáu.* (He drank the whole bottle of beer ~.) ⓑ*Kéuih ~ páaujó yāt chīnmáih (louh).* (He ran one kilometre without stopping.)

0490
➔yih/sāam háu luhk mihn 二／三口六面 (lit.) two/three mouths and six faces 兩／三個口六張臉

(idi.) A.PH (talk) face to face 當面說清楚 : *Néih yiu ~ tùhng kéuih góng chīngchó nīgihn sih ṁgwāan ngóh sih.* (You have to tell him ~ that it has nothing to do with me.)

hàuhlùhng 喉嚨 N throat 喉嚨 M go

0491
➔dauhsā hàuh 豆沙喉 (lit.) bean paste throat 豆泥做的喉嚨
(idi.) N rough voice 聲線沙啞 M fu/bá : ⓐ*Sēuiyihn kéuihfu haih ~, daahnhaih hóu singgám.* (Although she has a ~, yet it sounds sexy.) ⓑ*Néih fu ~, dím cheungdāk yuhtkūk a?* (You have a ~. How can you sing Cantonese opera?)

0492
➔dou hàuh ṁdou fai 到喉唔到肺 see 0388

0493
➔ngòhgūng hàuh 鵝公喉 see 0171

jéui 嘴/咀 N mouth, beak 嘴巴, 鳥的嘴 M go

0494 ✓
➔jéui 嘴(lit.) N mouth 嘴巴 M go
(idi.) BF (1) spout of a pot 壺的嘴 : *wùh* ~ (~) (2) spout of a kettle 大水壺的嘴 : *bōu* ~ (~) V kiss 吻 : ~ *kéuih* (~ him/her)

0495

→jīmjéui 尖嘴 (lit.) protruded/ sharp mouth 尖的嘴巴 (idi.) Adj. too particular about eating and drinking 對飲食很苛求 : *Kéuih hóu ~ ga, sóyíh kéuih m̀heui pèhng ge jáulàuh tùhngmàaih chāantēng ge.* (He is ~. So he never goes to cheap restaurants [of Chinese or Western food].)

0496

→ngàh jīm jéui leih 牙尖嘴利 (lit.) sharp teeth and sharp tongue 尖 的牙,銳利的嘴巴 (idi.) Adj. PH sharp-tongued and contentious 嘴不饒人 : *Kéuih sēuiyìhn nìhngéi saisai, daahnhaih góngyéh ~.* (Although he is young, he is ~ [in speaking].)

kyùhn(tàuh) 拳(頭) N/M fist; measure for a punch/ blow 拳頭; 拳擊的量詞 M go

0497

→màahng kyùhn dáséi lóuh sīfu 盲拳打死老師傅 (lit.) a random fist/ punch (of an ordinary man) can kill a highly experienced gungfu fighter 一個不懂拳術的人可 以打死一個熟諳功夫的人 (idi.) PH a novice can defeat a mentor 新人會勝老手: *Kéuih ngāamngāam hohksīk dá màhjeuk jauh yèhngsaai ngóhdeih nī géigo dájó géisahp nìhn ge, jànhaih ~.* (He just learned how to play mahjong, but he won a lot of money from us who knew how to play mahjong decades ago. The saying is right that ~.)

lóuh 腦 N brain 腦袋 M go

0498

→dāp tàuh dāp lóuh 耷頭耷腦 (lit.) head and brain droop 垂下的頭 跟腦子 (idi.) PH (1) in low spirits 沒精打采 的 : *Kàhmmáahn m̀gau fan, sóyíh gāmyaht ~.* (I didn't sleep enough last night. So I'm ~ today.) (2) (the way one walks) with one's head lowered 走路時垂下頭 : *Hàahnglouh ~ gám, móuh lèih sàhnhei.* (He walks ~, and that makes him look as if he is in low spirits.)

0499 ✓

→lóuhséun dōu meih sāangmàaih 腦囟都未生 埋 (lit.) PH even the fontanelles (of the baby) have not yet closed up (the skull) 嬰兒頭上的囟骨還未接合 (idi.) PH (said of youngsters) innocent and naive, not yet mentally mature 思想太單純,還未成熟 : *Wah jauh wah 'méihmaauh yúh jìwai bìhng juhng', kèihsaht hóudō chāamgā syúnméih ge yàhn ~.* (It is so said that beauty and wisdom are equally emphasized, but actually many contestants of the beauty pageant are ~.)

0500

→màih tàuh màih lóuh 迷頭迷 腦 (lit.) head and brain get lost 頭跟 腦都迷失了 (idi.) A.PH/PH (1) indulgently 很沉 迷 : ~ *yìhngau jísā chàhwú* (~ study purple clay teapots) (2) immerse oneself in 非常專注用

心：ⓐ *duhksyū duhkdou* ~ (~ one's studies) ⓑ ~ *jouhyéh* (~ one's work)

0501
➔ *m̀gīng daaihlóuh* 唔經大腦 (lit.) not through the brain 不經大腦 (idi.) PH not think before one says 說話不加思索： *Gam daaih go yàhn, góngyéh dōu ~ gé!* (You are such a grown up person. Why do you ~?)

0502
➔ *sihk lóuh* 食腦 (lit.) eat brain 吃腦子 (idi.) VO make a living by using intelligence and creativity 用智力及創意謀生： *Jīseun Fōgeih nīgo hòhngyihp fēisèuhng sēuiyiu ~ ge yàhnchòih.* (Talents who ~ are greatly needed in the sector of Information Technology.)

0503
➔ *tàuh daaih móuh lóuh, lóuh daaih sāang chóu* 頭大冇腦，腦大生草(lit.) a big head without a brain and a big brain just grows grass 頭大但沒有腦子,腦子大卻生草 (idi.) PH a stupid fool who does not use his brain 不懂思想的笨蛋： *"Boují wah yáuh go néuihyán hái gāaibīn béi yàhn ngāakjó géisahp maahn yānwaih kéuih bōngchan gógo yàhn máaih gáyeuhk." "Kéuih jānhaih ~, ~!"* ("It is reported in the newspaper that a woman was conned by a man on the street and lost hundreds of thousands of dollars in buying some fake medicine from him." "She really is ~.")

méih 尾 N tail 尾巴 M tìuh

0504
➔ *cháaichān néih tìuh méih* 踩親你條尾 (lit.) (I) tread on your tail (我)踏著你的尾巴 (idi.) PH (quite an offensive term in treating the addressee as an animal) offend you (不客氣的說話,把對方當作動物)開罪你： *Dímgáai gam ngok a? Ngóh ~ àh?* (Why are you so mad at me? Have I ~?)

0505
➔ *hóu tàuh hóu méih* 好頭好尾 (lit.) good head and good tail 好的頭跟好的尾巴 (idi.)PH go through something from beginning to end 既然開始了便把事情完成： *Néih geiyihn bōng kéuih jouhjó yātbun lo, jauh ~, bōng kéuih jouhmàaih kéuih lā.* (Since you've done half of the job for him, you'd better ~ and finish it for him.) (*A bridegroom and his bride would be requested by the guests to eat a chicken's head and rump at their wedding, which symbolizes that they'll have a good new life and a happy ending. The newly married couple would eat in a symbolic way by just licking the food.)

0506 ✓
➔ *méih 尾* (lit.) N tail 尾巴 M tìuh (idi.) N credit or distinction one gets in HKCEE 在香港中學會考中拿到優或良的成績 M tìuh： *"Wuihháau lódóu géidō tìuh ~ a?" "Seitìuh. Yāt A yih B yāt C."* ("How many ~?"

"Four. I've got one A two Bs and one C.") (* HKCEE is the Hong Kong Certificate of Education Examination. Students in Hong Kong are supposed to sit for this exam when they finish secondary school.)

0507

➡móuh méih fēi tòh 冇尾飛砣 (lit.) a shooting top becomes tail-less (when it flies off the string that holds it) 飛砣囉沒有了尾巴(,因爲飛脫了繫著它的繩子)
(idi.) PH a person whose whereabouts are hardly known by others so that it is difficult to get in touch with him 行蹤飄忽的人,別人很難找到他 : *Kéuih lóuhpòh jauhlàih sāang la, kéuih dōu m̀jī heuijó bīn, jingyāt ~.* (His wife is going to give birth to a baby very soon, and we still don't know where he's gone. He is just like a tail-less shooting top.) (*'Fēitòh' is a kind of thing that is used to shoot down something far away. Sometimes it can be used as an offensive weapon to shoot at people.)

0508

➡sáuméih 手尾 (lit.) hand and tail 手跟尾
(idi.) N (1) unfinished work 未做完的工作 M dī : *Ngóh yiu jouhmàaih dī ~ sīnji fonggūng.* (I have to finish my ~ before leaving the office.) (2) troubles (left behind) (留下的)麻煩事 M dī : ⓐ *Kéuih jouhchān yéh dōu yiu yàhn gān ~ ge.* (He needs others to settle his ~ every time he does something.) ⓑ *móuh ~ gān* (have no ~ to be resolved)

0509

➡ séui méih 水尾 (lit.) water end 水的終結
(idi.) N end of the prime time (of a trade) 某行業能夠賺錢的末期 : *Nīhòhng sēuiyihn hóuwán, daahnhaih yihgā yíhgīng haih ~.* (Although this is a profit making trade, now it's the ~.)

0510

➡tàuhméih 頭尾 (lit.) head and tail 頭跟尾巴
(idi.) A (said of the time spent) altogether 一共(花了的時間) : *Ngóhdeih nīchi heui Yahtbún léuihhàhng, ~ chātyaht.* (This time we went on a trip to Japan for ~ seven days.)

0511

➡tàuhtàuh méihméih 頭頭尾尾 (lit.) heads and tails 頭跟尾巴
(idi.) PH not the main part 不是主要部分 M dī : ⓐ *"Sihkjihng hóu dō sung bo!" "Dī ~/ sungtàuh sungméih m̀hóu yiu lo."* ("Oh, we've gotten a lot of left over foods [from the meal]." "We'd better throw them away since they are only the remains of the meal.") ⓑ *Dī choi jihnghaih yiu nyuhn ge bouhfahn, dī ~ jauh jaahkjó kéuih.* (We only want the tender part of the vegetable, so you'd better remove the rest of it.)

0512

➡wah tàuh síng méih 話頭醒尾 (lit.) speak of the beginning and one will induce the ending 說了開頭便知後面的說話是什麼

(idi.) PH a very clever person who will know what other people want to say by just hearing one or two words they utter 一個善解人意的聰明人： *Kéuih nīgo yàhn ~, m̀gwaaidāk lóuhsai gam jūngyi kéuih lā.* (He is ~. No wonder he has won the favour of his boss.)

0513

➔yāt tàuh yāt méih 一頭一尾 (lit.) one head and one tail 一個頭,一條尾巴
(idi.) PH (1) some here and some there, not being together orderly 次序亂了，一些在這裏,一些在那裏： *Gódī fāailóu, jāidou ~ gám, m̀ji dím wán.* (He puts the files ~. He makes it difficult for me to find them.) (2) both ends 兩端： *Nī tiuh gāai ~ dōu yáuh yāt gāan bihnleihdim.* (There is one convenience store at ~ of this street.)

0514

➔ yàuh tàuh dou méih 由頭到尾 (lit.) from head to tail 從頭到尾
(idi.) A.PH (1) from beginning to end 從頭到尾： ⓐ *Kéuih jēung fūng seun ~ joi tái yātchi.* (He read the letter ~ once again.) ⓑ *~ dōu haih kéuih góngsaai, ngóh móuh dāk góng.* (He dominated our conversation ~ and I couldn't even put in a word.) (2) the ins and outs 事情始末： *Kéuih jēung nīgihn sih ~ góngsaai béi ngóh tēng.* (He told me ~ of the event.)

mihn 面 N face 臉 M go/ faai

0515

➔béi mihnsīk yàhn/ PN tái 俾面色人睇 (lit.) let others see the color of one's face 給臉色別人看
(idi.) PH deliberately let others feel/ know that one is putting on airs 故意讓別人知道你的喜怒： *Ngóh lóuhyèh haih daaih yáuhchínlóu, ngóh nàaihnáai jauh sihsìh ~ ngóh ~.* (My father-in-law is a very rich man. My mother-in-law is always bossy to me.)

0516

➔béimín 俾面 (lit.) give face 給面子
(idi.) VO for one's sake 看在某人份上： *Kéuih ~ ngóh sīnji yùhnleuhng néih jā.* (He forgave you all for the sake of me.)

0517

➔béi yàhn siudou mihn wòhng 俾人笑到面黃 (lit.) face becomes yellow when being teased by others 被人取笑時臉孔變黃(idi.) PH feel very embarrassed when being teased by others 被人取笑感到很尷尬： *Hái yíhchìhn, yùhgwó néuihjái meih gitfān sāang jái jauh wúih ~.* (Formerly, if a girl had a baby before she was married, she would be teased by others and that would embarrass her.)

0518

➔chēutmín 出面 (lit.) put out the face 露出面孔
(idi.) A come out to face up to and settle problems on behalf of somebody else 站出來代人解決事

78

情：ⓐ*Gógo jaahpji geijé béi daihyih gāan bougún ge geijé dáchān, kéuihge jaahpjiséh doih kéuih ~ gou gógāan bougún.* (That magazine reporter was beaten by a newspaper reporter. The magazine company is going to sue the newspaper on behalf of him.) ⓑ *Ngóh ~ bōng néih tùhng daaih yìhlūng góngsou lā.* (I will go and bargain with the loan shark for you.) VO/ PH too obviously 太明顯：*Néih bōng kéuih bōngdou ~ (saai) ~.* (You are on his side ~.)

0519
➔dáam daaih sām sai mihnpèih háuh 膽大心細面皮厚 see 0383

0520
➔fáanmín 反面 (lit.) turn the face 把臉反過來
(idi.) VO (1) (said of friends) have a quarrel and then turn their back on each other 翻臉：*Léuhnggo pàhngyáuh waihjó chín ~.* (The two friends ~ for money.) (2) be irritated and burst into angry speech 動怒及罵人：*Ngóh joi chēui kéuih wàahnchín jē kéuih jauh jīkhāak ~ la.* (When I urged him to pay off his debts once again, he was ~.)

0521
➔láhéi faai mihn 挪起塊面
(lit.) make one's face tight 綳著臉孔
(idi.) PH wear a long face (to show unwillingness) 拉長臉孔(表示不願意的樣子)：ⓐ*Dī yeuhk hóu fú. Nīgo saimānjái hóu pa sihk. Yāt giu kéuih sihk kéuih jauh ~.* (The medicine is bitter. This child doesn't want to take it. Whenever you tell him to take it,

he ~.) ⓑ *Fógei mahn lóuhbáan gā yàhngūng louhbáan jauh ~.* (When the employees asked their boss to give them a payrise, he ~.)

0522
➔lohkmín 落面 (lit.) pull down the face of someone 把別人的臉拉下來
(idi.) VO make somebody lose face in public 令人當眾丟臉：*Kéuih haih daaihhohk haauhjéung, néih hái gam dō yàhn mihnchìhn wah kéuihdī hohksāang séuijéun dāi, jīkhaih ~ kéuih ~.* (He is the chancellor of the university. You said in front of so many people that the academic level of his students is low. You ~.) Adj. feel bad for having lost face 丟臉：*Kéuih haih daaih chyùhsī, néih hái yàhn mihnchìhn wah kéuih jyú ge yéh nàahnsihk, kéuih gokdāk hóu ~.* (He is a well-known chef, but you said before others that the food he made was terrible. He ~.)

0523
➔maakmín 擘面 (lit.) tear face 撕開臉
(idi.) VO see 0520(1)

0524
➔máhmihn 馬面 see 0319

0525✓
➔mihn 面 (lit.) N face 臉 M faai/go
(idi.) N (when changed into 'mín') (1) the outside of clothing 衣物的外面：*tong dái, mhóu tong ~* (iron the inside, not ~) (2) social face 面子：ⓐ*béi ~*

79

(give ~) see 0516 ⓑ *séung* ~ (favour somebody with one's presence) see 0538 BF (also 'mín') top, surface 上面, 表面 : ⓐ *tói* ~ (~ of a table) ⓑ *seunfūng* ~ (~ of an evelope)

0526
➔mihn chēngchēng 面青青 (lit.) face yellow green 臉呈青色 (idi.) PH (1) look pale (because of bad health) 臉色青白 (因爲健康不好) : *Kéuih yiu gáamfèih, sóyíh ṁgám sihkyéh, daahnhaih jauh ~ gám.* (Because she is on a diet [to lose weight], she dare not eat [so many] things, and that makes her ~.) (2) look frightened 面有懼色 : *Kéuih ~ jáulàih wahbéi ngóh tēng yīsāng yiu kéuih hōidōu.* (He came and told me in fear that the doctor wanted him to undergo an operation.)

0527
➔mihn chēng háusèuhn baahk 面青口唇白 (lit.) face green and lips white 臉跟口唇都青白 (idi.) PH look very pale 臉色很差 : *gēngdou* ~ (turn pale [because of fear])

0528
➔mihnhùhng 面紅 (lit.) face is red 臉發紅 (idi.) V blush 臉紅 : ⓐ*Kéuih hóu pacháu, giu kéuih kéihchēutlàih yíngóng kéuih jauh ~ ge la.* (He is very shy. He would ~ if you ask him to come out and give a speech [to an audience].) ⓑ *Kéuih faatgok yihngcho gógo yàhn haih kéuih lóuhgūng jīhauh jauh jīkhāak ~ la.* (When she found that she mistook

that man for her husband, she ~ [with embarrassment] at once.)

0529
➔mihn hùhng mihn luhk 面紅面綠 (lit.) face is red and green 臉變紅色和綠色 (idi.) PH (face) red with rage 臉紅耳赤 : ⓐ *nāudou* ~ (~) ⓑ *ngaaigāau ngaaidou* ~ (~ in a quarrel)

0530
➔mihn jójó 面左左 (lit.) each one turns his face to the left 各自把臉轉到左邊去 (idi.) PH not greet each other (because there is something wrong between them) 大家關係不好,見面也不瞅不睬 : *Kéuihdeih jihchùhng ngaaigāau jīhauh, gindóu mihn dōu ~.* (They did ~ when they met after they had a quarrel [some time ago].)

0531
➔mihn múng sām jēng 面懵心精 (lit.) face looks stupid but heart is clever 樣子愚笨,但內心精算 (idi.) PH one who appears like a fool but is shrewd at heart 裝蒜 : *Kéuih nīgo yàhn ~.* (He is ~.) also see 0212

0532
➔mihnpèih háu 面皮厚 (lit.) face skin is thick 臉皮厚 (idi.) Adj.PH (1) shameless 不知羞恥 : *Gógo yàhn gón kéuih dōu ṁjáu, jànhaih ~ la.* (That man won't go away even though I show him the door. He really is ~.) (2)

80

thick-skinned 不怕不好意思：see
0383

0533
➔mihnsīk m̀hóu 面色唔好
(lit.) color of the face is not good 臉
色不好
(idi.) PH not look well 氣色不佳 ：
*Kéuih nīpáai ~, haih m̀haih yáuh
behng a?* (He does ~. Has he been
sick recently?)

0534
➔mihn wòhng gwāt sau 面黃
骨瘦(lit.) face is yellow and bone
is thin 臉很黃,骨頭瘦
(idi.) PH be skinny and look pale
皮黃骨瘦 ： *Yānwaih gēifōng, dī
yàhn ngohdou ~.* (Because of the
famine, people there suffer from
starvation. They have become ~.)

0535
➔móuh mín 冇面 (lit.) no face
沒有面子
(idi.)Adj. losing face 丟臉 ：
*Lóuhbáan béi fógei laauh, gokdāk
hóu ~.* (The employer was scolded
by his employee. He felt he was
really ~.) also see 0522

0536
➔muhkháu muhkmihn 木口
木面 (lit.) wooden mouth and
wooden face 木做的臉孔
(idi.) PH one who rarely smiles,
poker-faced 不苟言笑的人面無表
情 ： *Kéuih nīgo yàhn, ~ gám, jīt dōu
m̀siu.* (He is ~. He won't laugh
even if you tickle him.)

0537
➔m̀yiu mín 唔要面 (lit.) throw
away face 不要臉
(idi.) Adj./ PH shameless 不知恥 ：
ⓐ *Léuhng hīngdaih waihjó jāang
sāngā dá gūnsī, daaihgā baau daaihgā
dī sēuiyéh, jānhaih ~.* (The two
brothers filed a lawsuit against each
other in the struggle over their
father's wealth. They made each
other's dirty secrets exposed. They
are really ~.) ⓑ *Gam ~ ge sih néih
dōu jouhdākchēut!.* (How dare you
do such ~ thing?)

0538
➔séungmín 賞面 (lit.) appreciate
face 賞給面子
(idi.) VO favour somebody with
one's presence 蒞臨增光 ：
ⓐ*Dōjeh ~!* (Thank you for coming.)
ⓑ*Ngóhdeih hōi lyùhnfūnwúi, néih
háh ~ lèh.* (We are going to have a
party. You would like to ~, wouldn't
you?)

0539
➔tái yàhn háumihn/ mihnháu
睇人口面／面口 see 0487

0540
➔tái yàhn mihnsīk 睇人面色
see 0487

0541
➔yàhn yiu mín, syuh yiu pèih
人要面，樹要皮 (lit.) PH man
needs a face, tree needs a bark 人要
面子，就好像樹要樹皮保護它 ：
Néih hái gam dō yàhn mihnchìhn

81

laauh kéuih, kéuih gánghaih nāu lā, ~,
~ ā ma. (You scolded him in front of
so many people. Of course he was
angry. You know, ~, ~.)

0542
→yáuh tàuh yáuh mihn/ mín
有頭有面 (lit.) have a head and a
face 有頭有臉
(idi.) PH a person of social status 有
社會地位的人 ： Kéuih hái
séhwúiseuhng ~./ Kéuih haih ~ ge
yàhn. (S/he is ~.)

**mòuhgún 毛管 N pores (of
the skin) 毛孔 M dī**

0543
→mòuhgún duhng 毛管 戙
(lit.) hair stands on end 毛豎起來
(idi.) PH (1) very frightened, make
one's flesh crawl, 毛骨悚然 ： Kéuih
góng gwáigú, tēngdou ngóhdeih ~ .
(He told us a ghost story which made
us ~.) (2) feel awful 覺得可怕 ：
Kéuih cheunggō àh? Ngóh ~ la. (Is he
going to sing? I'll ~.)

**ngaahktàuh 額頭 N
forehead 額頭 M go**

0544
→mèih dāi ngaahk jaak, móuh
lèih gwaigaak 眉低額窄，冇厘
貴格 (lit.) PH eyebrows are low and
forehead is narrow (,which make a
person look vulgar) 眉低壓目,額頭
不寬廣的人,樣子不高貴: Kéuih go
yéung ~, ~, dím wúih haih
yáuhchínlóu a? (His ~. How could it
be possible that he is a rich man?)

0545
→m̀sīk tái yàhn mèih tàuh
ngáahn ngaahk 唔識睇人眉
頭眼額 (lit.) not know how to read
another's eyebrows, head, eyes and
forehead 不懂看別人的眉毛,頭,眼
睛及額頭
(idi.) PH unable to be worldlywise
不懂看人臉色 ： Kéuih dōu ~, dím
lōu saigaai a? (He is ~. How can he
make a good living?)

0546
→ngaahktàuh seuhngbihn
séjyuh 額頭上便寫住 (lit.) it is
written on one's forehead 額上面寫
著
(idi.) PH can easily be found out by
people 很容易被人識別 ：
Waaihyàhn haih móuh yéung tái ga,
m̀tūng kéuih ~ mè? (You can't tell
who is a bad guy. Do you mean that
they ~ ?)

**ngáahn 眼 N eye 眼睛 M jek;
deui/ sēung**

0547
→baahkgaap/gap ngáahn 白鴿
眼 see 0105

0548
→chaahk mèih chaahk ngáahn
賊眉賊眼 (lit.) thief's eye-brows
and thief's eyes 賊的眉毛和眼睛
(idi.) PH look like a thief 樣子像個
賊 ： Fóchē seuhngbihn gam bīkyàhn,
kéihhái ngóh gaaklèih gógo yàhn ~
gám, ngóh dōu haih yiu síusāmdī hóu.
(It was so crowded on the train. The

man standing beside me ~. I'd better be aware of him.)

0549

➔chēui sōu lūk ngáahn 吹鬚碌眼 (lit.)blow one's beard and open wide one's eyes 吹鬍鬚跟張大眼睛 (idi.) PH blow one's top, be furious 非常生氣：*Kéuih nāudou* ~. (He ~/ is ~.)

0550

➔chéungngáahn 搶眼 (lit.) snatch eye(s) 把眼睛搶過來 (idi.) Adj. eye-catching, attractive 觸目,很吸引人：*Sīnyihm ge ngàahnsīk/ Sīnsīk béigaau* ~. (Bright colors are more ~.)

0551

➔chìhngyàhn ngáahn léuih chēut Sāisī 情人眼裏出西施 (lit.) one is taken for a beauty in the eyes of her lover 情人眼裏出西施 (idi.) PH love is blind 愛情是盲目的：*Kéuih yáuh gam dō kyutdím dōu yáuh yàhn háng chéui kéuih ge, mgwaaidāk juhkyúh wah ~ lā!* (She has so many defects in her personality, but still there is a man willing to marry her. That's just as the saying goes, ~.) also see 0241

0552

➔chòih bāthó louh ngáahn 財不可露眼 (lit.) money should not be exposed to the eyes (of others) 錢財不好被人家看見 (idi.) PH be well aware of one's money and hide it in some safe place 小心保護財物,放在別人看不見的地方：*~, néih jājyuh gam dō chín,*

faaidī jēung kéuih doihhóu lā. (~. You are holding so much money. Hurry up and put it in your pocket.)

0553

➔dāanngáahn 單眼 (lit.) single-eyed 一隻眼 (idi.) PH have only one eye 瞎了一隻眼睛：*Kéuih haih* ~ *ge.* (He ~.) ATT one-eyed 只有一隻眼睛的：*~lóu/ jái/ pó/ mūi* (~ man/ boy/ woman/ girl)

0554

➔dūk ngáahn dūk beih 篤眼篤鼻 see 0369

0555

➔fā dō ngáahn lyuhn 花多眼亂(lit.) too many flowers make the eyes blurred 花多眼亂 (idi.) PH too many choices 太多選擇,很難決定：*~, dōu mjī gáan bīngo hóu.* (There are ~. I don't know which one to choose.)

0556

➔ fó jē ngáahn 火遮眼 (lit.) eyes covered with fire 火把眼睛遮蓋 (idi.) PH eyes blazed with anger 眼睛充滿怒火：*Kéuih yātsih* ~ *saatjó yàhn, mjī dím syun.* (He flew into such a fury that he killed a man. He didn't know what to do then.)

0557

➔fongchèuhng sēung ngáahn táiháh 放長雙眼睇吓 (lit.) lengthen one's eyes and see 把眼睛放長來看東西

(idi.) PH wait and see (what one thinks is right) 等著瞧(你以為對的事發生)： *Kéuih jaahnmàaihsaai dī yāmgūng chín, móuh hóu bou ge. Ngóhdeih ~.* (He makes money by doing evil things. He will have retributive justice in the future. We just ~.)

0558
➔gām jīng fó ngáahn 金睛火眼 (lit.) gold pupils and fiery eyes 金睛火眼
(idi.) A.PH very attentive eyes 非常集中注意力： *Ngóhdeih gūngsī nīgo tāanwái jínchēut ge jyūbóu haih fēisèuhngjī mìhnggwai ge, néih yiu ~ gám táijyuh sīnji dāk a.* (The jewellery displayed by our company in this stall is very valuable. You have to watch it with ~.) PH tired out eyes (resulting from hard work) (工作辛勤使)眼睛非常疲累： *Yaht yauh jouh, yeh yauh jouh, ngàaihdou ~.* (He worked day and night. Now he has gotten ~.)

0559
➔gin chín hōi ngáahn 見錢開眼 (lit.) open wide one's eyes on seeing money 見了錢眼便張開
(idi.) PH feel excited when being offered money 別人有錢給他便覺得高興： *Dī tāamgūn ~, néih háng sái hāakchín jauh dāk ge la.* (The corrupt officials would ~. If you are willing to give bribes, you'll get the green light.)

0560
➔gin ngàh m̀gin ngáahn 見牙

唔見眼 (lit.) can see the teeth but not the eyes 只看見牙齒,不看見眼睛
(idi.) PH a very hearty smile 笑得很開心： *Nīgo a-pòh gindóu dī syūn làih taam kéuih, jauh siudou ~.* (This old lady had ~ when she saw her grandchildren come to see her.)

0561
➔héingáahn 起眼 (lit.) up the eyes 豎起眼睛
(idi.) Adj. easy to be seen 顯現出來： *Nīdī lāang nghngàahn luhksīk, sóyíh néih jīk ge fā m̀~.* (This kind of yarn is of different colors. So the pattern you knit is not ~.)

0562 ✓
➔hùhngmāau ngáahn 熊貓眼 (lit.) N panda's eyes 熊貓的眼睛 M jek; deui
(idi.) N (said of a person) shadows round the eyes 有黑眼圈的眼睛 M deui; jek： ⓐ *Ngàaihjó géi máahn tūngsīu jauh jīkhāak yáuh ~ la.* (I've been working the whole night through for these few days, and I got ~ very soon.) ⓑ *Kéuihge ngáahnbouh fajōng hóuchíh (deui) ~ gám.* (The cosmetics on her eyes made her look like a panda.)

0563
➔ jáamháh jek ngáahn 斬/眨吓隻眼 (lit.) blink one eye 一隻眼眨了一下
(idi.) PH (in giving a signal) wink at somebody 打眼色： *Kéuih heung ngóh ~, giu ngóh m̀hóu chēutsēng.* (He ~ me to show that he wanted me to keep quiet.)

0564 ✓

➔jáamháh ngáahn 斬/眨吓眼
(lit.) blink 眨一下眼睛
(idi.) A.PH in the blink of an eye 一瞬間 : ~ *jauh dou la.* (You'll be there ~.)

0565

➔jáungáahn 走眼 (lit.) gone the eyes 逃過眼睛
(idi.) VO (1) errors escape one's eyes 看漏了眼 : *Sēuiyihn ngóh hóu síusām gaaudeui, daahnhaih yáuhsìh dōu wúih ~.* (Although I am very cautious in doing proof-reading, still ~ sometimes.) (2) misjudge 判斷錯誤 : *Kéuih go yéung gam chūngmihng, ngóh yíhwàih kéuih duhksyū hóu lēk, dímjī kéuih háau daihmēi, jānhaih ~ la.* (He looks smart, and I thought that he was doing very well at school. How could I have known that he was placed last. I really ~ him.)

0566

➔jek ngáahn hōi, jek ngáahn bai 隻眼開,隻眼閉 (lit.) open one eye and shut the other 張開一隻眼,閉上另一隻
(idi.) PH shut ones eyes to, turn a blind eye to (and not interfere nor take action) 雖看見但不加干涉或採取行動 : *Dī mòuhpàaih síufáan jēung dī yéh báaisaai hái louhbīn maaih, dī gíngchaat jauh ~ (, m̀léih kéuihdeih).* (The licenseless hawkers put their things for sale on the roadside, but the police ~ it/them.)

0567

➔jyúnháh ngáahn 轉吓眼
(lit.) change eye 轉換眼睛
(idi.) see 0564

0568

➔mèih jīng ngáahn kéih 眉精眼企 (lit.) shrewd eyebrows and standing eyes 眉毛精明,眼睛豎起
(idi.) PH very smart looking 樣子精明 : *Nīgo hauhsāangjái ~, wah tàuh síng méih, jēunglòih yātdihng hóu lēk.* (This young man is ~. He will understand all what you mean when you just say a word. He certainly will have a very promising future.)

0569

➔ m̀gokngáahn 唔覺眼 (lit.) eyes are not aware 眼睛察覺不到
(idi.) PH not notice 沒注意 : ⓐ*Néih ~ m̀ ~ ngóh ge bīu hái bīn a? Ngóh m̀ ginjó a.* (Did you notice where my watch was? I lost it.) ⓑ *"Kéuih làihjó la, néih jī m̀jī a?" "Ngóh ~ bo!"* ("He's here. Do you know?" "Sorry, I did ~.") Adj.PH unnoticeable 不顯眼的 : *Nīdī yéh jāihái ~ ge deihfōng gánghaih móuh yàhn máaih lā.* (No wonder nobody buys these things. They are put in ~ place.)

0570

➔ móuh ngáahn tái 冇眼睇
(lit.) no eye see 沒有眼睛看
(idi.) PH too disappointed to see 很失望,不欲觀之 : ⓐ *Géi hīngdaih waihjó jāang sāngā dá gūnsī, jouh*

85

lóuhdauh ge jauh jānhaih ~ lo. (The brothers filed lawsuits against each other in the struggle over their father's property. The father was ~ that.) ⓑ*Dī gúpiu/ làuhga ditsèhng gám, (ngóh) jānhaih ~.* (The share/ flat prices have plunged so much that I am ~ them.)

0571
→ṁsīk tái yàhn mèih tàuh ngáahn ngaahk 唔識睇人眉頭眼額 see 0545

0572✓
→ngáahn 眼 (lit.) N eye 眼睛 M jek; deui/ sēung
(idi.) BF the eye of, having the shape of a human eye 像眼睛的形狀 : ⓐ *jām~* (~ a needle) ⓑ*fūng ~* (~ a typhoon) M measure for a needle 針 的量詞 : *yāt ~ jām* (one ~)

0573
→ ngáahnbaahk 眼白 (lit.) N sclera, whites of the eyes 眼球白色的 部分 : *Yáuh hùhngngáahnjing ge behngyàhn ~ bouhfahn wúih binsèhng hùhngsīk.* (The ~ of a patient who suffers red eye disease would become red.)

0574
→ngáahn baahkbaahk 眼白白 (lit.) eyes are very white 眼巴巴
(idi.) A.PH see something bad happen but cannot do anything about it 看見不好的事發生卻不能 阻止 : *Ngóh jēung dī chín jouhjó bun nihn ge dihngkèih chyùhnfún. Dímjī nī léuhnggo yuht leihsīk héijó hóudō, ngóh ~ ṁgin hóudō chín.* (I

had my money put in the bank on (fixed) deposit for six months. How could I have known that the interest rate would rise so much during these two months. I certainly have lost a lot of money, but I can't do anything about it.)

0575
→ngáahn bātgin wàih jihng 眼 不見爲淨 (lit.) if your eyes can't/didn't see it, then it's clean 眼不見爲淨
(idi.) PH better not worry about hygiene 不必那麼擔心衛生 : *"Jáugā chàhlàuh ge chyùhfóng dōu ṁhaih hóu gōnjehng, ngóh ṁhaih géi gám sihk kéuihdeih ge yéh." "~ ā ma! Pa mè jē!"* ("The kitchen of the restaurants and teahouses are not very clean. I'm a little worried when eating things there." "~, understand? There's no need to worry about it.")

0576
→ngáahn daaih tái gwolùhng 眼大睇過籠 (lit.) big eyes still miss it 眼睛大卻看不到
(idi.) PH fail to look at something carefully 看得不夠仔細 : *"Dímgáai ngóh wánṁ dóu boují seuhngbihn gódyuhn goubaahk gé?" "Nē, hái nīdouh lō, néih."* ("Why can't I find the advertisement in the newspaper?" "Hey, it's here. You miss it.")

0577
→ngáahnfā 眼花(lit.) eye flower 眼睛有花
(idi.) Adj. eyes blurred 眼睛昏花 : *Dágēi dájó géigo jūngtàuh jīhauh jauh*

yáuhdī ~. (After I've played TV games for hours, my ~.)

0578

➔ngáahnfāfā 眼花花 (lit.) eye flowers 眼睛有很多花
(idi.) PH/ A. PH eyes blurred 眼睛昏花 : ⓐ *Yámjó géi būi jáu jīhauh táiyéh jauh ~.* (My ~ after I drank several glasses of wine.) ⓑ ~ *táichojó* (~ and so see it wrong)

0579

➔ngáahnfó baau 眼火爆 (lit.) eyes burst into fire 眼睛裏的火爆炸
(idi.) PH eyes blaze with anger 怒氣沖天 : *Ngóh hóu jāng kéuih, táigin kéuih ngóh jauh ~ la.* (I hate him very much. My ~ when I see him.)

0580

➔ngáahn fut tóuh jaak 眼闊肚窄 (lit.) eyes are wide but the stomach is narrow 眼睛大,肚子小
(idi.) PH one's eyes are bigger than his stomach 想吃很多,可是吃不下 : *Jihjoh chāan yáuh hóudō yéh sihk, daahnhaih ngóh ~, jānhaih ṁdái la.* (There are lots of things to eat at a buffet. However, my ~. For me, it is not so worth eating.)

0581

➔ngáahn gāmgām 眼甘甘 (lit.) eyes fixed 定睛看
(idi.)A.PH fix one's eyes on, never take ones eyes off somebody, eye somebody up (and down)目不轉睛 : *Sihngyaht ~ gám mohngjyuh yàhn.* (He always/ never ~ me.)

0582

➔ngáahngok gōu 眼角高 (lit.) ending part of the eyes are high 眼尾的位置高
(idi.) PH/Adj.PH set a high standard in choosing one's spouse or a friend of the opposite sex 擇偶或選擇異性朋友的條件很高 : *Kéuih hóu ~ ge. Kéuih jihgéi haih sehksih, yùhgwó néih ṁhaih boksih, kéuih ṁwúih chói néih ge.* (She ~. She has a master's degree, so she won't associate with a man if he does not have a doctorate.)

0583

➔ngáahn gwahtgwaht 眼掘掘 (lit.) eyes fixed 定睛看
(idi.) PH/A.PH gaze at (someone) with malice 敵視別人 : ⓐ *Kéuih deui ngóh ~ gám, ngóh ṁjī géisih dākjeuihjó kéuih nē?* (He looked at me in an unfriendly way. I don't know when I have offended him.) ⓑ *Kéuih ~ gám mohngjyuh ngóh.* (He looked at me maliciously.)

0584

➔ngáahn hùhng 眼紅 (lit.) eyes red 眼睛紅色
(idi.) V jealous of, have green eyes 妒忌 : *Ṁhóu yānwaih yàhndeih jaahnchín dōgwo néih jauh ~ yàhndeih.* (Don't be ~ others because they earn more money than you.)

0585

➔ngáahn jáamjáam 眼斬斬/眨眨 (lit.) eyes blink and blink 眼睛眨著
(idi.) PH just blink one's eyes without a sign of remorse on one's face 臉上

沒有悔意,只是眨眼 : *Néih laauh kéuih kéuih jauh ~, laauhyùhn kéuih (kéuih) yauh haih gám.* (When you scold him, he ~, and after that he will do the same thing again.)

0586
→ngáahnjái lūklūk 眼仔碌碌
(lit.) little eyes roll here and there 小小的眼睛左右溜轉
(idi.) PH (said of babies or very small children) have lovely and cute eyes 嬰兒或小童可愛的眼睛 : *Nīgo bihbī ~, hóu dākyi!* (This baby ~. What a cute baby!)

0587
→ngáahn jūng dēng 眼中釘
(lit.) nail in one's eye 眼中釘
(idi.) N somebody one hates very much 你很憎恨的人 M go/ háu : *Kéuih dong ngóh haih ~.* (He treats me as a ~.)

0588
→ngáahnjyū 眼珠 (lit.) eye pearl 眼像珍珠
(idi.) N pupil 眼球的瞳孔 M jek; deui/ sēung : *~ wūjēutjēut.* (lovely dark-brown eyes)

0589
→ngáahn sāpsāp 眼濕濕 (lit.) eyes wet 眼睛濕了
(idi.) A.PH/PH with tears in one's eyes 眼中有淚 : *Ngóh mahn kéuih kéuihge lóuhgūng ge behngchihng dímyéung. Kéuih jauh ~ gám wah, "Yīsāng wah kéuih haih ngàahmjīng muhtkèih....."* (I asked her about the condition of her sick husband. She

said ~, "The doctor said he had terminal cancer......")

0590
→ngáahn táantáan 眼坦坦
(lit.) show the whites of the eyes 眼睛翻白
(idi.) PH a desperate look of a person when suffering heavy losses 遇到嚴重損失時的表情 : *Kéuih hohk yàhn jouh sāangyi, daahnhaih sihtdou ~.* (He did business just like others, but he lost all his money and became desperate.)

0591
→ngáahnyūn 眼冤 (lit.) eyes grieving 眼睛受冤
(idi.) Adj. feel disgusted (at/with something one sees), eyesore 看了覺得反感 : ⓐ *Kéuihdeih yāt hàahngmàaih jauh láam tàuh láam géng, táigin jauh ~.* (They [the two lovers] show intimacy when they see each other. I just ~ at it.) ⓑ *Kéuihdeih léuhng gūngpó sèhngyaht ngaaigāau dágāau, jānhaih ~.* (The husband and wife always quarrel and fight. What a wrong match!)

0592
→sāangjī māau yahp ngáahn 生滋貓入眼 (lit.) a cat with ringworm gets into one's eyes 生癬的貓兒入了眼睛
(idi.) PH eye somebody up (and down) 目不轉睛地看人 : *Kéuih yāt gindóu leng néui jauh ~ ge la.* (Whenever he sees a beautiful girl, he'll ~.)

88

0593

→séi ṁngáahnbai 死唔眼閉
(lit.) die with open eyes 死不瞑目
(idi.) PH (1) suffer grievance till one's dying day 至死不安 : *Kéuih yihgā behngdou jauhlàih séi la, go lóuhpòh juhng tùhng kéuih chìhn chāi ge jáinéui jāang kéuihdī sāngā, kéuih jānhaih ~ lo.* (Now he is dying in his bed, but his wife is still struggling over his wealth with the children by his first wife. He certainly ~.) (2) suffer grievance even after one's death 死後仍不安 : *Néih lóuhdauh dāk néih yātlāp jái, néih yauh gam ṁsāangsing, kéuih jānhaih ~.* (You are the only son of your [dead] father. But you don't tend to make good (in life). He certainly ~.)

0594

→seuhnngáahn 順眼 (lit.) smooth eyes 順眼
(idi.) Adj. feel alright when one looks at it, pleasant to one's eyes 看起來沒有問題，好看 : ⓐ*Ngóh gokdāk go jūng gwahái nīdouh ~ dī.* (I think it would be better if we hang the clock here.) ⓑ *Nīgāan gūngsī léuihbihn yáuh hóudō ṁgūngpihng ge sih, néih táiṁ ~ ge maih jáu lō.* (There are lots of unfair things in this company. If you don't like it, you'd better quit.)

0595

→síngmuhk 醒目 (lit.) wake up one's eyes 眼睛醒了
(idi.) Adj. (1) smart 聰敏 : *Nīgo saimānjái hóu ~.* (This child is very ~.) (2) smart and quick in movement 聰敏,身手快捷 : *Jouh yàhn yiu ~ dī, ṁhóu hóuchíh yātgauh faahn gám sín*

dāk ga. (Do be ~. Don't be inert and behave like a fool.)

0596

→táiṁgwo ngáahn 睇唔過眼
(lit.) look but cannot pass one's eyes 看不過去
(idi.) PH see that someone has really done something wrong or unfair (and be ready to do something about it) 覺得不公平,打算有所行動 : *Sīnsāang pīnsām bāanjéung, hóudō tùhnghohk dōu ~ jauh heung haauhjéung tàuhsou.* (The teacher is especially nice to the class representative. Many students think it's not fair to them. They complain about it to the principal.)

0597

→tīn móuh ngáahn lo 天冇眼囉 (lit.) Heaven has no eyes/is blind 天公沒有眼睛
(idi.) PH Heaven is a bad judge (when misfortune falls on the good or life is too kind to the wicked) 沒有天理,天不公平 : *Kéuih sānsān fúfú yéuhng daaih dī jáinéui, daahnhaih dī jáinéui jauh ṁléih kéuih, gáaudou kéuih yiu fangāai, jānhaih ~ lo!* (He worked very hard to raise his children. But they did not take care of him after they grew up. Now he is homeless and has to sleep on the street. ~!)

0598

→tīn yáuh ngáahn 天有眼
(lit.) Heaven has eyes/ can see 天公有眼睛
(idi.) PH Heaven is a good judge (when the innocents are vindicated [after suffering for a time] or the wicked are punished) 天公有理 : *Kéuih jouhjó gam dō waaih sih, hoih*

yàhn bāt chín, jēutjī béi gíngchaat jūkdóu, jānhaih ~ lo! (He had done so many evil things which are very harmful to people. Finally he was arrested by the police. It's true that ~!)

0599

➔yātngáahn gwāan chāt 一眼關七 (lit.) look at seven directions with just one eye 一隻眼睛看七個方位

(idi.) PH attentive to different things at the same time 同時注意不同的事情;眼觀六路 : *Jouh dīksí sīgēi ge yiu ~, yauh yiu tái haak, yauh yiu tái gāautūng bīuji, yauh yiu tái gāautūngchāai.* (A taxi-driver has to be ~. He has to look for passengers, look at the traffic signs and see if there is a traffic policeman.) (* Seven directions refer to all directions excluding the back [as in 'back and front'].)

0600

➔ yáuh ngáahn bātsīk Taaisāan 有眼不識泰山 (lit.) have eyes but not know the Mountain Tai 有眼不識泰山

(idi.) PH fail to recognize a person of importance 看見重要人物卻不知道 : *Néihdeih jānhaih ~, ngóh jauh haih néihdeih gūngsī ge júngchòih.* (You really ~. I'm the director of the company.)

0601

➔yáuh ngáahn mòuh jyū 有眼無珠(lit.) have eyes but not the pupils 有眼無珠

(idi.) PH (sarcastically) blind 諷刺

人盲目做事: *Ngóh yíhwàih kéuih haih lóuhsaht yàhn, dímjī kéuih ngāaksaai ngóhdī chín, ngóh jānhaih ~ lo!* (I thought that he was an honest man. How could I have known that he took all my money by fraud. I'm really ~.)

(ngáahn) mèih (眼)眉 N eyebrow 眉, 眉毛 M tìuh/ hòhng/ tòhng

0602

➔chaahk mèih chaahk ngáahn 賊眉賊眼 see 0548

0603

➔hóu mèih hóu maauh sāang sāsāt 好眉好貌生沙虱 see 0024

0604

➔mèih dāi ngaahk jaak, móuh lèih gwaigaak 眉低額窄，冇厘貴格 see 0544

0605

➔mèih jīng ngáahn kéih 眉精眼企 see 0568

0606

➔ngáahnmèihmòuh chèuhng 眼眉毛長 (lit.) eyebrow is long 眉毛長

(idi.) PH have no interest in doing (such) a time-consuming job 沒有興趣做需時太久的事 : *Jīk lāangsāam àh? Táigin jauh ~ lo!* (To knit a sweater? I ~ .)

0607
→ngáahnmèihmòuh tīutūng 眼眉毛挑通 (lit.) even eyebrows are exquisitely carved 連眉毛也雕刻得通透 (idi.) PH sharp-witted and cannot be easily cheated 人很精明,不易受騙：*Kéuih nīgo yàhn ~ ge, dím wúih séuhng néih dong ā?* (He is a person who is ~. How could he be tricked by you?)

0608
→séui jam ngáahnmèih 水浸眼眉 (lit.) water is going up to one's eyebrows 水浸上眉毛了 (idi.) PH going to meet with disaster 即將大禍臨頭：*Ngóhdeih sāam kèih móuh gūngláu, ngàhnhòhng wah yiu sāuláu, yihgā ~ la, néih faaidī séung baahnfaat lā.* (We didn't pay three instalments for our flat, and the bank is going to confiscate it. We are ~. Quickly think of a way to settle the problem.)

0609
→ tai ngáahnmèih 剃眼眉 (lit.) shave eyebrows 剃眉毛 (idi.) VO same as 'lohkmín', see 0522

ngàh 牙 N tooth 牙齒 M jek; pàahng

0610
→dá ngàhgaau 打牙較 (lit.) tap the jaw 敲打齒齦 (idi.) VO chat idly, have small talk, shoot the breeze 閒聊：*Baahngūng sìhgaan m̀hóu ~.* (People should not ~ during office hours.)

0611
→gin ngàh m̀gin ngáahn 見牙唔見眼 see 0560

0612
→góng daaihwah, lāt daaihngàh 講大話，甩大牙 (lit.) tell lies, then your molars will fall off 說謊話便會掉大牙 (idi.) PH a warning against children's telling lies 警誡孩子不好撒謊的說話：*Saimānjái m̀hóu góng daaihwah a, yānwaih, ~, ~.* (You children should not tell lies, because if you ~, ~.)

0613
→móuh ngàh lóuhfū 冇牙老虎 see 0258

0614
→ngáauhsaht ngàhgān 咬實牙齦 (lit.) bite one's gums hard 咬緊牙關 (idi.) A.PH tolerate bitterly, grind one's teeth 強忍：*Ngóh chōchō làihdou nīdouh ge sìhhauh, jouhgūng wán hóu síu chín, sāngwuht hóu kwannàahn, daahnhaih ngóh ~ ngàaihlohkheui, sīnji yáuh gāmyaht.* (When I first came here, I earned very little money from my job. Life was hard then. But I ~ and went on working hard to achieve a good life I have now.)

0615
→ngàhchaat 牙擦 (lit.) teeth are scrubbing 牙齒磨擦 (idi.) Adj. (1) boastful 喜炫耀自己：*Kéuih hóu ~ ga, wah jihgéi māt dōu dāk.* (He is ~ in saying that he

can do anything well.) (2) proud of oneself 自傲 : *Néih jauh hóyíh ~ lā, go jái jouh yīsāng, go néui jouh ginjūksī.* (You can be ~. Your son is a doctor and your daughter is an architect.)

0616

→ ngàh chaatchaat 牙擦擦 (lit.) teeth keep on scrubbing 牙齒不停磨擦 (idi.) PH boastful 炫耀自己 : *Kéuih sihngyaht ~ gám, mgwaaidāk yàhn mjūngyi kéuih.* (He is always so ~, no wonder people don't like him.) A.PH boastfully 很自豪地 : *Kéuih ~ gám wah, "Ngóh chùhnglòih meih syūgwo ge."* (He said ~, "I've never lost a game.")

0617

→ngàhchí dong gām sái 牙齒當金使 (lit.) teeth are used as gold 牙齒當作黃金使用 (idi.) PH keep one's word 言而有信 : *Sái māt chīm hahptùhng a? Ngóhdeih ~, gónggwo jauh haih ge la.* (Why should we sign a contract? We always ~. We'll take it seriously once we give you a promise.)

0618

→ngàh jáamjáam 牙斬斬(lit.) teeth are moving up and down 牙齒不停開合 (idi.) PH talkative and (tend to be) contentious 能言善辯 : *góngyéh ~ gám* (be ~ in one's speech)

0619

→ngàh jīm jéui leih 牙尖嘴利 see 0496

0620

→ngàhtung gám ge sēng 牙痛噉嘅聲 (lit.) make a sound as if one were suffering from toothache 像牙痛時的呻吟聲 (idi.) PH grumble (to show reluctance to do something) 抱怨(因不肯作某事) : *Sèhngyaht gwajyuh dágēi, giu kéuih jouhgūngfo jauh ~.* (He always occupies himself in playing TV/ video games. Whenever I tell him to do his homework, he ~.)

0621

→ngàhyīn 牙煙 (lit.) teeth and smoke 牙和煙 (idi.) Adj. dangerous 危險 : *Gógo jīupàaih béi daaihfūng chēuidou yiuhháh yiuhháh, jānhaih ~ la.* (The billboard was blown by the strong wind. It swung and was likely to fall. It was very ~.)

pei 屁 N fart 屁 M go; dī

0622

→bápei 把屁 (lit.) PH (said with contempt) it's not a big deal at all (語氣輕蔑)並不了不起 : *"Wa! Kéuihge bīu hóu leng bo!" "~!"* ("Oh, he has a beautiful watch!" "~!") (* 'Bápei' is much the same as 'bágwái', see 1141(2).)

0623

→chèuih fu fongpei→dō chí yāt géui 除褲放屁→多此一舉 (lit.) HIT take off trousers and let out gas→it's (a waste of time and) unnecessary to do so 把褲子脫去才放屁→不必這樣做 : *Yauh wah gūnghōi jīuping, kèihsaht haih*

92

yíhgīng loihdihngjó ge la, jānhaih ~ (→ ~). (It is said that the recruitment is open for application, but actually the successful applicant has already been chosen. It's like a person who ~.)

0624 ✓
➔fongpei 放屁(lit.)VO let out gas 放屁
(idi.) PH/ V nonsense, shit 胡說瞎扯: *"Kéuih hái boují seuhngbihn laauh néih wo." "Kéuih ~!"* ("He criticized you in the newspaper.""~!")

0625✓
➔pei 屁 (lit.)N fart 屁 M go; dī
(idi.) P a particle similar to 'gwái', but is much more limited in use. It rarely goes with other verbs other than 'yáuh'. 助語詞,與'鬼'相似,但用法很有限 , 多跟 '有' 一起 : *yáuh ~ yuhng* (what the hell use is it/ not useful at all)

0626
➔pei dōu ṁō go 屁都唔疴個
(lit.) not even let out gas 連屁也不放一個
(idi.) PH (said of a woman, usually abusive) shows no sign of having children 指女性(通常是責罵語)連生一個孩子的跡象也沒有 : *"Gitjó fān gam loih, lihn ~,"* go hóu sāmgāp séung póuh syūn ge gāpó wah. ("They have been married for such a long time, but she ~," said the mother-in-law, who was very anxious to have a grandchild.)

pèihfū 皮膚 N skin 皮膚 M dī

0627
➔chit yuhk bātlèih pèih 切肉不離皮 (lit.) when cutting the flesh, cut the skin too which still sticks to it 切肉時,連皮也一起切掉 (idi.) PH blood is thicker than water, be genetically related 親情濃厚 : *~, néih dá ngóh agō, jīkhaih dá ngóh, ngóh yiu bōng agō dáfāan néih.* (~. You beat my brother, that means you beat me too. I have to fight back for him.)

0628
➔dauhpèih 豆皮 (lit.) bean on the skin 皮膚上長了豆子
(idi.) N pocked face 麻臉 : ⓐ *Kéuihge mihn sāangmúhn ngamchōng, hóuchíh ~ gám.* (His face has so many pimples that it appears to be pocked.) ⓑ *~ lóu/ pòh* (a man/ woman with a ~)

0629
➔ngānpèih 韌皮 (lit.) tough skin 硬的皮
(idi.) Adj. naughty and disobedient 頑皮及不聽話 : *Nīgo saimānjái hóu ~, giu kéuih ṁhóu hái sōfádouh tiulàih tiuheui, wah gihk dōu ṁtēng.* (This child is ~. I've told him not to bounce on the sofa many many times, but he wouldn't listen.)

0630✓
➔pèih 皮 (lit.) N skin 皮膚 M faai; chàhng; dī
(idi.) N (1) peel, skin of fruit 水果的皮 M faai : *Ṁhóu jihnghaih sihk yuhk yiu lihn ~ sihk sīnji yáuhyīk.* (Don't just eat the pulp. It would do you good if you eat the ~ too.) (2)

93

dollar 元 ： *sahp géi* ~ (more than ten ~) (3) (when changed into a high rising tone: 'péi') running expenses 經營成本 ： *sūk* ~ (cut ~) BF (1) peel/ skin of (水果的)皮 ： *cháang/ hēungjīu/ sāigwā* ~ (~ of orange/ banana/ watermelon) (2) expenses 費用 ： ⓐ ~ *fai* (running ~) ⓑ (when changed into a high rising tone: '-péi') ： *hāan* ~ (save money by being thrifty)

0631
➔pèih gwōng yuhk waaht 皮光肉滑 (lit.) skin is bright and flesh is smooth 皮膚有光彩,肉很柔滑
(idi.) PH very good and smooth skin 狀態很好的皮膚 ： *Kéuih jauhlàih luhksahp seui ge lo bo, juhng haih ~ gám, m̀jī kéuih haih m̀haih sihkjó hóudō yinwō nē?* (She will soon be sixty, but she still has ~. I wonder if she has eaten a lot of bird's nest.)

0632
➔yàhn yiu mín, syuh yiu pèih 人要面,樹要皮 see 0541

sām　心 N heart　心 M go

0633
➔ chōu sām daaih yi 粗心大意 (lit.) coarse heart and big idea 粗心大意
(idi.)　Adj.PH　careless　and absent-minded 不夠細心 ： *Kéuih jouhyéh hóu ~ ge, néih yiu chēkchīngchó sīnji dāk a.* (He is very ~ in doing things. You certainly have to check [his work] carefully.)

0634
➔dáam daaih sām sai 膽大心細 see 0382

0635
➔dám sām dám fai 扰心扰肺 see 0387

0636
➔dihpmàaih sāmséui 疊埋心水 (lit.) fold up one's heart (water) 收拾心情
(idi.) PH give up doing one thing and try to concentrate on doing another 放棄做一件事,並嘗試專心做另一件事 ： ⓐ *Teuiyāu jīhauh, kéuih jauh ~ dáng jouh làaihláai.* (After she has retired, she just waits for her son's wedding.) ⓑ *Páau yeh máh syūsaai, bātyùh ~ fangaau bá la.* (I lost all my money in the horse racing tonight. I'd better go to bed instead.)

0637
➔ dōsām 多心 (lit.) many hearts 很多念頭
(idi.) Adj. be dillydolly, full of whims, a double-minded person 三心兩意 ： *"Ngóh yauh séung heui táihei, yauh séung heui yàuhséui, yauh séung heui hàahng gūngsī." "M̀hóu gam ~ lā! Faaidī kyutdihng lā."* ("I want to go to see movie, or go swimming or go window shopping." "Don't be ~. Hurry up and make up your mind.")

0638
➔fāsām 花心 (lit.) flowery heart 很多花的心
(idi.) Adj. (said of a man) be insatiable in love, fails to give his

mind to his lover (指男人)對愛情不專一 : *Kéuih hóu ~ ga, yātsih jēui nīgo néuihjái, yātsih yauh jēui gógo néuihjái.* (He is very ~. Now he is chasing after one girl but then he'll chase after another.)

0639
➜fāsām lòhbaahk 花心蘿蔔
(lit.) the heart of a turnip looks like a flower 蘿蔔的心好像一朵花
(idi.) N a man insatiable in love 對愛情不專一的男人 M go : *Kéuih jūngyi nīgo nàahmyán haih ~ làih ga. Ngóh jānhaih dahng kéuih dāamsām.* (The man she is falling in love with is ~. I'm really worried about her.)

0640
➜fónglòhng syuh → yāttìuh sām 枌榔樹→一條心 (lit.) a coir-palm tree→has only one heart 枌榔樹→(只有)一條心
(idi.) HIT (said of a man) loves his girlfriend/ wife heart and soul (指男性)對愛情專一 : *A-Wóng deui néuih pàhngyáuh/ taaitáai jānhaih hóyíh wah ~ → ~.* (We can say that Wong ~.)

0641
➜fūisām 灰心 (lit.). grey heart 灰色的心
(idi.) Adj. feel very disappointed and want to give up 很失望,打算放棄 : ⓐ *Sātbaaihjó géichi jīhauh, kéuih (gokdāk) hóu ~.* (He ~ after having failed for several times.) ⓑ *Mhóu ~, gaijuhk lóuhlihk lā.* (Don't ~. Keep trying.)

0642
➜hāaksām 黑心 (lit.) black heart 黑色的心
(idi.) Adj. wicked minded (hoping that misfortune will fall on others) 心腸不好（希望別人有壞事發生）: *Kéuih hóu ~ ga, sihngyaht mohng ngóhdeih léuhng gūngpó ngaaigāau/ ngóh béi lóuhbáan cháau yàuhyú.* (He is very ~. He always hopes that I would quarrel with my husband [/wife] / I would be fired.)

0643
➜ hahp/ngāam sāmséui 合／啱心水 (lit.) meet one's heart water 合心意
(idi.) Adj.PH one's cup of tea, to one's liking 自己所喜歡的 : *"Yáuh móuh gáandóu ~ ge dāanwái a?" Gógo deihcháan gīnggéi mahn go haak.* (*"Have you found a flat that is ~?" the real estate agent asked his client.)

0644
➜ háu bāt deui sām 口不對心
see 0462

0645
➜háu sih sām fēi 口是心非
see 0467

0646
➜hóusām dāk/ yáuh hóu bou 好心得／有好報 (lit.)PH recompense will go to the good 善有善報 : ~, *chéng gokwái gyūn dōdī chín lā.* (~. Please give more money [for charity].)

95

0647

➔hóu sāmdéi 好心地 (lit.) good heart base 心很好

(idi.) Adj.PH kind-hearted 心很善良 : *Kéuih nīgo yàhn hóu ~ ga, táigin yàhn yáuh kwannàahn jauh jīkhāak bōng yàhn ge la.* (He is a very ~ person. Whenever he sees that others are in trouble, he'll immediately help them out.)

0648

➔hóusām jeuhk lèuih pek 好心著雷劈 (lit.) be kind-hearted but in turn be struck by thunder 做好事卻被雷打

(idi.) PH help/ kindness is not appreciated, but is resented instead 幫助別人，對別人好反而被怪責: *Ngóh bōng kéuih jāphóu dī yéh, kéuih juhng laauh ngóh gáau kéuih dī yéh, jānhaih ~.* (I tidied up the things for him, but he blamed me for meddling with his things. My ~.) (* It is a more emphatic way of saying than 0649.)

0649

➔hóusām m̀dāk hóubou 好心唔得好報 (lit.) be kind-hearted but have no recompense in return 做好事沒有好的報應

(idi.) PH good intention is not appreciated 別人不領你的好意 : *Bōng kéuih jouhyéh, dōjeh dōu móuh yāt sēng, jānhaih ~.* (I helped him [to do things], yet he didn't even say 'thank you' to me. The saying is true that my ~.)

0650

➔hóusām m̀ pa jouh 好心唔怕做 (lit.)PH there's no harm to do good deeds 好事不妨去做 : *"Nīdouh giu ngóh gyūnchín, gódouh yauh giu ngóh gyūnchín, bīn gyūndāk gam dō a?" "Óh, ~ gé."* ("This charity has asked me to donate money. That one also asks me to do so. How can I afford to donate so much money to them?" "Oh! ~.")

0651

➔hūngsām lóuhgūn 空心老倌 (lit.) heartless opera actor/ actress (who has a nice-looking appearance but not the art of performing opera) 外表美麗但沒有表演藝術的戲曲演員

(idi.) N a person who is outwardly gorgeous but not substantial 華而不實,外表奢華,其實內裏空虛的人 M go : *Kéuih jeuk mìhngpàaih, jā leng chē, dī néuih mìhngsīng yíhwàih kéuih haih gūngjí, kèihsaht kéuih haih ~ làih ge jī ma.* (He wears clothes of well-known brands, and drives an expensive car. The movie/TV actresses take him for a rich dandy, but actually he is not/ ~.)

0652

➔ louh yìuh jī máhlihk, yaht gáu gin yàhnsām 路遙知馬力，日久見人心 see 0313

0653✓

➔mohsām 磨心 (lit.) N heart/ pivot of a grindstone 石磨的心／轉軸 M go

(idi.) N a person suffering from his being a negotiator between two opposing persons/ parties 替意見不同的人或團體作調停而覺得辛苦 M go : *Ngóh wah jauh wah haih jyúyahm jē, kèihsaht yáuhsih haih lóuhsai tùhng tùhngsih (jīgāan) ge ~ làih ge ja.* (It is so said that I am the section head, but sometimes I find it a hard job to meditate between my boss and my colleagues.)

0654
→**móuh sām** 冇心 (lit.) no heart 沒有心
(idi.) A unintentionally 不是故意 的：*Ngóh ~ ngāak néih ga, haih kéuih giu ngóh m̀hóu góngbéi néih tēng jī ma.* (I didn't mean to lie to you. It's he who asked me not to tell you [the truth].) PH not do something intentionally 不是故意 做的：*Ngóh haih ~ ga, néih m̀hóu gwaai ngóh a.* (I did ~. Please don't be angry with me.)

0655
→**ngámjyuh go lèuhngsām** 揞 住個良心 (lit.) cover up one's conscience (with one's hands) 用手 掩蓋良心
(idi.) A.PH against one's conscience 違背良心：ⓐ*~ jouh waaihsih* (do evil things ~) ⓑ*~ góng* (say it ~)

0656
→**paak sāmháu** 拍心口 (lit.) pat one's chest 拍胸口
(idi.) A.PH give a bold promise 大 力承諾：*Kéuih ~ deui ngóh wah, "Nīgihn sih, bāauhái ngóh sānseuhng. Néih m̀sái gēng."* (He ~ to me and said, "I'll tackle the problem for you. Don't be afraid.")

0657
→**pīnsām** 偏心 (lit.) heart is not

right in the middle 心不在正中的位 置
(idi.) V favour/ show partiality to somebody 偏袒某人：ⓐ*sīnsāang ~ máuhgo hohksāang* (the teacher ~ a certain student) ⓑ*fuhmóuh ~ máuhgo jáinéui* (the parents ~ a certain child) Adj. (said of elders or superiors) fail to be fair (in showing partiality to somebody) (長輩或上級 因偏袒某人而)不公正：*sīnsāang hóu ~* (the teacher ~)

0658
→**sāam sām léuhng yi** 三心兩 意(lit.) three hearts and two ideas 三心兩意
(idi.) PH be dillydolly, full of whims, a double minded person 有太多念 頭,不專心：see 0637

0659
→**sàhnsām** 神心 (lit.) god's heart 神的心
(idi.) Adj. (said of Chinese) religious, devout (worshipers of the gods in Chinese folklore) 對中國民間所膜拜 的神很虔誠：*Kéuih hóu ~ ga, jiumáahn dōu jōnghēung baaisàhn.* (She is very ~. Every morning and night, she burns incense and worships her god[s].)

0660 ✓
→**sām** 心(lit.)N heart 心 M go
(idi.) N core (containing the seeds of fruits) 水果的心 M go：*Nīgo pihnggwó/ léi ge ~ laahnjó.* (The ~ of this apple/ pear is rotten.)

97

0661

➔ **sāmbehng** 心病 (lit.) disease in heart 心的病

(idi.) N (1) something that bothers you 心裏的不安 : ~ wàahn sēui sāmyeuhk yī (you need the right remedy to heal what bothers you) (* The example sentence is also an idiomatic expression.) (2) covert conflict (between people) 人與人之間心中不和 : Kéuihdeih léuhnggo yáuh ~. (There is ~ between them.)

0662

➔ **sāmdō** 心多 (lit.) many hearts 心多

(idi.) Adj. (1) too suspicious 太多疑心 : "Néih nīpáai sèhngyaht dōu gam yeh fāan, hái ngoihbihn jouh mēéh a?" taaitáai mahn. "Néih m̀hóu gam ~ lā, ngóh hái gūngsī hōi wúi ā ma!" lóuhgūng wah. ("Recently you got home so late. What did you do?" asked the wife. "Don't be ~. I had business meetings," said the husband.) (2) see 0637

0663

➔ **sām dōu sahtsaai** 心都實晒 (lit.) even heart tightens 連心也縮緊了

(idi.) PH disappointed and worried 失望及擔心 : Gūngsī ge jīkyùhn tēnggin wah yiu chòihyùhn jauh ~. (When the staff learned that some of them were going to be laid off, they were ~.)

0664

➔ **sāmfàahn** 心煩(lit.) heart is in trouble 心煩

(idi.) Adj. feel troubled 心緒不寧 :

Kéuih yāt lámhéi yiu sé leuhnmàhn jauh ~ la. (Whenever he thought of writing a thesis, he ~.)

0665

➔ **sām gógeui, háu gógeui** 心嗰句，口嗰句 see 0483

0666

➔ **sāmhòhn** 心寒 (lit.) heart is cold 心寒

(idi.) V feel terrible 心裏覺得可怕 : Dī bōktàuhdóng sīnbātsīn jauh bōkwàhn néih, joi ló néih dī chín, tēnggin dōu ~. (The head-bashing robbers will hit your head from behind first. They then take away your money while you are unconscious. People ~ when they hear about this.)

0667

➔ **sāmjūk** 心足 (lit.) heart feels enough 心裏覺得足夠

(idi.) Adj. content, satisfied 心滿意足 : ⓐ M̀hóu wah gā yàhngūng la, m̀cháau yàuhyú ngóh yíhgīng hóu ~ la. (I won't think about getting a raise [in my salary], I would be ~ if I were not fired.) ⓑ Jungjó luhkkahpchói sāam jéung dōu juhng m̀ ~ àh? (You are the third prize winner of the Mark Six, and still you are not ~?)

0668

➔ **sāmngāp** 心嗑 (lit.) heart is covered by something 心被一些東西遮蓋著

(idi.) Adj. upset, frustrated 覺得失望不安 : Kéuihge behng yījó gam noih dōu juhng meih hóu, ngóh jānhaih ~. (He has undergone medical treatment for such a long time, yet he didn't recover. I'm really ~.)

0669

➔sāmséui 心水 (lit.) heart water 心裏的水
(idi.) ATT one's cup of tea 合心意的 : ⓐ *Néih haih chēutméng ge máhpihnggā, gāmyaht ge choisih, néih yáuh mātyéh ~ máh a?* (You are a famous horse-racing commentator. Do you have any favourite horses in today's event?) ⓑ *Hái Hēunggóng hóu nàahn máaihdóu ~ láu.* (It's difficult to buy a flat that is ~ in Hong Kong.) N (1) (one's) liking 合心意的 : *hahp/ ngāam* ~ see 0643 (2) mind 頭腦 : ~ *chīng* (clear-headed)

0670

➔sām sīsī 心思思 (lit.) heart keeps on thinking 心不停在想
(idi.) A.PH thinking of (trying to do something) 想做一件事 : *Ngóh gaaijó yīn móuh géi noih, yihgā yauh ~ séung sihkfāan.* (I quit smoking for a short time, but now I am ~ smoking again.)

0671

➔sāmsyūn 心酸 (lit.) heart is/feels sour 心酸
(idi.) V feel very sad (about something tragic) (對慘事) 覺得悲傷 : *Hái gāautūng yingoih jījūng séimòhng ge séijé, kéuihdeih ge gāsuhk haamdou hóu chāilèuhng, tēngdóu ge yàhn dōu (gokdāk) ~/ tēngdou néih sām dōu syūn.* (The kinfolk of those killed in the traffic accident cried grievously, which made us ~.)

0672

➔sāmtáahm 心淡 (lit.) heart is insipid 心裏淡而無味
(idi.) V lose interest (because of failure) 因失敗而失去興趣 : *Kéuih yahpjó yùhlohkhyūn gam dō nihn juhng meih hùhng, kéuih yáuh dī ~ la.* (He has been in showbiz for so many years but he is not yet popular. He is now disappointed and ~.)

0673

➔sāmtàuh gōu 心頭高 (lit.) heart is high 心在高處
(idi.) PH too ambitious, set one's goal too high 心志太高 : *Yihgā dī daaihhohk bātyihpsāng jānhaih ~ ge, yāt bātyihp jauh wah géi nihn jīloih yiu wán géi baak maahn.* (Nowadays, university graduates are ~. They want to earn millions of dollars within a few years.)

0674

➔sāmtàuh hou 心頭好 (lit.) N (most) favourite thing 心裏所喜愛的東西 M dī : ⓐ "*Yéuhng gāmyú hóu màhfàahn ge.*" "*Móuh baahnfaat lā, nīdī haih ngóhge ~.*" ("It's very troublesome to raise gold fish." "No one can blame me. This is my ~ to do.") ⓑ *Chīn gām nàahn máaih ~.* (Although one is willing to spend a lot of money [/one thousand nuggets of gold], one can still hardly buy one's ~.) (* The example sentence is also an idiomatic expression.)

0675

➔sāmyúhn 心軟 (lit.) heart

becomes soft 心變得軟
(idi.) V give in (to somebody's plea) (經不起人家懇求而)動搖 ： ⓐ *Kéuih sēuiyihn ngāi néih, néih dōu m̀hóu gam faai ~.* (Although he pleaded with you for this, you shouldn't ~ so quickly.) ⓑ *Kéuih nīgo yàhn hóu yùhngyih ~ ge.* (She is one who will ~ very easily.)

0676
→sām yūkyūk 心郁郁 (lit.) heart keeps on moving 心不停在動
(idi.) see 0670

0677
→yàhn lóuh sām bātlóuh 人老心不老 (lit.) old in age but young at heart 年紀雖老但心裏覺得年輕
(idi.) PH (derogatory) want to do what a young person would do even in one's old age (貶義)老了還想做年青人做的事 ： *Kéuih jingyāt ~, luhkchātsahp seui yàhn juhng bāau yihnāai.* (He doesn't act his age at all. Although he is in his sixties, he still has a mistress.)

0678
→yàhnsām móuh yim jūk 人心冇厭足 (lit.) PH be never content/ satisfied 人永不感到滿足 ： see 0049

0679
→yàhnsām yuhk jouh 人心肉做 (lit.) human heart is made of flesh 人的心是用肉做的
(idi.) PH not be so hard-hearted 不會那麼狠心 ： *Yíhchihn kéuih sēuiyihn deui ngóh m̀hóu jē,*

daahnhaih yihgā kéuih gam cháam, hàaih, ~, ngóh dōu wúih bōng kéuih gé. (Although he treated me badly before, I would ~ and I will help him instead because he is now in such a bad condition.)

0680
→yáuhsām 有心 (lit.) have heart 有一個心
(idi.) PH thank you (for your regards) 多謝(關心) ： *Néih hóu ma? Hóu, ~.* (How are you? Fine, ~.) Adj.PH be concerned about 關注 ： *Kéuih hóu ~ ga, nihnnihn dōu geidāk ngóhge sāangyaht.* (He is much ~ me and every year he can remember my birthday.) A really want to (do something) 真的想(做) ： *Néih (haih) ~ máaih sīnji hóu mahn gachihn.* (Don't ask about the price unless you ~ buy it.)

0681
→yáuh sām m̀pa chìh, sahpyuht dōu haih baainihn sìh 有心唔怕遲，十月都係拜年時 (lit.) PH one should not be afraid of being late if one really wants to see one's friends; October is still a good time for a new year's greeting 有誠意就不用怕太遲，十月也是拜年的好時候 ： *"Ngóh chēutnín nihn jūng sīnji hóyíh gin néihdeih." "M̀gányiu, ~, ~."* ("I won't be seeing you until in the middle of next year." "Never mind, ~.")

0682
→yīusām yīufai 抆心抆肺 see 0389

100

sāmgōn 心肝 **N heart and liver** 心和肝

0683

➔**dīkhéi sāmgōn** 的起心肝
(lit.) lift up heart and liver 把心與肝拿起來
(idi.) A.PH make up one's mind (and act on it) 下定決心(真的去做)：*Juhng yáuh géigo yuht jauh yiu wuihháau la, juhng m̀faaidī ~ duhksyū?* (You only have a few months for your Hong Kong Certificate of Education Examination. Why do you still not ~ to prepare for it?)

0684

➔**lāaijái lāai sāmgōn, lāai néui lāai nghjohng** 孻仔拉心肝，孻女拉五臟 (lit.) one's youngest son extracts his heart and liver while one's youngest daughter extracts his viscera 幼子牽扯一個人的心與肝,幼女牽扯一個人的五臟
(idi.) PH the youngest son is sometimes favored by his parents but the youngest daughter, all the time 幼子極得父母寵愛,幼女則父母只寵愛她：*"Kéuih gwái gam sek kéuih ge sai néui." "Gánghaih lā ~, ~."* ("He loves his youngest daughter very much." "Sure, ~, ~.")

0685

➔**móuh sāmgōn** 冇心肝 (lit.) no heart or liver 沒有心和肝
(idi.) Adj.PH/ PH absent-minded, memory is bad 沒有記性：*Dímgáai néih gam ~ a, taatáai ge sāangyaht dōu m̀geidāk?* (Why are you so ~? You forget even your wife's birthday.)

0686

➔**sāangjái m̀jī jái sāmgōn** 生仔唔知仔心肝 (lit.) you give birth to a baby but you don't know how its heart and liver are 就算兒子是你生的,你也不知他的心和肝是怎樣的
(idi.) PH even parents can hardly know what their children are thinking 父母很難知道子女的心意：~. *Hòhfong haih kèihtā yàhn.* (~, not to mention someone else.)

0687

➔**sāmgōn bóubui** 心肝寶貝
(lit.) heart and liver are valuables 心和肝是寶貝
(idi.) N one's most precious thing(s) 一個人最寶貴的東西：ⓐ*Nīdī yéh ngóhdeih wah haih laahpsaap, daahnhaih kéuih jauh donghaih ~.* (We say that these are trash, but he regards them as his ~.) ⓑ*kéuihge ~ jái/néui* (his darling son/ daughter)

0688

➔**sāmgōnding** 心肝蒂 (lit.) the base of one's heart and liver 心和肝最重要的部分
(idi.) N most beloved one 最心愛的人 M go：*Kéuih géisahp seui yàhn dāk yāklāp néui, nīgo néui jauh haih kéuihge ~.* (He is now middle-aged. He has only one daughter, who is his ~.)

sān 身 **N/M body; measure meaning 'the whole body'**身體 ; 全身 **M go**

0689

➔**chēutsān** 出身(lit.) put out the body 出身

(idi.) N one's family or education background 一個人的家庭或教育背景：*Kéuih ge ~ hóu dāimèih..* (He is a person of humble birth.) V telling others one's family or education background 顯示一個人的家庭或教育背景： ⓐ *Kéuih ~ mihngmùhn mohngjuhk, ngóh jauh ~ kùhngfú gātihng.* (He comes from an illustrious clan but I, a poor family.) ⓑ *Kéuih ~ mihnghaauh.* (He received his education from a prestigious school/ university.) VO start to make one's own living 開始賺錢自立： *Kéuihdī jáinéui yíhgīng ~ la, kéuih yihgā ngōnlohk la.* (His children ~. Now he has no more financial burden of his family.)

0690
➔chīsān 黐身 (lit.) stick to body 黏著身體
(idi.) Adj. (1) clingy 常依附大人： *Go màhmā wah, "Ngóhgo néui hóu ~ ge."* (The mother said, "My little daughter is very ~.") (2) clinging 形影不離：*Kéuihge néuih pàhngyáuh hóu ~ ge.* (He has a ~ girlfriend.) (3) (said of a job) so busy that one cannot pull oneself away from it even for a short while：*Kéuih hái chàhchāantēng jouh sāungán ge. Nī fahn gūng hóu ~ ge.* (He works as a cashier in a cafeteria. His job is ~.)

0691
➔chīsān chīsai 黐身黐世 (lit.) stick to one's body 黏著身體
(idi.) PH cling to (somebody) 痴纏： ⓐ *Go màhmā góng, "Ngóhge jái sihngyaht ~, hàahnghōi yātjahn dōu*

haam." (The mother said, "My little boy always ~ me. He'll cry even if I go away just for a while.") ⓑ *Kéuihdeih léuhnggo ~.* (The two lovers ~ each other [in public].)

0692
➔chī sān gōuyeuhk 黐身膏藥 (lit.) medical adhesive 黏著身體(患處)的膏藥
(idi.) N a person who always clings to somebody 常痴纏著別人的人： *Ngóhge jái/ néuih pàhngyáuh hóuchíh ~ gám.* (My little son/ girlfriend is like a ~.)

0693✓
➔chòih dō sānjí yeuhk 財多身子弱 (lit.) PH (said of a person) rich but weak in health 有錢可是身體不太好
(idi.) PH (sarcastically) good pay but little work (諷刺的說話)高薪但工作少： *"Ngóhdeih bouhmùhn ge a-táu, sèhngyaht jíhaih gin kéuih tái boují, kīng dihnwá ge jà bo." "Kéuih ~ā ma."* ("Our department head just reads newspapers and talks on the phone all the time." "Don't you know that he has ~/is ~?")

0694 ✓
➔dohksān dehngjouh 度身定做 (lit.) PH tailor-made 由裁縫做衣服
(idi.) PH devise something just for somebody 特別爲某人而設： *Nīgo kehkbún haih dahkbiht waih néih ~ ga.* (The script was solely written for you.)

0695

→fan go sān lohkheui 瞓個身落去 (lit.) make one's body lie down 把身體躺下

(idi.) PH put all one's money and effort into (a certain kind of investment) 把所有金錢精力放在一種投資事業上 : *Kéuih waihjó baahn nībún jaahpji, ~.* (He ~ running this magazine.)

0696

→gwosān 過身(lit.) pass the body 身體過去了

(idi.) VO pass away, die 逝世,死 : *Hóu noih móuh kéuihge sīusīk, yùhnlòih kéuih ~ jó ~ lo.* (I have not heard from him for a long time. It turns out that he has ~.)

0697

→jāusān 週身 (lit.) round the body 環繞身體

(idi.) A all over (one's body) 全身 : ~ *jan/ hàhn/ sāpsaai/ gwāttung/ m̀ōnlohk* (tremble/ feel itchy/ get wet/ have sore bones/ feel uneasy ~)

0698

→jāusān dōu, móuh jēung leih 週身刀,冇張利 (lit.) carry knives all over one's body, but none of them is sharp 全身佩刀,但沒有一張是鋒利的

(idi.) PH Jack of all trades, a person who has different kinds of knowledge but is expert in none 懂很多東西,但沒有專長的 : *Kéuih sīk chaapfā, pāangyahm tùhng waahkwá, daahnhaih ~, ~.* (He knows how to arrange flowers, do cooking and draw pictures. But he is ~.)

0699

→jāusān m̀jeuihchòih 週身唔聚財(lit.) money does not stay on any parts of one's body 錢財不留在身上

(idi.) PH feel uneasy all over 全身感到不安 : ⓐ*Hàahng yauh m̀ haih, chóh yauh m̀haih, ngóh ngáanghaih (gokdāk) ~ gám.* (I ~ all the time. Neither taking a walk nor sitting down could make me feel alright.) ⓑ *Jeukjó nīgihn sāam ngóh ngáanghaih (gokdāk) ~ gám.* (I always feel there must be something wrong after I put on this dress.)

0700

→jāusān m̀jihyìhn 週身唔自然 (lit.) feel unnatural all the body 全身不安

(idi.) PH feel uneasy all over 全身覺得不自然 : see 0699

0701

→kwansān 困身 (lit.) body is confined 身體被困

(idi.) Adj. (said of a job) to have to stay at the workplace for very long time 指工作需要員工長時間留在工作地點 : *Hái jáugā jouh làuhmín haih hóu ~ ge, gēifùh yàuh jiu jouhdou máahn.* (As a waiter in a restaurant, one has to work almost all day [from morning till night].)

0702

→laahn sān laahn sai 爛身爛世 (lit.) broken all over one's body 全身破爛

(idi.) PH put on worn out/shabby clothes 穿破爛／襤褸的衣服 :

Yihgā chìuhlàuh hīng jeukdou ~ gám. (Now it's trendy to ~.)

0703

→ làih pòuhsaat gwo gōng → jih sān nàahn bóu 泥菩薩過江→自身難保 (lit.) clay god crosses a river→ it cannot save even itself (from drowning) 泥菩薩過江→自身難保 (idi.) HIT one cannot protect even oneself, not to mention others 自己也幫不了自己(何況他人) : ⓐ *Kéuih jihgéi dī gūngfo dōu gáaum̀dihm, jing sówaih ~ → ~, néih bātyùh mahn daihyíh go lā.* (He has many problems with his studies. The saying is right that he ~. You'd better ask somebody else for help.) ⓑ *Kéuih cháaulūngjó gúpiu, ~ → ~, néih juhng hóu mahn kéuih jechín?* (He got burned on the stock market. He ~. You should not ask him to lend you money, should you?)

0704

→ lásí séuhng sān 挪屎上身 (lit.) get shit and put it on one's body 拿糞便往身上放 (idi.) PH (1) get oneself into trouble 自找麻煩 : *Ngóh nīgo gaiwaahk yuht jouh yuhtm̀dihm, nīchi jānhaih ~ la.* (My project is getting more and more difficult. I find I have ~.) (2) do something worthless and bad for oneself 做對自己有害無益的事: *Néih bōng kéuih wàahn daaihyíhlūng ge jaai àh? Jānhaih ~!* (You are going to pay the debts to the loan shark for him? You certainly ~!)

0705

→ lātsān 甩身 (lit.) off the body 脫身 (idi.) VO (1) get away from 逃脫,逃避 : *Kéuih góngyéh gāi dēung m̀tyúhn gám, ngóh wah yiu gón sìhgaan sīnji hóyíh ~.* (He kept on talking and showed no sign of stopping. I told him I was in a hurry before I could ~ him.) (2) be freed from 免於 : ⓐ *Búnlòih gūngsī paai ngóh heui, sāumēi ngóh behngjó sīnji hóyíh ~.* (Our company had planned to send me there. Later I was sick, and so I was ~ going.) ⓑ *Kéuih yihgā jái daaih néui daaih, hóyíh ~ lo.* (Now that his children have grown up, he can be ~ the financial obligations to his family.)

0706

→ mòuh jaai yātsān hēng 無債一身輕 (lit.) no debt makes your whole body light 無債一身輕 (idi.) PH feel released when one gets out of debt, feel light-hearted if one is not in debt 付清債或不負債便覺得輕鬆 : ⓐ *Gūngyùhn láu, ~.* (I feel released after I have paid all the installments on my flat.) ⓑ *Ngóh m̀ ūngyi jāang yàhn chín ge, ~ ā ma.* (I don't like to owe anybody money, you see, one would ~.)

0707

→ saatdou màaih sān 殺到埋身 (lit.) killing is near 快被人殺 (idi.) PH will soon be dealt with 快要被人整治: *Jóu páai kéuihdeih ge bouhmùhn chòihyúhn, yihgā dou ngóhdeih la, ~, dímsyun a?* (Some of

104

the staff were laid off in their department not long ago. Now it's our turn. We'll ~. What can we do about it now?)

0708
➔sān 身 (lit.) body 身體
(idi.) M the whole body 全身 : ⓐ *yāt* ~ *hohn* (bathe in sweat) ⓑ *yāt* ~ *sāpsaai* (wet to the skin) ⓒ *yāt* ~ *ngáih* (see 0023) ⓓ *m̀séi yāt* ~ *sàahn* see 0082

0709
➔sān gwōng géng leng 身光頸靚 see 0402

0710
➔sānhàhn 身痕 (lit.) body is itchy 身體發癢
(idi.) V (1) itch for, have a strong desire 渴望 : *Hóu noih móuh heui chāamgā móuhwúi la, yihgā* ~ *séung tiuháh móuh.* (I haven't been to a dance for a long time. Now I ~ a dance.) (2) feel uneasy for being unable to do something one likes 因不能做自己喜歡的事而感不安 : ⓐ*Kéuih yāt m̀dá màhjéuk jauh* ~ *ge la.* (He would feel uneasy when he cannot play mahjong.) ⓑ *Nīgo saimānjái hóu yáih, màhmā wah, "M̀dá néih (néih) jauh* ~ *la."* (The child is very naughty. His mother said, "Won't you feel happy if I don't beat you?") ⓒ*Yáuh chín jauh* ~ . (Once a person gets money, he would think of spending it.)

0711
➔sān joih fūk jūng bāt jī fūk

身在福中不知福 (lit.) PH be unaware that one is living in blessing 身在福中不知福 : *Yáuhdī lohkhauh deihkēui ge saimānjái, móuh syū duhk, yauh yihngyéuhng bāt lèuhng, Hēunggóng ge saimānjái jauh* ~. (The children in some undeveloped regions have no opportunity for education, and they suffer from malnutrition. But the children in Hong Kong are ~.)

0712
➔sān yáuh sí 身有屎 (lit.) body has shit 身上有糞便
(idi.) PH secret and filthy behaviour 不見得光又不光彩的事 : *"Kéuih m̀jūngyi yàhndeih góng fānngoihchìhng ge sih ge bo!" "Gánghaih lā, kéuih* ~." ("He doesn't like people talking about another's extramarital affairs." "Of course, he himself has the same problem.")

0713
➔sìhng/ sèhnggo sān fan (saai) lohkheui 成個身瞓(晒)落去 see 0695

sāttàuh 膝頭 N knee 膝蓋 M go

0714
➔sāttàuh daaihgwo béi 膝頭大過脾 (lit.) knee is bigger than thigh 膝蓋比腿大
(idi.) PH (formerly said of drug addicts) skin and bone 非常瘦(以前說吸毒者) : *Kéuih jānhaih saudāk chāilèuhng la,* ~. (He is awfully thin. He is just ~.)

105

- 0715

➔sāttàuh gíu ngáahnleuih 膝
頭揇眼淚(lit.) dry one's tears with
his knees 用膝蓋抹乾眼淚
(idi.) PH grieve or even shed tears 情
況可悲，會令人流淚 : *Gónghéi
dájeung gójúng chāilèuhng(faat) jauh
~ lo.* (Talking about the miseries of
war would make one ~.)

sáu　手 N hand 手 M jek; deui/
sēung

0716

➔baahksáu hīnggā 白手興家
(lit.) prosper one's family with white/
empty hands 白手興家
(idi.) PH achieve a successful life with
one's own hands 用一雙手創出成功
之路 : *Kéuih chōchō lohklàih
Hēunggóng ge sihhauh, yātgo sīn dōu
móuh, sāumēi kéuih ~, yihgā juhng
haih séhwúi mihngláuh tīm.* (When he
first came to Hong Kong [from
mainland], he had not a penny to his
name. Later, he ~, and now he has
become a celebrity in the
community.)

0717

➔chansáu 趁手(lit.) while you
have a hand 趁有手
(idi.) A (1) might as well do some
manual work 趁機會 : *Wàahngdihm
néih chēutgāai, ìngōi ~ bōng ngóh
dámjó dī laahpsaap ā.* (As you are
going out, would you take out the
garbage for me, please?) (2) avail
oneself of an opportunity 把握機
會 : *"Hóu ~ máaih la wei,
maaihyùhn jauh móuh ge la,"* go

síufáan wah. ("You should buy one
since they are here. You can't buy
any one of them after this." said the
vendor.)

0718

➔chéungsáu 搶手 (lit.) snatch
with hand 用手搶
(idi.) Adj. (said of commodities)
extremely welcome （貨物）很受歡
迎 : *Nīdī yéh hóu ~, yātjàhngāan jauh
maaihsaai la.* (These things are ~ (by
users). They are sold out in a short
while.)

0719

➔chēutsáu 出手(lit.) stretch out
hand 伸出手
(idi.) VO (1) (extend one's hand to)
beat somebody （出手）打人 :
*Kàuhjing gínggou gógo jūkkàuhyùhn
yānwaih kéuih ~ dáyàhn.* (The referee
warned that fooballer against beating
his rival.) (2) offer a price or
remuneration 出價或酬勞 : *Kéuih
haih daaih mihngsīng, néih ~ gam dāi
kéuih gánghaih ìmbōng néih paakhei
lā.* (He is a very popular movie star,
but if you offer him that little money
to star in your movie, he will
certainly say no.) (3) manage
something by oneself 親自做 : *Nīdī
gam síu ge sih, sáimāt daaihlóu néih ~
heui jouh a?* (It's not a big deal. Why
should we bother you, our gang boss,
to do it?)

0720

➔chòih dou gwōnggwan sáu,
yih fong nàahn sāu 財到光棍
手，易放難收 (lit.) PH once the
money goes to the conman's hand, it

is very difficult to get it back 錢財到了騙子手中,就很難取回 : *Jing sówaih ~, ~. Kéuih ngāakjó néihdī chín, néih séung lófāan, géi nàahn lo.* (Just as the saying goes, ~, ~. You want to get back the money he cheated you of? It's not that easy.)

0721

→chōu sáu chōu geuk 粗手粗腳 see 0405

0722

→daahngūng sáu 彈弓手 (lit.) a hand with a spring 裝上彈弓的手
(idi.) N (1) (finger problem) trigger finger (手指的一種病) 彈弓手: *Ngóhge sáujígūng binsihng ~, yiu jouh síu sáuseuht.* (My thumb has become a ~, it needs a small operation.) (2) (said of children) be tricky in playing finger guessing game 小童玩猜拳時出手狡猾: *Néih chēut ~, dong néih syū.* (You are ~. You're supposed to be out.)

0723

→dō sáu 多手 (lit.) many hands 很多手
(idi.) A be too curious and touch 因爲好奇想摸一下 : *Ngóh ~ móháh kéuih jauh laahn la.* (I'm ~ it. After that, it broke.) Adj. be too curious and touch 因爲好奇想摸一下 : *Mhóu gam ~!* (Don't touch!) also see 0407

0724

→dō sáu dō geuk 多手多腳 see 0407

0725

→gaap sáu gaap geuk 夾手夾腳 see 0408

0726

→gáausáu 攪手 (lit.) stirring hand 攪東西的手
(idi.) N a person who takes the initiative 發起行動的人 M go : *Nīchi bahgūng/ yàuhhàhng, bīngo jouh ~ ga?* (Who is the ~ in this (industrial) strike/ demonstration?)

0727

→jēng yàhn chēut háu, bahn yàhn chēut sáu 精人出口,笨人出手 see 0474

0728

→jé sáu jé geuk 姐手姐腳 see 0418

0729

→jí sáu waahk geuk 指手劃腳 see 0419

0730

→jósáu làih, yauhsáu heui 左手嚟,右手去 (lit.) come at the left hand and go at the right 從左手來,又從右手去
(idi.) PH money just comes and goes 錢賺回來很快又花去了 : ⓐ*Ngóh chēutjó lèuhng jauh jēung dī chín gāausaaibéi taaitáai, jing sówaih ~, ~.* (After I get my pay check, I give it to my wife. Just as the saying goes, ~.)
ⓑ *Kéuih wán géidō chín dōu móuh dāk jihng, ~, ~.* (No matter how much money he earns, he never has any money left. His ~.)

0731
→jouh sáu geuk 做手腳 see 0420

0732
→jóyauhsáu 左右手 (lit.) left hand and right hand 左手跟右手
(idi.) N right hand man (of a boss), very helpful assistant 好幫手 : *Kéuih haih ngóhge ~. Ngóh móuh kéuih m̀dāk.* (He is my ~. I can't do without him.)

0733
→kīksáu 棘手 (lit.) hand gets stuck 手給卡住
(idi.) Adj. tough (case), thorny (matters), very difficult to solve 很難解決的事情 : *Gíngfōng gokdāk nīgihn ngon hóu ~, yānwaih sītái béi yàhn jáamjó tàuh tùhng sáují geukjí.* (The police find it a ~ case because the head, fingers and toes of the found body were cut off.)

0734
→lohksáu dá sāamgāang 落手打三更(lit.) put the hand down to beat a drum three times as an indication of the third time period at night 用手打三下更鼓報時
(idi.) PH make mistakes just when starting (to do something) 一開始便做錯 : *Kéuih gāmjīu jīngsàhn fóngfāt, yāt hōigūng jauh ~.* (He is in low spirits this morning, and he ~ to work.)

0735
→m̀ hóu sáu geuk 唔好手腳 see 0424

0736
→móuh sáuméih 冇手尾 (lit.) no hand or tail 沒有手和尾
(idi.) Adj. fail to put the things back after use 用完東西不放回原處 : *Nīgo yàhn hóu ~, dī yéh jáuwàih pehk.* (This is a person who ~. He just puts things anywhere he likes.)

0737
→ ngáau sáugwā 拗手瓜 (lit.) arm-wrestling 用前臂把別人的前臂壓下來
(idi.) VO compete 競爭 : *Nīgo dihnsih tòih tùhng gógo dihnsihtòih ~, néih gú bīngo wúih yèhng ā?* (This TV company ~ with that one. Which one do you think will win?)

0738
→ pàhsáu 扒手 (lit.) stealing hand 扒手
(idi.) N pickpockets 專門偷人錢包的小偷 M go : *Yàhn dō ge deihfōng, yiu síusām dī ~ a.* (You have to beware of ~ in crowded places.)

0739
→sāamjek sáu 三隻手 (lit.) three hands 三隻手
(idi.) N pickpocket 扒手 (* It is not so commonly used as 'pàhsáu' nowadays.) : see 0738

0740
→ sāangsáu 生手(lit.) raw hand 生的手
(idi.) N inexperienced factory worker 沒有經驗的工廠工人 : *Gwónggou wah, "Búnchóng jīuping daaihleuhng gūngyàhn, mòuhleuhn ~ suhksáu dōu*

fūnyìhng." (The advert. says, "We need a great many workers in our factory. Anybody, inexperienced or experienced, is welcome.") Adj. (said of factory workers) green, inexperienced, not skilled 指工廠工人沒有經驗, 不熟練 : *Nīgo gūngyàhn sānlàih ge, sóyíh hóu ~.* (This worker is new here, so he may have problems with his work.)

0741

➔ sái wàahng sáu 使橫手
(lit.) use the horizontal/wrong hand 用橫/錯的手
(idi.) A.PH use dirty or illegal methods 用不正當或不合法的手段 : *Dī jyuhhaak m̀háng būnchēut, go daaih yihpjyú jauh ~ sāuláu, peiyùhwah dihntāi tìhng dihn, jínglaahn séuijai, yauh giu dī hāak séhwúi ge yàhn háidouh chēutyahp.* (The tenants do not want to move out, so the landlord of the whole building ~, such as by causing power cuts of the lift, cutting off the water supply and opening the gate for the triads to come and go.)

0742

➔sānsáu 新手(lit.) new hand 新手
(idi.) N greenhorn, novice of a skill 沒有經驗剛開始一門手藝的人 : *Nīgo bāsí sīgēi haih ~, sóyíh yáuhsìh gwojó jaahm (kéuih) dōu m̀jī.* (He's a new bus driver. Sometimes he doesn't know that he has missed a bus stop but just drives on.)

0743 ✓

➔sáu 手(lit.) N hand 手 M jek; deui/ sēung

(idi.) M (1) measure for 'one transaction' of stocks and shares or foreign currencies 一次股票或外幣買賣的量詞 : *máaih/maaih yāt~gúpiu* (buy/sell ~ of stocks) (2) measure for 'a set of tiles/cards' one has gotten in a game of mahjong/poker 玩麻將或紙牌時所拿到的一套牌 : *Nī~ páai hóu hóu/yeuhk.* (I've gotten an upper/a lower hand.)

0744

➔sáubáan haih yuhk, sáubui dōu haih yuhk 手板係肉, 手背都係肉 (lit.) palm is flesh, the back of the palm is also flesh 手掌是肉,手掌的背也是肉
(idi.) PH be in a dilemma as to which person one should take sides with 左右爲難,不知幫誰好 : *Bàhbā tùhng màhmā ngaaigāau, ~, ~, ngóh dōu m̀jī dím jouh hóu.* (My father was quarreling with my mother. I was ~. I simply didn't know what to do.)

0745

➔sáudō 手多 (lit.) many hands 手很多
(idi.) Adj. see 0723

0746

➔sáu dōdō 手多多 (lit.) very many hands 手非常多
(idi.) PH/A.PH touch anything one likes 亂摸東西 : ⓐ*Daaih yàhn giu saimānjái, "M̀hóu sèhngyaht ~ gám lā."* (Adults tell the kids, "Behave yourselves and don't ~.") ⓑ ~

dálaahn yàhndeih ge yéh (~ and break other's things)

0747
→ sáu dō geuk dō 手多腳多 see 0428

0748
→ sáugán 手緊 (lit.) hands are tight 手很緊張
(idi.) Adj. hard to make ends meet 手頭緊, 週轉不靈 : *Nīpáai hóu ~, yiu mahn pàhngyáuh jechín sái.* (Recently I've found it very ~. I have to ask my friends to lend me some money.)

0749
→ sáugeuk m̀hóu 手腳唔好 see 0429

0750
→ sáugwā héi jín 手爪起腱
(lit.) biceps are bulging 前臂及臂都隆起
(idi.) PH very strong arms 手臂很強壯 : *Kéuih ~, móuh yàhn gám hā kéuih.* (He has ~. No one would try to bully him.)

0751
→ sáuhah 手下 (lit.) below hand 手下面
(idi.) N subordinate, people who work under you 下屬 M go : *Kéuih haih ngóh ~.* (He works under me.)

0752
→ sáuhei 手氣 (lit.) air of hand 手氣
(idi.) N luck in gambling 賭錢的運氣 : *Gāmyaht ~ hóu chā, syū jó hóudō*

chín. (I have no ~ today. I've lost much money.)

0753
→ sáu mòhng geuk lyuhn 手忙腳亂 see 0431

0754
→ sāusáu 收手 (lit.) take back the hand 把手收回
(idi.) VO stop doing 停手不幹 : ⓐ *Jouh māt dá kéuih a? Hóu ~ lo bo!* (Why do you beat him? Stop!) ⓑ *Ngóh yèhngmàaih nīchi chín jauh ~ la.* (I'm now winning some money. I'll stop betting after this.)

0755
→ sáutàuh 手頭 (lit.) hand and head 手跟頭
(idi.) N one's finanical situation at a particular time 一個人在某一個時期的經濟情況 : ⓐ *Nīpáai ~ hóu gán/ hóu sáugán* (see 0748) ⓑ *Yìhgā ~ sūngdī.* (Now it's easier for me to make ends meet.)

0756
→ sáu(tàuh)seuhng 手(頭)上
(lit.) on hand and head 手跟頭上
(idi.) A on hand 手上 : *~ móuh chín, séung máaih gúpiu/ láu dōu m̀ dāk lā.* (I have no money ~. I can't buy stocks and shares/ a flat even though I want to.)

0757
→ sáu tìhng háu tìhng 手停口停 see 0484

110

0758

➔sóngsáu 爽手 (lit.) pleasant hand 爽快的手

(idi.) Adj. (1) quick and smooth 做事很快 : ⓐ *Kéuih jouhyéh hóu ~.* (He is ~ in doing things.) ⓑ *Wai, ~ dī lā!* (Hey, hurry up! [You are a bit slow.]) (2) willing to spend or give money 願意花錢 : ⓐ *máaihyéh hóu ~* (~ in buying things) ⓑ *Mahn kéuih jechín, kéuih dōu hóu ~ ge.* (If you ask him to lend you money, he won't say 'no'.)

0759

➔suhksáu 熟手 (lit.) ripe/cooked/mature hand 熟的手

(idi.) N experienced/skilled factory workers 有經驗,熟練的工廠工人 : *Sāangsáu yàhngūng síudī, ~ jauh dōdī.* (The inexperienced workers earn less money, the ~ earn more.) Adj. (said of factory workers) experienced, skilled 工廠工人很有經驗,很熟練 : *Ngóh hái nīgāan chóng jouhjó géigo yuht dōu juhng meih hóu ~.* (Although I've been working in this factory for a few months, still I can't do my work very well.)

0760

➔syún sáu laahn geuk 損手爛腳 see 0432

0761

➔tok sáujāang 托手睜 (lit.) support the elbow 托著手肘

(idi.) VO refuse to help 拒絕幫忙 : *Daaihgā hóu pàhngyáuh, mhóu ~ lā.* (We are good friends. Please don't ~ me.)

0762

➔yàhn dō sáu geuk lyuhn 人多手腳亂 see 0436

0763

➔yāt sáu yāt geuk 一手一腳 see 0440

0764

➔yáuh(fāan) géiháh sáansáu 有(番)幾吓散手 (lit.) have learned some Chinese gungfu fighting 略懂功夫

(idi.) PH quite skillful in 頗有技巧 : *Kéuih jyúsung/dábō ~ ge bo!* (Oh, he is ~ cooking/playing ball games.)

sáují 手指 N finger 手指 M jek

0765

➔gām sáují 金手指 (lit.) gold finger 金色手指

(idi.) N backbiter 在背後中傷別人的人 : *Bōsí gāmyaht laauh ngóh, wah yiu gong ngóh kāp, yùhnlòih néih haih ~.* (Our boss scolded me today. He said I would be demoted. Now I see that you are the ~.)

0766

➔jáam sáují (gaaidóu) 斬手指(戒賭) (lit.) cut the fingers (and not gamble any more) (爲了戒賭)把手指斬了

(idi.) PH have/show a strong decision to quit the bad habit of gambling 顯示極大決心戒除賭博這種不良嗜好 : *Nītàuh wah ~, gótàuh yauh heui dóu, jānhaih móuhdāk gau.* (He just said that he ~, but then he went gambling again.

There's no way for him [to stop gambling].)

0767

→meih dou luhksahp luhk, m̀hóu siu yàhn sáují kūk 未到 六十六，唔好笑人手指曲 (lit.) if one is not yet sixty-six years old, he should not laugh at someone else who has crooked fingers 還沒到六 十六歲，就不要笑別人有彎曲的手 指 (idi.) PH do not tease others too easily/ soon 不要隨便／太早取笑 別人 : *"Ngóh m̀wúih hohk kéuih gám, ga go kùhnggwái."* *"~, ~. Néih yáuh gēiwuih gitfān sīnji syun lā."* ("I won't marry a poor guy, like her." "~. You can say/do that only when it comes the time that you are going to get married.")

0768

→sahpjek sáují yáuh chèuhng dyún 十隻手指有長短 (lit.) of the ten fingers, some are long and some are short 十個指頭之中，有些 長有些短 (idi.) PH not all roses, not every one is equally good within a group 不是 人人都那麼出色 : *"Kéuih jihgéi hóu lēk, daahnhaih dī jáinéui jauh m̀ haih gam lēk, yáuh yātgo juhng hóu chā tìm."* *"Haih gám ge la, ~ ā ma."* ("He has been doing very well in life, but not all of his children have done as well as he. One of them is doing very badly." "It's always so. Haven't you heard of the saying ~?")

0769

→sáují ngáauchēut 手指拗出

m̀ngáauyahp 手指拗出唔拗入 (lit.) fingers are bent outwards but not inwards 把手指彎出去,不把它 彎入來 (idi.) PH take sides with outsiders, but not one's group members 幫外 人不幫自己人 : *Néih ~, yàhndeih maih hā ngóhdeih lō.* (You ~. That's why people bully us.)

0770

→sáují ngáauyahp m̀ngáauchēut 手指拗入唔拗 出 the opposite of 0769

sí 屎 N shit, faeces, excrement, dung 糞便 M dūk; dī

0771

→dāam sí dōu m̀tāusihk 擔屎 都唔偷食 (lit.) even if a person carries shit (on both ends of the carrying-pole), he won't steal it to eat 挑糞也不會偷來吃 (idi.) PH (a humorous way of saying that a person is) extremely honest (幽 默的說法，一個人)極誠實 : *"Wa! Néih jēung gam dō chín jāihái kéuihdouh àh?"* *"M̀sái gēng, kéuih nīgo yàhn ~, ngóh hóu fongsām."* ("Wow, you left so much money with him." "Don't worry. He's ~. I don't worry about it myself.")

0772

→gáusí laahpsaap 狗屎垃圾 see 0195

0773

→sān síhāang 新屎坑 (lit.) new public toilet 新的公廁

112

(idi.) PH new thing(s) which is of great interest (to people) but will be put aside like trash later 新的東西,得到人們喜愛,但不久會被棄置一旁： ⓐ *"Máaihjó gógihn wuhngeuih béi kéuih jīhauh jauh sèhngyaht yiu wáan." "~ ā ma."* ("After I bought him the toy, he plays with it all the time." "To him, it's a ~.") ⓑ *"Gógāan chīukáp síhchèuhng ngāamngāam hōi ge sihhauh, hóudō yàhn bōngchan, yihgā jauh paak wūyīng." "Dī yàhn ~ lō."* ("Many people went to buy things at that supermarket when it started business here, but now business is bad there." "People like new things just for a short time.")

0774

➔sān síhāang dōu yáuh sāamyaht hēung 新屎坑都有三日香 (lit.) even the new public toilet smells good for (the first) three days 新的公廁也有三天不臭
(idi.) PH particular interest in new thing(s) which will last just for a short time 對新的東西特別喜愛,但不會長久： *"Gógāan poutáu hōijó jēung géigo láihbaai dōu juhng gam hóu sāangyi." "~ lā."* ("That shop opened a few weeks ago, and business has been so good." "People have ~.")

0775 ✓

➔sí 屎 (lit.) N shit, faeces, excrement, dung 糞便 M dūk; dī
(idi.) Adj. poor (in performance, skill or quality) (表現,技術或品質)差劣： ⓐ *"Kéuih tekbō dím a?" "Hóu ~."* ("How is he at playing football?" "Very ~.") ⓑ *"Kéuih sé góbún syū*

dím a?" "~ yéh." ("How's the book he wrote?" "It's trash.") ⓒ *sí kíu* (~ and useless solution) see 0003 ⓓ *yātdaahm sātòhng yātdaahm sí* see 1031

0776

➔sihkbáau faahn dáng sí ō 食飽飯等屎疴 (lit.) eat enough then wait to shit 吃飽了飯就等拉屎
(idi.) PH be tired of being idle and want to do something meaningless 閒得不耐煩想做些無聊事： *Kéuih jihgéi m̀sái jouhyéh gwái gam dākhàahn, jauh yiu ngóhdeih gáau māt gáau maht, néih gú ngóhdeih hóuchíh kéuih gám, ~ mē!* (He doesn't have to do anything and has much free time. But he wants us to do this and that. Does he think that we are ~ just like him?)

0777

➔sihk sí là 食屎啦 (lit.) PH (a term of abuse) go eat shit (罵人語)吃屎吧： *Bōsí wah, "Néih m̀hóu joi chihdou la." Go gūngyàhn wah, "~! Ngóh m̀lōu la."* (The boss said, "Don't be late [for your work] any more." The worker said, "~! I quit.")

0778

➔sihk sí ō faahn 食屎疴飯 (lit.) eat shit but pass out rice 吃屎卻拉飯
(idi.) PH be ungrateful (which is contrary to human nature from the viewpoint of Chinese) 忘恩負義(中國人認爲不合人性)： *Kéuih deui néih gam hóu, yauh gaausīk néih gam dō yéh, néih m̀jíwah móuh dōjehgwo*

kéuih, juhng gaapmàaih kèihtā yàhn hā kéuih, néih jānhaih ~. (He was so nice to you and had taught you so many things. However, you not only did not thank him, but also ganged up with other people and bully him. You are really very ~ to him.)

0779

→sihk sí sihkjeuhk dáu 食屎食著豆 (lit.) eat shit which turns out to be beans 吃屎原來是豆

(idi.) PH misfortune turns into good fortune, a blessing in disguise 因禍得福 : *Kéuih námjyuh laauhyùhn go lóuhsai ïnngāam jïhauh jauh jáuyàhn ge la, dímjï go lóuhsai gokdāk kéuih hóu yáuh douhléih, juhng sïngjó kéuih kāp tīm. Kéuih nïchi jānhaih ~ lo.* (He planned to quit his job after having criticized his boss to his face. However, his boss thought that he was right and promoted him. For him, ~ this time.)

0780

→Sōujāu sí 蘇州屎 (lit.) shit at Sōujāu 蘇州的屎

(idi.) N troubles left unsolved 留下的未解決的麻煩 M dī/ dēui : *Kéuih chihjó jīk, daahnhaih kéuih yáuh hóudō yéh meih gáaudihm, làuhdāi dī ~ béi ngóh jauh jáujó la.* (He quit his job. However, there are many things that were not finished by him. He left behind him troubles for me to settle and quit.)

tàuh 頭 N head 頭 M go

0781

→béi go tàuh néih dong dang

chóh 俾個頭你當櫈坐 (lit.) you can have my head and sit on it like a stool 我把頭給你,你可以當是櫈子坐上去

(idi.) PH (like a swear word saying that something is) impossible (像咒語以表示某事)不可能發生 : *Kéuih wúih faatdaaht ?! Ngóh ~ a!* (He will make a fortune?! That's ~!)

0782

→chēuttàuh 出頭 (lit.) put out one's head 露出頭

(idi.) A see 0518 V (short form of 'chēut yàhn tàuh deih') become famous and successful in life (是 '出人頭地' 的簡短說法) 有名氣及成功

: *Hōigóng dōu yáuh wah, "Gūng jih bāt ~." Dágūng dím wúih faatdaaht ā!* (As the saying goes, "The Chinese character for 'gūng'[工] symbolizes that there is no breakthrough in one's life as an employee." How could it be possible for the salaried class to make a fortune?)

0783

→dāptàuh dāplóuh 耷頭耷腦
see 0498

0784✓

→gwōngtàuh 光頭 (lit.) PH/ VO bald head 禿頭

(idi.) V just pass (the Hong Kong Certificate of Education Examination/ HKCEE with no distinctions or credits) (在香港中學會考中)僅僅合格(沒有任何優或良的成績) : *"Wuihháau sihngjīk dím a?" "~ lō."* ("What are your results in the HKCEE?" "~.") also see 0506

114

0785

→hám tàuh/ táu màaih chèuhng
撼頭埋牆 (lit.) hit one's head
against the wall 把頭撞向牆
(idi.) PH punish oneself (to show
deep remorse) 感到很懊悔而懲罰自
己的方法： ⓐ *Gāmyùhng fūngbouh*
jīhauh, sēuiyìhn wah sihtsaai dī chín,
daahnhaih m̀tūng ngóh yiu ~ mè!
(After the economic turmoil, I lost
all my money in business. Do you
mean that I have to ~ by ~?) ⓑ *Ngóh*
mìhngjī gójek máh wúih yèhng ge,
daahnhaih móuh máaih, gitgwó baau
daaih láahng, ngóh yihdāk ~. (I knew
very well that the horse would
win, but I didn't bet on it. Later it
won as the dark horse. I'd rather ~
by ~.)

0786

→hímgwo taitàuh 險過剃頭
(lit.) more dangerous than shaving
the head 比剃頭更危險
(idi.) PH barely avoid failure or
escape danger 險象環生, 僥倖逃
過： *Háausi luhksahp fān hahpgaak,*
ngóh háaudóu luhksahp dím lìhng yāt
fān, jānhaih ~. (The passing grade of
the exam is 60, and I got 60.01. I
almost failed.)

0787

→hóu tàuh hóu méih 好頭好
尾 see 0505

0788

→láam tàuh láam géng/ gai 攬
頭攬頸/髻 see 0396

0789

→màih tàuh màih lóuh 迷頭迷
腦 see 0500

0790

→móuh gam daaih ge tàuh jauh
m̀hóu daai gam daaih ge/ déng
móu 冇咁大嘅頭就唔好戴咁
大嘅／頂帽(lit.) don't wear such a
big hat if you do not have such a big
head 沒有那麼大的頭就不要戴那
麼大的帽子
(idi.) PH don't live beyond your
means 不要生活與收入不相稱： ~,
néih sāuyahp gam síu, jauh m̀hóu nám
máaih láu máaih chē la. (~. You have
such a low income, you shouldn't
think of buying a flat or a car.)

0791

→móuh gam daaih ge tàuh
m̀daaidāk gam daaih ge/ déng
móu 冇咁大嘅頭唔戴得咁大
嘅／頂帽 (lit.) if your head is not
that big, you can't wear such a big hat
沒有那麼大的頭就不可以戴那麼大
的帽子
(idi.) PH one's livelihood is
commensurate with one's income 生
活與收入相稱： "*Kéuih yauh yáuh*
láu yauh yáuh chē, yauh yáuh gūngyàhn,
jānhaih sāileih la." "~, *kéuih haih*
ngàhnhòhng júng gīngléih, gánghaih dāk
lā." ("He has a flat, a car, and has hired
a maid servant. Terrific!" "~. He is
the general manager of a bank. He
certainly can afford it.")

0792

→mòuhlèih tàuh 無厘頭 (lit.)
no head 沒有頭

(idi.) ATT unreasonably humourous 不合情理的／無端的幽默 ： ~ *dihnyíng/ deuibaahk* (~ movie/ dialogue) (* 'Mòuhlèih tàuh' is a different brand of humour developed in Hong Kong movies in the 90s.)

0793

➔pāi go tàuh béi néih dong dang chóh 批個頭俾你當櫈坐
(lit.) I'll cut my head off and let you sit on it like a stool 把頭砍下讓你當櫈子坐
(idi.) PH a more emphatic way of saying than 0781

0794

➔sāam tàuh luhk bei 三頭六臂(lit.) three heads and six arms 三頭六臂
(idi.) PH very capable person, wear different hats 非常能幹的人 ： *Jouh bouhmùhn a-táu yiu yáuh ~ sīnji dāk, yauh yiu jāngchéui jīyùhn, yauh yiu gúnléih jīkyùhn, yauh yiu heui lyùhnlok kèihtā bouhmùhn.* (The department head has to be a ~. He needs to fight for resources, oversee his staff and be a liaison between departments.)

0795

➔sahpgo gwōngtàuh gáugo fu 十個光頭九個富 (lit.) PH of the bald, nine out of ten are rich 十個禿頭的人有九個是有錢的 ： *"Néih sáimāt pa gwōngtàuh jē, ~ ā ma!" "Hósīk ngóh haih daih sahpgo lē."* ("You don't have to worry about going bald. Don't you know that ~?" "It's a pity that I'm the tenth one.")

0796

➔sáisāp go tàuh 洗濕個頭
(lit.) wash the hair and it has become wet now 洗頭時把頭髮弄濕
(idi.) PH have started doing something which is unredeemable 一開始做一件事便沒法回頭 ： ⓐ*Nīgihn sih néih yiu séung chīngchó sīnji hóu jouh a. Yùhgwó m̀haih, ~ jauh hóu nàahn gáau ge la.* (You have to think clearly before doing this. It will be difficult to work it out once you ~.) ⓑ *Ngóh gúm̀dou nīgihn sih wúih gam màhfàahn ge, yihgā ~, wàihyáuh ngàaihlohkheui hái lā.* (I didn't expect that it would be that troublesome. Since I ~, I have to go through with it. That's all I can do.)

0797✓

➔tàuh 頭 (lit.)N head 頭 M go
(idi.) N (when changed into high rising tone, 'táu') head of 主管 ： *Néihdeih ge bouhmùhn, bīngo jouh a ~ a?* (Who is the ~ your department?) BF (1) enemy 敵人 ： *(séi) deui ~* ([sworn] ~) also see 0269 (2) (when changed into a high rising tone, '-táu') the head person 居主導地位的人 ： ⓐ *sih* ~ (boss, employer) ⓑ *chaahk* ~ (leader of the thieves) ⓒ*pun* ~ (subcontractor of construction work) PH as in 'Adj./V néih go tàuh' which means 'Shit! Absolutely not.', Adj./V 個屁 ： ⓐ *"Hóu pèhng wo." "Pèhng ~!"*("It's cheap." "~!") ⓑ *"Gābāan yáuh móuh chín béi ga? "Béi ~!"* ("Shall we have extra pay for working overtime?" "~!") (* Literally, 'néih go tàuh' means 'your head'.)

0798

➔tàuhhokdéng chēutyīn 頭殼頂出煙 (lit.) smoke comes out of one's scalp 頭上冒煙
(idi.) PH be in a state of great fury 氣得七竅生煙 : *nāudou* ~ (~)

0799

➔tàuhméih 頭尾 see 0510

0800

➔tàuhtàuh méihméih 頭頭尾尾 see 0511

0801 ✓

➔tàuhtung 頭痛(lit.) V/ N have a headache/ headache 頭痛
(idi.) Adj. headache causing : ⓐ*Hái Hēunggóng, jyuhngūk haih jeui ~ ge mahntàih.* (In Hong Kong, to find a house to live in is the most ~ problem.) ⓑ*Nīgihn sih gáaudou ngóh tàuh dōu tungmàaih.* (It gives me a headache.)

0802

➔tàuhtung yī tàuh, geuktung yī geuk 頭痛醫頭，腳痛醫腳 see 0433

0803

➔wahtàuh síng méih 話頭醒尾 see 0512

0804

➔yāttàuh mouhséui 一頭霧水
(lit.) fog and mist all over one's head 滿頭是霧跟水
(idi.) PH get lost (in understanding something) 摸不著頭腦 : *Néih góngdou ngóh ~.* (I ~ in what you say.)

0805

➔yāt tàuh yāt méih 一頭一尾 see 0513

0806

➔yàuh tàuh dou méih 由頭到尾 see 0514

0807

➔yáuh tàuh yáuh mihn/ mín 有頭有面 see 0542

tàuhfaat 頭髮 N hair 頭髮 M tiuh; dī

0808

➔yáuh tàuhfaat bīngo séung jouh laatlēi ā 有頭髮邊個想做鬠鬠吖(lit.) no one would like to have favus if he has hair 有頭髮的人,誰想生頭皮癬呢
(idi.) PH can do nothing but 被環境所迫才這樣做 : *"Kéuih gāan poutáu hóu jaahnchín ge bo, dímgáai yiu maaihjó kéuih a?" "Hàaih, ~! Kéuih yiu maaih poutáu wàahn dóujaai ā ma."* ("He made much money from his shop. Why did he want to sell it?" "He ~ sell it. He needs money to pay his gambling debts.") (* Favus is a kind of skin disease on a person's scalp, which will make his hair fall out.)

tóuh 肚 N belly, abdomen, tummy 肚子 M go

0809

➔baautóuh 爆肚 (lit.) explode the abdomen 爆開肚子
(idi.) VO (said of opera actors) ad

117

lib, improvise, make up new lines of dialogue or new words of songs in a play (in not strictly following or when forgetting the script) (戲曲演員)表演時不依足或忘記劇本,即時創作出新對白或唱詞 : *Dī yàhn wah yínyùhn ~ haih yānwaih móuh duhksuhk kehkbún, kèihsaht ~ ge nàahndouh juhng gōu.* (People say that actors ~ because they did not study the script well. In fact, ~ requires much more skill because it is more difficult to ad lib than to just follow the script.) (* 'Baautóuh' can be viewed as a kind of creative process in drama and was originally adopted by Cantonese opera actors on stage.)

0810
→báautóuh 飽肚 (lit.) full up stomach 吃飽了的肚子
(idi.) A (when taking medicine) after meal 飯後(吃藥) : *Nī dī yeuhk yiu ~ sihk, yùhgwó m̀haih wúih lá waih.* (you should take this medicine ~, otherwise it will hurt your stomach.)

0811
→bējáu tóuh 啤酒肚 (lit.) beer belly 肚子滿是啤酒
(idi.) N beer gut, pot-belly, a man who has a belly like a barrel for beer 大肚子的男人,身型像載啤酒的桶 M go : *Séuhngjó nihngéi ge nàahmyán, hóudō dōu yáuh go ~.* (Many older men have a ~.)

0812
→daaihtóuh 大肚 (lit.) big tummy 大的肚子
(idi.) VO be pregnant (when the abdomen gets big) 懷孕 (腹部凸出來) : *Kéuih ~ jīhauh jauh m̀jouhyéh la.* (When she was ~, she quit her job.) ATT (1) pregnant 懷孕 : ~ *pó* (~ woman) (2) of/ for pregnant woman 孕婦的 : ~ *sāam* (clothes for a ~)

0813
→díngtóuh 頂肚 (lit.) support the tummy/ stomach 把肚子頂住
(idi.) VO (1) satisfy hunger 解餓 : *Ngóh yìhgā hóu tóuhngoh, yiu sihk dī yéh ~ sīn.* (I'm very hungry now. I need [to eat] something to ~.) (2) (said of food) can satisfy hunger for a longer time (食物)吃了可以使人比較長時間不會感到飢餓 : *Sāléut dím hóyíh ~ a? Sihk faahn sīnji hóyíh ~ gā ma.* (How can salad ~? Only [eating] rice can.)

0814
→go tóuh dá gú 個肚打鼓 (lit.) (it's like) beating a drum in the belly 肚子裏打鼓
(idi.) PH very hungry 肚子很餓 : *Ngóh yìhgā (ngohdou) ~.* (I am ~ now.)

0815
→hīn chèuhng gwa tóuh 牽腸掛肚 see 0378

0816
→hūngtóuh 空肚 (lit.) empty stomach 空的肚子
(idi.) A (when taking medicine) before meal, fast 飯前(吃藥) : *Nī dī yeuhk ~ sihk yáuhhaauhdī.* (This medicine will be more effective if you take it ~.)

118

0817

➔jihk chèuhng jihk tóuh 直腸直肚 see 0379

0818

➔lágōu tóuhpèih 挪高肚皮
(lit.) pull up (the clothes to show) the belly 把衣服扯高露出肚皮
(idi.) PH (unnecessarily) reveal something that is private 不必要地揭露自己的私人情況 : *Ngūkkéi ge gīngjài chihngyìhng m̀hóu góngbéi yàhn jī a, m̀sái ~ béi yàhn tái ge.* (Don't tell others about the finanical situation of our family. You don't need to ~ to others.)

0819

➔ngáahn fut tóuh jaak 眼闊肚窄 see 0580

0820✓

➔tóuh 肚 (lit.) N belly, abdomen, tummy 肚子 M go
(idi.) M be filled with/ a belly of 一肚子: ⓐ *yāt ~ hei* (see 0821) ⓑ *yāt ~ fó* (~ anger)

0821

➔yāttóuh hei 一肚氣 (lit.) a belly of rage 一肚子氣
(idi.) PH anger (without vent) 心裏很生氣 : *Kéuih jouhyéh jouhdou ~, m̀jī dím faatsit.* (He doesn't know how to give vent to the ~ he gets from his job.)

waih 胃 N stomach (as the digestive organ) 胃 M go

0822

➔hōiwaih la néih 開胃喇你

(lit.) you really have a good appetite 你胃口很好
(idi.) PH be greedy about one's benefits 奢望 : ⓐ *Gam pèhng ge jáujihk yáuh yùhchi silk, ~!* (You expect to have shark's fins soup on so cheap a menu. You are just imagining.) ⓑ *Hùhngsīk bouhyúh gínggou jauh m̀sái fāangūng, néih ~!* (You expect to have a day off when a red rainstorm warning is in force. You must be dreaming.)

yíhjái 耳仔 N ear 耳朵 M jek; deui/ sēung

0823

➔boktàuh gōugwo yíh 膊頭高過耳 see 0373

0824

➔daaih yíhlūng 大耳窿 (lit.) big ear hole 大的耳腔
(idi.) N loan shark 放高利貸的人 M go : *Je ~ (ge) chín jīkhaih séi louh yāttiuh.* (If you borrow money from a ~, you are going to be marked for death.)

0825

➔gaak chèuhng yáuh yíh 隔牆有耳(lit.) walls have ears 隔牆有耳
(idi.) PH someone can (over)hear outside (of the room) (房間)外邊的人會(偷)聽到 : *Néih laauh lóuhbáan m̀hóu gam daaihsēng lā, yānjyuh ~ a.* (Don't speak so loudly when criticizing your boss. Keep in mind that ~.)

119

0826

→jejó lùhngyíh Chán jek yíh 借咗聾耳陳隻耳 (lit.) borrow the ear of the deaf-mute Chan 借了聾子阿陳的耳朵

(idi.) PH (1) not listen 沒聽到：*Ngóhdeih góng gam noih, néih dōu m̀jī ngóhdeih góng māt àh? Néih haih m̀haih ~ a?* (We have been talking for so long and you still don't know what we are talking about. Are you ~ing?) (2) turn a deaf ear to, give no heed to 聽了卻置之不理：*Ngóh laauh kéuih kéuih jauh ~.* (He ~ me when I blame him.)

0827

→jóyíh yahp, yauhyíh chēut 左耳入，右耳出 (lit.) go in the left ear and out the right one 從左邊的耳朵入,卻從右邊的耳朵出來

(idi.) PH forgetful, go in one ear and out the other 沒有記性：*Néih nītàuh góng, kéuih góttàuh m̀geidāk, ~, ~.* (He always forgets what you have just said. He is ~.)

0828

→móuh yíhsing 冇耳性 (lit.) have not the nature/function of the ear 沒有耳的性質/功能

(idi.) Adj. memory is bad, forgetful 記性不好：*Kéuih nīgo yàhn hóu ~, néih yiu góng dō géi chi kéuih sīnji geidāk.* (His ~. You have to tell him a few more times before he can remember.)

0829

→ngáauh yíhjái 咬耳仔 (lit.) bite ear 咬耳朵

(idi.) VO whisper 耳語：*Kéuihdeih léuhnggo háidouh ~, saisēng góng, daaihsēng siu.* (The two of them ~ to each other. They talked in a low voice, but laughed loudly.)

0830✓

→yíh 耳 (lit.)N ear 耳 M jek;deui/ sēung

(idi.) BF handle of a cup 杯的把手 M jek/ go：*Būi ~ laahnjó.* (The ~ is broken.)

0831

→yíhbīn fūng 耳邊風 (lit.) wind (blowing) beside the ears 耳朵旁邊的風

(idi.) N no heed 聽了但置之不理：*Kéuih dong ngóh ge syutwah haih ~.* (He gave ~ to my words.)

0832

→yíhjái yúhn 耳仔軟 (lit.) ear is soft 耳朵軟

(idi.) PH/ Adj.PH easily believe what others say especially slanders 容易聽信別人說話，尤其是讒言：*Ngóhdeih bōsí hóu ~ ga. Sóyíh ngóhdeih yiu tokjyuh kéuih hahbihn gógo jyúyahm.* (Our boss would very ~. So we have to flatter the section head who works under him.)

0833

→yíhjyū 耳珠(lit.) ear pearl 耳朵像珠

(idi.) N earlobe 耳垂 M go：*Táiseung sīfú wah ~ daaih yauh háuh ge yàhn chòihwahn wúih hóu hóu.* (A Chinese physiognomy master would tell you that a person with large and thick ~ would be very lucky in making money.)

yīu 腰 N waist 腰 M tìuh

0834
→móuh yīugwāt 冇腰骨 (lit.) have no backbone 沒有脊骨
(idi.) Adj. PH (of people) spineless, cowardly and unreliable 沒有骨氣, 懦弱及不可靠 : *Kéuih nīgo yàhn jānhaih hóu ~. Búnlòih ngóhdeih gónghóu heung lóuhbáan tàihchēut yigin, daahnhaih kéuih yāt gindóu lóuhbáan m̀haih géi gōuhing jauh m̀gám chēutsēng.* (He is a ~ person. We agreed to express our opinions to our boss. But when he saw that the boss was a little not pleased, he kept his mouth shut.)

0835
→tāantāan yīu 攤攤腰 (lit.) lying down waist 躺下的腰
(idi.) PH (1) be dead tired 累得要死 : ⓐ*guihdou* ~ (~) ⓑ*jouhdou* ~ (do hard work until ~) (2) to a very great extent 很厲害 : *sihtdou* ~ (suffer huge losses in business/ investments)

0836
→yīu yùhn bui háuh 腰圓背厚 (lit.) waist is round and back is thick 腰圓背厚
(idi.) PH plump figure 身材飽滿 : *Kéuih ~, hóu yáuh fūkhei.* (S/he has a ~. S/he certainly will have a life of bliss.)

yuhk 肉 N flest 肉，肌肉 M gauh; faai; dī

0837
→beihgōlūng móuh yuhk 鼻哥窿冇肉 see 0368

0838
→chit yuhk bātlèih pèih 切肉不離皮 see 0627

0839
→gwātyuhk 骨肉 see 0446

0840
→heiyúk 戲肉 (lit.) flesh of a play 一齣戲的肉
(idi.) N climax of a play or movie 戲劇電影的高潮 M chèuhng : *Góchēut hei ge gwónggou seuhngbihn wah "Chèuhngchèuhng ~", daahnhaih ngóh jauh gokdāk muhndou chāugān.* (The movie's advert. says, "Every episode has a ~." However, I felt extremely bored [when seeing the movie].")

0841
→jām m̀gātdou yuhk m̀jī tung 針唔拮到肉唔知痛 (lit.) one will feel no pain until he is pricked by a needle 人不被針刺到就不會覺得疼痛
(idi.) PH one just feels alright until one suffers misfortune 不好的事若不發生在你身上, 你就不會覺得痛苦 : ~, *gūngmouhyùhn m̀sái chòihyùhn, gánghaih m̀jīdou sīyàhn gūngsī chòihyùhn ge cháamfaat lā.* (~. The civil servants are rarely laid off. They certainly don't understand the misery the staff of private corporations will suffer when being laid off.)

121

0842
➔pèih gwōng yuhk waaht 皮光肉滑 see 0631

0843
➔sáubáan haih yuhk, sáubui dōu haih yuhk 手板係肉，手背都係肉 see 0744

0844
➔yàhnsām yuhk jouh 人心肉做 see 0679

0845✓
➔yuhk 肉 (lit.) N flesh 肉 M gauh;faai;dī
(idi.) N pulp, flesh of fruits 水果的肉 M dī : Mhóu jihnghaih sihk ~, yiu lihn pèih sihk sīnji yáuhyīk. (Don't just eat the ~. It will do you good if you eat the peel too.) BF (when changed into a high rising tone, '-yúk') the inner part (inside a cover) 裏面(被外層包著)的部分 :
ⓐ seun~ (letter inside an envelop) ⓑ bīu~ (~ of a watch) ⓒ fógēi ~ (~ of a cigarette lighter)

0846
➔yuhkchek 肉刺 (lit.) flesh is painful 肌肉刺痛
(idi.) Adj. painfully upset (for having bought something that is too expensive) 買了太貴的東西之後覺得心疼 : Kéuih nīgo yàhn hóu gūhòhn ge, máaih gam gwai ge yéh kéuih hóu ~/ yuhk dōu chekmàaih. (He is a stingy person. He felt ~ after he bought such expensive things.)

0847
➔yuhkgán 肉緊 (lit.) flesh is tight 肌肉緊張
(idi.) Adj. excited 緊張興奮 : Dī máh jauhlàih chūnggwo jūngdím ge sihhauh, dī máhmàih dōu hóu ~ gám daaihsēng ngaai, "Faaidī lā, faaidī lā!" (When the horses are running to the winning-post, the punters cry out loudly, "Quick, quick!") V worry (because one cannot do the things he wants others to do) 不能做自己想別人做的東西而緊張 : Jáinéui mkàhnlihk duhksyū fuhmóuh dōu msái gam ~ ge. (Even though the children don't study hard, their parents need not ~ so much.)

0848
➔yuhk joih jāmbáan seuhng 肉在砧板上(lit.) meat is right on the chopping block 肉在砧板上
(idi.) PH at the mercy of 任人宰割／擺佈 : Go deihcháan daaihwòhng ge jái béi yàhn bóngga. Yìhgā ~, kéuih jíyáuh tēng dī féitòuh wah béi suhkgām. (The son of the property tycoon was kidnapped. Now he is ~ the gang. All what his father can do is pay the ransom that the gang has demanded.)

0849
➔yuhkmàh 肉麻 (lit.) flesh is numb (肌)肉麻(痺)
(idi.) Adj. feel disgusted (when seeing/hearing something that is unnatural or awful) 肉麻,看到或聽到不自然或兀突的事而感到討厭 : ⓐ Hái Hēungggóng, yùhgwó paaktō ge yàhn hái yàhn mihnchìhn yauh láam yauh sek, kèihtā yàhn jauh wúih gokdāk

hóu ~. (In Hong Kong, if lovers hug and kiss each other in public, others would ~.) ⓑ *Kéuih sébéi néuih pàhngyáuh ge chihng seun gwái gam* ~. (The love letters he wrote to his girlfriend made us ~.)

0850
➔yuhksyūn 肉酸 (lit.) flesh is sour 肌肉酸了
(idi.) Adj. (1) ugly 難看 : *go yéung hóu* ~ ([said of a person] looks ~) (2) awful 兀突 : ⓐ*dī jih (sédāk) gam* ~ (handwriting is bad) ⓑ *Fūk wá (waahkdāk) hóu* ~ . (The picture looks ~.)

0851
➔yuhktung 肉痛 (lit.) flesh is painful 肌肉疼痛
(idi.) Adj. see 0846

123

3. Colors

baahksīk 白色 N white 白色

0852 ✓

→baahk 白 (lit.)Adj. white 白 (idi.) BF (1) in vain, unrewarding 徒勞無功,白費 : ⓐKéuih chéng nīchāan ngóhdeih m̀haih ~ sihk ga. Ngóhdeih yiu bōngfāan kéuih jouhyéh ga. (The meal he treated us to is not a free one. We have to do him a favour in return.) ⓑ "Kéuih būnjó la, daahnhaih sāumēi léuhnggo yuht móuh gāaujōu, béi kéuih ~ jyuh," go yihpjyú wah. ("Now he has moved, but for the last two months, he lived here without paying any rent," said the landlord.) ⓒJáulàuh fātyìhngāan jāplāp, lóuhbáan jáujó lóu. Nīgo yuht móuh lèuhng chēut, ~ jouh. (The restaurant was suddenly closed down and our boss has run away. We won't get any pay for this month.)ⓓ Néih yingjīng gógāan gūngsī giu néih dáng kéuihdeih ge dihnwá, ngóh gú néih dōu haih ~ dáng ge jē. Néih bātyùh sānchínggwo daihyih fahn gūn bá lā. (The company you went for an interview told you to just wait for their call. I think you'll just wait ~. You'd better apply for another job.) (2) (in cooking) without using any seasonings 沒有加任何調味品 的 : ⓐ~ chit gāi (boiled chicken which is chopped to pieces when being served) (* Usually, people eat it with finely chopped ginger and salt.) ⓑ~ saahp dáan (boiled egg) ⓒ ~ cheuk hā see 0067 (3) (cook)

without any meat 沒有肉一起煮 的 : ⓐ ~ saahp tōng (vegetable soup ~) ⓑ ~ jūk (congee/ rice gruel ~) (4) only : ~ faahn (rice ~)(* People say it when they order rice in restaurants.) V become white 白了: tàuhfaat ~ jó (hair has ~)

0853

→baahkbaahk 白白 (lit.) double white 很白 (idi.) A in vain, unrewarding 徒勞無 功,白費 : ⓐNgóhdeih yeukjó kéuih yámchàh, daahnhaih kéuih móuh làih, ngóhdeih hái chàhlàuh ~ dángjó kéuih géigo jūngtàuh. (We had agreed to have tea with him, but he didn't come. We waited for him for hours in the teahouse ~.) ⓑ Jóu jī néih wúih bōng kéuih ge, ngóh jauh m̀sái ~ sāai gam dō sihgaan jīngsàhn yauh làih bōng kéuih lā. (If I knew beforehand that you were going to help him, I wouldn't have wasted my time and energy on him.)

0854

→baahkjehng 白淨 (lit.) white and clean 潔白乾淨 (idi.) Adj. fair (complexion) 皮膚白 皙 : ⓐKéuih sāangdāk hóu ~. (She has ~ complexion.)ⓑKéuih dī pèihfū ~ jó. (She now has ~ skin.)

0855

→baahk jí hāak jih 白紙黑字 (lit.) white paper and black written words 白紙黑字

(idi.) PH in black and white, in writing or in print 正式的寫下來 : *Háugóng m̀syunsou, yiu ~ sélohklàih sīnji dāk.* (A verbal promise/ agreement cannot guarantee anything. We want it ~.)

0856
→baahk mūngmūng 白濛濛 (lit.) white and blurred 又白又朦朧
(idi.) PH all white 白濛濛 : ⓐ *tàuh faat ~* (~ hair) ⓑ *Kàhmmáahn sèhngmáahn lohksyut, yihgā ngoihbihn ~.* (It snowed all night last night. Now it's ~ outside.)

0857
→baahk sàaihsàaih 白晒晒 (lit.) PH just white 只是一片白色 : *Yáuh héihing sih jauh m̀hóu jeuk ~ ge sāam lā.* (Don't put on ~ clothes for a happy occasion.)

0858
→chīngbaahk 清白 (lit.) clear and white 清白
(idi.) Adj. innocent, not guilty 無罪 : *Gógo yìhfáan wah, "ngóh móuh saatyàhn, ngóh haih ~ ge."* (The suspect said, "I didn't kill anybody. I'm ~.")

0859
→fèihfèih baahkbaahk 肥肥 白白 (lit.) PH chubby and white 胖胖白白 : *Kéuih sāangjó yātgo ~ ge bìhbī, hóu dākyi.* (She gave birth to a ~ baby. It's very lovely.)

0860 ✓
→ gāau baahkgyún 交白卷 (lit.) VO hand in a blank answer sheet 交白卷
(idi.) VO unrewarding, fail to accomplish a mission 無功而還 : ⓐ *Yātgo máhpihngyàhn wah, "Nīgo kèhsī gāmyaht ~."* (A horse-race commentator said, "This jockey didn't win any races today.") ⓑ *Hohkhaauh paai kéuihdeih heui chāamgā béichoi, daahnhaih kéuihdeih ~ fāanlàih.* (Our school sent them to take part in the contest, but they came back empty-handed.)

0861
→láaihbaahksīk 奶白色 (lit.) milky white 像奶的顏色
(idi.) N cream-colored, beige 乳白色 : *~ ge gāsī* (~ furniture)

0862
→máih(baahk)sīk 米 (白) 色 (lit.) the white colour of rice 像米的白色
(idi.) N beige 米(白/黃)色 : *buhng chèuhng yàuh ~* (paint the wall ~)

0863
→sái baahkbaahk 洗 白 白 (lit.) wash the white 洗白色
(idi.) PH (said of babies or very young children) take a bath (小兒語) 洗澡 : *Bìhbī, màhmā tùhng néih ~.* (My darling baby, mother is going to give you a bath.)

0864
→syutbaahk 雪 白 (lit.) Adj.

snowy (white)雪白：~ *ge mòuhgān*
(~ towel)

0865

➔(hóuchíh) syut gam baahk
（好似）雪咁白 (lit.) PH as
white as snow 像雪那樣白：*Gihn
baahk sēutsāam hóuchíh ~.* (The
white shirt is ~.)

0866

➔táibaahk 睇白 (lit.) see white
看見白色
(idi.) A it is obvious 眼看：*Gógo
jūkkàuh pìhngseuhtyùhn wah, "~
sehyahp ge la, dímjī go bō johng
chyúh."* (The football match
commentator said, "~ that he will
score a goal, but he fails because the
ball just hits the goal post.")

**chàhsīk 茶色 N tea color,
(transparent) brown 茶色，
（透明）棕色**

0867

➔chàhsīk bōlēi 茶色玻璃
(lit.) N brown glass 棕色玻璃：~
chēung/ mùhn (~ window-pane/
door)

**chēngsīk 青色 N light green
青綠色**

0868

➔bīuchēng 標青 (lit.) raise the
green 高舉青色
(idi.) Adj. outstanding 出眾：
sihngjīk hóu ~ (performance is ~)

0869

➔chēngbaahk 青白 (lit.)
yellow-green and white 青色和白色
(idi.) Adj. pale 蒼白：*mihnsīk hóu*
~ (look ~) also see 0526 and 0527

0870

➔chēng bībī 青啤啤 (lit.)
PH an emphatic way of saying
'yellow-green' 很青：*Ngóh m̀jūngyi*
~ *ge chēunglím.* (I don't like ~
curtains.)

0871

➔chēng leng baahkjehng 青
靚白淨(lit.) green, pretty, white and
clean 青嫩,好看,白皙和乾淨
(idi.) PH young, pretty/ handsome
and have a fresh complexion 年輕又
皮膚白皙：*Ngóh yahlèhng seui jái
gójahnsí, ~, m̀jī géidō néuihjái
jūngyi ngóh.* (When I was in my
twenties, I was ~. Lots of girls
were fond of me.)

0872

➔chóuchēngsīk 草青色(lit.) N
greyish green (usually the color of a
soldier's uniform) 帶灰的綠色,通常
是軍服的顏色：~ *ge gwānfuhk* (~
uniform for soldiers)

0873

➔gēngchēng 驚青 (lit.) fear the
green 害怕青色
(idi.) Adj. be frightened and feel
uneasy 害怕和不安：*"Baih la,
gīngléih fāanlàih la, ngóhdeih juhng
meih gáaudihm dī yéh." "Néih m̀sái
gam* ~. *Kéuih m̀wúih laauh
ngóhdeih ge."* ("Oh, that's too bad!

The manager is coming and we still haven't gotten everything ready." "Don't ~. He won't blame us for that.")

0874
→kàhmkàhm/kám chēng 噙噙青 (lit.) snatch the green 把青色擒住
(idi.) Adj. PH/ A. PH do something hastily 做事匆忙： *Gwo máhlouh m̀hóu ~ gám a, yiu táichīngchó yáuh móuh chē sīnji hóu gwo a.* (Don't cross the road so hurriedly . Make sure that there are no cars coming before crossing the road.)

chóisīk 彩色 **ATT colour** 七彩的

0875 ✓
→chātchói 七彩 (lit.) N/ATT a riot of color, colorful 七彩
(idi.) PH serious, severe 很厲害：
ⓐ *béi lóuhsai laauhdou* ~ (be ~ly scolded by the boss) ⓑ *(cheunggō) johngbáan johngdou* ~ (make too ~/ many mistakes [in singing] for not keeping to the beat) ⓒ *behngdou* ~ (be ~ly ill)

fūisīk 灰色 **N grey** 灰色

0876 ✓
→fūi 灰 (lit.) N grey 灰
(idi.) Adj. dim 暗淡： *Kéuih gokdāk nīgo saigaai hóu ~, jihgéi yauh móuh yàhnsāng lohkcheui, sóyíh kéuih séung jihsaat.* (He could not see the bright side of life nor did he have

any pleasure in life [i.e. he has been suffering all his life]. Therefore he wanted to commit suicide.)

0877
→fūisīk deihdaai 灰色地帶
(lit.) grey area/zone 灰色地帶
(idi.) N ambiguous case 模稜兩可
M go： *Yáuhsih faatleuht dōu yáuh ~.* (Sometimes there is ~ in law.)

gāmsīk 金色 **N golden** 金色
0878
→gāmngàuh 金牛 (lit.) gold cow 金的牛
(idi.) N a HK\$1,000 bill/note 港幣一千元大鈔 M jēung ： *yāt jēung ~ (a ~)*

0879 ✓
→gāmwòhngsīk 金黃色 (lit.) N golden yellow/brown 金黃色
(idi.) N (deep fry the ingredients until they are) golden brown (炸食物至變)金黃色 ： *jadou bin ~* (deep fry it until it becomes ~)

gútùhngsīk 古銅色 **N colour of bronze, reddish-brown** 赤褐色

0880
→gútùhngsīk 古銅色 (lit.) colour of bronze, reddish-brown 赤褐色
(idi.) N color of sun-tanned skin 曬黑了的皮膚的顏色 ： *Kéuih dī pèihfū saaidou bin ~.* (He has sun-tanned skin [like the deep shade of bronze].)

hāaksīk 黑色 N black 黑色

0881
→dōnghāak 當黑 (lit.) in the dark 在黑暗之中
(idi.) V unlucky 運氣差 : *Jānhaih ~, mòuh dyūndyūn béi lóuhsai laauh.* (I am ~. I was blamed by our boss and yet I don't know why.)

0882 ✓
→hāak 黑 (lit.) Adj. black, dark 黑
(idi.) Adj. in bad luck, unlucky 運氣差 : *Nīpáai hóu ~, dóuchàn dōu syū.* (Recently I've been ~. I lose money every time I bet.) RVE become black 變成黑色: ⓐ *jĕung baahk tàuhfaat yíhm ~* (dye the white hair black) ⓑ *saai ~ (tan)* V (1) become black 黑了 : *dihnsihgēi ge wámín ~ jó* (blackout of TV screen) (2) become dark 暗了: ⓐ *Tīn ~ jó* (It's already dark.) ⓑ *pèihfū ~ jó* (have darker complexion/tanned)

0883
→hāakbaahk 黑白 (lit.) ATT black and white 黑白 : *~ dihnsih/ fēilám/ séung/ pín* (~ TV/ film/ photograph/ movie)

0884
→hāakdái 黑底 (lit.) black as the background color 黑色做背景
(idi.) N member of a triad society 黑社會會員 : *Kéuih haih ~, néih ṁhóu tùhng kéuih lòihwóhng gam dō a.* (He is a ~. Don't associate with him so often.)

0885
→hāak māmā/ māngmāng/ mahkmahk 黑麻麻／孟孟／墨墨 (lit.) PH pitch-dark, pitch-black 很黑 : *Yānwaih tìhng dihn, sóyíh jāuwaih ~.* (Because there is a power blackout here, so it is ~ everywhere.)

0886
→hāak séhwúi 黑社會 (lit.) black society 黑色社會
(idi.) N gang/secret society 黑社會, 幫會 M go : *yahp ~* (join the ~)

0887
→hāakwá 黑話 (lit.) black word 黑色的說話
(idi.) N argot (used among triads) 黑社會的人說的隱語 M dī : *Hāak séhwúi ge yàhn yuhng ~ mahn néih, yùhgwó néih ṁsīk yuhngfāan ~ daap, kéuihdeih wúih dá néih.* (If you are questioned by a triad using ~ but you cannot answer him using the same kind of words, you will be beaten up by him.)

0888
→tàuhtàuh pungjeuhk hāak 頭頭碰著黑 (lit.) wherever one goes, one meets with the black 到處遇到黑色
(idi.) PH a string of bad luck, everything goes wrong 到處碰釘,運氣很差 : ⓐ *Làihdou Hēunggóng, jānhaih ~ la, wán go chānchīk, dímjī kéuih būnjó ngūk, séung wah wán gūng jouh, yauh yuhnggāam gīngjai sēuiteui, yìhgā lihn go wuhjiu dōu*

129

m̀ginjó tīm. (I've had ~ since I came to Hong Kong. I looked for one of my relatives, but he had moved. I planned to look for a job, but it happens that there is an economic downturn here. Now I have even lost my passport.) ⓑ*Gāmyaht jānhaih ~.* *Jīujóu fāangūng daaih sākchē chihdou, ngaanjau heui ngàhnhòhng lóchín, dímjī pàaih chèuhng lùhng, móuh lódou, fonggūng fāan ngūkkéi līp tìhngdihn, yiu hàahng sahpgéi chàhng làuhtāi.* (~ today. In the morning I was late for work because of a terrible traffic jam. I went to the bank to get some money at noon, but there was a long queue, and so I left. When I came home from the office, there was a power cut in the lift. I had to climb more than ten flights of stairs.)

hùhngsīk 紅色 N red 紅色

0889

➔daaih hùhng daaih jí 大紅大紫 (lit.) extremely red and extremely purple 大紅大紫
(idi.) PH extremely successful in showbiz 在演藝事業中非常成功 : *Yínyùhn fanlihn bāan ge hohksāang, yáuh géidō go jēunglòih wúih ~ ā?* ([Could anyone have guessed] How many trainees in the actor training course would become ~ in the future?)

0890✓

➔hùhng 紅(lit.) Adj. red 紅
(idi.) Adj. successful in showbiz 在演藝事業中成名 : *Kéuih yihgā haih hóu/ daaih ~ ge dihnyíng mìhngsīng.* (Now he is a very popular movie star.) V (1) become successful in showbiz 在演藝事業中成名 : *Kéuih meih ~ gójahnsí, mātyéh hei dōu paak. Yihgā ~ jó la, jauh gáan hei paak.* (Now that he has ~, he only stars in the movies he likes, but before he didn't have any choice.) (2) become red 紅了: *yānwaih pacháu, sóyíh faai mihn ~ jó* (blush because of shyness) also see 0528 and 0529 RVE make popular 使成名 : *Kéuih béi cheungpín gūngsī búng ~.* (He was made (a) very popular (singer) by the disc company.) BF blood 血 : ⓐ*gāi ~* (chicken ~) see 0123 ⓑ*jyū ~* (pig ~) see 0223

0891

➔ hùhng baahk yih sih 紅白二事 (lit.) red event and white event 紅白二事
(idi.) PH happy occasions and funerals 喜事和喪事 : *~ jauh haih yuhng hùhngsīk tùhng baahksīk làih bíusih.* (~ are signified by the colours of red and white.)

0892

➔hùhng bōkbōk/ gwàhng-gwàhng 紅卜卜／轟轟 (lit.) PH very red 很紅 : ⓐ*Kéuih chàh yīnjī chàhdou faai mihn ~.* (She put so much rouge on her face that it looked ~.)ⓑ*Dī saimānjái dungdou faai mihn ~.* (The children's faces are red with cold.)

0893

➔hùhngdái 紅底 (lit.) red as the background color 紅色做底色

130

(idi.) N a HK $100 bill/note 港幣一百元鈔票 M jēung：*yāt jēung* ~ (~)

0894

→hùhngdou faat jí 紅到發紫
(lit.) so red that it becomes purple 紅得發紫
(idi.) PH people in show business reach the peak of their career 在演藝事業中非常成功：*Géisahp nihn chìhn, kéuih hái dihnyínggaai ~, daahnhaih gú m̀dou, kéuih yìhgā jouh hātyī.* (He was a megastar [in the movies] decades ago, but who would have thought that he is a beggar now.)

0895

→hùhngsih baahksih 紅事白事 see 0891

0896

→m̀hùhng m̀hāak 唔紅唔黑
(lit.) not red nor black 半紅不黑
(idi.) PH not popular enough in show business 在娛樂圈不怎麼受歡迎：*Kéuih hái yùhlohkhyūn lōujó gam dō nihn dōu juhng haih ~ gám.* (He has been in showbiz for so many years and yet he is ~.)

0897

→mùihgwaihùhng(sīk) 玫瑰紅(色) (lit.) N rosy 玫瑰紅色：*~ ge seunfūng* (a ~ envelope)

0898

→sāamfān ngàahnsīk séuhng/dong daaihhùhng 三分顏色上／當大紅 (lit.) expect to dye something scarlet with just three Chinese grams of pigment 只有三分

顏色便以爲可以把東西染成大紅色
(idi.) PH think too highly of oneself, take something trivial for a big deal 自視過高, 把小事當作了不起的事：*Gīngléih jaan kéuih géi geui kéuih jauh ~, yíhwàih jihgéi hóu lēk.* (Our manager just praised him. He took it for a big deal and thought he himself was a very capable man.)

làahmsīk 藍色 N blue 藍色

0899

→bóulàahmsīk 寶藍色 (lit.) precious blue 寶貴的藍色
(idi.) N royal blue 寶藍色：*~ ge lāu* (a ~ jacket)

0900

→tīnlàahmsīk 天藍色 (lit.) N sky blue 天藍色：*~ ge tói bou* (~ table cloth)

0901

→wùhséuilàahm(sīk) 湖水藍 (色)(lit.) as blue as lake water 像湖水的顏色
(idi.) N acid blue 湖水藍色：*~ ge kwàhn* (an ~ skirt)

luhksīk 綠色 N green 綠色

0902

→choiyihpluhk(sīk) 菜葉綠 (色) (lit.) N as green as vegetable leaf 像菜葉的綠色：*Lāp yúk ~.* (The piece of jade is ~.)

0903

→chóuluhksīk 草綠色 (lit.) N as green as grass 草青色：*Kéuih jeuk sāam luhksīk ge toujōng, chan ~*

ge hàaih tùhng sáudói. (Her dark green suit matches her shoes and her handbag which are ~.)

0904

➔luhksīk wòhpìhng 綠色和平 (lit.) PH Green-peace 綠色和平 : ~ haih yātgo wàahnbóu jóujīk. (~ is an organization for environmental conservation.)

0905

➔pìhnggwóluhk(sīk) 蘋果綠(色) (lit.) N apple green 像青皮蘋果的綠色 : Go būi haih ~. (The cup is ~.)

ngàahnsīk 顏色 N colour 顏色 M júng/ jek

0906

➔chīngyātsīk 清一色(lit.) all in one colour 全都是一種顏色 (idi.) N (in mahjong game) purity hand with all the tiles of the same category, royal flush (麻將)清一色 A (1) all (of the same gender) 全部都是男／女性 : Nībāan ~ haih néuih hohksāang. (The students in this class are ~ girls.) (2) uniformly 一律 : Dī sihjái dōu ~ jeuksaai hùhng sāam hāak fu. (All the waiters put on red shirts and black trousers.)

0907✓

➔ngh ngàahn luhk sīk 五顏六色 (lit.) colorful, gaudy 顏色繽紛 (idi.) PH (said of illness) serious (病) 很嚴重 : behngdou ~ (be ~ly ill)

sīkséui 色水 N colour 顏色

0908

➔sihyàuh lōu faahn→jíng sīk jīng séui 豉油撈飯→整色整水 (lit.) add (dark brown) soy sauce to (white) rice→just play tricks with colors 把(深啡色的)醬油加在(白色的)飯上→只是調弄顏色 (idi.) HIT tend to mislead others 有意誤導別人 : Kéuih sihngyaht hóuchíh hóu mòhng gám, kèihsaht kéuih ~ → ~ béi lóuhsai tái jī ma. (He appears as if he is very busy, actually he just ~ our boss [into thinking that he is hard-working.])

wòhngsīk 黃色 N yellow 黃色

0909

➔daahnwóngsīk 蛋黃色 (lit.) N as yellow as a yolk 像雞蛋黃的顏色 : ~ ge sēutsāam (a shirt ~)

0910

➔lìhngmūngwòhng(sīk) 檸檬黃(色) (lit.) N as yellow as a lemon 像檸檬的黃色 : Dī síubihn ~. (The urine is ~.)

0911

➔souwòhng 掃黃 (lit.) sweep the yellow 掃除黃色 (idi.) ATT anti-vice 掃除色情架步的 : Gíngfōng chóichéui ~ hàhngduhng. (The police conducted an ~ operation.) V clean up a place by removing the sex dens, (said of policemen) conduct anti-vice operation 掃除色情架步, (警察)採取剷除色情架步的行動 :

Wohnggok yáuh hóudō sīkchihng gabouh, gíngchaat sihsih heui gódouh ~. (There are many vice dens in Mongkok. The police always go there to ~.)

0912 ✓

→wòhng 黃(lit.) Adj. yellow 黃 (idi.) N pornography 色情 : ⓐ~, *dóu, duhk haih séhwúi sāam hoih.* (~, gambling and drugs are the three vices that can ruin our society.) ⓑ*sou* ~ see 0911 V become yellow 黃了 : ⓐ *gihn baahk sēutsāam ~jó* (the white shirt has ~) ⓑ *béi yàhn siu dou mihn* ~ see 0517 ⓒ : *mihn ~gwāt sau* see 0534

0913

→wòhng kàhmkàhm 黃噙噙 (lit.) PH the emphatic way of saying 'very yellow' 很黃 : *Kéuih móuhfajōng gójahnsí, faai mihn ~ gám.* (When she doesn't put on any make-up, her face looks ~.)

0914

→wòhng máhkwá 黃馬褂 (lit.) yellow jacket (for men) 黃色的 馬褂 (idi.) N relative of the boss 老闆的 親戚 M go : ⓐ~ *gánghaih ìnsái hóuchíh ngóhdeih gám, jouhdāk gam sānfú lā.* (It's true that the ~ need not work as hard as we do.) ⓑ*Kéuih tùhng lóuhbáan ge ját yātchái jouhyéh, kéuih ìngám dākjeuih nīgo ~.* (He works with the nephew of his boss, so he dare not offend him / the ~.)(* 'Wòhng máhkwá' is the yellow ceremonial jacket bestowed by the

Chīng emperors [1644–1911] on their relatives or officials who have achieved distinction.)

0915 ✓

→wòhngsīk 黃色(lit.)N yellow 黃色 (idi.) ATT vice, pornographic 與色 情有關的 : ⓐ~ *gabouh* (a ~ den) ⓑ ~ *wábou* (~ magazines)

wū 烏 BF black 黑色

0916

→wū dēungdēung/sèuhsèuh 烏啄啄／蛇蛇 (lit.) PH (1) be in the dark 對一件事毫不知情 : *Gūngsī jauh làih yiu chòihyùhn la, néih juhng ~ gám.* (Our company is going to lay off some people, but you are still ~.) (2) muddled 糊塗 : *jouh yàhn ~ gám* (be ~ in everything)

0917

→wū jēutjēut 烏卒卒(lit.) PH lovely (and shining) black 黑得(發 亮)可愛 : *Nīgo saimānjái ge tàuhfaat/ ngáahnjyū ~.* (The hair/ pupils of this child is/ are ~.)

133

4. Cooking and Food

I. Jyúfaat (ways of cooking)

baahk 白 **BF cook something without any meat or using any seasonings** 用開水煮,不加肉類或任何調味品

0918
→baahkcheuk 白灼 (lit.) V lightly boil (without using any seasonings) 用開水稍煮熟 (不加任何調味品) : ⓐ*Nīdī choi, ~ jīhauh, gādī hòuhyàuh jauh dāk ge la.* (~ these vegetables. Top with oyster sauce before serving.) ⓑ *~hā* see 0067

0919
→baahksaahp 白烚 (lit.) V (1) boil (usually a longer time) without using any seasonings 用開水煮熟,不加任何調味品 : ~ *dáan* (boiled egg) (2) boil without any meat 不用肉煮的 : *Dī choi hóyíh ~.* (The vegetables can be ~.) also see 0852 (2) and (3)

baau 爆 **V blast, explode** 爆炸

0920✓
→baau 爆 (lit.) V blast, explode 爆炸
(idi.) V (1) (when stir-frying) brown the ingredient(s) in boiling hot oil 把烹調材料拋進燙油裏 : *jēung dī gēung, chūng, syuntàuh ~ háh kéuih*

sīn (brown the ginger, spring union and garlic first) (2) reveal a secret/ scandal to the public 把秘密／醜聞公開 : *Gógo yáuhchínlóu béi yàhn lahksok, yùhgwó kéuih m̀béichín, dī dáaitòuh jauh jēung kéuihdī cháumàhn heung sānmàhngaai ~ saaichēutlàih.* (The rich man was blackmailed by the thugs. If he refused to pay them money, they would reveal his dirty secrets to the press.)

bōu 煲 **V boil, cook with a lot of water** 用頗多的水煮

0921
→bōu dihnwá jūk 煲電話粥 (lit.) cook rice gruel on telephone 打電話的時候煮粥
(idi.) VO talk so long (time) on the phone (that even rice gruel could have been cooked during that period of time) 在電話中談了很久(甚至連粥也可以在那段時間內煮好) : *M̀hóu sèhngyaht ~ lā, jójyuh yàhndeih yuhng dihnwá.* (Don't always ~. You may inconvenience others who want to use the phone.)

0922
→bōu móuh máih jūk 煲冇米粥 (lit.) cook congee without rice 煮沒有米的粥

(idi.) VO make idle promise, make a promise but not intend to keep it 答應 別人但不會實行：*Yauh wah jōngsāu gāan ngūk, gam noih dōu meih gin kéuih wán yàhn fāanlàih jouh, ngóh tái kéuih dōu haih ~ ge jē.* (He said that he would have the house refurbished, but he hasn't gotten anybody to do it. I think he just ~.)

cháau 炒 V sauté, stir-fry 炒

0923✓

→cháau 炒(lit.) V sauté, stir-fry 炒
(idi.) V (1) (the short form of 'cháau yàuhyú') fire (an employee) 解僱：*béi gūngsī ~ jó* (be ~ by the company) see 0086 (2) speculate 投機：*~ láu/ gúpiu/ ngoihbaih* (~ on property/ stocks and shares/ in foreign currencies) (3) scalp tickets, make a profit by selling tickets on the black market 黑市炒賣 票：ⓐ*~ fēi (~)* ⓑ*Dī jūkkàuhmàaih máaih ~ fēi.* (The football fans buy tickets on the black market.) also see 0356

0924 ✓

→cháaumàaih yātdihp 炒埋一 碟 (lit.) PH get all the ingredients stir-fried together and put them on one plate 把所有材料一起炒及放在 一個碟上面
(idi.) PH make up one thing by means of different elements 把不同 的元素放在一起做成一個新的組 合：*Nī géigo hohksāang chìhngdouh mtùhng, daahnhaih ngóh mléih la, ngóh jēung kéuihdeih ~, jauh hóyíh hōibāan*

la. (These students are of different levels. But I don't care. I will just put them together to make up one class.)

dahn 燉 V stew 燉

0925 ✓

→dahn dūnggū 燉冬菇 (lit.)
VO stew mushroom 燉冬菇
(idi.) VO be demoted as a kind of punishment to those in governmental disciplinary departments, especially to policemen of middle or lower ranks 政府紀律部隊職員降職,尤 指中低級警察：*Gógo binyī gíngtaam (béi seuhngsī) ~, yiu jouh bunnihn gwānjōng (gíngchaat).* (He was demoted from plain-clothes officer to uniformed constable for six months.)

guhk 焗 V bake 焗

0926✓

→guhk 焗(lit.) V bake 焗
(idi.) Adj. stuffy, no fresh air 空氣 不流通：*Gāan fóng sēuiyihn yáuh láahnghei jē, daahnhaih chóhmúhn yàhn, yauh sāanmàaihsaai dī chēung, gwái gam ~.* (Although the room is air-conditioned, it is filled with people and all the windows are shut. It's terribly ~.)

gwán 滾 V boil 水開了

0927✓

→gwán 滾 (lit.) V boil 水開了
(idi.) V cheat 欺騙：*Kéuih tàuhlóuh gáandāan, hóu yùhngyih béi yàhn ~.*

136

(S/he is so naive that s/he will be easily cheated by others.)

0928

→yātméi kaau gwán 一味靠滾
(lit.) the only way of cooking is to boil 只用熱水燙的煮法
(idi.) PH (said of a person) always cheats others 常常欺騙人 : *Kéuih nīgo yàhn, ~.* (He is a person who ~.)

gwo láahnghòh 過冷河 VO (said of noodles and pasta) put in cold water after the fisrt boiling and before cooking again (粉麵等)第一 次煮沸後放在冷水中，然後再煮

0929

→gwo láahnghòh 過冷河 (lit.) cross cold river 渡過冷的河
(idi.) VO (1) (said of noodles or pasta) put in cold water after the first boiling and before cooking again (粉 麵等) 第一次煮沸後放在冷水中， 然後再煮 : *Fán tùhng mihn dōu yiu ~.* (Noodles or pasta need to be ~.)
(2) (said of high ranking civil servants in Hong Kong) mandatory unemployment for a period of time after his (early) retirement 香港高級 公務員(提早)退休之後一段時間內 不得任職任何機構 : *Kéuih ~jó ~ jíhauh hái yātgāan gwokjai gāmyùhng gēikau wándóu fahn hóu gūng.* (He now has a good job in an international financial corporation after his ~.)

jyú 煮 V cook 煮

0930

→jyú 煮 (lit.) V cook 煮
(idi.) V backbite, speak ill of somebody (who is not present) (在 背後) 說人壞話 : ⓐ *Kéuih heui gīngléihdouh ~ (gwái) néih.* (He went to our manager's office and ~ you.) ⓑ *jyúdoulàih jauh sihk* see 1038

luhk 淥 V lightly boil, rinse in hot water, scald (in order to clean) 在沸水中稍煮或稍清洗

0931

→luhk 淥 (lit.) V lightly boil, rinse in hot water, scald (in order to clean) 在沸水中稍煮或稍清洗 : ⓐ*gwán séui ~ jyūchéung* see 0220 ⓑ*gwán séui ~ geuk* see 0413

suhk 熟 V/Adj. cooked, well done 熟了

0932

→yātwohk suhk 一鑊熟 (lit.) get all the ingredients cooked in one pan 把所有材料放在一個鍋裏煮熟
(idi.) PH kill everyone including oneself (mostly by setting something on fire) 同歸於盡 (多是放火) : *Gógo chīsinlóu fongfó sīu gāan ngūk, námjyuh daaihgā ~.* (That crazy man set fire to the house because he wanted to kill everyone, including himself.)

II. Sihkmaht (food)

bāau 包 N Chinese bun 包子 M go

0933
→haambāau 喊包 (lit.) crying bun 哭的包子
(idi.) N cry-baby, baby/ child who likes to cry all the time 常喜歡哭的小孩 M go : *Nīgo ~ làih ge, yūkdī jauh haam.* (It is a ~. It cries very easily.)

0934
→maaih daaih bāau 賣大包
(lit.) sell big Chinese bun 賣大的包子
(idi.) PH offer a good bargain to the other side(s) 在買賣之中讓對方得到很多好處 : *Gógāan deihcháan gūngsī yauh sung jōngsāufai yauh sung leuhtsīfai, ~.* (That property company will pay the refurbishment and the lawyer's fees [for each purchase]. The flat buyers will greatly benefit from this.)

béng 餅 N cake 餅 M go

0935
→daaih béng 大餅 (lit.) big cake 大的餅
(idi.) N quite an old colloquial term for a one-dollar coin in Hong Kong 香港一元硬幣的舊的俗稱 M go

0936
→sái daaih béng 洗大餅 (lit.) wash big cake 清洗大的餅
(idi.) VO clean dishes in a restaurant 在食肆中當清洗碗碟的工作 : *Kéuih hái jáuhàuh jouh ~ ge.* (He ~.)

0937
→yātgo béngyan 一個餅印
(lit.) (cast from) the same cake mould 同一個餅模 (做出來的)
(idi.) PH (said of parents and children or siblings) look the same (父母子女或兄弟姊妹之間)樣貌極相似 : *Kéuihge jái tùhng kéuih gáanjihk haih ~.* (His son looks just like him.)

bōlòh 菠蘿 N pineapple 鳳梨 M go

0938 ✓
→bōlòh 菠蘿 (lit.)N pineapple 鳳梨 M go
(idi.) N roughly made bomb 土製炸彈 M go : *Yáuh yàhn hái gāai seuhngbihn fong ~, jaséi géigo yàhn.* (Someone put a ~ on the street and some people were killed by it.)

0939
→gām bōlō 金波蘿 (lit.) gold pineapple 金色的波蘿
(idi.) N one's darling son/ daughter/ grandchildren 寶貝兒子/女兒/孫兒 M go : *Kéuih dong kéuihge syūn haih ~.* (He treats his grandchild like a ~.)(* Actually, 'bōlō' is a container for holding wine and should be written '叵羅'.)

cháang 橙 N orange 橙, 橘子 M go

0940

→lòhdái cháang 籠底橙 (lit.) oranges put at the bottom of the bamboo basket 放在竹籠最下面的橙 (idi.) N worst students 成績最低／差的學生 M go; dī : *Lēk ge hohksāang háisaai A bāan, làuhfāan dī ~ béi ngóh gaau.* (The smart students are all placed in class A. The ~ are for me to teach.)

choi 菜 N vegetable 蔬菜 M pō; gān

0941

→sāanggwāt daaihtàuh choi→ jungwaaih 生骨大頭菜→ 種 (縱)壞 (lit.) bony turnip→ (it) grows wrong 纖維硬化了的大頭菜→是栽種得不好 (idi.) HIT (said of children) be spoiled 子女被慣壞了 : *"Kéuihdī jáinéui, yauh yīn yauh jáu, yauh mtēng fuhmóuh wah."* "*Hàaih, ~→ ~ lō.*" ("His son and daughter smoke and drink. Moreover, they don't listen to their parents." "Oh, they are ~.")

0942 ✓

→yèhchoifā 椰菜花 (lit.) N cauliflower 花椰菜 M gān; pō (idi.) N a kind of venereal disease, a wart, papule 疣 (一種性病) : *sāang ~* (to have ~)

0943

→yèhchoitàuh 椰菜頭 (lit.) the top part of a cauliflower (formed by a ball of flower buds) 椰菜上端有很多花蕾的部分

(idi.) N very curly hair 頭髮很鬖曲 M go: *tàuhfaat lyūndou hóuchíh (go) ~ gám* (~ like ~)

dáan 蛋 N egg 雞蛋 M jek/ go

0944

→baahksaahp dáan 白焓蛋 see 0919 (1)

0945 ✓

→dáan 蛋 (lit.) N egg 蛋 M jek/ go; dā (idi.) NU (score) zero 零(分) : ⓐ *háausi sihk ~* (get a ~ in the examination) ⓑ *sihk/ syū gwōngdáan* (score zero in a match, game or contest)

0946

→gāmngàhn dáan 金銀蛋 (lit.) gold and silver egg 金色和銀色的蛋 (idi.) N (chickens') eggs and ducks' eggs prepared in lime (*It is a dish of food which can be prepared either by stir-frying or steaming.) 雞蛋和皮蛋一起煮的餸菜,炒或蒸都可以 M dihp, go : *Nīchi haih ngóh daih yātchi sihk ~.* (This is my first time to eat ~.)

0947

→hòhbāau dáan 荷包蛋 (lit.) purse/walletlike egg 像錢包的雞蛋 (idi.) N egg fried on one side and then folded up/ egg fried on both sides 煎雞蛋的時候把一邊翻上/兩邊都煎的蛋 M go/jek : *jīn ~* (fry an egg)

0948

→I.Q. lihngdáan IQ 零蛋 (lit.)

Intelligence Quotient is zero 智商零分
(idi.) PH very stupid 愚蠢 : *Gam gáandāan ge sou néih dōu m̀sīk gai, jānhaih ~.* (You can't do even so simple a sum, you are really ~.)

0949
→lihng (gāi) dáan 零 (雞) 蛋
(lit.) zero egg 零的雞蛋
(idi.) NU (score) zero 零 (分) : *mahksyū ~* (get a ~ in dictation)

0950
→maaih hàahm ngaapdáan 賣鹹鴨蛋 (lit.) sell salted ducks' eggs 賣鹹(的)鴨蛋
(idi.) PH die, pass away 死了 : *heuijó ~* (have ~)

0951
→mōkhok gāidáan 剝殼雞蛋
(lit.) an egg with its shell removed 碌了殼的雞蛋
(idi.) PH/ N white and smooth skin of the face 又白又滑的臉蛋 : *Yuhngjó ngóhdeih (chēut) ge wuhfūbán jīhauh, néihge pèihfū jauh wúih hóuchíh ~ gám ge la.* (After using our skin care cosmetics your face will be like ~.)

0952
→taaiyèuhng dáan 太陽蛋(lit.)
sun-like egg 太陽蛋
(idi.) N (said of fried egg) sunny side up 只煎一邊的蛋 M jek/ go : *~ hóu nàahn sīufa.* (Eggs cooked ~ are too hard to digest.)

dáu 豆 N bean, pea 豆 M lāp; gān

0953
→báauséi hòhlāandáu 飽死荷蘭豆 (lit.) the Holland peas die of overeating 青豆飽得要死
(idi.) PH (said of a person) disgusts others by being too proud 一個人太驕傲令人討厭 : *Sihngyaht wah jihgéi dím lēk dím lēk, jānhaih ~.* (He always boasts about his achievements, and that makes me sick.)

0954
→dauhdēng 豆丁 (lit.) tiny pea 小豆
(idi.) N very young and small child 細小孩童 M go : *Yíhchìhn gin kéuih, ~ gam saigo, yìhgā yauh gōu yauh daaih.* (When I last saw him, he was a ~ . Now he is tall and big.)

0955
→dauhlàih 豆泥 (lit.) beans and mud 豆跟泥
(idi.) Adj. sloppy, low standard, not imposing 差勁,簡陋 : *Kéuih gāan poutáu hóu ~ ge ja, deihfōng yauh sai, jihnghaih dāk yātgo fogei ja.* (His shop is very simple. The place is small, and there is only one shopkeeper.)

0956
→dauhsā sīk 豆沙色 (lit.) N the colour of red bean paste 紅豆泥的顏色 : *~ ge toupōng* (a woman's suit in ~)

0957 ✓

→**hùhngdauh/dáu sā 紅豆沙**

(lit.) N red bean soup 紅豆湯 M wún

(idi.) N blood (for transfusion) (用來輸血的) 血漿 M bāau : *Yáuh behngyàhn yiu syūhyut, ló bāau ~ làih lā.* (There is a patient who needs a blood transfusion. Please get me a packet of ~.)

0958

→**jīmàh luhkdáu 芝麻綠豆**

(lit.) sesame seeds and green beans 芝麻綠豆

(idi.) Adj. PH (1) miscellaneous, trivial, of small importance 瑣碎,微不足道 : ⓐ *Yātyaht yuhng géidō chàhyihp nīdī gam ~ ge sih, jouh gīngléih ge jauh ṁsái léih lā.* (As a manager, you don't need to know such small thing as how much tea is/how many (kilograms of) tea leaves are consumed in one day.) ⓑ *Nīdī haih ~ ge sih/ cho làih ge jī ma, néih sáimāt gam nāu jē.* (This is just a small thing/ mistake. You don't need to be so mad.) (2) low-ranking (official) 官職低微 : *Jouh go ~ gūn jī ma, sáimāt gam ngok a?* (You are just a ~ official. You should not be so fierce [with me].)

0959

→**tòhng chī dáu, séui kāu yàuh 糖黐豆,水溝油** (lit.) (it's easy to have) sugar sticking to beans, (but it's hard to have) water mixing with oil 用糖黏著豆很容易,想水跟油融合在一起就很難

(idi.) PH the two very different ways people get along with one another: sometimes they enjoy being together, sometimes they don't 人們相處時的兩種截然不同的情況:很融洽及不咬絃 : *"Kéuihdeih léuhng hīngdaih, hóu gójahnsí jauh ~, ngaaigāau gójahnsí jauh ~." "Saimānjái haih gám ge la."* ("Sometimes the two brothers can get along very well with each other. But when they quarrel, they turn their back on each other." "Children are always so.")

dauhfuh 豆腐 N bean curd 豆腐 M jyūn; gauh

0960 ✓

→**dauhfuhjā 豆腐渣** (lit.) N residue of soybeans in making bean curd or soybean milk 磨豆漿或做豆腐時的黃豆渣滓 M dī

(idi.) N constructions which are of very poor quality and are dangerous 質素很差又有危險性的建築物 : ⓐ ~ gūngchìhng (~) ⓑ *Sìhngginsēung tāu gūng gáam líu, héichēutlàih ge láu binsìhng ~.* (The contractors use insufficient and poor materials, so the houses they built are poor and dangerous.) ⓒ *Sìhmàhn séi hāan séi dái, dímjī máaihjó ge haih ~ láu.* (Some people in Hong Kong work very hard to save money [to buy a flat]. How could they have known that the flats they bought are ~.)

0961 ✓

→**dauhfuhyéun 豆腐膶** (lit.) N

bean curd cube 小方塊豆腐 M gauh
(idi.) N very small (area) (面積)細小：
*Kéuih gāan ngūk/ poutáu hóuchíh ~ gam
sai.* (His house/shop is ~ [like a ~].)

0962
➔làhmgwo dauhfuh 腍過豆腐
(lit.) PH (even) softer and easier to be
mashed up than bean curd 比豆腐還
軟,還易爛： *"Buhng chèuhng juhng
~,"* *gógo jōngsāulóu yātmihn (yuhng
dihnjyun) jyun chèuhng yātmihn wah.*
("The wall is ~," said the decorator
while he was drilling the wall [with an
electric drill].)

**faahn 飯 N cooked rice 飯 M
wún**

0963
➔cháau láahngfaahn 炒冷飯
(lit.) fry left-over/ stale rice 把吃剩的飯
再炒來吃
(idi.) VO repeat the same old thing,
rehash, no novelty 重覆,沒有新意：
*Kéuih nīchi ge yíngóng tùhng seuhngchi
ge chāmdō yātyeuhng, ~ jē.* (His
speech this time is much the same as
the last one. He just ~.)

0964
➔chèuhngkèih faahnpiu 長期
飯票 (lit.) long term rice ticket 長期
飯票
(idi.) N husband (a man who can make
a woman a living for the rest of her
life) 丈夫 (一個可以供養女人一輩
子的男人) M jēung： *Yihgā juhng
yáuh yahn gokdāk néuihyán msái gam*

lēk, wándóu jēung ~ jauh dāk ge la.
(Nowadays, there are still some people
who think that women do not need to be
successful. It is good enough for them
to find a ~.)

0965
➔láahngfaahn choijāp 冷飯菜
汁 (lit.) N/ PH stale rice and left-over
food or sauce (usually given to
beggars) 吃剩的飯和菜(通常用來施
捨給乞丐) M dī： *Yātgo hātyī hāt faahn
sihk gójahnsí wúih góng, "Yáuh mē ~,
sīséháh lā!"* (When a beggar begs for
food, he would say, "Do you have any
~? Please give me some.")

0966
➔lēu faahn ying 嘍飯應 (lit.)
spit the rice (while eating) and say yes
把飯吐出來以便說聲'好'
(idi.) PH give an agreement without
hesitation and unconditionally 毫不考
慮及無條件地答應： *Wòhng síujé giu
Jēung sīnsāang pùih kéuih heui, Jēung
sīnsāang jauh jīkhāak ~.* (Miss Wong
asked Mr. Jeung to go with her and he
immediately said yes.)

0967
➔lihnmáahn chìhn, faahn hauh
yīn 年晚錢，飯後烟 (lit.) PH for
ordinary people, what they need for
new year is money; and for smokers, all
what they need after a meal is a
cigarette 普通人過年的時候最需要
錢,而煙民在飯後最需要的是煙：
"Yāt sihkyùhn faahn jauh dāamjyuh háu

yīn." "~, ~ ā ma." ("You smoke a cigarette just after you finish your meal." "Hey, you know ~, ~.")

0968 ✓
➜yātgauh faahn 一嚿飯 (lit.) a lump of rice 一團飯
(idi.) PH (said of a person) not smart or active enough 不夠精明活躍 : *Sihngyaht kéihháidouh, dōu m̀sīk bōngsáu, (hóuchíh) ~ gám.* (You just stood there the whole time and did not lend a (helping) hand. You are dumb like ~.)

fāansyú 番薯 N yam 洋芋 M go/ gauh; gān

0969 ✓
➜daaih fāansyú 大番薯 (lit.) N big yam 大洋芋 M gauh
(idi.) N very fat and stupid person 又胖又笨鈍的人 M gauh : *Kéuih sèhng gauh ~ gám.* (He is a ~ just like a ~.)

gāi 雞 N chicken 雞 M jek; gān

0970
➜baahkchit gāi 白切雞 see 0852 (2)

0971
➜fèihgāichāan 肥雞餐 (lit.) fat chicken meal 有肥雞吃的餐
(idi.) N gratuity/ incentive/ golden handshake (*It is a sum of money given as a kind of compensation to a civil servant who has been invited to retire early.) 特惠金(給建議提前退休的公

務員的錢) : ⓐ *sihk* ~ (opt to take the ~) ⓑ ~ *binjó yúhgap chāan sahmjí āmchēun chāan.* (~ has been reduced to a pigeon meal or even a quail meal, i.e. that kind of money has become less and less.)

0972
➜gāi 雞 see 0107–0152

0973
➜yàhndeih chēut gāi, néih chēut sihyàuh 人哋出雞, 你出豉油 (lit.) others offer a chicken but you just offer soy sauce 人家給你雞, 你只提供醬油
(idi.) PH one still cannot afford the expenses even though the largest portion is paid by others 人家出了最大份的錢你也負擔不來 : *Ngóhge chānchīk wah yùhgwó ngóh heui Gālàhdaaih taam kéuih, kéuih jauh bāau sihk bāau jyuh. Daahnhaih ~, ~ dōu m̀ dihm lā, ngóh lihn jeui pèhng ge gēipiu dōu móuh chín máaih.* (One of my relatives said I could stay in her house if I went to visit her in Canada. But ~, [because] I don't even have the money to buy the cheapest plane ticket.)

gāt 桔 N tangerine 桔 M go

0974
➜dāk go gāt 得個桔 (lit.) get a tangerine 得到一個桔
(idi.) PH get nothing 甚麼也沒有(拿到) : ⓐ *Jouhdāk gam sānfú dōuhaih ~,*

gogo yuht ge yàhngūng dōu sáichīng. (I ~ even though I work so hard. My salary is used up every month.) ⓑ *"Bōsí sé néihge bougou sédāk hóu hóu bo!" "Maih ~! Kéuih wahjó gūngsī sihtgán bún, ìnhóyíh joi sīngyàhn."* ("Hey, you got a very good report from our boss." "So what? I'll ~ out of it. He has already told me that our company was losing money and he could not give anyone a promotion.")

0975

→sàhnchìhngāt → yām gōn 神前桔→陰乾 (lit.) tangerines offered to the god(s) → they dry up slowly 供奉在神前的桔→不知不覺地愈來愈乾)

(idi.) HIT (usually said of money) becomes less and less (通常指錢財)愈來愈少 : *Tūngjeung gam sáileih, dī chín jáihái ngàhnhòhng jauh hóuchíh ~ gám → ~.* (Inflation is so serious. If you put your money in the bank, it will ~.)

0976

→wahngāt 運桔 (lit.) bring the tangerines here and there 把桔帶來帶去

(idi.) V meddle with no sincerety 瞎弄東西,沒有誠意 : *"Yauh yiu ló nīgo béi kéuih tái, yauh yiu ló gógo béih kéuih tái, táiyùhn yauh ìmmáaih, ~ ga kéuih,"* go sauhfoyùhn wah. ("I had to take this out and take that out for her to look at. But she didn't buy any one of them. She simply ~," said the saleslady.)

gēung 薑 N ginger 薑 M gauh; gān; faai

0977

→búndeih gēung ìmlaaht 本地薑唔辣 (lit.) locally grown ginger is never hot 本地種的薑不辣

(idi.) PH grass is always greener on the other side of the fence, local talents are inferior to foreign ones 本地的人材不及外國的好 : *"Kèihsaht Hēunggóng jauh yáuh daaihbá jyūngā lā, sáimāt chéng ngoihgwok ge jyūngā ā." "~ ā ma!"* ("Actually, there are lots of experts in Hong Kong. We don't need to consult foreign experts." "Don't you know that ~?")

0978 ✓

→gēung 薑 (lit.)N ginger 薑 M gauh ; gān; faai

(idi.) Adj. gutsy, shrewd and daring 膽子大,不畏強權 : *Gam gau ~ a, gindóu chāailóu dōu ìm pa.* (How ~ you are!/ How dare you behave like that before me! You are even not afraid of the police.) (*A suspect showing contempt would be teased like this after having been intercepted by a policeman.)

0979

→gēung yuht lóuh yuht laaht 薑越老越辣 (lit.) the longer the time that ginger grows, the hotter it tastes 薑越老越辣

(idi.) PH (said of man) the older one grows, the more experienced and capable he is 人越老經驗越豐富,本領也越

大 ： *Nīgihn sih, Chánjái gáauìndihm, jēutjī béi Lóuh Jēung gáaudihmjó sóyíh wah lē, ~, jānhaih móuh cho ge.* (Young Chan couldn't manage it. In the end, it was settled by Old Jeung. That's why people say ~. It's really right.)

gwā 瓜 N gourd, melon 瓜 M go; gauh; gān

0980 ✓

→daaih dūnggwā 大冬瓜 (lit.)N big winter melon/white gourd 大冬瓜 M go

(idi.) N very fat man 大胖子 M go ： *Kéuih sihng sāambaak bohng, hóuchíh go ~ gám.* (He weighs almost three hundred pounds [i.e. 136.5 kilos]. He is like a ~.) (*Winter melons are the largest of all kinds of melon or gourd.)

0981

→dūnggwā dauhfuh 冬瓜豆腐 (lit.) winter melon and bean curd 冬瓜 [和豆腐]

(idi.) PH misfortune or even death 不測甚至死亡 ： *Ngóhdeih chyùhngā ge sāngwuht dōu haih kaausaai kéuih ge la, yihgā kéuih sauhjó chúhng sēung, yùhgwó yáuh mātyéh ~, ngóhdeih jauh ìnjī dím syun lo.* (He is the breadwinner of our family. Now he is seriously injured, and if something worse happens to him, what shall we do then?)

0982

→fúgwāgōn 苦瓜乾 (lit.) dried bitter gourd 乾的苦瓜

(idi.) N a sad look 苦著口臉 ： ⓐ

Sihngyaht haam, hóuchíh ~ gám. (You always cry. You wear ~ like a ~.) ⓑ ~ *gám ge mihnháu* see 0457

0983 ✓

→gwā 瓜 (lit.) N gourd, melon 瓜 M go; gauh; gān

(idi.) V die 死 ： *Kéuih ~ jó lo.* (He ~.) RVE die of 死於 ： *Gógo chaahklóu béi gíngchaat hōichēung dá ~ jó lo.* (The thief was shot dead by the policeman.)

0984

→tàhng lang gwā, gwā lang tàhng 藤扒瓜，瓜扒藤 (lit.) (like) melon and vine entangled with each other 瓜跟藤纏繞在一起

(idi.) PH (things or relations) interrelate with each other 事情或關係糾纏不清 ： ⓐ *Nī gāan gūngsī léuihbihn ge yàhnsih gwāanhaih hóu fūkjaahp, ~, ~ gám.* (There are very complicated personal relationships between people in this company, just like ~.) ⓑ *Nīdī sih ~, ~ gám, gáaudou ngóh tàuh dōu tungmàaih.* (These things ~. They give me a headache.)

hā 蝦 N shrimp, prawn 蝦 M jek; gān

0985

→hā 蝦 see 0067–0070

0986

→lyūngūng hāmáih 攣弓蝦米 (lit.) small curvy dried shrimp 彎彎的小乾蝦

(idi.) PH being curvy, not straight 形
狀彎彎的, 不直的 : *Hàahng tùhng
chóh dōu yiu sānjihk tiuh yīu, m̀hóu
hóuchíh ~ gám.* (You have to straighten
your back up when you walk or sit.
Don't hunch your back like a ~.)

**háaih 蟹 N crab 螃蟹 M jek;
gān**

0987
→háaih 蟹 see 0071–0077

**hēungjīu 香蕉 N banana 香蕉
M jek; bohng**

0988 ✓
→hēungjīu 香蕉 (lit.) N banana
香蕉 M jek ; bohng
(idi.) N (a teasing term for) young
Chinese born overseas (嘲笑語) 海外出
生的華僑青年 M jek : *Nījek ~,
jìhnghaih sīk tēng Jūngmàhn, m̀sīk góng
ga.* (This ~ can only understand Chinese.
He cannot speak Chinese.) (* 'Hēungjīu'
is used to mean young Chinese born
overseas because it is yellow outside but
white inside.)

0989 ✓
→hēungjīu pèih 香蕉皮 (lit.)N
banana skin 香蕉皮 M faai; dī
(idi.) N trap 陷阱 : *béi ~ yàhn cháai*
(set a ~ for somebody [by making him
slip on a banana skin]) (*Instead of
'hēungjīu pèih', some people would
say 'sāigwā pèih', i.e. water melon
rind/skin.)

0990 ✓
→sihk/yaak jīu là 食／喡蕉啦
(lit.) PH eat banana 吃香蕉吧
(idi.) PH (a term of abuse) go eat shit
(罵人語)吃屎吧 : "~ *!*" "*Néih sīn
là!*("~!" "After you!") also see 0777

**hóisīn 海鮮 N seafood 海鮮 M
gān; júng**

0991
→hóisīn ga 海鮮價(lit.) price of
seafood 海鮮的價錢
(idi.) N changeable price according to
the demand of the market 根據市場
需求而作出價格的變動 : *Yàuhhaak
dō jó, jáudim ge fóng binsihng ~.* (As
more and more tourists come, the price
of the hotel rooms fluctuates as does the
price of seafood.)

0992
→yàuhséui hóisīn 游水海鮮
(lit.) swimming seafood 游泳的海鮮
(idi.) N very fresh seafood 非常新鮮
的海鮮 M dī : ⓐ *Jáugā ge yùhgōng
léuihbihn yáuh hóudō ~.* (There is a lot
of ~ in the fish tank in that restaurant.)
ⓑ *sāangmáahng ~* (~ which is still
alive) also see 0070 and 0102

**jāai 齋 N vegetarian food 齋
M dihp; go/meih; júng**

0993
→hōijāai 開齋 (lit.) break fast 破
齋
(idi.) VO win after failure(s), break a
losing streak (多次)失敗之後終於勝

利：ⓐ*B deuih hái seuhngbun chèuhng sihk gwōngdáan, hahbun chèuhng ~ la.* (Team B scored zero in the first half. It scored for the first time in the second half.) ⓑ*daih sei hyūn páai sīnji ~* (have lost 12 straight games in mahjong then win the 13th)

0994 ✓
➜jāai 齋 (lit.) N vegetarian food 齋 M dihp; go/ meih; júng
(idi.) BF exclusively, only 淨,只是： ⓐ *~ jūk* (rice porridge with no other ingredients) ⓑ*~ fē* (black coffee) ⓒ*~ tōk* (just talk [without any visual aids or entertaining performance] like in a talk show)

0995
➜sihk jāai bāyùh góng jing wah 食齋不如講正話 (lit.) it's better to say the right words than to go vegetarian 吃齋菜不如說對的話
(idi.) PH it's better to tell the truth/ have some straight talking 不如說真話：*~ā, néih gyūnchín béi chihsihn gēigwāan haih hóu, bātgwo kéuihdeih yáuh hóudō hàhngjingseuhng ge jīchēut. Néih bātyùh jihkjip jēung dī chín sīsébéi hātyī juhng hóu.* (~. It's good for you to donate money to the charities. However, they have to spend a lot of money on the running expenses. You'd better give your money to the beggars yourself.)

je 蔗 N sugar cane 甘蔗 M tiuh; lūk

0996
➜jejā báan 蔗渣板 (lit.) N boards made of fibres of crushed sugar cane 用壓了蔗汁的甘蔗纖維做的 (木)板 M faai：*Nī go gwaih ge mùhn dōu haih yuhng ~ jouh ge ja.* (The doors of this cupboard are ~.)

jīndēui 煎堆 N fried sesame seeds ball 煎堆 M go

0997
➜láahng sáu jāp go yiht jīndēui 冷手執個熱煎堆 (lit.) pick up a hot sesame seeds ball with a cold hand 冷的手拾到一個熱的煎堆
(idi.) PH encounter good opportunity unexpectedly 很意外地遇到好機會：*Kéuih yihmàhn jīhauh wúihláuh fāanlàih Hēunggóng, háifāan yíhchìhn ge hokkhaauh jouh doihfo. Dímjī go haauhjéung fātyihn séijó, haauhdúngwúi jauh chéng kéuih jouh haauhjéung, kéuih dōu syundākhaih ~ lo.* (He came back to Hong Kong after having emigrated to a foreign country. He then worked as a substitute teacher in the school he had worked in before. No one could have known that the principal died suddenly. The board of directors of the school offered him the post of principal. He could be regarded as lucky for having ~.)

0998
➜lihnmáahn jīndēui → yàhn yáuh ngóh yáuh 年晚煎堆→人有我有 (lit.) fried sesame seeds balls

at the end of the year→I want to get one just like others 新年的煎堆→別人有我也要有 (idi.) HIT do what other people would do in their secular life 做世俗人所做的事 : *Lóuhpòh, ngóhdeih bātyùh sāangfāan go bihbī, ~ → ~ ā ma.* (My darling wife, let's have a baby. Let's ~, and that's all I want.)

júng 糭/粽 N glutinous rice dumpling 糭/粽 M jek

0999

→jeukdou hóuchíh jek júng gám 着到好似隻糭嘅 (lit.) dress like a glutinous rice dumpling 穿得好像一隻糭子 (idi.) PH wrap oneself up in heavy clothes 穿了厚的衣服 : *Nīdouh dūngtīn, dungdou lihnghah yihsāamsahp douh, dī yàhn jeuk sāam ~.* (It's twenty or thirty degrees below zero here in winter, so people ~ like a ~.)

1000

→meih sihk ńghyuht júng, hòhn yī bātyahp lúhng 未食五月糭，寒衣不入櫳 (lit.) PH winter clothes should not be put in the chest before you eat the bamboo leaf dumpling of the Dragon Boat Festival 還未吃過端午節的糭子，就不要把冬天的衣服放在衣箱裏 : *M̀hóu gam faai sāumàaih dī dūngtīn sāam lā, ~, ~ ā ma!* (Don't put away the winter clothes so soon. Don't you know that ~?)

jyū 豬 N pig 豬 M jek

1001

→jyū 豬 see 0211–0241

laahtjīu 辣椒 N pepper 辣椒 M jek

1002 ✓

→laahtjīujái 辣椒仔 (lit.) N small peper 小的辣椒 M jek (idi.) N (said of a person) short but smart and sharp 短小精幹,不容易被人欺負的人 M jek : *Kéuih sēuiyìhn saisailāp, daahnhaih ~ làih ga.* (Although he is a short guy, he is like a ~.)

lìhnjí 蓮子 N lotus seed 蓮子 M lāp

1003

→lìhnjíyùhng 蓮子蓉 (lit.) lotus seeds paste (used as the main filling of mooncakes or other dessert cakes) (*People normally call it 'lìhnyùhng'.) 蓮蓉(用來作月餅或甜餅的餡料) (idi.) N very sweet smiling face 很甜的笑容 : *Kéuih yāt gindóu go syūn jauh ~ gám ge mihnháu ge la.* (Whenever he sees his grandchild, he wears a ~.)

máih 米 N rice 米 M lāp; gān

1004

→chàaih máih yàuh yìhm (jeung chou chàh) 柴米油鹽(醬醋茶) (lit.) firewood, rice, oil, salt (, sauce, vinegar and tea) 柴米油鹽(醬醋茶)

(idi.) PH (the seven) daily household necessities 每一個家庭每天的生活必需品：*Kéuih múihgo yuht ge sānséui yiu yuhnglàih gāau ngūkjōu, séuifai dihnfai, juhng yáuh ~, dōu yiu kéuih fukjaak.* (His monthly salary is used to pay the rent, the water bill and the electricity bill, and still he has to buy ~.) (*The expression can be preceded by 'hōimùhn chātgihn sih'. The two segments literally mean: when you open the door and go into a house, you need to use ~.)

1005
→dākmáih 得米 (lit.) have gotten rice 得到了米
(idi.) V attain/reach one's goal 達到目的：*Ngóh jēuijó Chàhn síujé gam noih, kéuih jēutjī yīngsihng gabéi ngóh la. Ngóh nīchi ~ la!* (I've been courting Miss Chan for such a long time, and finally she has promised to marry me. This time I get what I want.)

1006
→dóumáih 倒米 (lit.) pour out somebody else's rice (from his bowl) 把別人(碗中)的米倒出來
(idi.) V cause others to suffer loss 使別人有損失：*Dī jīkyùhn deui dī haak móuh láihmaauh, jīkhaih tùhng sihtáu ~.* (If an employee is rude to the customers, he will ruin his employer's business.)

1007
→dóumáih sauhsīng 倒米壽星

(lit.) (like) the God of Longevity throwing away rice 把米倒掉的壽星
(idi.) N one who causes others to suffer loss 使別人有損失的人 M go：*Yihgā gīngjai ṁhóu, kéuih juhng gón haak, kéuih jingyāt ~.* (Now the economy is bad here, but he still scares away the customers. He is really like ~.)

1008
→mahnmáih 問米 (lit.) ask for rice 問米
(idi.) VO go to a psychic to communicate with the dead (usually one's kinfolk) 找靈媒與鬼(通常是死去的親人)溝通：~ *pó* (a woman psychic)

1009
→máihfaahn bāanjyú 米飯班主 (lit.) rice/ meal giver 給飯別人吃的人
(idi.) N people from whom one can earn a living 可以讓你有辦法生活的人 M go：*Dī haak haih ngóhdeih ge ~ làih ga, ṁhóu dākjeuih kéuihdeih a.* (Our clients are ~. Don't make them feel bad.) (* 'Bāanjyú' is actually the operator of a Cantonese opera troupe who makes up the cast list each time a [new] play will be staged.)

1010
→ṁchau máihhei 唔嗅米氣 (lit.) not even smell the odour of rice 連米的氣味也沒聞過
(idi.) PH not have experience of life (and thus not sensible enough) 缺少人生經

驗及不通情達理： *Lēngjái lēngnéui dōu ~ ge, tùhng kéuihdeih góng gam dō jáan sāaihei jē.* (The young guys and girls do ~ and are not sensible enough. It's just a waste of time to talk to them.)

1011
→m̀pa máih gwai, ji pa wahn jaih 唔怕米貴，至怕運滯 (lit.) PH one should not be afraid of the price of rice having gone up; all one should be afraid of is bad luck 不怕米 的價錢貴，最怕是交上霉運 ： *"Sātyihp gam noih dōu meih wándóu gūng jouh, jánhaih cháam la." "Juhkyúh dōu yáuh góng, ~, ~ ā ma."* ("I've been out of work for such a long time and yet I can't find a new job. How bad!" "As the saying goes, ~, ~. Don't you know about that?")

1012
→sihkbáau mòuh yāu máih 食飽無憂米 (lit.) eat enough of carefree rice 吃飽了令人無憂無慮的米 (idi.) PH not having any worries about one's livelihood 生活無憂無慮 ： *Gūngmouhyùhn haih tit faahnwún, kéuihdeih ~, sóyíh yāt tēngginwah yiu sīyìhngfa jauh gwái saat gam chòuh.* (Civil servants all have very secure jobs and they never worry [about their jobs]. That's why they made a strong outcry on learning that [some of the] governmental departments are going to be privatized.)

1013
→yātyeuhng máih yéuhng

baakyeuhng yàhn 一樣米養百樣人 (lit.) feed different kinds of people with just one kind of rice 用一種米養不同種類的人 (idi.) PH there are different kinds of people in the world (and so do not expect them to behave like you or have the same opinion as you) 世界上有各種各樣的人(所以不能希望別人和你一樣)： *~, néih haih gám, yàhndeih meih bīt haih gám.* (~. Others may not act or think the way you do.)

ngaap 鴨 N duck 鴨子 M jek

1014
→ngaap 鴨 see 0163–0170

1015 ✓
→tihnngaap/ ngáap 填鴨 (lit.) N roast Peking duck 北京烤鴨 M jek (idi.) N students who are compelled to study as much as they can 被逼要念很多書的學生 ： *Hēunggóng ge hohksāang hóuchíh ~, kéuihdeih sauh ge gaauyuhk jauh haih ~ sīk gaauyuhk.* (Students in Hong Kong are like ~. The kind of education they receive is spoon-fed education.)

ngàuhyuhk 牛肉 N beef 牛肉 M faai; gān

1016 ✓
→ngàuhyuhkgōn 牛肉乾 (lit.) N thin dried beef 牛肉乾 M faai (idi.) N ticket issued by a traffic warden 交通警察發出的告票 M jēung : *sáudóu ~ (get a ~)*

150

pàaihgwāt 排骨 N pork ribs 排
骨 M gauh; dihp; gān

1017 ✓

➔pàaihgwāt 排骨 (lit.) N pork
ribs 排骨 M gauh; dihp; gān
(idi.) N skinny/ bony person 很瘦的
人：*saudou hóuchíh ~ gám* (~ as thin
as ~)

sāammàhnjih 三 文 治 N
sandwich 三文治 M gihn; faai; gauh

1018 ✓

➔sāammàhnjih 三 文 治 (lit.) N
sandwich 三文治 M gihn; faai; gauh
(idi.) ATT the sandwiched 夾在中間
的：*Ngóhdeih dī ~ gāaikāp, māt yéh
fūkleih dōu héungsauhmdóu.* (We
are ~ class. We don't have the
benefits entitled to the upper class and
the lower classes.)

sūnggōu 鬆糕 N Cantonese
sponge cake 粵式蛋糕 M go/
gauh

1019

➔sūnggōu hàaih 鬆糕鞋 (lit.) N
thick high-healed shoes (like
Cantonese sponge cake) 厚底高鞋
(像廣東的蛋糕) M deui; jek：*Jeuk ~
yiu síusām, hóu yùhngyih náuchān geuk.*
(You have to take care when wearing ~.
You'll very easily sprain/get injured by
twisting your ankles.)

syùhjái 薯仔 N potato 馬鈴薯 M
go; gān

1020

➔syùh 薯 (lit.) potato 馬鈴薯
(idi.) Adj. not smart 不聰明伶俐：
*Sēuiyìhn kéuih go yéung hóu ~,
daahnhaih kéuih go yàhn hóu hóu.*
(Although he doesn't look smart, he is a
good person.)

tōng 湯 N soup 湯 M wún; go

1021

➔mtōng mséui 唔湯唔水 (lit.)
neither soup nor water 不是湯也不是
水
(idi.) PH (1) do one's work halfway and
make a mess of it 工作半途而廢,變得
一團糟：*Néih jouhyéh jouhdou
yātbun jauh mjouh, yihgā ~ gám,
bīngo tùhng néih jāp sáuméih a?* (You
only ~. Who would finish it for you?)
(2) not good enough：*Dī gājéung
dāamsām yùhgwó nīgāan hohkhaauh
tēuihàhng móuhyúh gaauhohk jīhauh,
dī hohksāang ge yīngmàhn jauh wúih
bindāk ~.* (The parents are very anxious
about their children because once the
policy of teaching students in their native
language is implemented in this school,
the students' proficiency in English
might decline.)

tóng 糖 N candy, sweets 糖果 M
M lāp; bāau

1022

➔jaahn lāp tóng, siht gāan
chóng 賺粒糖，蝕間廠 (lit.) earn
a piece of candy but lose a factory 賺到
一粒糖卻虧蝕了一間工廠

(idi.) PH penny gain, thousands of pounds loss 因少失大, 賺很少蝕很多：*Búnlòih ngóh cháau gúpiu yáuh dāk jaahn ge, dímjī gāmyùhng fūngbouh yāt làih, jauh cháam lo, hàaih ~, ~.* (I would have earned some money by speculating on stocks and shares. However, my investments are worth nothing now because of the economic downturn. The saying is true that ~, ~.)

tōngyún 湯丸 **N glutinous rice ball** 湯丸 **M go/ lāp**

1023

→néuihyán tōngyún 女人湯丸 (lit.) woman's glutinous rice ball 女人吃的丸子
(idi.) N ladies' man, a man popular among ladies 得女性喜愛的男性：*Gwái gam dō néuih tùhnghohk dahkdāng dá dihnwá béi kéuih mahn gūngfo. Kéuih jing yāt ~ làih ga.* (Many girl classmates deliberately ring him up and ask him to help with their homework. He is really a ~.)

yàuh 油 **N oil** 油 **M dihk; dī; gān**

1024

→dihnggwo tòih yàuh 定過抬油 (lit.) safer than carrying oil with a pole 比用肩挑油還穩當
(idi.) PH have much confidence in 十分有把握：*Nīchi háausi, ngóh ~, yānwaih ngóh sīk daapsaai dī si tàih.* (I ~ the exam because I knew all the answers to the questions on the exam paper.)

yàuhjagwái 油 炸 鬼 **N Chinese doughnut** 油條 **M tiuh**

1025

→gaakyeh yàuhjagwái→móuh lèih fóhei 隔夜油炸鬼→冇厘火氣 (lit.) Chinese doughnut deep fried/made the previous night→the heat is all gone 昨天晚上弄好的油條→一點也不熱了
(idi.) HIT very good-tempered person who never gets angry 脾氣很好, 從不發怒的人：*Kéuih nīgo yàhn, hóuchíh ~ gám → ~. Néih laauh kéuih kéuih dōu m̀wúih nāu ge.* (He is a ~. He won't get mad even if you scold him.)

yéun 膶 **N animal liver** 動物的肝 **M go**

1026 ✓

→gāmngàhn yéun 金銀膶(lit.) N fat pork wrapped in dried and preserved pig's liver 用醃製好的乾的豬肝包著的肥豬肉 M tiuh; gān
(idi.) N Rolex watch with gold and platinum band 勞力士表的一種款式, 表帶用 K 黃金或白金做成 M go：*Kéuih daai ge ~, m̀jī haih jān dihng gá ge nē.* (I wonder if the ~ he is wearing is a real one or a fake one.)

yìhm 鹽 **N salt** 鹽 **M jah; dī**

1027 ✓

→diu yìhmséui 吊鹽水 (lit.)VO (medical) receive an intra-venous infusion (of saline), give a patient an I.V. drip 接受鹽水注射
(idi.) VO (said of factory workers)

152

have not enough work to do (and so they can only earn money little by little to support their families. This situation is just like a patient who is having a saline drip/ I.V.) 工廠工人開工不足, 錢只能一點一點的賺(如接受鹽水注射的人)：*Yihgā hóudō Hēunggóng ge gūngchóng būn séuhngheui daaihluhk, búndeih ge gūngyàhn jauh (m̀gau yéh jouh)* ~. (Nowadays, many Hong Kong factories have moved to mainland China, and the local workers ~.)

1028
→gā yìhm gā chou 加鹽加醋
(lit.) add salt and vinegar 加鹽添醋
(idi.) PH exaggerate 轉述事情時誇大：*Kéuih sìhsìh góngyéh ~ gám, seun kéuih jauh séi (fó) la.* (He always ~ in what he says. You'll be in trouble if you believe him.)

yú 魚 N fish 魚 **M tìuh; gān**

1029
→yú 魚 see 0085–0104

III. Yámsihk (eating and drinking)

**bējáu 啤酒 N beer 啤酒 M
būi; jēun; gun**

1030
→bēbē kéuih 啤啤佢 (lit.)
beer him 啤一下他
(idi.) PH let's have beer 讓我們喝
些啤酒: *Ngóhdeih deuih bō yèhngjó,
yìhgā heui sihkfaahn, ~.* (Our ball
team wins. Now we go to eat and
~.) (*'Bē', the transliteration of
'beer', is now used as a verb in
Cantonese.)

**daahm 啖 M a mouthful of
一口**

1031
→yātdaahm sātòhng
yātdaahm sí 一啖砂糖一啖屎
(lit.) (to give/ be given) a mouthful
of granulated sugar and then a
mouthful of shit (被別人餵以)一口
砂糖之後一口糞
(idi.) PH a (fake) praise followed by
a/an intended criticism 欲抑先揚,
先 假 意 稱 讚 然 後 責 備 : ⓐ
"*Kàhmyaht lóuhsai gin néih, dím a?*"
"*Kéuih béi ngóh tái kéuih sé ngóh ge
bougou.*" "*Dím a?*" "*~.*" ("Our boss
wanted to see you yesterday. What
happened then?" "He showed me the
report he wrote about me." "How
was it?" "There was ~.") ⓑ *Kéuih
góngyéh ~. Kéuih séung laauh néih
jīchìhn, wúih jaanháh néih sīn.*
(~. This is the way she talks. She

will praise you before criticizing
you.)

**haap 呷 V take a sip 吞一小
口**

1032
→haapchou 呷醋 (lit.) take a sip
of vinegar 吃醋
(idi.) VO envy, be jealous of 妒忌 :
*Màhmā jíhaih máaih yéh béi
mùihmúi wáan, gājē ~ la.* (The
mother bought a toy only for the
younger sister. The elder one ~
her.)

lōu 撈 V mix 混在一起

1033
→yùhchi lōu faahn 魚翅撈飯
(lit.) have shark's fins for rice 魚翅
下飯
(idi.) PH have a sumptuous meal
(especially for the shareholders when
the stock market is booming) 奢侈
的飯餐(尤其是股市興旺時股民吃
飯的奢侈情形) : ⓐ *Nīpáai gúsíh
gam wohng, ngóhdeih chāanchāan dōu
hóyíh ~.* (The stock market is
enjoying a boom. We can have
shark's fins for every meal.) ⓑ *Yáuh
chín jauh wah ~ jē, móuh chín jauh
sihk hàahmyùh chēngchoi lō.* (You can
~ when you are rich, but salted fish
and vegtetables when you have no
money.)

mōk 剝 V peel off, strip, shell 剝

1034

→mōk fāsāng 剝花生 (lit.) open up the shell of the peanut (and eat) 把花生剝開(來吃)
(idi.) VO be in the way of two lovers 防礙兩個情侶談戀愛 : *Yàhndeih léuhnggo paaktō, ngóhdeih m̀hóu ~, jójyuh yàhndeih lā.* (The two lovers are having a good time. We should stay away and not ~.)

sihk 食 V eat 吃

1035

→daaih sihk sai 大食細 (lit.) big eats small 大吃小
(idi.) PH the powerful ones gain advantages at the expense of the weak 強凌弱, 弱者犧牲在強者手下 : ⓐ*Gúsíh daaih héi daaih dit, haih dī daaihngohk háidouh gáaugáaujan jī ma, kéuihdeih jauh jaahn daaih chín, dī síu gúmàhn jauh sihtdou ngaai gaumehng, nīdī giujouh ~ ā ma.* (The fluctuations on the stock market were caused by those speculative tycoons. As a result, they made a lot of money, but the ordinary investors/shareholders suffered heavy losses. This is what we call ~.) ⓑ*Gógāan daaih bougún joi chēut yātjēung sān boují, séungwah ~, chéungmàaih kèihtā boují ge duhkjé.* (That big newspaper agency is publishing yet another newspaper. They are going to attract readers of other newspapers.)

1036

→joh sihk sāan bāng 坐食山崩 (lit.) sitting idle, one can eat up even a mountain (of food/ wealth) 坐吃山空
(idi.) PH one's money will be used up one day if he does not secure his own living by seeking sources of income 人不應坐著不做事, 應設法維持生活 : *Sēuiyihn kéuih yáuh jīkchūk jē, daahnhaih yùhgwó joi wánm̀dóu gūng jouh, jauh wúih ~ ge lo wo.* (Although he has some savings, he will use it up if he cannot find a new job.)

1037

→jūngjūng jihkjihk, jūngsēui hātsihk 忠忠直直，終須乞食 (lit.) PH (a sarcastic way of saying that) an honest person will end up begging on the street (諷刺的說法) 忠實的人只會做乞兒 : *"Kéuih nīgo yàhn jānhaih jūngjihk la." "Yáuh mēéh yuhng ā, ~, ~."* ("He is a very honest person." "What is the good of it? Can't you see that ~?")

1038

→jyúdoulàih jauh sihk 煮到嚟就食 (lit.) when the cooked food is given to you, you just eat it 煮好的東西放到你面前，你就把它吃了好了

155

(idi.) PH take the undesirable thing that happens/is given to you 逆來順受 : *"Gógo haak deui néihge bouhmùhn ṁmúhnyi, gīngléih yiu laauh néih bo." "~lā."* ("That client was not satisfied with your department, and our manager is going to blame you." "I'll take it as it comes.")

1039
→ngájái sihk wòhnglihn, yáuh fú jihgéi jī 啞仔食黃蓮,有苦自己知(lit.) A deaf-mute eats the bitter seeds of coptis chinensis. He has no way to express the bitterness to others. 啞巴吃黃蓮,只有他自己知道很苦
(idi.) PH suffer the ugly truth (which is better not known by others) 不想告訴別人的苦況 : *Taaitáai yìhm kéuih sung ge gitfān jāunihn geinihm ge láihmaht ṁgau mìhnggwai. Kèihsaht, kéuih gāmyaht sīnji jīdou jihgéi cháau yàuhyú, daahnhaih yauh ṁgám góngbéi taaitáai jī, jānhaih ~, ~.* (His wife didn't like the gift he bought for their wedding anniversary because it was not valuable enough. Actually, he just found out today that he had been fired, but he was afraid to tell his wife. All he could do was ~.)

1040
→ngóh sihk yìhm dōgwo néih sihk máih 我食鹽多過你食米

(lit.) the salt I ate is more than the rice you ate/ I eat salt more often than you eat rice 我吃的鹽比你吃的米多/我吃鹽比你吃米的時間多
(idi.) PH I have more experience of life than you do 我的人生經驗比你豐富 : *A mā ~. Ngóh yāt tái kéuih go yéung jauh jīdou kéuih ṁhaih hóu yàhn làih ge la,"* màhmā deui go néui góng. ("As a mother, ~. With just one look, I can tell that he is not a good man," said the mother to her daughter.)

1041
→saatsihk 煞食 (lit.) Adj. (1) attractive, appealing 吸引人,討人喜歡 : *Nīgo yuhtkehk yínyùhn ge bākpāai gūngfū jeui ~.* (The martial arts of this Cantonese opera actor is most ~ [to the audience].) (2) winning move/tactics that one is good at using 能令人取勝的 : *Nīgo móhngkàuhyùhn yuhng kéuih jeui ~ ge yātjīu, chèuhngchāu, sóyíh yèhngjó.* (The tennis player used a ~, i.e. a long distance strike, and so he won.)

1042
→saihyuhn dong sihk sāangchoi 誓願當食生菜 (lit.) take an oath is like eating lettuce 發誓就好像吃生菜
(idi.) PH (derogatory) it's so easy to swear an oath (貶義)發誓是非常容易的事 : *"Kéuih wah kéuih hóyíh saihyuhn móuh tùhnggwo daihyihgo*

néuihjái heui gāai." "*Baih joih kéuih ~ lē."* (He said he could swear an oath that he had never gone out with another girl." "But that doesn't mean anything because for him, ~.")

1043
→sānfú wánlàih jihjoih sihk 辛苦搵嚟自在食 (lit.) PH since one works hard to earn a living, one should enjoy his meals leisurely 辛苦工作賺錢, 就應該 悠閒地享用每一頓飯: *Fongga ge sihhauh hóudō Hēunggóng yàhn jūngyi heui chàhlàuh taan chàh, ~ ā ma.* (People in Hong Kong like to have tea in restaurants during holidays. [They think] ~, you know.)

1044
→sēuigā sihk méih wú 衰家 食尾糊 (lit.)PH (in mahjong) the worst player/ the player with the worst luck wins the last game (out of 16 games) (打麻將時)運氣最差的 人只在(四圈之中的)最後一次糊 出: *~, ngóh yiu jāpwái.* (I am the worst winner. I only won the last game. I want to exchange seats with you [i.e. the other three players].)

1045
→séung sihkjó yàhn jek gēui mè 想食咗人隻車咩(lit.) (you) want to eat the piece of 'chariot' (that belongs to your rival when playing a Chinese game of chess), don't you?

你想把人家的棋子 "車" 吃掉麼? (idi.) PH be overcovetous, expect to get too much from others 太貪心,想 佔人家太多便宜 : *"Kéuih séung tùhng ngóhge néui gitfān lē, jauh yiu béi yātbaak maahn láihgām, yātbaak wàih jáujihk......" "Néih ~!"* ("If he wants to marry my daughter, he has to give me one million dollars for the betrothal and one hundred tables (of food) for the banquet......" "Are you going to be that ~?")

1046 ✓
→sihk baahkgwó 食白果 (lit.)VO eat white/ empty fruit 吃白 果
(idi.) VO rewardless, without success 徒勞無功 : *Yātgo máhmàih syūsaai dī chín jīhauh wah, "Gāmyaht ~."* (A punter, after having lost all of his money, would say, "I was unsuccessful [in horse-racing] today.") (* 'Baahkgwó' actually are ginkgoes. Literally 'baahkgwó' means 'white nut', but figuratively it means 'blank result/fruitless'.)

1047
→sihk chāt gam sihk 食七咁 食(lit.) eat as those people do on the forty-ninth day (i.e. 7x7=49) after their kinfolk's death 像一個人死後 第四十九天,他的親屬吃的情形 (idi.) PH eat and drink as much as possible at a free meal 別人請客, 所以大吃大喝 : *Gāmchāan yáuh yàhn chéng, ngóhdeih yātyū ~ lo.* (Someone else will pay for this meal. Let's ~.)

1048

→ sihk daaihwohk faahn 食大鑊飯 (lit.) eat rice cooked in (the same) big wok (一起)吃用大鍋煮的飯
(idi.) PH happily exploit resources from the government 享用政府資源：*Jingfú gok bouhmùhn dōu haih ~ ge, jouhdāk hóu m̀hóu m̀sái gēng.* (All governmental departments ~. They don't have to worry at all whether they have a good performance or not.)

1049

→sihkdāk hàahmyùh dáidāk hot 食得鹹魚抵得渴 (lit.) if you eat salted fish, you are supposed to have tolerance for thirst 吃鹹的魚乾就得忍受口渴之苦
(idi.) PH be prepared to bear the consequences of what one has done 要承受自己作事的後果：*~, néih tàuhjī gam gōu fūnghím ge yéh, yiu yáuh sāmléih jéunbeih haih chèuihsih wúih siht daaih bún ge.* (~. You invest your money in high-risk items. You should be prepared for the heavy losses you would suffer.)

1050

→sihkdāk sih fūk 食得是福 (lit.) PH those who can eat a lot are blessed people 可以吃很多東西的人是有福的：*"Néih sihk gam dō yéh, m̀pa fèih àh?" "~ ā ma."* ("You eat so much. Aren't you afraid of gaining weight?" "You know ~.")

1051 ✓

→sihkfán 食粉 (lit.) VO eat rice noodles/ powder 吃粉
(idi.) VO take drugs (* 'Fán' is the short form of 'baahkfán', i.e. heroin.) 吸白粉（即海洛英）：*Hauhsāangjái móuh sāmgēi duhksyū m̀gányiu, hohk yātmùhn sáungaih dōu hóyíh wán sihk, jeui baih jauh haih ~.* (It's not something serious if youngsters do not put effort into their studies. They still can earn a living if they learn some skill. The worst thing for them to do is to ~.)

1052

→sihk gāi wú 食雞糊 (lit.) eat chicken's gruel 吃雞的米糊
(idi.) PH (in mahjong) win the least money in one game 打麻將時勝出，但是贏的錢是最少的：*Néih ~ jiht ngóh baaupàahng, néih jānhaih sēui la!* (You ~ but spoiled my grand slam [owing to your priority of taking our winning tile]. It's too bad of you!)

1053

→sihk gáu daaih gwái 食九大簋 (lit.) eat nine courses of food placed in bronze containers offered to a king 吃九道用銅器盛載的菜餚,像皇帝那樣
(idi.) PH have a sumptuous feast/banquet 參加盛宴：*Gāmmáahn yáuh yàhn chéngyám, ~.* (Somebody invited us to a banquet in a restaurant. We are going to have a ~ [like that of a king].) (*A

conventional Cantonese banquet is made up of nine main courses.)

1054

→sihk gūkjúng 食穀種 (lit.) eat one's seed corn 吃老本

(idi.) VO use one's own savings (while jobless) (失業時)要用平日的積蓄 ： *Yùhgwó joi wánm̀dóu yéh jouh, jauh yiu ~ ge la.* (I have to ~ if I still can't find a new job.) (*A Chinese farmer would reserve some of the seed corn for the next plantation after every harvest.)

1055

→sihkgwo fāan chàhm meih 食過翻尋味 (lit.) come again for the delicious food one has had before 吃過之後再來吃

(idi.) PH come again for the benefits one has had before 食髓知味 ： *"Nīgāan poutáu, seuhnggo yuht sīnji béi chaahk dágip, nīgo yuht yauh béi chaahk dágip." "Gánghaih lā, dī cháak ~ ā ma, gógāan poutáu gam yih lohksáu."* ("The shop was robbed only last month. It is robbed again this month." "Of course, the thieves ~. They found it easy to rob that shop.)

1056

→sihkgwo yeh jūk 食過夜粥 (lit.) have eaten mid-night rice gruel before 吃過夜裏的粥

(idi.) PH have learned some Chinese kungfu before 學過中國功夫 ：

Kéuih ~ ga. Néih tùhng kéuih dá wúih sihtdái ga. (He ~. You would lose if you fight with him.) (*Formerly, people would have rice gruel for a mid-night snack after practicing martial arts at their teacher's place.)

1057 ✓

→sihk ja wú 食詐糊 (lit.) the winning of mahjong turns out to be a mistake 打麻將糊錯了

(idi.)VO against one's expectation 期望錯誤,希望落空 ： ⓐ*Kéuih hóu hahn (sāang) jái, kéuih dōu yíhwàih nīchi lóuhpòh saht sāang jái, dímjī ~.* (He extremely hoped to have a son. He thought that his wife would certainly give birth to a baby boy this time. However, things just happened ~.) ⓑ*Nī kàuh sehyahp la! Dímjī kàuhjing wah yuhtwaih, m̀syun. Nīchi ~ la.* (He kicked a goal, but the referee said he kicked the ball off-sides and so the goal wouldn't count. This time he shot the ball in vain.)

1058

→sihkjó fóyeuhk 食咗火藥 (lit.) have eaten gunpowder 吃了火藥

(idi.) PH fly into a fury 非常生氣及發怒 ： *Kéuih ~ àh? Gam ngok laauh yàhn gé?* (Has he eaten gunpowder? Why is he reviling others so furiously?)

1059 ✓

→sihk lìhngmūng 食檸檬
(lit.) VO eat lemon 吃檸檬
(idi.) VO (usually said of a man) be refused by a woman either to dance with him or to go on a date (指男性)被女性拒共舞或出外 ： ⓐ *"Néih yáuh móuh yeuk kéuih heui gāai a?" "Yáuh, bātgwo ~ jē."* ("Have you tried to make a date to go out with her?" "Yes, I have, but she said no.") ⓑ *M̀jī dímgáai gāmmáahn sèhngmáahn ~.* (I don't know why the girls refused to dance with me all night tonight.)

1060

→sihk lòhsī 食螺絲 (lit.) eat screw 吃螺絲釘
(idi.) VO (said of broadcasters) make mistake when reading a script 廣播員讀錯稿 ： *Béi dōdī sìhgaan yuhbeih jauh m̀wúih ~ lā.* (More preparation will save you from ~.)

1061

→sihk m̀báau yauh ngohm̀séi 食唔飽又餓唔死 (lit.) you would not have too much to eat nor would you suffer from hunger 吃不飽又餓不死人的
(idi.) PH manage to make a living (with a moderate amount of money earned from a secure job) 工作穩定但收入中等 ： *Gaausyū nī fahn gūng, ~, daahnhaih faatdaaht jauh móuh fán lo.* (As a teacher, you can ~, but you can't get rich.)

1062

→sihk sāibāk fūng 食西北風 (lit.) eat northwest wind 吃西北風
(idi.) PH suffer from hunger, have nothing to eat 捱餓,沒東西吃 ： ⓐ *Ngóh hēimohng faaidī wándóu yéh jouh lā, yùhgwó m̀haih jauh yiu ~ ge la.* (I hope I could find a job soon. Otherwise I will ~.) ⓑ *Dī jōimàhn wah, "Yùhgwó dī lèuhngsihk juhng meih wahndoulàih, ngóhdeih gāmmáahn jauh yiu ~ ge la."* (The people who suffered from the catastrophe said, "If the food has not come yet, then we'll ~ tonight.)

1063

→sihk tàuhwùh, syū lāt fu 食頭糊，輸甩褲 (lit.)PH (in mahjong) the winner of the first game will suffer heavy losses in later games, such that even his trousers will fall off (打麻將時)第一次糊出的人後來會輸得很慘,連袜子也會脫掉 ： *~, ~, hóuchói néih sihk/ yèhng daihyāt pōu páai jē.* (~. It's lucky for me that you won the first game.)

1064

→sihk tīn wú 食天糊 (lit.) eat heavenly rice gruel 吃天上的稀飯
(idi.) VO (in mahjong) win at the very beginning of a game after one has gotten all the tiles right (打麻將)遊戲一開始時已拿了全對的牌,所以贏了 ： *Nī pōu páai, kéuih ~.* (In this game, he ~.)

1065

➜sihk tōháai faahn 食拖鞋飯
(lit.) eat slippers rice 吃拖鞋飯
(idi.) PH same as 1070

1066

➜sihkwú 食糊 (lit.) eat rice
congee 吃米糊
(idi.)VO win a game of mahjong 打
麻將糊／贏了 ： *Kéuih dájó seigo
hyūn (páai) sīnji ~ yātpōu ~.* (He
only won one game within the four
rounds/ out of sixteen games.)

1067

➜sihk wún mín, fáan wún dái
食碗面，反碗底 (lit.) after
having eaten a bowl of rice, one turns
the bowl upside down 吃完飯,把碗
反過來(使碗底朝天)
(idi.) PH ungrateful 忘恩負義 ：
*Kéuih yáuh laahn gójahnsí ngóh
bōng kéuih. Yihgā kéuih gíngyihn
wah ngóh ṁhóu, jingyāt ~, ~.* (I took
care of him when he was in
adversity. How could I have known
that he would criticize me now. He is
~ [to me].)

1068

➜sihk yàhn ṁlēu gwāt 食人
唔嘟骨 (lit.) suck a man down
without spitting his bones 吃人但
不把他的骨吐出來
(idi.) PH take advantage of others
relentlessly 毫不留情地奪取別人
的利益 ： ⓐ *Gódī daaihyíhlūng,
jingyāt ~, néih je síusíu chín jauh yiu*

wàahn géisahp púih. (The loan sharks
~. Although you borrow only a
small amount of money from them,
you still have to return ten times the
amount to them.) ⓑ *Godī
deihcháansēung jingyāt ~ ge, yātchek
jauh yiu maaih sèhng maahn ngàhn.*
(The property merchants ~. They
sell a flat for almost ten thousand
dollars per square foot.)

1069

➜sihk yèh faahn, jeuk lá yī
食爺飯，著嫲衣 (lit.) eat the rice
(given) by father, wear the clothes
(made) by mother 吃爸爸(給)的飯，
穿媽媽(做)的衣服
(idi.) PH (said of children) be well
supported by parents 有父母好好供
養的子女 ： *Yihgā dī hauhsāangjái,
~, ~, bīndouh jīdou fuhmóuh wán
chín gāannàahn ā?* (Nowadays, the
youngsters are ~. They rarely know
that their parents have to work very
hard to support them.)

1070

➜sihk yúhn faahn 食軟飯
(lit.) eat soft rice 吃軟的飯
(idi.) PH live on the earnings of
one's wife/girlfriend who is a
prostitute 依賴妻子或女友賣淫為
生 ： *Nīgo nàahmyán jānhaih jihngaak,
~.* (This man is really very mean.
He ~.)

1071

➜tái sung sihk faahn 睇餸食

161

飯 (lit.) take a look at the (number of) dishes/ how much food there is while eating rice/ a meal 一面吃飯一面看看有多少菜

(idi.) PH use money carefully according to the budget/ one's income 量入爲出 : *Ngóhdeih ge gīngfai yáuhhaahn, ngóhdeih yiu ~, m̀hóu lyuhn sái chín.* (We only have limited funds. We should ~ and should not spend money at random.)

1072
➔ tùhng tòih sihkfaahn, gokjih sāuhàhng 同檯食飯，各自修行 (lit.) although people eat at the same table, everyone of them practices his own religious rules 就算是在同一張桌子吃飯,每個人都自己修行

(idi.) PH (1) people in the same group have little interaction with one another 同一個團體內的人沒有交流 : *Sēuiyihn hái tùhngyātgāan hohkhaauh gaausyū, daahnhaih dī sīnsāang dōu haih ~, ~ ge.* (There is very little interaction between the teachers though they teach at the same school.) (2) mind your own business 不要理會別人怎樣做 : ~, ~, *néih m̀hóu léih yàhndeih gam dō lā.* (~, and don't interfere in other people's affairs.)

yám 飲 V drink, eat (soup)
喝, 吃 (湯)

1073
➔ yám tàuh daahm tōng 飲頭

啖湯 (lit.) take the first sip of the soup 喝第一口湯
(idi.) PH be the first to gain advantage 比別人先得到好處 : *Jóu géi nìhn maaih pòuhtāat ge poutáu ~, yìhgā sīnji maaih ge poutáu jíhaih séuiméih.* (The [cake] shops that started to sell Portugese egg tarts a few years ago had made money from them. Those who start to do this business now will find that it is the end of the prime time of this profit-making business.)

IV. Meihdouh (tastes)

fú 苦 Adj. bitter 苦

1074 ✓
→fú 苦(lit.)Adj. bitter 苦
(idi.) Adj. hard, difficult 艱苦,困
難 : *sāngwuht hóu* ~ (lead a ~ life)

1075
→hàahmfú 鹹苦(lit.) salty and
bitter 鹹跟苦
(idi.) N hardships in life 生活的艱
苦 : *m̀ngàaihdāk* ~ (cannot endure
~)

hàahm 鹹 Adj. salty, salted 鹹

1076
→bun hàahm bun táahm 半鹹
半淡 (lit.) half salty and half
insipid 一半鹹一半淡
(idi.) PH (usually said of accent) not
accurate enough in speaking a new
language or dialect, less than perfect
說一種新的語言說得不夠正確 :
Kéuih góng Jūngmàhn góngdāk ~
gám, hóu hóusiu. (His less than perfect
Chinese is very amusing to us.)

1077 ✓
→hàahm 鹹 (lit.) Adj. salty,
salted 鹹
(idi.) BF pornographic, erotic 色情
的 : ~ *syū/ dáai* (~ books/ videos)

1078
→hàahmsāp 鹹濕 (lit.) salty
and wet 又鹹又濕

(idi.) Adj. (said of a man) nasty, dirty
男人好色 : *Yàhn bīk ge deihfōng,
yiu síusām dī* ~ *lóu a.* (You need to be
aware of those ~ guys in crowded
places.)

1079
→m̀hàahm m̀táahm 唔鹹唔
淡 (lit.) neither salty nor insipid 不
鹹不淡
(idi.) see 1076

hēung 香 Adj. fragrant, good smell 香

1080 ✓
→hēung 香 (lit.) Adj. fragrant,
good smell 香
(idi.) V (1) fail 失敗 : *Jóyihk daaih
geuk yāt seh, táibaahk sehyahp ge la,
dímjī* ~ *jó.* (The left wing makes a
high kick. Obviously he should have
scored a goal, but he didn't.) (2) lose
the game 比賽輸了 : *Nījek máh
yātlouh dōu líhngsīn, dímjī làhm méih
~, jauhlàih dou jūngdím ge sihhauh béi
daihyih jek máh gwojó.* (This horse is
leading all the way, but it ~ in the
end. It is overtaken by another horse
when it is very close to the winning
post.)

laaht 辣 Adj. hot, spicy 辣

1081 ✓
→laaht 辣 (lit.) Adj. hot, spicy
辣

(idi.) Adj. cruel, drastic 毒辣, 狠毒 : *Hāak séhwúi deuifuh yàhn ge sáudyuhn haih hóu ~ ge.* (The triads take ~ measures to deal with their enemies.)

1082
➔sēunglaaht 雙辣 (lit.) doubly spicy 雙倍的辣
(idi.) N (in mahjong) double perfect score (打麻將)大滿貫 : *sihk ~* (win the ~)

1083
➔yáuh laaht yáuh m̀laaht 有辣有唔辣 (lit.) some are spicy and some are not 有些辣有些不辣
(idi.) PH there are advantages and disadvantages (in doing one thing) 做一件事有好處也有壞處 : *Yihmàhn lē, ~. Ngoihgwok haih yáuh dōdī màhnjyú, daahnhaih yihk yáuh hóudō yàhn sātyihp.* (~ in emigrating to other places. Although you can enjoy more democracy in foreign countries, you will also find that many people are unemployed.)

meih 味 N taste, smell 味道, 氣味 M júng; jahm/ buhng

1084
➔wòhmeih 和味 (lit.) harmonious in flavour 味道調和
(idi.) Adj. (when talking about a large sum of money) terrific, fantastic (指一筆可觀的錢)不得了, 太好了 : ⓐ *Kéuih jēung bāt*

teuiyāugām chyùhnyahp ngàhnhòhng sāu leihsīk, múihgo yuht yáuh maahn géi yihmaahn mān, dōu géi ~. (He'll get ten or twenty thousand dollars of monthly interest from the pension he deposited in the bank. ~!) ⓑ *Nī kèih Luhkhahpchói ge leuihjīk jéunggām yáuh sāmchīngéi maahn, yíngjān ~.* (The accumulated dividend of this time's Mark Six jackpot is over thirty million dollars. It's really ~.)

syūn 酸 Adj. sour 酸

1085 ✓
➔syūn 酸 (lit.) Adj. sour 酸
(idi.) Adj. (1) sad, sorrowful 難過 : *sām ~* see 0671 (2) sore 酸痛 : ⓐ *Yāt fāanfūng lohkyúh, ngóh jauh yīu ~ bui tung ge la.* (I'll have a pain in my back on windy or rainy days/ whenever the weather is bad.) ⓑ *yuhksyūn* see 0850

táahm 淡 Adj. plain, insipid, not savoury enough 淡, 味道不濃

1086 ✓
➔táahm 淡 (lit.) Adj. plain, insipid, not savoury enough 味道淡
(idi.) Adj. lose interest, be indifferent 失去興趣 : ⓐ *Gīnggwo gam dō bāthahng ge sih jīhauh, kéuih jouh yàhn jouhdou ~ saai.* (After having suffered so much misfortune, he found that life didn't mean much to him.) ⓑ *Kéuih yíhchìhn hóu jūngyi sipyíng ge, yihgā ~ jó lo.* (He liked

taking pictures very much before. But now he ~ in it.) © *sām* ~ see 0672

tìhm 甜 Adj. sweet 甜

1087 ✓

→tìhm 甜 (lit.) Adj. sweet 甜
(idi.) Adj. (lovely) sweet 可愛 : ⓐ
go yéung hóu ~ (look ~) ⓑ *siudāk hóu* ~ (have a ~ smile)

1088

→tìhm syūn fú laaht 甜酸苦辣 (lit.) sweet, sour, bitter and spicy 甜酸苦辣
(idi.) PH the pleasures and hardships in life 生命中快樂跟痛苦的事 : *Ngóh dōu géisahp seui yàhn lo, mātyéh ~ dōu ngàaihgwo lā.* (I'm old now. I have experienced all ~.)

5. Culture

I. Gaauyuhk (education)

duhksyū 讀書 VO study (with books), attend school, receive education 念書, 上學, 受教育

1089
➔duhk séi syū, séi duhksyū, duhksyū séi 讀死書, 死讀書, 讀書死 (lit.) PH not know how to apply what one learns, study by rote learning and there's no future for one's studying hard 讀死書, 死讀書, 讀書死 (*~, ~, ~ are criticisms on students who are the victims of the education system of Hong Kong.) : *Hēunggóng ge hohksāang ~, ~, ~.* (The students in Hong Kong do ~, ~ and ~.)

1090
➔duhk sípín 讀屎片(lit.) study diapers 念尿布
(idi.) VO (a term of abuse at students or scholars) what damn books you have studied! 念甚麼鬼書來！ : *Néih sauhgwo gam dō gaauyuhk dōu juhng jouh waaih sih, néih ~ lā néih.* (You have been well educated but you still do evil things. ~!)

1091
➔duhkwaaih sīsyū 讀壞詩書 (lit.) one has studied poetry and books and yet is bad (in one's behaviour) 念了詩和書本,行為卻不好

(idi.) PH well educated but bad in conduct 雖受高深教育,但品行差 : *Yáuhdī jūnghohksāang yauh sihkyīn yauh hái chīukāp síhchèuhng tāuyéh, jānhaih ~.* (Some secondary school students smoke and steal in supermarkets. They are~.)

1092
➔pùih taaijí duhksyū 陪太子讀書 (lit.) accompany the crown prince and study with him 陪太子念書
(idi.) PH join one's superior or beloved one(s) in doing something 參與上司或所愛的人要做的事 : ⓐ "*Dímgáai néih làih máhchèuhng a?*" "*Ngóh ~ jē. Ngóh lóuhsai yiu làih ā ma!*" ("How come you are here at the race course?" "I just follow my boss. He wants to come.") ⓑ *Yìhgā dī saimānjái duhksyū, fuhmóuh juhng gánjēung, yáuhsìh dōu yiu duhkmàaih yātfahn, jing sówaih ~.* (Nowadays, parents are anxious about their children's studies so much that sometimes they have to study together with them. It's just as the saying goes, ~.)

1093
➔tīnsyū 天書(lit.) heavenly book 天書

(idi.) N a book showing you the keys to success 一本教你取得成功的書 M bún/bouh ： *wuihháau* ~ (~ in the HKCEE, also see 0506)

1094
→yāt mihng yih wahn sāam fūngséui, sei jīk yāmgūng ńgh duhksyū 一命二運三風水，四積陰功五讀書 (lit.) destiny comes first, luck second, geomancy third, to do good deeds without being known fourth, and to study (books) fifth 一命二運三風水,四積陰功五讀書
(idi.) PH although one's lot is predestined, yet one can still make good in life by being benevolent or receiving education 命運好不好是上天註定,但人爲因素如行善及接受教育,也可以改善命運 ： *Néih séung yáuh hóu ge chìhntòuh àh? Duhk dōdī syū lā, ~, ~ ā ma.* (You want to have a good future?! Put more effort into your studies and study more because ~, ~.)

1095
→yātbún tūngsyū táidou lóuh 一本通書睇到老 (lit.) read/ use the same Chinese almanac/ calendar till one's old age 一本通書用到老
(idi.) PH fail to be flexible (in doing things in sticking to old principles too much) 做人墨守成規,不夠靈活 ： *Ṁtùhng ge hohksāang jauh yiu yuhng ṁtùhng ge gaaufaat, ṁhóu ~,*

wíhngyúhn dōu yuhng yātgo gaaufaat. (You should use various teaching methods when teaching different kinds of students. Try to be flexible and not to use the same old method all the time.)

fahohk 化學 N chemistry 化學

1096 ✓
→fahohk 化學 (lit.) N chemistry 化學
(idi.) Adj. fragile, feeble, not durable 脆弱,不耐用 ： ⓐ *Nīdī yéh yuhng léuhng yuhng jauh laahn, jānhaih ~ la.* (These things broke after I used them one or two times. They are really ~.) ⓑ *Jouh yàhn jānhaih ~ la. Kéuih chìhnyaht juhng hóudeihdeih ge, gāmyaht jauh dēngjó la.* (Life is so ~ ! Everything was fine with him two days ago, but he died today.)

fō 科 N/M subject, course; measure for a subject/ course 科目;科目的量詞

1097
→gáau bīnfō a 攪邊科呀 (lit.) what subject/ course are you meddling in? (你)攪甚麼科目？
(idi.) PH what the hell are you doing/ going to do/ do you want? ： *Néihdeih bāan yéh kàhmyaht jínglaahn ngóhdeih poutáu ge mùhn, gāmyaht yauh làih ~?* (You damn guys broke the door of my shop yesterday, and ~ today?)

→síuyìhfō 小兒科 (lit.) N pediatrics 小兒科

(idi.) N very simple thing to do 很簡單的技倆 : *Daaih chyùhsī wúih gokdāk jīndáan haih ~ jē.* (A chef would think that to fry an egg is a ~.) Adj. (1) very simple (and not requiring any skill) 簡單又不需要甚麼技巧 : *Faatyìhngsī wah sáitàuh haih hóu ~ jē.* (A hair designer would say that to wash one's hair is ~.) (2) not a big deal, nothing serious 不算很嚴重 : *Néihdeih gódouh yihkāp deihjan, ~ lā, ngóhdeih nīdouh chātkāp a.* (You had an earthquake measuring two [on the Richter scale] in your place, it's ~. We had one measuring seven here.)

gīng 經 BF classic books 經書

1099 ✓

→sāam jih gīng 三字經 (lit.) N the three-character primer (*Formerly it was the first book Chinese children were supposed to study.) 三字經 (以前中國小孩第一本要念的書) M bún/ bouh

(idi.) N foul language 粗言穢語 M dī : *Tái kéuih ngoihbíu sīmàhn, dímjī yāt chēutháu jauh góng ~.* (He looks like a well cultured person. How could I have known that he starts his speech with ~.)

gīngjai 經濟 N economics, economy 經濟

→gīngjai 經濟 (lit.) N economics, economy 經濟

(idi.) Adj. economical, money saving 省錢 : *Heui daaih chāantēng sihk gánghaih gwai lā, heui faaichāandim sihk maih ~ dī lō.* (It is certainly expensive to eat in a big restaurant. We can economize if we go to a fastfood shop.)

séjih 寫字 VO write (Chinese characters) 寫字

1101

→ m̀jī go cháu jih dím sé 唔知個醜字點寫 (lit.) not know how to write the character for 'shame' 不懂寫 '醜' 字

(idi.) PH shameless 不知羞恥 : *Yìhchìhn yùhgwó néuihjái jēui làahmjái, dī yàhn jauh wúih wah go néuihjái ~.* (In the past, if a girl chased after a boy, people would criticize her and said that she was ~.)

1102

→yāt jih gam chín 一字咁淺 (lit.) as easy as the Chinese character for 'one' 像 '一' 字那麼容易

(idi.) PH as easy as ABC 非常淺易 : *Kéuih dímgáai bōng néih? ~ lā, kéuih séung néih bōngfāan kéuih jī ma.* (Why did he help you? It's very easy to understand. He just wants you to help him in return.)

sī 詩 N poem, poetry 詩 M sáu

1103

→suhk duhk Tòhngsī sāam baak sáu, m̀wúih yàhm sìh yáh wúih tāu 熟讀唐詩三百首，唔會吟時也會偷 (lit.) PH if you study hard the three hundred selected poems of the Tang Dynasty (618 – 907 A.D.), you can easily write a poem by picking some lines from them even though it is not your own work 把唐詩三百首都讀熟了,就算真的不會吟詩,也會隨口念幾句 : *~, ~, jokmán dōu haih yātyeuhng, néih tái dōdī jauh wúih sédāk hóu ge la.* (~, ~. This is the same case with writing compositions. You must read more before you can write well.)

1104

→yàhmsī dōu yàhmm̀lāt 吟詩都吟唔甩 (lit.) even though you recite poems, you can't escape 吟詩也不能逃避

(idi.) PH see 0259

siuwá 笑話 N joke 笑話 M go

1105 ✓

→siuwá 笑話 (lit.) N joke 笑話 M go

(idi.) PH it's ridiculous, it's too absurd 太可笑了,豈有此理 : *~ ! Ngóh haih lóuhbáan, ngóh yiu tēng néih wah!* (~ ! I am the boss and [do you mean] I have to listen to you!)

waahk 劃 M a stroke of a Chinese character 劃

1106

→sahp waahk dōu meih yáuh yāt pit 十劃都未有一撇 (lit.) not a stroke out of ten (of a Chinese character) is drawn 十劃的字一劃也還未寫得出來

(idi.) PH it's far too early to predict the accomplishment of a task 太早說／預期事情的成果 : *"Néih géisí póuh syūn a?" "Héih! ~. Ngóhge jái gitfān móuh géi nói jī ma."* ("When will you have a grandchild?" "Oh, it's far too soon for me to tell. My son just got married not long ago.")

yùhnjí 原子 N atom 原子 M lāp/ go

1107 ✓

→yùhnjí 原子(lit.)N atom 原子 M lāp

(idi.) ATT new product of the 1960's 一九六零年代的新產品 : ⓐ ~ *bāt* (ball-point pen) ⓑ ~ *lāp sāuyāmgēi* (transistor radio) ⓒ ~ *maht* (stretch socks)

II. Màhnyùh (recreation)

báan 板 N beat of Chinese operatic songs 中國戲曲的節拍 **M go**

1108 ✓

➡ johngbáan 撞 板 (lit.) VO sing to the wrong beat/out of rhythm when singing Cantonese operatic songs 唱粵曲走板

(idi.) VO run into trouble 產生麻煩 ﹕ *Kéuih nīgo yàhn hóu leuhnjeuhn, giu kéuih jouhyéh jauh ~ dōgwo sihkfaahn.* (He is a clumsy person. He ~ more often than he eats.)

cheunggō 唱 歌 VO sing (songs) 唱歌

1109 ✓

➡ cheung 唱 (lit.) V sing 唱

(idi.) V speak ill of someone 說人壞話 ﹕ ⓐ *Kéuih jáuwàih ~ kéuihge lóuhbáan hóu hāakbohk.* (He told everybody that his boss was very mean to them.) ⓑ *Yùhgwó ngóhdeihge fo yáuh mahntàih, jauh yātdihng yiu teuifāan chín béi yàhn, yùhgwó m̀haih, jauh wúih béi yàhn ~ ge la.* (If there's something wrong with the things we sell, we must give the money back to the customers. Otherwise, we'll be criticized by them and lose our good reputation.)

1110

➡ cheunghóu 唱 好 (lit.) sing well 唱得好

(idi.) RV say something good about 說好話 ﹕ ~ *gúsíh* (~ the stock market)

1111

➡ cheungsēui 唱 衰 (lit.) sing badly 唱得差

(idi.) RV bad-mouth, say something bad about , speak ill of 說壞話 ﹕ ~ *Hēunggóng* (~ Hong Kong/ give a negative report on Hong Kong)

1112 ✓

➡ m̀ngāam kī 唔啱 key (lit.) PH sing out of tune 唱歌走音

(idi.) PH cannot get along well with each other 不咬絃 , 合不來 ﹕ *Kéuihdeih léuhnggo dōu ~ ge, néih giu kéuihdeih hahpjok jáan sāaihei jē.* (The two of them ~. It's a waste of time for you to ask them to work together.)

1113

➡ móuh nījī gō(jái) cheung 冇呢枝歌(仔)唱 (lit.) there's no such song for you to sing/ nobody sings this song anymore 沒有這首歌的了／人們不唱這歌了

(idi.) PH there's no such a good thing any more 再沒有那麼好的事了 ﹕ *Yíhchìhn sóyáuh gūngmouh yùhn dōu haih tit faahnwún, daahnhaih yihgā ~ lo, yānwaih jingfú yiu yuhng hahpyeukjai.* (Before, civil servants would rarely be fired. They had very secure jobs. But ~ because new civil servants are employed on contract.)

dék 笛 N flute 笛子 M jī

1114

→ m̀ tēng kéuih jī dék 唔聽佢枝笛 (lit.) not listen to his flute (but just sing your own way) 不聽他吹的笛子(只管自己唱)
(idi.) PH not listen to (the advice of) a certain person (but just do it one's own way) 不聽某人的說話只管自己做：Kéuih giu yàhn m̀ hóu máaih gójek sān gú (piu), daahnhaih dī yàhn ~, gitgwó siht daaih bún. (He told others not to buy the new stocks, but they did not listen to him. As a result, they lost a lot of money.)

hòhchē 合尺 N musical notes of Cantonese operatic songs 粵曲的音名

1115

→ hahpsaai hòhchē 合晒合尺 (lit.) sing the notes (of an operatic song) correctly 把(戲曲的)歌的音調都唱對了
(idi.) PH entirely satisfy one's demands, to one's liking, really one's cup of tea, 全合心意：Néih séung wán gāan ngūk yauh yiu pèhng jōu yauh yiu jihng yauh yiu gāautūng fōngbihn, nīgāan jauh ~ lā. (You want to rent a flat which is cheap, quiet, and convenient. This one can ~.)

kūk 曲 N songs (especially Chinese operatic songs) 歌曲 (尤指中國戲曲裏的歌曲) M sáu/ jī/ jek

1116

→ kūk bāt lèih háu (, kyùhn bāt lèih sáu) 曲不離口(，拳不離手) (lit.) songs should not stay away from one's mouth (and fist boxing, one's hands) 曲不離口(,拳不離手)
(idi.) PH (in singing) practice makes perfect (,which is the same with fist-boxing) 多練習才唱得好(, 拳術也是一樣)：Néih séung cheunggō cheungdāk hóu, jauh yiu sìhsìh lihn jaahp sīn ji dāk, hōigóng dōu yáuh wah ~ ā ma. (If you want to sing well, you need to practise very often. People always say ~. You should know that.)

1117

→ lātkūk 甩曲 (lit.) off the song 脫了曲
(idi.) VO (in singing operatic songs) forget the word(s) or lag behind the note(s)/ music 忘了歌詞或追不上拍子音樂(尤指戲曲)：Daaih lóuhgūn sèhngyaht ~, yáuh móuh gáau cho a. (The famous opera actor often ~. He should not have sung so badly.)

póu 譜 N musical score 歌譜 M go

1118

→ lèihpóu 離譜 (lit.) deviate from/ not follow the score while singing 唱歌時不跟著歌譜去唱

(idi.) VO/ Adj. unreasonable, ridiculous 不合道理 : *Kéuih yahtyaht fāangūng chìhdou jóuteui ~ saai daaih ~/ jānhaih hóu ~.* (Every day he comes to office late and leaves early. He's gone too far [for not following the office hours].)

1119 ✓

➔ **móuh póu** 冇譜 (lit.) PH (sing) without a score (唱歌但)沒有歌譜
(idi.) PH/ Adj. (said of a person) unreliable (for lacking general principles of life) 指人不可靠因爲缺乏普通做人的原則 : *Kéuih jānhaih ~ ge, chìhjó sèhng go jūngtàuh juhng meih dou.* (He is really ~. He is over an hour late and yet he hasn't come.)

tàahn 彈 V play musical instruments 彈奏樂器

1120

➔ **daahngālóu dájiu→móuh tàahn** 蛋家佬打醮→冇(壇→)彈 (lit.) the boat people have a religious service to offer deliverance to the ghosts→they don't need an altar 水上人家舉行宗教活動超渡亡魂→他們不需要祭壇
(idi.) HIT perfect, there is no complaint 沒有瑕疵,十分好 : *Gógāan jáugā ge choi tùhng dī fógei, jānhaih ~ → ~.* (The food and the service at that restaurant are ~.) (*A pun is made on 壇 [altar] and 彈 [criticize]. Both of them are pronounced '*tàahn*'.)

1121

➔ **sīk tàahn m̀sīk cheung** 識彈唔識唱 (lit.) only know how to play a musical instrument but not know how to sing 只會彈奏樂器,不會唱
(idi.) PH criticize others (for doing something badly) but cannot do it oneself 只會批評別人做得不好,自己卻不會做 : *Sèhngyaht wah ngóh jyúsung m̀hóusihk, ~, néih jyúbéi ngóh tái ā.* (You always say that I can't cook well. You just ~. Why don't you make a dish yourself [and let's see if it's good]?)

1122 ✓

➔ **tàahn** 彈 (lit.) V play a musical instrument with fingers 彈奏樂器
(idi.) V criticize 批評 : ⓐ *Yáuh yàhn ~ gógo gōsīng cheunggō m̀sīk táuhei.* (Some people criticize that singer's breathing techniques.) ⓑ *Kéuih ~ ngóh jyú sung (jyúdāk) m̀hóusihk.* (He ~ me that I couldn't cook well.)

1123

➔ **yáuh jaan móuh tàahn** 有讚冇彈 (lit.) PH just give praise and no criticism 只有讚賞,沒有批評 : ⓐ *Tàihhéi nīgo hohksāang, gogo sīnsāang dōu ~.* (All the teachers would ~ to this student when talking about him.) ⓑ *Lóuhbáan deui néihge gaiwaahk ~.* (Our boss ~ to your project.)

1124

→yáuh tàahn móuh jaan 有彈
有讚 (lit.) PH just criticize and give
no praise 只有批評,沒有讚賞 :
*Kéuih nīgo yàhn hóu yīmjīm ge,
mātyéh dōu ~.* (He is always so
critical. He ~ to everything.)

1125

→yáuh tàahn yáuh jaan 有彈
有讚 (lit.) PH criticize and also
praise 有批評也有讚賞 :
*"Lóuhbáan deui ngóhge gūngjok dím
a?" "~ lā."* ("What does our boss
think about my work?" "He ~.")

**taaigihk 太極 N Chinese
shadow boxing, tai chi 太極拳
M tou**

1126 ✓

→sá taaigihk 耍太極 (lit.) VO
play shadow boxing 打太極拳
(idi.) VO refuse implicitly/indirectly
婉拒,推搪 : *Giuchān kéuih gyūnchín
kéuih dōu ~.* (Every time I ask him
to donate money, he ~.)

**tiumóuh 跳舞 VO dance 跳
舞**

1127 ✓

→tiu chóukwàhn móuh 跳草
裙舞 (lit.) VO dance hula hula 跳
呼拉舞
(idi.) VO refuse to give a prompt
promise and try to act peevishly 不立
刻答應並鬧彆扭 : *Gógo néuih
ngaihyùhn chíhjyuh yìhgā daaih hùhng,*

*sóyíh dihnsih gūngsī giu kéuih juhkyeuk
gójahnsí kéuih jauh daaih ~.* (Relying
on the fact that she is extremely
popular now, that lady artist ~ when
the TV company asked her to renew
her contract.)

**wá 畫 N picture, painting,
drawing 畫,圖畫 M fūk/ jēung**

1128 ✓

→wuhnwá 換畫 (lit.) VO
(said of cinemas) change to a new
movie 戲院上映新的電影
(idi.) VO have a new boy/ girlfriend
有了新的男／女朋友 : *Kéuih nīgo
yàhn hóu fāsām, hóu faai jauh ~ ge la.*
(He is like a playboy. He always ~.)

**yāmngohk 音樂 N music 音樂
M sáu/ jī/ jek; dī**

1129

→chìuhjāu yāmngohk→jihgéi
gu jihgéi 潮州音樂→自己顧
自己 (lit.) Swatowese music→ (it
sounds like saying that) one looks
after oneself 潮州音樂→(聽起來像
說)自己照顧自己
(idi.) HIT (1) go Dutch 各人攤分費
用 : *"Nī chāan bīngo chéng a?"
"Móuh a, ~ → ~."* ("Who is going to
pay for our meal?" "No one. We
have to ~.") (2) you have to take
care of yourself (since there is no
one who can give you help) 要自己
獨自處理事情(因為沒有其他人可
以幫忙) : *Nīpáai gogo dōu mòhng,
jing sówaih ~ → ~, jauhsyun néih*

gūngfo yáuh mahntàih, dōu móuh yàhn hóyíh bōng néih. (Everyone has been busy recently. ~. Even if you have problems with your studies, no one can help you.)

III. Gwaaiyih kahp Seunyéuhng (spiritual beings and beliefs)

baatgwa 八卦 **N the Eight Trigrams** 八卦

1130 ✓

➔baatgwa 八卦 (lit.) N the Eight Trigrams 八卦

(idi.) Adj. nosy, curious to know about others' secrets 愛理別人閒事 : ⓐ *Yàhndeih jouh mèéh gwāan néih mèéh sih jē, m̀hóu gam ~ lā.* (What others have done has nothing to do with you. Don't be so ~.) ⓑ *~ jaaphjī* (gossip magazine) N an eight-trigram charm 爲風水迷信而懸掛的八卦(鏡) M go : *Fūngséui sīfú wah ngóhdeih yiu gwa go ~ hái mùhnháu dóng saat.* (The geomancy expert advised us to hang ~ on the main door to resist the evil forces [that came towards us/ our house].) (* 'Baatgwa' is a kind of charm used by Chinese to ward off evil. It is a small octagonal tablet on which are carved or painted the eight trigrams. A mirror in the middle of it is believed to have magical power to reflect evil back to its source.)

1131

➔baatgwa pó/ baatpòh 八卦婆 / 八婆 (lit.) eight-trigram woman 八卦婆娘

(idi.) N nosy and gossipy women 愛理別人閒事及說人是非的女人 M go : *Ngóhdeih sāanmàaih mùhn sīnji góng, yùhgwó béi dī ~ tēngdóu jauh baih la.* (Let us close the door before

we talk about it. It would be bad if we are overheard by those ~.)

1132

➔bingwa 變卦 (lit.) change (the arrangement of) the trigrams 變卦

(idi.) VO (1) change one's mind 改變主意 : *Kéuih yīngsihng tùhng ngóhdeih hahpjok, yihgā yauh ~.* (He has promised to cooperate with us, but now he ~.) (2) change something already planned 改變已定好的計劃 : *Búnlòih dihnghóu ge gaiwaahk yihgā yáuh bingwa la.* (Our well-made plan has to be changed.)

chìhnsai 前世 **N the previous life** 前生

1133

➔chìhnsai m̀sāu 前世唔修 (lit.) fail to do good deeds/ be ascetic in one's previous life 前生沒有行善／修行

(idi.) PH Oh, it's too bad/ Oh, how tragic! 噢,真慘 : *Kéuih jānhaih ~ lo, gajeuhk go gám ge lóuhgūng.* (~ ! Why did she marry such a man [in this life? Had she done something bad in her previous life?])

faht 佛 **N Buddha** 佛祖

1134

➔faht dōu yáuh fó 佛都有火 (lit.) even Buddha has fire 連佛也火了

(idi.) PH even people of very good temper are made angry 連脾氣最好的人也不能忍受,也火了: *Chau saimānjái sēuiyihn wah yiu yáuh noihsing jē, daahnhaih yáuhsih jānhaih ~.* (People say that you need to have much patience to take care of your children, but sometimes ~.)

1135
→ *gáauchēut go daaihtàuh faht* 攪出個大頭佛 (lit.) come up with a big head Buddha 弄出一個大頭的佛
(idi.) PH turn something into a blunder 把事情攪得一塌糊塗: *Kéuih gáau pāattih ~. Kéuih dehng gódaat deihfōng yùhnlòih yíhgīng yáuh yàhn dehngjó. Dī sihkmaht heiséui yauh sungjó làih, yihgā m̀jī dím hóu.* (He made a blunder in organizing the party. It turned out that the place had already been booked by someone else, and now all the food and drinks have been sent here. We don't know what to do about this.)

1136
→ *m̀tái jāng mihn dōu tái faht mihn* 唔睇僧面都睇佛面 (lit.) even if you don't look at the monk's face, you shoud look at Buddha's face 不看僧臉看佛臉
(idi.) PH do someone a favour either for the sake of A or B 不看在甲的份上,也看在乙的份上: *Néih bōngháh ngóh lā! Ngóh tùhng néih bàhbā tùhng néih lóuhbáan dōu haih hóu pàhngyáuh, néih ~ ā.* (Please help me! I am a good friend of your father and your boss. You ~.)

1137
→ *múhn tīn sàhn faht* 滿天神佛 (lit.) gods and Buddhas are all there in heaven 滿天神佛
(idi.) PH things turn out to be upheavals and chaos 事情變得一團糟: *Ngóhdeih bōng kéuih gáau yíncheungwúi. Kéuih yātsih yauh wah gói yahtkèih, yātsih yauh wah gói deihdím, yihgā yauh wah yiu wuhn ngohkdéui, béi kéuih gáaudou ngóhdeih ~.* (We organized a concert for him. But then he said he would change the date. Later he said he would change the place, and now he said he was going to change the band. We are muddled and annoyed by him.)

1138
→ *waih yàhn waih dou dái (, sung faht sung dou sāi)* 爲人爲到底(,送佛送到西) (lit.) PH When you do a favour for someone, you should do it till the whole thing is done. (It's like escorting Buddha to the West. You must go with Him until He arrives at the destination.) 幫人做事要徹底完成才好(,好像送佛要送達西方): *"Néih bōng kéuih sung gāsī heui, yauh bōng kéuih būnjáu dī gauh gāsī, jānhaih hóu yàhn." "~ ā ma."* ("You helped him take the new furniture to his house and helped him take away the old

177

furniture. That was very nice of you." "You know, ~.")

1139
→yàhn jāang yātdaahm hei, faht jāang yātlòuh hēung 人爭一啖氣，佛爭一爐香 (lit.) man would strive for a mouthful of air and Buddha, a burner of incense sticks 人爭一口氣, 佛爭一爐香 (idi.) PH strive for success and try not to be despised by others 爭氣不被人家看扁 : ~, ~. *Kéuih sēuiyihn táisíu ngóh jē, daahnhaih ngóh m̀wúih sēui béi kéuih tái ge.* (He looks down on me, but I won't let him crow over me/ do it. I will ~.)

1140
→yàhn yiu yī jōng, faht yiu gām jōng 人要衣裝，佛要金裝 (lit.) PH man needs good dress to make him look nice, and Buddha needs gold to make Him look dignified 人要打扮才好看,好像佛要用金來裝飾一樣 : *Hōi góng dōu yáuh wah, ~, ~, dábaanháh jānhaih leng hóudō ge.* (As the saying goes, ~, ~. You'll certainly look much nicer if you dress up.)

gwái 鬼 N ghosts, spirits, demons, devils, souls 鬼 M jek

1141
→bá gwái 把鬼 (lit.) PH (1) it's entirely useless 這樣做完全沒有用 : *Nīgihn sih dōu m̀gwāan kéuih sih, néih*

giu kéuih làih ~ mè. (This has nothing to do with him. ~ for you to call him to come.) (2) it's bad, nothing is great at all 很差,沒甚麼了不起 : *"Kéuih chéng néih sihk ge yùhchi chāan dím a?" "~! Yùhchi tōng jauh jān."* ("How was the shark's fin meal he treated you to?" "~! There was much more soup than shark's fins.") also see 0622

1142
→diu hēu gwái 吊靴鬼 (lit.) boot following ghost 常跟在你靴子後的鬼 (idi.) N a person who always goes after you 常跟在你背後的人 M jek : *Sèhngyaht gānjyuh ngóh, hóuchíh jek ~ gám.* (You follow me all the time. You are like a ~.)

1143
→dō go hēunglòuh dō jek gwái 多個香爐多隻鬼 (lit.) one more incense stick burner, (you have to worship/ you would invoke) one more ghost 多一個焚香的爐,便要多拜／會多引來一隻鬼 (idi.) PH the more one arranges things (for other people), the more troublesome it will become 越多作人事安排便越麻煩 : *"Ngóhdeih bōsí ge sailóu jouh fu gīngléih, yìhgā kéuih yauh béi go yījái yahplàih jouh jyúyahm." "~. Ngóhdeih jouhyéh yiu síusāmdī ji dāk la."* ("The younger brother of our boss is the assistant manager of our company, and now our

boss has made the younger sister of his wife a section head." "~. We'd better be careful in our work.")

1144
→fāangwái(lóu) 番鬼（佬）
(lit.) foreign devil 洋鬼子
(idi.) N (*It is much the same as 'gwáilóu.') see 1157

1145
→gingwo gwái dōu pa hāak 見過鬼都怕黑 (lit.) once having seen a ghost, one becomes fearful of the dark 見過鬼的人就會害怕黑暗的地方
(idi.) PH a burned child dreads fire 驚弓之鳥 : Kéuih hái daaihluhk máaihgwo laahnméih láu jīhauh, jauh m̀gám joi hái daaihluhk máaihláu, kéuih wah ~ wóh! (He had paid the down payment of a flat on the mainland, but it turned out that the buyers would never know when the construction work would be finished. He said he would never buy any flat on the mainland again because ~.)

1146
→gin yàhn góng yàhn wá, gin gwái góng gwái wá 見人講人話，見鬼講鬼話 (lit.) speak human language to man, and speak devil's language to devils 見了人便說人(愛聽)的說話,見了鬼便說鬼(愛聽)的說話
(idi.) PH speak speculatively to different kinds of people one deals with 遇到不同的對象就有不同的應對 : Kéuih ~, ~, hóu sīk lōu ge. (He ~. He is a smoothie.)

1147
→gūhòhn gwái 孤寒鬼 (lit.) mean ghost 吝嗇鬼
(idi.) N meanie, cheap-skate 很吝嗇的人 M go : Kéuih nīgo ~, néih séung kéuih chéng néih sihk yātchāan àh, néih m̀sái jíyi. (You want him, the ~, to treat you to a meal? You'd better not expect him to do so.)

1148 ✓
→gwái 鬼 (lit.) N ghosts, spirits, demons, devils, souls 鬼 M jek
(idi.) N foreigners, especially Westerners 外國人,尤指西方人 M go ; dī : ⓐgaau dī ~ hohk Jūngmàhn (teach ~ Chinese) ⓑtùhng dī ~ jouh sāangyi (do business with ~) (* 'Gwái' meaning foreigners is a short form of 'gwáilóu', also see 1157 N) BF foreign guy 外國人 : ⓐ Méihgwok ~, Yīnggwok ~ (American ~, British ~) (*'Lóu' can be used here instead of 'gwái'.) ⓑ hāak ~ (negro, Blacks) P (when used after 'māt' or inserted in an RV compound) the damn 是語助詞, 表示討厭 : ⓐ Néihdeih háidouh gáau māt ~ yéh a? (What the hell are you doing here?) ⓑ Kéuih m̀síusām dá ~ laahn dī yéh. (He was careless and broke the things.) ⓒ béi kéuih sihk ~ saai (all eaten by him) PN (1) I, me 我 : Kéuih gam gūhòhn, ~ jūngyi kéuih a. (He is such a stingy person. How

179

would ~ fall in love with him?) (2) other people 別人,人家： ⓐ *Gaaklèih poutáu yauh gáamga yauh daaih jahngsung, ngóhdeih jauh māt dōu móuh, ~ làih bōngchan ngóhdeih mē?* (The shop next door is having a big sale and giving lots of coupons to customers. But we aren't doing either in our shop. Who on earth will come and buy our things?) ⓑ*Néih góngyéh gam saisēng, ~ tēngdākdóu mè.* (You are speaking in such a low voice. How can ~/ I hear you?)

1149
➔gwái dá gam 鬼打咁 (lit.) the way a ghost beats you 像鬼打你 (idi.) A. PH (much the same as 'gwái gam') see 1152

1150
➔gwái dá gwái 鬼打鬼 (lit.) a ghost fights with another ghost 鬼打鬼
(idi.) PH be on bad terms with one another because of a covert struggle 關係不和,明爭暗鬥 ： *Dī jíkyùhn sèhngyaht ~, gūngsī ge yihpmouh yauh dím wúih hóu ā!* (The staff members are ~. How can the business of the company be good?)

1151
➔gwái fó gam leng 鬼火咁靚 (lit.) as beautiful as ghost fire 像鬼火那麼漂亮
(idi.) PH exceedingly beautiful 漂亮得不得了 ： ⓐ*Kéuih jeuk ge*

máahnjōng ~. (The evening dress that she wore was ~.) ⓑ *Kéuih dábaandou ~ chēutgāai.* (She dressed herself in ~ costume and then went out.) (* 'Gwáifó' by itself is 'firefly', which is seen by people as 'ghost fire'.)

1152
➔gwái gam 鬼咁 (lit.) the way a ghost would be like 像鬼那樣
(idi.) A exceedingly 非常 ： ~ *leng/ sēui* (~ pretty/ bad)

1153
➔gwáigwáidéi 鬼鬼哋 (lit.) look a little like a ghost 有點像鬼
(idi.) PH look a little like a foreigner 樣子有點像洋人 ： *Kéuihge yéung (yáuhdī) ~.* (He ~.)

1154
➔gwáigwái syúsyú 鬼鬼祟祟 (lit.) ghosts and the disasters they bring to man 鬼及它帶來的災害
(idi.) PH look sneaky (as if one is doing something stealthily) 樣子鬼祟 ： *Kéuih jihngjínggái gám hàahngyahplàih, go yéung ~ gám.* (He walked in quietly, and he ~.) A. PH sneakily 鬼鬼祟祟 ： *Kéuih ~ gám hàahngyahplàih, hóuchíh séung tāuyéh gám.* (He walked in ~, as if he wanted to steal.)

1155✓
➔gwáijái 鬼仔 (lit.) N young ghost, child ghost 小鬼 M jek

180

(idi.) N young male Westerners 年輕男性洋人 M go : *Kéuih béi kéuihge jái duhk ~ hohkhaauh.* (He sends his son to a school for Westerners' children.)

1156
➔gwái jē ngáahn 鬼遮眼 (lit.) eyesight blocked by a ghost 被鬼遮蓋了視線
(idi.) PH stupidly overlook something (at a certain moment) 不知爲甚麼一時看不見 : *Dímgáai ngóh dōngsih táiìmgin gé, jānhaih ~.* (Why didn't I see it at that time? I really had made a silly mistake for not noticing it.)

1157
➔gwáilóu 鬼佬 (lit.) male ghost 男性的鬼
(idi.) N foreigners, male Westerners 洋人，男性洋人 M go : *Hái Hēunggóng, néih hóyíh gindóu hóudō ~.*(You can see many ~ in Hong Kong.) ATT foreign, Western, exotic 洋,西方,外國 : ⓐ*Kéuih yáuh go ~ méng, giujouh A-Paul.* (He has an English name, Paul.) ⓑ *~ chàh* (jasmine tea, a kind of Chinese tea favoured by Western people) ⓒ *~ lèuhngchàh* (beer, a kind of drink considered by Hong Kong Cantonese to be similar in effect to Chinese herb tea) ⓓ *~ yuhk* (sweet and sour pork, a Chinese dish favored by many Western people) ⓔ *dī ~ yéh* (things initiated/ produced by ~ people) ⓕ *ngóhge ~ pàhngyáuh* (my friend

who comes from ~ places) ⓖ *Kéuih heuijó Méihgwok géinihn, hohkmàaihsaai dī ~ yéh, gindóu yàhn yauh láam yauh sek.* (He has been in the States for a few years, and is much influenced by ~ culture. Now he will hug and kiss you whenever he sees you.)

1158
➔gwáimūi 鬼妹 (lit.) ghost's younger sister 鬼的妹妹
(idi.) N young female Westerners 年輕女性洋人 M go : *Yáuhdī ~ jeuksāam béigaau daaihdáam.* (Some ~ are accustomed to wearing sexy clothes.)

1159
➔gwái paak hauhméih jám 鬼拍後尾枕 (lit.) ghost taps the back of one's head 鬼拍人的脖子後方
(idi.) A. PH let out a secret unknowingly 不自覺地洩露了秘密 : *Nīgo beimaht, búnlòih kéuih séi dōu ìmháng góng ge, sāumēi jauh ~ góngjó chēutlàih.* (At first, he tried his best not to tell the secret, but later, he ~.) (*'Hauhméih jám' is the rear part of one's head that rests on the pillow when one is lying in bed.)

1160
➔gwáipòh 鬼婆 (lit.) ghost woman 鬼婦人
(idi.) N women Westerners 洋婦 M go : *Gógāan yaujihyún chéngjó go ~ gaau Yīngmán, sóyíh hóudō gā jéung*

181

bouméng. (That kindergarten has a ~ to teach English, so many parents want their children to be enrolled.)

1161

➔gwái sēng gwái hei 鬼聲鬼氣 (lit.) ghost's voice and ghost's mood 鬼的聲音和鬼的語氣
(idi.) PH (1) speak with a foreign /Western accent 說話有(西)洋人口音 : *Tēng kéuih góngyéh ~ gám, yùhnlòih kéuih haih jūksīng.* (He ~. I later realize that he is overseas [young] Chinese.) (2) speak in a funny and unnatural voice 說話作狀不自然 : *Néih jouh mèéh góngyéh ~ gám a? Jinggīngdī lā!* (Why do you ~? Be serious.)

1162

➔gwái séuhngsān 鬼上身 (lit.) ghost goes up to one's body 鬼走上人的身體
(idi.) PH (said of a person) be taken over by a ghost/ devil 人被鬼纏著 : *Gógo mahnmáihpó yihgā sáu jan geuk jan, hóuchíh ~ gám.* (The hands and the feet of the woman psychic are shaking as if she were ~.)

1163

➔gwái sihk làih gám sēng 鬼食泥噉聲 (lit.) it sounds like a ghost eating mud 像鬼吃泥的聲音
(idi.) PH groan, moan 抱怨, 或表示不願意的聲音 : *Giu kéuih jouh dō síusíu yéh jē jauh ~.* (He ~ when I told him to do just a little more work.)

1164

➔gwáisyú 鬼祟 (lit.) ghost and disaster 鬼跟災禍
(idi.) Adj. sneaky 鬼祟 : ⓐ*Kéuihge yéung hóu ~.* (He looks ~.) ⓑ*Kéuih jouhyéh hóu ~.* (He is ~ in his behaviour.)

1165

➔gwáitàuhjái 鬼頭仔 (lit.) small ghost leader 小的鬼領導
(idi.) N informer (who is a triad member and who gives information about his gang to the police/ who informs against the rest of the gang) (向警察提供他所屬幫會情報的)線人 M go : *Dímgáai chāailóu jīdou ngóhdeih hái nīdouh hōipín gé, haih m̀haih néih jouh ~ a?* (How come the cops know that we are going to have a gang fight here? Are you the ~?)

1166

➔gwái waahk fùh 鬼劃符 (lit.) (like) a ghost drawing a Taoist talisman 鬼寫道教的符咒
(idi.) PH (derogative) illegible (cursive writing) 難以辨認的草字 (貶義) : *séjih hóuchíh ~ gám* (the handwriting is like ~)

1167

➔jáan gwái 盞鬼 (lit.) Adj. special and cute 特別又有趣 : *Kéuih chitgai ge tihmbán, yinwō jéléi, dōu géi ~ ge bo.* (The dessert, birds' nest jelly, he designed is ~.)

1168

→jáugwái 走鬼 (lit.) gone the ghost 鬼走了

(idi.) VO (said of hawkers) flee (policemen) (小販)逃避警察 : *Yāt yáuh chāaiyàhn waahkjé síufáan gúnléih déui làih, dī mòuh pàaih síufáan jauh yiu ~ la.* (The licenseless hawkers have to ~ when policemen or members of the General Duties Team come.)

1169

→jáugwái 酒鬼 (lit.) wine ghost 酒鬼

(idi.) N alcoholic, drunkard 嗜酒的人 M go/ jek : *Kéuih lóuhgūng haih ~, yámjeui jáu jauh deng yéh lohk gāai.* (Her husband is an ~. When he is drunk, he throws things out on the street.)

1170

→jónggwái 撞鬼 (lit.) bump into a ghost 碰到鬼

(idi.) VO (1) (said of a person) be haunted by a ghost 見到鬼並給鬼纏著 : *Kéuih jihchùhng gómáahn bunyé heuiyùhn fàhnchèuhng fāanlàih jīhauh jauh hóuchíh chīchīdéi gám, mtūng kéuih ~ jó ~?* (Since he came back from the graveyard late that night, he seemed as if he were out of his mind. Could it be possible that he was ~?) (2) a term of abuse received when bumping into others 碰撞到別人時被罵之語 : *~ néih àh/ mè!* (How come you bump into me, you ghost?)

also see 0113 (3) damn you 去見鬼吧 : *~ àh/ mè! Gam jóu chòuhséng yàhn.* (~! You wake me up so early with that loud noise.)

1171

→jouh gwái dōu mlèhng 做鬼都唔靈 (lit.) even if one were a ghost, one would be unable to exercise his supernatural power 就算做鬼,也不能施法

(idi.) PH cannot do anything to help 一點也幫不上忙 : *Kéuih yihgā ~ lā, mèeh chín dōu móuhsaai, juhng dím hóyíh bōng néih wàahnjaai a?* (Now he ~ you. He has lost all his money. How can he help you pay your debts?)

1172

→kùhnggwái 窮鬼 (lit.) N ghost of no money 窮的鬼

(idi.) N a person as poor as a church mouse 窮光蛋 M go/ jek : *A néui, dímgáai yáuhchínlóu néih mga, ga go ~ jē?* (My daughter, why do you marry ~ instead of a rich man?)

1173

→laahndóu gwái 爛賭鬼 (lit.) broken gambling ghost 破爛的賭錢的鬼

(idi.) N a person too indulged in gambling, a habitual gambler 嗜賭的人 M go/ jek : *Kéuih jingyāt ~, móuh chín dōu yiu jechín heui dóu.* (He is really ~. Even if he has no money to gamble, he borrows it from others.)

1174

→laahngwái 爛鬼 (lit.) rotten ghost 腐爛的鬼

(idi.) ATT useless, very cheap 沒用的或一錢不值的 : ⓐ*Nīdī ~ yéh, juhng m̀dámjó kéuih?* (Why have you still not thrown away these ~ things?) ⓑ*Nīgo ~ bīu, béi (ngóh) dōu m̀yiu a, kéuih jauh donghaih bóu.* (I wouldn't take this ~ watch even if you give it to me for free, but he takes it as a gem.)

1175

→láahngwái 懶鬼 (lit.) lazy ghost 懶的鬼

(idi.) N lazy person 懶人 M go/jek : *Sihkjó faahn wún dōu m̀sái, jingyāt ~.* (You don't even wash the dishes after the meal, you are really a ~.)

1176

→noih gwái 內鬼 (lit.) inside ghost 裏面的鬼

(idi.) N spy (who seeks information about an organization he works in) (收集一個機構情報的)內奸 M go : *Ngóh sīyih ngóhdeih gūngsī yáuh ~, yùhgwó m̀haih, yàhndeih dím wúih jīdou ngóhdeih ge gīngyihng chaakleuhk nē?* (I suspect that there is a ~ in our company. If not, how come others know our logistic strategies?)

1177

→sēuigwái 衰鬼 (lit.) bad ghost 不好的鬼

(idi.) ATT bad, damnable 壞的,可惡的 : *Kéuihge ~ lóuhgūng dásihng kéuih gám yéung.* (Her ~ husband beat her in such a terrible way.) N (1) damnable person 可惡的人 M go : *Nīgihn sih m̀hóu béi A-Chán go ~ jīdou a.* (Don't let Chan, the bad guy, know it.) (2) (a very intimate term said by a woman to her man) honey, darling, sweetheart (女子對男子很親密的叫法)你這冤家 : *Yàhndeih dōu m̀jī géi gwajyuh néih a, ~!* (~, I miss you so much!)

1178✓

→sēuigwái 水鬼 (lit.) water ghost 水的鬼 (* After a person is drowned, he will become a water ghost.)

(idi.) N frogman 蛙人 M go : *Gíngfōng paai ~ dálàauh sītái.* (Some ~ were sent by the police to get the dead out from the sea.)

1179

→syùhntàuh gēng gwái, syùhnméih gēng chaahk 船頭驚鬼,船尾驚賊 (lit.) be afraid of seeing a ghost at the bow and a thief at the stern 怕在船頭碰到鬼,又怕在船尾遇到賊

(idi.) PH too many worries 太多憂慮 : *Jouh sāangyi, néih pa sihtbún, cháau gúpiu, néih pa cháaulūng, néih ~, ~, bātyùh jēung dī chín jāihái ngàhnhòhng lā.* (You are afraid of losing money in doing business or in speculating on the stock market.

You have ~. You'd better put your money in the bank.)

1180✓

→tai séi gwái 替死鬼 (lit.) N a person dies on behalf of someone else 替死鬼 M go/ jek
(idi.) N scapegoat 代罪羔羊 M go/ jek : *Nīdāan yéh búnlòih haih kéuih mē ge, bātgwo kéuih jauh wán néih jouh ~.* (He was supposed to be held responsible for this. However, he has made you the ~.)

1181

→yàhn lóuh jēng, gwái lóuh lèhng 人老精，鬼老靈 (lit.) PH a person will be more clever the older he grows, a ghost will be more powerful the longer the time it is a ghost 人老了就變得聰明,做鬼久了,它就變得法力強 : *Ngóh hauhsāang gósih jauh béi kéuih hāp jē. ~, ~. Ngóh yìhgā géi'ah seui lo, juhng dím wúih béi kéuih wánbahn ā.* (When I was young, I was bullied by him. However, ~, ~. Now I am in my middle age/ already old, so he can't take advantage of me any longer.)

1182

→yàhn sai gwái daaih 人細鬼大 (lit.) man small and ghost big 人小鬼大
(idi.) PH too young to do what adults do or know what adults know 太年輕去做大人做的事或知道大人才應知的事 : *Yìhgā dī hohksāang ~,*

sahplèhng seui jauh hohk yàhn paaktō. (Nowadays students are ~. They start dating when they are in their teens.)

1183

→yáuh chín sáidāk gwái tēui mòh 有錢使得鬼推磨 (lit.) with money, you can make a ghost move the (heavy) grinder (for you) 要是有錢,連鬼你也可以叫它爲你推磨
(idi.) PH money can do anything 錢是萬能的 : *Kéuih yìhgā m̀háng bōng néih jouh jē, ~, néih béi dōdī chín kéuih (kéuih) jauh háng ge lā.* (Now he refuses to do it for you. However, ~. He will say yes if you give him more money.)

1184

→yeh gwái 夜鬼 (lit.) night ghost 夜裏的鬼
(idi.) N a person energetic at night time and so he goes to bed late 晚上精神好並遲睡的人 : *Ngóh jóu fan jóu héi, kéuih jauh haih ~.* (I go to bed early and get up early. As for him, he is ~.)

1185

→yuht kùhng yuht gin gwái 越窮越見鬼 (lit.) the poorer one becomes, the more ghosts he will encounter 越窮越多見鬼
(idi.) PH the poorer one is, the more money he needs to make ends meet/ the more financial problems he will

185

have 越窮越多需要錢才能解決的問題：*Lèuhngméih yíhgīng móuh māt chín, nī géi yaht gūngjung gakèih, ngàhnhòhng yauh sāanmùhn, gāmyaht go jái behngjó yiu tái yīsāng, jānhaih ~.* (I won't have money until the coming payday. We have public holidays these few days and the banks close. Today my son got sick and he has to go to see a doctor. The saying is right that ~.)

jīng 精 BF goblins, elves, spirits, demons 精靈,妖精

1186
→jīnglīng 精 靈 (lit.) elves, goblins, spirits 精靈 (*When used literally, it should be 'jīnglìhng', with the second syllable retaining its low falling tone.)
(idi.) Adj. (said of children) smart and lovely 伶俐可愛： ⓐ *Nī go saimānjái hóu ~.* (This child is ~.) ⓑ *Bìhbī ge ngáahn hóu ~.* (The baby has a pair of ~ eyes.)

1187
→lóuhyàhnjīng 老人精 (lit.) old man elf 老人小精靈
(idi.) N children who behave like adults 小孩行為像成年人 M go： ⓐ *Chāamgā Gōsīng Mòuhfóng Daaihchoi gódī saimānjái, gogo dōu haih ~.* (Children who took part in that Singers Imitation Contest all sang and danced like adults.) ⓑ *wùhlèihjīng* see 0361

mō 魔 BF/N demons, devils, evil spirits 妖魔

1188
→douh gōu yāt chek, mō gōu yāt jeuhng 道高一尺，魔高一丈 (lit.) if the god is one foot tall, then the devil is ten feet tall 道高一尺,魔高一丈
(idi.) PH the bad is always more capable than the good 壞人永遠比好的人有本領：*Sēuiyìhn gíngfōng sìhsìh souwòhng, daahnhaih ~, ~, gódī sīkchìhng gabouh hóu faai yauh hōifāan.* (The police carry out anti-vice operations very often. However, ~, ~. The vice dens can always resume business soon afterwards.)

pòuhsaat 菩薩 N Bodhisattva 菩薩 M go

1189
→ m̀pa sihn chòih nàahn sé, ji pa pòuhsaat m̀lèhng 唔怕善財難捨，至怕菩薩唔靈 (lit.) PH we don't worry about that people are not willing to give money for charity, what we most worry about is that the Bodhisattvas do not answer our prayers 不擔心其他人是否願意用錢做善事，最擔心是菩薩不靈驗： ⓐ *Néih gyūn gam dō chín béi gógāan míu àh!?"* "*M̀gányiu lā, ~, ~ ā mā."* ("You donated so much money to that temple!" "There's nothing bad. You know ~, ~.") ⓑ *làih pòuhsaat gwo gōng→jih sān nàahn bóu* see 0703

sāam bóu dihn 三寶殿 N/ PW Buddhist temple dedicated to Triratna (i.e.) the triad of Buddha, the dharma, and the sangha 供奉三個菩薩的佛殿 M gāan

1190

➔mòuh sih bāt dāng sāam bóu dihn 無事不登三寶殿 (lit.) if one has no problems, one does not go to the temple of the three Buddhas 無事不登三寶殿
(idi.) PH I come because I have some problems 因爲有事, 所以才來 (找你): *"Dímgáai gam hóu làih wán ngóh a?"* *"~. Ngóh yáuh dī sih yiu tùhng néih sēunglèuhng."* ("It's so nice for you to call on me, but what's up?" "~. I have something that I need to discuss with you.")

sàhn 神 N gods, deities, immortals, spiritual beings 神 M go/ wái

1191

➔baaidāk sàhn dō jih yáuh sàhn beiyauh 拜得神多自有神庇佑 (lit.) PH if you worship your god(s) more often, it/ they will certainly bless you in return 多拜神, 神就自然會保祐你 : *"A-pòh, néih gam sàhnsām a!"* *"Óh, ~ ā ma."* ("Hi, madam, you are so pious." "You should have known the saying that ~.")

1192

➔bánsàhn dōu móuh geui jān

稟神都冇句真 (lit.) not a single word is honest even in one's prayers 稟告神明時也沒有一句說話是真的
(idi.) PH (said of a person) totally unreliable (人)全不可靠 : *Kéuih nīgo yàhn, ~, néih seun kéuih (góng) jauh séifó la.* (He is ~. It will be troublesome if you believe what he says.)

1193

➔hohksàhn 鶴神 (lit.) god of crane 鶴神
(idi.) N a damn guy (who makes things bad for people) 令人倒霉的人 M go : *Kéuih jīngyāt ~ làih ge, béi kéuih gáauwāangsaai ngóhdeih nīgihn sih.* (He spoiled the whole thing we were doing. He's a ~.)

1194

➔hohksàhn 學神 (lit.) god of learning 學習的神
(idi.) N a person who learns to drive in his tutor's car. In the front and at the back of the car, there hangs a cardboard with a character 學 written on it in red 駕駛學生在老師車子裏學習開車, 車子前後都掛著一個寫有紅色「學」字的牌 M go : *Jāchē ge yàhn gindóu ~ dōu wúih yeuhng kéuihdeih.* (Drivers would give way whenever they see a student driver's car.)

1195

➔sàhn bātjī, gwái bātgok 神不知, 鬼不覺 (lit.) god doesn't know, neither does ghost 神不知, 鬼不覺
(idi.) PH escape the eyes of all the

people (when doing something stealthily) 別人全不察覺(你偷偷做的事)：*Néih hāu kéuih hàahnghōi jauh yuhng jēung gá kāat wuhnjó kéuih jēung jān kāat, gám jauh ~ lā.* (When he goes away, take his credit card and replace it with this fake one. Sure, you can ~.)

1196

➔sàhn gōu sàhn daaih 神高神大 (lit.) as tall and big as a god 像神那麼高大
(idi.) PH tall and big (figure) 身材魁梧：*Kéuih (sāangdāk) ~ hóuchíh joh sāan gám.* (He is ~, and looks like a hill.)

1197

➔sàhngwan 神棍 (lit.) god's staff/ rod 神的杖
(idi.) N a conman who cheats people in the name of a god or a religious sect 假借神或教派的名義去行騙的騙徒 M go/tìuh：*Dī ~ jyūnhaih haak yàhn, wah néih faahn nīyeuhng faahn góyeuhng, yihnhauh giu néih sáichín baaisàhn fagáai, móuhfēi haih séung ngāak néihdī chín jē.* (A ~ always tries to intimidate you by saying that you have committed this or that kind of offence against the gods, which can be dispelled by buying offerings and worshipping the gods. All they want is to make money.)

1198

➔sàhnhéiséuhnglàih 神起上 來 (lit.) start to behave like a god 忽然好像神一樣
(idi.) PH suddenly start to do very well (as opposed to one's general performance) 忽然表現得很好,跟平時不一樣：*Nīgo hohksāang pihngsìh ge sìhngjīk hóu chā, daahnhaih nīchi háausíh kéuih fātyìhngāan ~, háaudāk géi hóu.* (The general performance of this student is poor, but in this exam, he ~ and his results are quite good.)

1199

➔sàhn jāng gwái yim 神憎鬼厭 (lit.) both gods and ghosts disgust him/ her 神憎鬼厭
(idi.) PH (said of a person) very disgusting and hated by others 非常令人討厭憎恨的人：*Dī hāak séhwúi sihsìh heung dī poutáu sāu bóuwuhfai, jānhaih ~.* (The triads always extort protection fees from the shops. They are really ~.) also see 0293

1200

➔sàhnsàhn fafa 神神化化 (lit.) PH be a little bit odd in one's behaviour 行為有點古怪：*Kéuih nīgo yàhn ~ gám, yáuhdī yàhn yíhwàih kéuih haih chīsin ge.* (He is ~. Some people think he is crazy.)

1201

➔sàhnsām 神心 see 0659

1202

➔sàhnsándéi 神神哋 (lit.) a little bit like a god 有一點像神

(idi.) PH cannot function well and sometimes will develop problems 操作不太好,有時會有故障 : *Nīgo dihnlóuh ~, yáuhsih ngóh séung dámjó kéuih lohkgāai.* (This computer ~. Sometimes I want to throw it out on the street.)

1203

➔sàhnsándéi gīng 神神哋經 (lit.) PH a little ill mentally 精神有點問題／不正常: *Ngóh táigin kéihhái ngóh pòhngbīn ge yàhn jih yihn jih yúh, hóuchíh yáuhdī ~ gám, sóyíh ngóh faaidī jáuhōi.* (I saw the man standing beside me talking to himself. He looked as if he was ~. Therefore, I hurried up and stayed away from him.)

1204

➔sàhn tēui gwái ngúng 神推鬼 (lit.) pushed by gods and ghosts 被鬼神推使 (idi.) PH be urged to do something for no reason 無緣無故的去做一件事 : *Ngóh dōu gú gúsíh wúih lam ge la, daahnhaih ~ yauh yahpjó fo, yihgā cháam la.* (I did guess there would be a slump on the stock market. However, I didn't know why I still bought more stocks. Now I am really suffering heavy losses.)

1205

➔saih sàhn pek yuhn 誓神劈願 (lit.) swear by god and chop one's oath 向神大力發誓 (idi.) PH swear blind 矢口發誓 :

Ngóh mahn kéuih yáuh móuh fán jouh gógihn sih, kéuih jauh ~ wah móuh. (I asked him if he had a hand in doing that. He ~ that he had not.)

1206

➔sēuisàhn 衰神 (lit.) bad god 不好的神 (idi.) N (disgusting) bad guy 瘟神 (罵人語) M go : *Kéuih jingyāt ~, dálaahnsaai ngóhdī yéh.* (He is really a ~ having broken all my things.)

1207

➔tipcho mùhnsàhn 貼錯門神 (lit.) tape the pictures of the two door gods on the wrong sides 反貼門神 (idi.) PH be at odds with each other 大家見面不瞅不睬 : *"Dímgáai kéuihdeih léuhnggo (hóuchíh) ~ gám a?" "Kéuihdeih kàhmyaht ngaaijó gāau ā ma."* ("Why don't the two of them greet and talk to each other?" "They had a quarrel just yesterday. Didn't you know that?")

1208

➔wàahndāk sàhn lohk 還得神落 (lit.) PH (1) one should thank god for having been saved from a disaster 人應酬謝神恩,因爲倖免於難 : *Góga bāsí sātsih, ngóh jāangdī chóhjó kéuih ge la, nīchi jānhaih ~.* (That bus had an accident. I had almost gotten on it. This time I ~.) (2) one should thank god for having succeeded in doing a very difficult thing 人應酬謝神恩，因爲僥倖成功：*Gógāan mihng haauh síuhohk yáuh sāamsahp go wái jē, daahnhaih jauh yáuh sāamchīn yàhn sānchíng. Ngóhge jái háaudóu, jānhaih ~ lo!* (That prestigeous primary school has only thirty places. However, three thousand students applied for the enrollment. My son is a successful applicant. I really ~.)

1209

→yahp ngūk giu yàhn, yahp míu baaisàhn 入屋叫人，入廟拜神 (lit.) PH You greet people when you go into their house, and so you are supposed to worship gods when you enter a temple 到人家裏，要跟人打招呼；來到廟裏，就要拜神：*Yàuhhaak làih chāamgūn nīgāan míu, dōu wúih baaiháh sàhn ~, ~ ā ma.* (When tourists visit this temple, they also worship the gods [in the temple]. You know ~, ~.)

1210

→yahttáu m̀hóu góng yàhn, yehmáahn m̀hóu góng sàhn 日頭唔好講人，夜晚唔好講神 (lit.) don't talk about others by day nor the spiritual beings by night 白天不要談別人，晚上不要談鬼神 (idi.) PH speak of the devil 一說曹操，曹操就到：*"Tēngginwah A-Chán jyunjó gūng bo. A! Kéuih làih la. Hóujoih ngóhdeih móuh góng kéuih sihfēi jē." "Sóyíh wah lē, ~, ~."* ("I heard that Chan had changed job. Oh! Here he comes! Luckily, we were not gossiping about him." "That's why people say, ~, ~.")

sàhnsīn 神仙 N fairies, immortals, supernatural beings 神仙 M go/ wái

1211

→baatsīn gwohói → gok hín sàhntūng 八仙過海→各顯神通 (lit.) the eight immortals of Taoism cross the sea → each one of them has to develop his own supernatural power 八仙過海→各顯神通 (idi.) HIT each one has to try his best to attain his goal 各方面都要盡顯本領以達到目的：*Waihjó jāang Saigaai Būi jūkkàuh béichoi ge boyíngkyùhn, géi gāan dihnsihtòih jauh yiu ~ → ~ la.* (In order to compete for the rights to broadcast the World Cup Soccer, the TV companies, ~ → ~, trying their best to attain their goal.)

1212

→dāk séuhngchòhng hīn péih kám, dāk jouh wòhngdai séung sīng sīn 得上床掀被冚，得做皇帝想升仙 (lit.) after one is allowed to get into bed, he wants to take the sheet to cover himself ; and after one becomes king, he wants to become an immortal too 可以上床睡，就想拿被子蓋自己，做了皇帝就連神仙也想做

(idi.) PH be never content, always ask for more 得寸進尺,貪得無厭 : *Go jyuhhaak yīukàuh ngóh bāau séuidihn, ngóh yīngsihng kéuih, sāumēi yiu ngóh wuhn láahngheigēi, ngóh dōu yīngsihng kéuih, yihgā juhng yiu ngóh gáam jōu tīm, jingyāt ~, ~.* (My tenant wanted me to pay the water bill and the electricity bill for him, I said yes. Later he wanted me to install a new air-conditioner for him, and I did that, too. But now he wants me to reduce his rent. He is really ~, ~.) also see 0049

1213
➔ **gwojó hói jauh sàhnsīn** 過 咗海就神仙 (lit.) having crossed the sea, one will become a fairy 過 了海便是神仙
(idi.) PH (1) how good it would be if one succeeds in cheating others 瞞 天 過 海 : *Ngóhdeih jēung dī baahkfán chòhnghái hàhngléih léuihbihn, m̀béi hóigwāan jīkyùhn gímchàhdóu, gám ~ lā!* (We hid the drugs in our luggage. We were so careful that they were not spotted by the customs officers. ~ !) (2) how nice it would be if one has overcome an obstacle 過了難關就好了 : *Ngóh juhng yáuh yātgo yuht ge siyuhngkèih. ~ lo!* (There's still one month before I can finish the probationary period [of my job]. ~ !)

1214
➔ **mòuh jīn mòuh sin, sàhnsīn**

nàahn bin 無氈無扇,神仙難 變 (lit.) no blanket and no fan, even a fairy cannot undergo a transformation 無氈無扇,神仙難變 (idi.) PH even a very capable person cannot do anything with very limited resources 資源有限,就算很有本領 也不能做些什麼 : *Jingfú béi gam síu jīyùhn, ngóhdeih bouhmùhn dím hóyíh faatjín a? ~, ~ lā.* (How can our department develop with such limited resources from the government? You know ~, ~.)

1215
➔ **sīn dōu m̀sīn** 仙都唔仙 (lit.) fairy but also not fairy 是仙也不是仙 (idi.) PH pennyless, not having a cent 窮得一分錢也沒有 (*Actually, the 'sīn' in this expression is the transliteration of 'cent'.): *Chēutlèuhng dī chín yíhgīng sáisaai la, yihgā ~, wàihyáuh mahn pàhngyáuh jejyuh dī chín yuhng sīn lā.* (I've already spent all my salary. Now I am ~. The only thing I can do is to borrow money from my friend and use it for the time being.)

1216✓
➔ **sīngsīn** 升仙 (lit.) VO ascend to heaven and become a fairy/ immortal 升天做神仙
(idi.) VO (1) the indirect way of saying 'to die' '死'的另一種說法 : ⓐ*Néih léuhngyaht dōu m̀háng sihkyéh, séung ~ àh?* (You refused to eat for two days. Are you going ~?)

ⓑ *"Gógo lóuh baak juhng háidouh ma?" "Gauhnín ~ jó ~ lo."* ("Is that old man still there?" "He ~ last year.") (2) a mixed code of the Cantonese word 'sīng' (i.e. go up to, promote to) and the first syllable of the English word 'senior' 升上高級的職位,'仙' 是英文'senior'的第一個音節 : *Néih hái daaihhohk jouhjó gam noih dōu juhng meih ~ àh?* (You've been working for the university for such a long time and yet you have not been ~ ?) (*A pun or a joke can be made on this example since 'sīngsīn' can mean 'to die'.)

1217
➔Wòhngdaaihsīn➔ yáuh kàuh bīt ying 黃大仙➔有求必應 (lit.) the great immortal Wong➔ whatever you pray for, he will make it come true 黃大仙➔有求必應 (idi.) HIT (a person who) always says yes to others' request 從不拒絕別人請求的人 : *Yàhnyàhn dōu wah kéuih haih hóuhóu sīnsāang, gánghaih lā, kéuih haih ~ → ~.* (Everybody says that he is a very good person. Sure, because he ~ → ~.) (*Sometimes a goal keeper in a football match would teasingly be called 'Wòhngdaaihsīn', because every time his rival makes a shoot [i.e. yáph kàuh], the ball will certainly hit the goal [i.e. bīt yīng]. However, it is good for a basketball or football player to be called 'Wòhngdaaihsīn', because he scores every time he shoots.)

Sauhsīnggūng 壽星公 N the God of Longevity 壽星 M go
1218
➔sauhsīng 壽星 (lit.) N the God of Longevity 長壽之星 M go (idi.) N a person who has a birthday 當天生日的人 M go : ⓐ~ gūng/ pó/ jái/ néui (a man/ woman/ boy/ girl ~) ⓑdóumáih ~ see 1007 ⓒ ~ gūng diugéng → yìhm mehng chèuhng see 0403

sìhngwòhng 城隍 N city god 城隍 M go
1219
➔gahnjyuh sìhngwòhng míu dōu m̀kàuhfāan jī hóu chīm 近住城隍廟都唔求番枝好簽 (lit.) since you live near the city god's temple, why don't you (go there and) cast a bamboo stick telling your good fortune? 既然住在城隍廟附近,爲甚麼不去求一枝好的簽呢 (idi.) PH why don't you make good use of a favorable situation you are in 既然形勢比別人好,爲甚麼不把握這個機會 : *Séung faatdaaht jauh yiu jung luhkhahpchói, néih ngūkkéi làuhhah jauh haih (máhwúi) tàuhjyujaahm, néih dōu m̀heui máaih. ~ ?* (You won't become rich unless you win the Mark Six. There's a Jockey Club betting office downstairs of your apartment, but you never go and buy the Mark Six. ~ ?)

1220
➔gahnjyuh sìhngwòhng míu

kàuhfāan jī hóu chīm 近住城隍廟求番枝好簽 (lit.) live near the temple of the city god, so it's more convenient to (go there and) cast a bamboo stick telling one's good fortune 住在城隍廟附近,求得一枝好的簽總比別人方便 (idi.) PH make good use of a (more) favorable situation one is in (than others) 近水樓台先得月;形勢比別人優勝,較易得益 : *Ngóh sīk gógāan jáugā ge gīngléih, sóyíh fàahnmòhng sìhgaan dōu m̀sái dehngtói, ~ ā ma.* (I am a friend of the manager of that restaurant, so I don't have to make a reservation even during busy hours. I just ~, you know.)

1221

→séuigwái sīng sìhngwòhng 水鬼升城隍 (lit.) the water ghost is promoted to city god 水鬼變了城隍 (idi.) PH (said of a person of lower rank and who one despises) gets a promotion (一個較低級及你看不起的人)升級 : *~, kaau tok (daaih geuk) jī ma.* (He ~ all by flattering the boss.)

tàuhtōi 投胎 VO be reborn/ reincarnated (as human) 投胎, 轉世

1222

→gónjyuh (heui) tàuhtōi mè 趕住(去)投胎咩 (lit.) be in a hurry to be reborn 趕著去投胎 (idi.) PH (a term of abuse) be in a hurry to go to hell (罵人語) 趕著去死麼 : *Gam gāp, ~ mè!* (You are in such a hurry. Are you ~?) (*According to Buddhism, a person has to die first before he will be reborn.)

tóudéi 土地 N the God of Earth 土地神 **M go**

1223

→yìhmchōng tóudeih/ déi→ hàahmsāp baakfú 鹽倉土地→鹹濕伯父 (lit.) HIT the God of Earth in the storehouse for salt→a dirty old man 在鹽倉裏的土地神→色迷迷的中／老年男人 : *Géisahp seui yàhn, yāt gindóu leng néui jauh ngáahn gāmgām gám mohngjyuh yàhn, jìngyāt haih [~ →] ~.* (Although he is in his middle/ old age, he stares at beautiful girls whenever he sees them. He is really [~ →] ~.) (* 'Yìhm' [salt] is salty, i.e. hàahm. It is also a little wet, i.e. sāp. 'Hàahmsāp' means nasty, dirty, see 1078. The God of Earth is also addressed as 'baakfuh', but the changed tone of 'fuh' into 'fú' is used for someone one despises.)

wàhnpaak 魂魄 N soul 魂魄

1224

→sāam wàhn m̀ginjó chāt paak 三魂唔見咗七魄 (lit.) one's three souls and seven spirits detached from his body 不見了三魂和七魄 (idi.) PH be scared to death 嚇得魂不附體 : *haakdou ~ (~)* (*It is believed

193

among Chinese that there are three souls and seven spirits inside a man's body.)

1225

→sātwàhn 失魂 (lit.) lose one's soul 失去魂魄

(idi.) Adj. be absent-minded 精神恍惚及沒有記性 ： ⓐ *Kéuih nīpáai hóu ~, sèhngyaht m̀geidāk nīyeuhng m̀geidāk góyeuhng.* (He has been very ~ recently. He always forgets this or that.) ⓑ ~ *yú* see 0097

1226

→sātwàhn lohkpaak 失魂落魄 (lit.) lose one's soul and drop one's spirit 失了魂魄

(idi.) PH (1) be seriously scared 驚惶失措 ： *Kéuih jónggwái jīhauh, haakdou ~.* (After he saw a ghost, he was ~.) (2) cannot concentrate and cannot feel settled 精神恍惚 ： *Jouh māt nīpáai néih ~ gám a? Yáuh mēéh sāmsih a?* (Why can't you ~? Do you have something on your mind that is bothering you?)

1227

→wàhnpaak dōu m̀chàih 魂魄都唔齊 (lit.) one's soul is not all there inside his body 魂魄不全

(idi.) PH be scared to death (驚恐得)魂不附體 ： *haakdou ~ (~)* (*see 1224)

yāmgūng 陰功 N covert good deeds 不被人知的善事

1228

→yāmgūng 陰功 (lit.) covert good deeds 不被人知的善事

(idi.) ATT evil 邪惡 ： ⓐ *Kéuih saatyàhn fongfó, jouhjó hóudō ~ sih.* (He killed and burned others. He did a lot of ~ things.) ⓑ ~ *chín* (money one earns by doing ~ things) PH for god's sake one should not have done that/ such a thing should not have happened 天啊,他不應該這樣做/這樣的事不應該發生 ： ⓐ ~ *lo! Kéuih dámdāi go bihbī jauh jáujó lo.* (She dumped her baby and left. ~!) ⓑ ~ *lo! Gāan ngūk sīusihng gám.* (The house was so badly damaged by fire. ~!) ⓒ ~! *Go baakyēpó béi go jái gónchēutlàih.* (The old woman was driven out from her son's house. ~!)

yèhsōu 耶穌 N Jesus 耶穌

1229

→góng yèhsōu 講耶穌 (lit.) talk about Jesus 講耶穌

(idi.) VO being too kind to others in explaining in detail and counseling patiently 太仁慈地詳加解釋及耐心輔導 ： *Jihnghaih sīkdāk ~, néih yiu fahtháh kéuihdeih jí dāk gā ma.* (You only know how to ~ [but that won't help]. You need to punish them.)

Yìhmlòhwòhng 閻羅王 N the Ruler of Hades, the King of Hell 閻王

1230

→tùhng Yìhmlòhwòhng gaak

194

jēung jí 同閻羅王隔張紙 (lit.)
just a sheet of paper in between a man
and the Ruler of Hades 跟閻君只是
一紙之隔

(idi.) PH might easily die 很容易送
命 : ⓐ *Yìhchìhn fōhohk móuh gam
jeunbouh, néuihyán sāang bihbī jauh
hóuchíh* ~ *gám.* (In the past, people
knew little about science. Women ~
during the delivery of a baby.)
ⓑ *Kéuih jānhaih hóuchói lo,
gaudākfāan. Kéuih sēungdāk gam
chúhng, jānhaih* ~ *ja.* (He is lucky that
he can be saved and is still alive. He
~ because he was seriously wounded.)

195

IV. Yàhnsāng jiwai (wisdom of life)

bánsing 品性 N personality, temperament, character 性格

1231

→gōngsāan yih gói, bán/ búnsing nàahn yih 江山易改, 品／本性難移 (lit.) PH it's easy to change the reign of a country, but it's hard to change the character of a person 江山易改,品／本性難移 : ⓐ *"Giugihk kéuih kàhnlihkdī duhksyū dōu m̀tēng." "~, ~. Láahn yàhn haih giu m̀tēng ge."* ("No matter how I urge him to study hard, he won't listen to me." "~, ~. You can't make a lazy person move.") ⓑ *~, ~, néih m̀hóu hēimohng hóyíh góibin yatgo yàhn. (~, ~. So don't expect that you can change a person.)

béi(gaau) 比(較) V compare 比較

1232

→yàhn béi yàhn, béiséi yàhn 人比人,比死人 (lit.) PH when a person compares himself with others, he'll become agitated upon finding that he has been suffering loss or is much inferior to others 人比人, 氣死人 : *"Daaihgā dōu haih yātyeuhng ge jīkkāp, dímgáai kéuihge fūkleih hóudī gé?" "~, ~. M̀hóu léih yàhn gam dō lā."* ("We are in the same rank. Why are they entitled to more fringe benefits?"

"~, ~. Don't bother about others that much.")

bouying 報應 N recompense, retribution 報應 M dī

1233

→sihn yáuh sihn bou, ngok yáuh ngok bou 善有善報,惡 有惡報 (lit.) PH a good person will get recompense and a bad person will get retribution 善有善報,惡有惡報 : *~, ~, yeuhkyihn meih bou, sihsàhn meih dou.* (~, ~. If there is not yet any recompense or retribution, it's just a matter of time.) (*The last two segments of the example sentence can be taken as the ending part of the first two ones.) also see 0646 and 0649

chìh 遲 Adj. late 晚了,遲到

1234

→chìhdou hóugwo móuh dou 遲到好過冇到 (lit.) PH it's better late than never 遲到比沒有到／永不 到 好 : *Gwo máhlouh yùhgwó hùhngdāng jauh yiu tìhng, géi míuh jūng jí ma, ~.* (Don't cross the road when the red light is on. It only takes you a few seconds, and ~.)

1235

→chìh làih/ lòih sīn séuhng ngohn 遲嚟／來先上岸 (lit.) the last comer becomes the first to go

ashore 晚來的人早些登上岸邊
(idi.) PH last come, first served 來得
晚比來得早更有利 ： *Kéuih chìhgwo*
ngóh yahp gūngsī jouh, daahnhaih ~,
kéuih sīngjó kāp, ngóh dōu meih sīng.
(He joined our company later than I.
However, ~. He's gotten a promotion,
but I haven't yet.)

**chòih 財 BF/N money, wealth
錢, 財富**

1236
➔chòih saan yàhn ōnlohk 財
散人安樂 (lit.) people would feel
peaceful when their money is gone/
spent 錢財花光了,人就會安寧些
(idi.) PH the troubles that money
brings will disappear once the money
is gone 錢財沒有了,則它帶來的麻
煩也會消失 ： *Léuhng hīngdaih*
sihngyaht waihjó jāang sāngā
ngaaigāau, bàhbā lāuhéiséuhnglàih,
jēung dī chín gyūnsaaibéi chìhsihn
gēigwāan. Yìhgā ~, móuhdāk jāang ā
ma. (The two brothers always
quarreled over their father's wealth.
Their father became angry and gave
all his money to the charities. Now, ~.
There's nothing for them to scramble
for.) also see 0693

1237
➔faatchòih laahpbán 發財
立品 (lit.) PH value self-discipline
after one becomes wealthy 人富有
了就注意修行 ： *Nīgo daaih*
deihcháan sēung hóyíh góng haih ~.

Kéuih faatjó daaht jīhauh yauh
duhksyū yauh gyūnchín béi daaihhohk.
(We can say that this property
developer ~. After he has become
rich, he studies [at school] and
donates money to universities.)

1238
➔m̀haih néih chòih m̀yahp
néih doih 唔係你財唔入你袋
(lit.) if it's not your money, it won't go
into your pocket 不是你的錢財,不
會走進你的口袋
(idi.) PH money will only go to the
right person 錢只會給值得有它的
人 ： *"Máaihgihk Luhkhahpchói dōu*
m̀jung." "Gánghaih lā, ~." ("No matter
how many times I bought the Mark
Six, I have never won." "Of course,
~.") also see 0699 and 0720

1239
➔sauh yàhn chìhnchòih, tai
yàhn sīujōi 受人錢財,替人消
災 (lit.) PH if you accept other
people's money, you are supposed to
ward off evil for them 要了人家的
錢,就要替人家消災解難 ： *~, ~. Néih*
jouhdāk kéuihge bóubīu, jauh yiu doih
kéuih dóng jídáan. (~, ~. Since you
are (employed as) his bodyguard, you
are supposed to shield him against
bullets with you body.)

1240
➔síu chòih m̀chēut, daaih
chòih m̀yahp 小財唔出，大財

唔入 (lit.) if you do not give a little money out, no big fortune will come in/ to you 小財不出,大財不入 (idi.) PH nothing venture, nothing gain 不作小小犧牲,就沒有大收穫 : ~, ~. *Néih lihn géisahp mān Luhkhahpchói dōu m̀máaih, yauh dím wúih faatdaaht ā.* (~, ~. You don't even want to spend thirty or forty dollars to buy the Mark Six, how would you become rich?)

chūngmìhng 聰明 Adj. clever, smart 聰明

1241

➜chūngmìhng yāt sai, chéun deuhn yātsìh 聰明一世，蠢鈍一時 (lit.) one has been wise all one's life, but would be stupid at one time 一生人都聰明,可是一時之間卻很愚笨 (idi.) PH even a wise man would be foolish sometimes 聰明人一時糊塗 : *Kéuih haih leuhtsī, nīchi dōu béi yàhn ngāak, jānhaih ~, ~ lo!* (He is a lawyer but he was conned this time. It's true that ~, ~.)

dá 打 V fight 打架

1242

➜ m̀dá m̀sēungsīk 唔打唔相識 (lit.) PH no fight, no acquaintance 不打不相識 : *A-Gaap tùhng A-Yuht dágāau, sāumēi kéuihdeih faatgok daaihgā dōu haih A-Bíng ge pàhngyáuh, sóyíh wah lē, ~.* (A fought

with B. Later they found out that they both were friends of C. This is just as the saying goes, ~, ~.)

daaih síu 大小 N the big and/ or the small 大跟/或小

1243

➜yān síu sāt daaih 因小失大 (lit.) save the small at the expense of the big 因小失大 (idi.) PH penny gain, pound loss 得到小小好處,卻失去其他好多好處 : *Ngóh táigin deihhá yáuh yātgo yātmān ngán, séungwah jāphéi kéuih, dím jī ditjó go n̄ghmān lohk hāangkèuih, nīchī jānhaih ~ lo.* (I saw a one-dollar coin on the ground. When I tried to pick it up, a five-dollar coin of mine dropped into the gutter. This is just as the saying goes, ~.) also see 1367

dóu 賭 V gamble,bet 賭錢

1244

➜bāt dóu sih yèhngchìhn 不賭是贏錢 (lit.) PH not to gamble is money-winning 不賭是贏錢 : *Dī yàhn dóuchín (ge muhkdīk) haih séung yèhngchín jī ma, kèihsaht ~ lā.* (People gamble in order to win money. Actually, ~.)

1245

➜géi chàhng gingwo dóujái máaih tihndeih ā 幾曾見過賭仔買田地吖 (lit.) PH has anyone

198

ever seen a (habitual) gambler buy land/properties? (*The tacit answer is 'no'.) 何／不曾見過賭徒置業 ： *"Kéuih wah kéuih jī sóyíh gam laahndóu, haih yānwaih séung yèhng daaih chín máaih láu wóh." "Hàaih, ~."* ("He said the reason why he indulged in gambling was that he wanted to win a large sum of money to buy a flat." "Oh no. ~?")

1246
➔laahndóu 爛賭 (lit.) broken by gambling 因賭錢而破爛了 (idi.) Adj. indulged in gambling 沉迷賭博 ： ⓐ *Kéuih jī sóyíh je daaihyíhlūng chín, haih yānwaih taai ~ lō.* (The reason why he borrows money from loan sharks is because he is too ~.) ⓑ *~ gwái* see 1173 (* 'Laahn', i.e. broken, can also be used as an adverb meaning 'indulgently'.)

1247
➔sahp dóu gáu pin 十賭九騙 (lit.) PH of gambling, you will be cheated nine times out of ten 十賭九騙 ： *~, chūnkeih m̀hóu dóuchín a!* (~, so you should by no means gamble.)

1248
➔syūchín gāai yàuh yèhngchìhn/ chín héi 輸錢皆由贏錢起 (lit.) PH people lose money in gambling all because they win first 輸錢全因為先前贏了錢而引致的 ： *"Kéuih héisáu yèhng ge,*

sāumēi syūfāansaai." "~ ā ma." ("In the beginning he won, but later he lost all the money (he won)." "Sure, ~.")

fūk 福 N blessing, bliss, good luck 福, 福份, 好運

1249
➔daaihlaahn bātséi, bīt yáuh hauh fūk 大難不死，必有後福 (lit.) PH a person can expect good fortune after he has a narrow escape from death 大難不死，必有後福 ： ⓐ *"A-Wóng chóh góga fēigēi sātsih, hóuchói kéuih séiṁheui."* *"~, ~. Giu kéuih máaihfāan jēung Luhkkhahpchói lā."* ("The plane Wong took had an accident, and luckily he didn't die." "~. You can tell him to buy Mark Six.") ⓑ *yihsyūn jih yáuh yihsyūn fūk* see 0332 ⓒ *sihkdāk sih fūk* see 1050 ⓓ *sān joih fūk jūng bāt jī fūk* see 0711

gā 家 N/M family; measure for a family, a factory, or a shop 家庭; 家(量詞)

1250
➔dūnggā m̀dá dá sāigā 東家唔打打西家 (lit.) quit (the job in) this company and join another one (for a new job) 不在這裏工作也可以到別的地方工作 (idi.) PH there's no permanent employment in the world 世間上沒有永久固定的工作 ： *Bōsí cháau néih yàuhyú néih maih wángwo daihyih fahn*

199

gūng lō, ~ jé! (You were fired by your boss. You can simply look for a new job. You know ~!)

1251
➔gāgā yáuh bún nàahn nihm dīk gīng 家家有本難念的經 (lit.) every family has a Buddhist sutra that is difficult to chant 家家有本難念的經 (idi.) PH every family has its own problems 每個家庭都有自己的問題 : *"Néihdeih léuhng gūngpó dōu yáuh gam hóu ge gūng jouh, sāngwuht yīnggōi bātsìhng mahntàih ge bo." "Hàaih, ~, néih m̀jī gam dō ge la."* ("You and your wife/ husband have such good jobs, there shouldn't be any problems with your livelihood." "Oh, ~. You don't know much about us.")

1252
➔gā wòh maahnsih hīng (, gā sēui háu bāt tihng) 家和萬事興 (,家衰口不停) (lit.) PH a family in harmony would achieve prosperity, but if the family members quarrel all the time, that would cause the family to fall into a decline 家庭和諧,會興盛(,但如果家中常有爭吵,則家庭會衰敗) : *~, yáuh mēéh sih maih daaihgā chóhdāi sēunglèuhngháh lō, sáimāt gam chòuh a?* (~. Let's sit down and talk about the problem. Why should we quarrel?/We don't need to quarrel.)

1253
➔jāp syū hàahng tàuh, cháamgwo baaihgā 執輸行頭,慘過敗家 (lit.) being the first one to suffer loss is worse than losing the wealth of the family 比人家先吃虧比敗了家中財富更慘 (idi.) PH never be late in grasping benefits 千萬不要比別人遲得到利益 : *Gógāan chīukāp sìhchèuhng gāmyaht hōimohk, tàuh ńghsahp go guhaak béi yihsahp mān jauh hóyíh yahm ló yéh. Ngóhdeih faaidī heui lo, ~, ~ ā ma.* (Today is the first day of business of that supermarket. It offers a free shopping spree to the first fifty customers for just paying twenty dollars. Let's go quickly. You know, ~, ~.)

1254
➔yātgā pìhnyìh léuhnggā jeuhk 一家便宜兩家着 (lit.) PH (it seems that one side is making a profit, but actually) both sides will benefit 大家都有好處 : *Go poutáu lóuhbáan deui yihpjyú góng, "Gīngjai gam chā, yùhgwó néih gáam ngóh jōu, jauh ~. Yùhgwó m̀haih, ngóh yiu jāplāp, néih yiu dīuhūng go pouwái, jauh leuih dau leuih lō."* (The shopowner said to the landlord, "The economy is bad here. If you reduce the rent [of the shop], then it will be ~. Otherwise, I'll have to close down my shop, and nobody will rent it, then it will be bad for both of us.")

gaisou 計數 **VO do a sum** 計算

1255

→síu sou pa chèuhng gai 小數怕長計 (lit.) PH an ever growing amount though small will become a large sum 少數怕長計 : *Sēuiyihn múihgo yuht kau yātbaak mān, daahnhaih ~, yātnihn jauh kau yātchīn yihbaak mān ge lo bo!* (Although only one hundred dollars are deducted each month, ~. By the end of the year, one thousand and two hundred dollars would have been deducted.)

gíng 景 **N view** 風景, 景物 **M go**

1256

→lóging 攞景 (lit.) get a view 取景 (idi.) VO (said of film making or picture taking) on location, look for a background 拍電影或拍照時取景 : *Ngōi tùhng ngóh yíng jěung séung ā, ngóh séung ~ nīgo ~.* (Would you take a picture of me, please? I want to ~ this ~ as the background for my picture.)

1257

→lóging dihng jahnghing 攞景定贈興(慶) (lit.) Do you mean to take pictures (of me with a camera) or give me anger? 取景還是贈送惱怒 (idi.) PH (Are you really happy for me/him or) do you want to make me/him angry? 你(是真的為我高興抑或是)要令我生氣? : *Néih mihngjī kéuih tùhng néuih pàhngyáuh dengjó bōu juhng mahn kéuih géisí chéngyám, néih ~ a?* (You know very well that he has broken up with his girlfriend, but you still ask him when he will give his wedding banquet. ~?) (*The focus of the expression is on 'jahnghing', and 'ging' in 'lóging' rhymes with 'hing' in 'jahnghing'.)

góng 講 **V speak, talk, say** 說

1258

→góng dō cho dō 講多錯多 (lit.) PH the more one speaks, the more mistakes he'll make 說得越多, 錯得也越多 : *~, sóyíh yáuhsih mchēutsēng juhng hóudī.* (~. Sometimes it's better to keep one's mouth shut.)

gúlóuh 古老 **Adj. old fashioned, be out** 古老

1259

→gúlóuh dong sìhhīng 古老當時興 (lit.) PH the old-fashioned is treated as a trend 把舊的款式當新的 : *"Yìhgā dōjó yàhn jeuk tòhngjōng sāamfu bo!" "~ ā ma!"* ("Now there are more people wearing traditional Chinese costume." "You know, ~.")

hòhng 行 **N/M line of business, walk of life; measure for a trade** 行業; 行業的量詞

1260

→tùhnghòhng yùh dihk gwok
同行如敵國 (lit.) people in the
same trade regard each other as
enemies 同行如敵國
(idi.) PH there's always keen
competition between people in the
same trade 同一行業之間競爭劇
烈 : *Sēuiyihn wah ~ jē, daahnhaih
léuhnggāan gūngsī ge lóuhbáan hái
yàhn mihnchihn dōu yáuh góng yáuh
siu ga.* (Although we say ~, the
bosses of the two [competing]
companies appear to be very friendly
to each other in public.) also see
1705.

jaai 債 N debt 債 M bāt; dī

1261

→chèuhngmehng jaai,
chèuhngmehng wàahn 長命
債，長命還 (lit.) life time debts
take a life time to pay off 長命的債
要一輩子才可清還
(idi.) PH pay large debts little by
little (and so it will take one a long
time to be out of debt) 太多的債要
慢慢清償 : ⓐ *"Ngóh chàhng láu
yiu gūng yihsahp nihn."* *"~ lō!"* ("I
have to pay installments for my flat
for twenty years." "Well, ~.") ⓑ
mòuh jaai yātsān hēng see 0706

1262

→yàhnchìhng gángwo jaai 人
情緊過債 (lit.) PH to buy and

send a gift is more urgent than
paying a debt 送禮比還債更迫切 :
*"A-Chán hahgo láihbaai gitfān
chéngyám. Ngóhdeih yiu faaidī jouh
yàhnchìhng."* *"Gánghaih lā, ~."*
("Chan invited us to his wedding
banquet next week. We should
hurry up and buy him a gift." "Sure,
~.")

jáu 走 V run 跑

1263

→meih hohk hàahng sīn hohk
jáu 未學行先學走 (lit.) learn to
run before learning to walk 還沒有
學會走路便學跑
(idi.) PH too impatient to jump to the
next phase 太急不及待要到第二個
步驟 : *Yātgo hohk sé Jūngmàhn jih
móuh géi nói ge ngoihgwok hohksāang
séung hohk Jūnggwok syūfaat, kéuih ge
sīnsāang wah, "Néih joi hohk noihdī
sīn lā, ~."* (A foreign student wants to
learn Chinese calligraphy shortly after
he has started to learn how to write
Chinese characters. His teacher says,
"Spend more time to learn to write
characters before you pick up
calligraphy. You are ~.")

1264

→sāamsahp luhk jeuhk, jáu
wàih seuhng jeuhk 三十六
着，走爲上着 (lit.) among the
thirty-six tactics, 'to flee' is the best
one 三十六着,走爲上着

(idi.) PH it would be best for one to run away (from the scene) 逃離現場是最佳辦法 : *Hōipín ge sihhauh, ngóh faatgok kéuihdeih yàhn dō, ngóhdeih yàhn síu, sóyíh ngóh ~, ~.* (When we started the [gang] fight, I found that they had more men than we did. So I thought ~, ~.)

jēng 精 Adj. too smart, too clever, shrewd 太聰明

1265

➔chèuih bahn yáuh jēng 除笨有精 (lit.) take away foolishness and there is cleverness 除去愚笨就有聰明

(idi.) PH it's still worth doing (though it may not be an easy job) (雖然事情或許不易做,可是還是)值得做 : *Heui ngàhnhòhng jouh làuhyúh ngonkit yiu béi hóudō leihsīk, daahnhaih yùhgwó dī làuhga héi, maih ~ lō.* (After you have gotten a mortgage from the bank, you have to pay a lot of interest. But ~ in case the flat prices would rise.)

1266

➔jēnggwāijó 精歸咗(lit.) PH always thinking of the benefits to one's self 太精乖了,太爲自己的好處著想 : *Kéuih nīgo yàhn sēuiyihn sauhgwo gōusām gaauyuhk, daahnhaih jouhyéh jauh ~.* (Although he is well educated, he is ~ when it comes to work.)

jī 知 V know 知道

1267

➔yeuhk yiu yàhn bāt jī, chèuihfēi géi mohk wàih 若要人不知,除非己莫爲 (lit.) if you don't want others to know, you should not have done it 若要人不知,除非己莫爲

(idi.) PH there's no absolute secret in the world 世界上沒有絕對的秘密: *"Néih m̀hóu jēung nīgo beimaht góngbéi yàhn jī." "~, ~, ngóh m̀góng yàhndeih dōu wúih jī lā."* ("Don't let others know the secret." "~, ~. People will find it out even if I don't tell them.") also see 0117

kùhng fu 窮富 N poverty and/ or wealth 貧窮跟/或有錢

1268

➔bouh kùhng nàahn dái, bouh fu nàahn tái 暴窮難抵,暴富難睇 (lit.) PH a sudden fall into poverty is hard to endure, and a sudden gain of wealth will make it difficult for others to tolerate one's arrogance (*The second segment is more often used than the first one.) : *Sówaih ~, ~. Kéuih fātyìhngāan sīngjó jouh júng gīngléih, gánghaih béi mihnsīk ngóhdeih tái lā.* (As the saying goes, ~, ~. He would certainly make us feel that he is superior to us since he was suddenly promoted to general manager.)

léih 理 BF/N reason 道理

1269

➔bōng léih bāt bōng chān 幫理不幫親 (lit.) take sides with reason, but not with blood relationship 幫理不幫親 (idi.) PH uphold justice regardless of personal relationships 主持公道,不考慮人的關係 ： *Kéuih bàhbā hái līp léuihbihn toutàahm béi yàhn wah, kéuih ~, dōu hyun kéuih bàhbā ṁhóu gám jouh.* (His father was criticized by others for having spit in the lift. He ~ and asked him not to do that.)

leih hoih 利害 N the good and/or the bad of doing something 利害, 利弊

1270

➔yáuh (yāt) leih bīt yáuh (yāt) hoih 有(一)利必有(一)害 (lit.) if there is any benefit, there must be harm, too 有利必有一害 (idi.) PH there's no absolute benefit in anything 沒有絕對有利益的事 ： *Dihnlóuh sēuiyìhn wah deui yàhnleuih yáuh hóu daaih ge gunghin, daahnhaih dihnlóuh behngduhk yauh hóu màhfàahn, sóyíh wah lē, ~.* (Although computer is a great contribution to human life, computer viruses are very troublesome. That's why people say ~.) also see 1083

maahn 慢 Adj. slow 慢

1271

➔maahn gūng chēut sai fo 慢工出細貨 (lit.) PH slow work makes a product delicate and perfect 慢慢做才會做出精細的貨物 ： *"Nī tou sāijōng yiu yātgo yuht sīnji jouhhóu àh?" "Haih a, ~ ā ma. Néih ṁséung mē?"* ("It will take you one month to make a Western suit [for me]?" "Yes, sir. You know, ~. Don't you want a good tailored suit?")

nàahn 難 Adj. difficult 難

1272

➔maahn sih héitàuh nàahn 萬事起頭難 (lit.) PH in doing everything, it is difficult at the beginning 萬事起頭難 ： *~, ngóhdeih gūngsī hōitàuh gó géi nìhn sihtbún, hóujoih sāuṁēi nìhnnìhn jaahnchín.* (~. Our company had lost money for the first few years. Luckily, it made money every year later.)

1273

➔sēung gin hóu, tùhng jyuh nàahn 相見好，同住難 (lit.) PH it's better to see each other from time to time than to live together (because there would be conflicts and disputes) 有時見見面就很好, 一起住就不好 (因爲會發生衝突爭執) ： *Sēuiyìhn ngóhdeih haih hóu pàhngyáuh, daahnhaih ~, ~. hái sūkse léuihbihn, ngóhdeih ṁwúih jouh tùhngfóng ge.*

(Although we are good friends, we won't be roommates in the dormitory because ~, ~.)

sānfú 辛苦 **Adj. hard, fatigued** 辛苦

1274

→yáuh jih m̀joih, ló fú làih sān 有自唔在，攞苦嚟辛 (lit.) give up the easy way of doing things but take the hard way 有舒服的方法不用,卻要用吃力的方法
(idi.) PH prefer to do something the hard way 偏要辛苦： ⓐ *"Néih jyuh gam gōu, m̀daap līp, yiu hàahng làuhtāi! Dímgáai ~, ~ a?" "Ngóh séung gáamfèih ā ma."* ("Your house is so high up in this building. You don't use the lift. You climb the stairs instead. Why do you ~, ~?" "I want to keep fit, you know.") ⓑ *sānfú wánlàih jihjoih sihk* see 1043

sēui wohng 衰旺 **N bad luck and/or good luck** 運氣壞跟/或運氣好

1275

→yàhn yáuh sāam sēui luhk wohng 人有三衰六旺 (lit.) man has three good times and six bad times 人有時運氣差,有時運氣好
(idi.) PH there are always times of adversity or prosperity in life 人生必有失意或得意的時候 ： *"Hàaih, gāmnihn tàuhtàuh pungjeuhk hāak." "Néih m̀sái gam sāmngāp, ~, chēutnín*

hàahngwahn dōu m̀díng lē." ("Oh! I am having a string of bad luck this year." "Don't be so upset. ~. Maybe you will have good luck next year.")

tāamsām 貪心 **Adj. greedy, convetous** 貪心

1276

→tāam jih bin go pàhn 貪字變個貧 (lit.) the character for 貪 (i.e. covetous, greedy) becomes the one for 貧 (i.e. poverty) 貪字變了貧字
(idi.) PH lose much money because of covetousness 因爲貪心,所以損失了很多錢財 ： *Kéuih yíhwàih gúsíh juhng wúih sīng, dímjī gāmyaht daaih dit, nīchi ~ la.* (He thought the share prices would still be on the rise. How could he have known that they plunged today. This time he ~.)

yúhn ngaahng 軟硬 **Adj. soft and/ or hard** 軟及/ 或硬

1277

→sauh yúhn m̀sauh ngaahng 受軟唔受硬 (lit.) can bear softness but cannot tolerate hardness 吃軟不吃硬
(idi.) PH (said of people) yield to gentle measures but not tough ones 可屈服於懷柔手段,卻不會屈服於強硬的手段 ： *Kèihsaht dī saimānjái haih ~ ge. Yùhgwó néih dádāk kéuih dō, kéuihdeih juhng wúih yáihdī tīm.* (In fact, children ~. They'll become naughtier if you beat them so much.)

205

6. Everyday Objects

bō 波 N ball 球 M go

1278 ✓

→bō 波 (lit.) N ball 球 M go
(idi.) N (1) woman's breast 女性乳房 M go (2) typhoon signal 風球 : *Yìhgā ché sāam houh ~ jē, chìhdī wúih ché baat houh.* (Now ~ no. 3 is in force, and no. 8 may be hoisted later.) N/ M gear of a car 汽車的變速指示 : ⓐ*jyun/tong* ~ (shift ~) ⓑ*jyun/ yahp yih* ~ (shift into second [~]) ⓒ *jihduhng ~ chē* (an automatic [i.e. a car with automatic transmission/gears]) (*The other kind of car is called 'gwanbō chē'.)

bōu 煲 N/M pot, kettle; measure meaning 'a pot/kettle of' 鍋, 壺; 量詞:一鍋/壺 M go

1279

→baaubōu 爆煲 (lit.) blast the kettle 鍋爆了
(idi.) VO the secret is exposed 秘密讓大家知道了 : *Kéuih bāau yihnáai ge sih ~ jó ~ la, sóyíh taaitáai yiu tùhng kéuih lèihfān.* (His affair has already ~. That's why his wife wanted to divorce him.)

1280 ✓

→chàhbōu 茶煲 (lit.) N tea kettle 沏茶的水壺 M go
(idi.) N a transliteration of the English word 'trouble' 是英文'麻

煩'一字的音譯 : *Néuihyán haih ~.* (Women are ~.)

1281

→dāanlíu tùhngbōu → yāt gwán jauh suhk 單料同煲→一滾就熟 (lit.) a kettle made of thin plate of copper→as soon as the water boils, the food (inside the kettle) is done 用薄銅片做的鍋→水一開,食物就煮熟了
(idi.) HIT said of a woman whom a man can seduce very easily by flirting with her just a little (指女性) 只需要逗她一點兒,她便會跟你變得相熟 : *Kéuih haih sauhgwo gōusām gaauyuhk ge néuihjái, mhaih gódī ~ → ~ ga.* (She is much educated, and she's not the kind of woman who ~ → ~.)

1282

→dengbōu 揼煲 (lit.) throw away the sandpot and break it 把沙鍋砸破
(idi.) VO (said of lovers) break up (with each other) 指情侶分手 : *Kéuihdeih léuhnggo paakjó géigo yuht tō jauh ~ jó ~ lo.* (The two lovers have already ~ after dating for just a few months.)

1283

→diu sābōu 吊沙煲 (lit.) hang (up) the earthen pot (because there's nothing to cook) (因爲沒東西煮,所以)把沙鍋吊起

(idi.) VO starve 要揸餓 :
*Ngāamngāam yuhngsaai dī chín,
tīngyaht sīnji chēutlèuhng,
gāmmáahn yiu ~ la.* (I've used all
my money. I won't get my pay
check untill tomorrow. So tonight
we have to ~.)

1284
➔kūbōu 箍煲 (lit.) mend the
cracked sandpot (usually by putting
wires around it) 修補破裂的沙鍋
(通常用鐵線圍著它)
(idi.) VO try to make up/ not to
break up with one's lover 試圖挽
回愛情 : *Néih tùhng néuih
pàhngyáuh ngaaijó gāau àh?
Faaidī ~ la, yùhgwó m̀haih jauh wúih béi
yàhn chéungjó heui ge la.* (You had a
quarrel with your girlfriend? Hurry
up and ~. Otherwise, she would be
stolen away by another man.)

1285✓
➔sābōu ngāangchāang 沙煲
罌罉 (lit.) PH sandpot, jar and
kettle 沙鍋,罌跟壺 M dī
(idi.) N pots and pans 炊具 M dī :
Móuh ~, dím jyúfaahn a? (There isn't
any ~. How to cook a meal then?)

bou 布 N cloth 布 M faai; pāt

1286
➔yātpāt bou gam chèuhng
一疋布咁長 (lit.) as long as a
bolt of cloth 像一疋布那麼長
(idi.) PH very long story to tell 說
起來話長的事 : *Kéuih dímyéung
wánfāan sātsaanjó ge fuhmóuh?
Gónghéilàih jànhaih ~.* (How was he

reunited with his lost parents? It's
~.)

**boyāmtúng 播音筒 N
megaphone 擴音器, 傳聲筒 M go**

1287 ✓
➔boyāmtúng 播音筒 (lit.) N
megaphone 擴音器, 傳聲筒 M go
(idi.) N one who likes to talk about
others' secrets 愛說人家秘密的
人 : *Kéuih jingyāt haih ~ làih ga,
yùhgwó kéuih jīdou néih ge
beimaht, jauh chyùhn saigaai ge
yàhn dōu jī ge la.* (S/He really is ~.
If s/he knows your secret, then
everyone in the world will know it
too.)

**būi 杯 N/M cup; measure
meaning 'a cup of' 杯子; 量
詞: 一杯 M go/jek**

1288
➔mahnbūi 問杯 (lit.) ask the
cup 問問杯子
(idi.) VO cast horoscope (by using
two small pieces of wood) (用兩塊
小木片)占卜 : *Yáuhdī màihseun ge
yàhn wúih heui míu ~, táiháh pòuhsaat
yáuh mātyéh jísih.* (Some super-
stitious people go to the temple to ~.
They want to see what divine
revelation the dieties have for them.)

**chàaih 柴 N firewood 柴 M
tiuh; gān**

1289
➔chàaih máih yàuh yìhm
(jeung chou chàh) 柴米油鹽
(醬醋茶) see 1004

1290

➡chàaihtòih 柴台 (lit.) firewood and stage (for performance) 柴跟戲台 (idi.) VO hoot at, make catcalls 喝倒彩 : *Gógo gōsīng dāngtòih cheunggō ge sihhauh jáuyām, béi dī gūnjung ~ / gūnjung ~ kéuih ~.* (That singer sang out of tune when he was having a live performance. The audience ~ him.) (* 'Chàaihtòih' might have been made up of 踩台, which means to stamp on the stage [on seeing a poor performance].)

1291

➡chàaih wāwā 柴娃娃 (lit.) firewood doll 柴做的娃娃 (idi.) PH/ A. PH do something not seriously like playing games 做事不認真,兒戲 : *Nīgo dihnsih jitmuhk wuhnjó géigo hauhsāangjái jouh jyúchìh. Kéuihdeih jouh jitmuhk ge sihhauh ~ gám.* (That TV program has new hosts. They are very young and they host the program in a ~ way.)

1292

➡chòhnghahdái pochàaih → johng daaih báan 床下底破柴→撞大板 (lit.) chop firewood under the bed→ (the chopper would) hit the wooden frame of the bed 在床底下砍柴→(砍柴的刀)撞到了床的大木板 (idi.) HIT run into big trouble 碰到大麻煩 : *Tàuhsīn tùhng ngóh hái līpdouh ngaaigāau ge néuihyán, yùhnlòih haih bōsí ge a mā, nīchi jānhaih ~ → ~ la. Táipa bōsí wúih cháau ngóh.* (The woman who just quarreled with me in the lift is the

mother of our boss. This time I ~ → ~. I'm afraid our boss will fire me.) also see 1108

1293

➡daaih hóu chàhmhēung dong laahn chàaih 大好沉香當爛柴 (lit.) very good aloeswood is taken for rotten wood 上好的沉香被當作是朽木 (idi.) PH precious thing is regarded as rubbish 好的東西被當作是不值錢的東西 : *Kéuih bàhbā jihngdāi béi kéuih gó géigauh gú yúk sēuiyìhn m̀haih géi héingáahn, daahnhaih hóu jihkchín. Dímjī kéuih jauh sungjó béi yàhn, jānhaih ~.* (The pieces of jade that his father left him were very precious, though they were not very attractive. However he gave them to others. This is just as the saying goes, ~.)

1294

➡fai chàaih 廢柴 (lit.) useless firewood 沒用的木柴 (idi.) N (said of a man) useless thing (指男性)廢人 M tiuh : *Kéuih gaausyū yauh m̀dāk, jouh hàhngjing yauh yāttaap wùhtòuh, jingyāt ~.* (He can't teach well and is incompetent in administration. He is really a ~.)

1295

➡gwōnggwan(lóu) yuhjeuhk móuhpèih chàaih 光棍(佬)遇著冇皮柴 (lit.) a naked-rod (guy) meets a skinless-log 光禿棍子遇到沒有皮的木柴 (idi.) PH a swindler is fooled by another swindler 騙子也被人欺騙 : *Ngóh séung ngāak kéuihdī chín, dímjí béi kéuih ngāakjó ngóhdī chín, nīchi jánhaih ~ lo.* (I wanted to con him out of his money, but as a result he got money from me. This time it's just as the saying goes, ~.)

1296

➜lāaichàaih 拉 柴 (lit.) pull firewood 拉動木柴

(idi.) VO die, be dead 死 : *Kéuih ~ jó ~ lo.* (He's ~.) (* 'Lāaichàaih' now is not so commonly used as 'dēng [goi]', see 1340.)

1297

➜lóuh chàaih 老柴 (lit.) old firewood 老的木柴

(idi.) N (said of a man) old thing (說男性) 老傢伙 M tiuh : *Gó tiuh ~ gam ngok ga!* (That ~ is so fierce!)

1298

➜náumàhn chàaih 扭紋柴 (lit.) firewood of twisted grain 紋理扭曲的木柴

(idi.) N a person who always shows irrational disagreement and whom people find it hard to handle 常鬧彆扭的人 M go/ tiuh : *Gógo jōuhaak jingyāt ~ làih ge. Kéuih m̀haih láu nīyeuhng jauh haih láu góyeuhng. Néih wah béifāan ngongām kéuih, kéuih jauh wah yiu jyuhgau (sihgaan) sīn. Dou kéuih jyuhgau la, kéuih yauh yiu néih béi būnchīnfai, yùhgwó m̀haih jauh chihdī sīnji būnjáu.* (That tenant is really ~. You give him this but he wants that. I'd tried to give him back the deposit, but he wanted to*

stay untill the end of the lease. Then he asked for money to pay the moving company. He said unless I agreed, otherwise he wouldn't move out.)

1299

➜ngáauchàaih 拗 柴 (lit.) break firewood 把柴枝拗折

(idi.) VO twist/sprain one's ankle 腳踝骨扭傷 : *Kéuih jáudāk taai faai, deihhá yauh waaht, fātyihn jek geuk yāt wāt jauh ~ jó ~ lo.* (He ran too fast, and the ground was wet. Suddenly he ~.)

1300

➜ saudou hóuchíh tiuh chàaih gám 瘦到好似條柴噉 (lit.) PH (said of a person) as thin as a piece of firewood/ a rail 指人骨瘦如柴 : *Néih sèhngyaht gáamfèih m̀sihkyéh, ~, bīndouh hóutái ā.* (You always want to keep fit and do not want to eat. You are ~. Do you think that makes you look good?)

chek 尺 M/N foot; ruler 尺 M bá

1301

➜dāk chyun jeun chek 得寸進尺 (lit.) get an inch, then want to have one foot (i.e. ten inches in Chinese system of measurement) 得寸進尺

(idi.) PH (1) insatiable/ never satisfied 貪得無厭 : *Dī mòuhpàaih síufáan ~. Chōsih kéuihdeih hái ngūkchyūn ngoihbihn báaidong, móuh yàhn léih, yìhgā jauh yahplàih ngūkchyūn báaidong.* (The licenseless hawkers are ~. At the beginning, they

210

put up their stalls outside our housing estate. Since nobody told them to go away, now they even do business inside our place.) (2) go on taking advantage of or bullying others (because one has not been challenged) 繼續找別人的好處／欺負別人（因別人沒有反抗）：*Néih ìnhóu ~ bo! Ngóh ìnchēutsēng néih jauh dong ngóh behng māau.* (Don't ~, and don't take me for a sick cat because I stayed silent on the matter.) see 0255

1302

➔néih ging ngóh yāt chek, ngóh ging néih yāt jeuhng 你敬我一尺，我敬你一丈 (lit.) you offer me one foot and I'll offer you ten in return 你敬我一尺,我敬你一丈 (*There are ten Chinese feet in one 'jeuhng'.)
(idi.) PH I'll be much more respectful to you if you respect me first 你尊敬我,我更尊敬你：*"Néih sáimāt gam haakhei a?" "Óh, ~, ~ jē!"* ("You don't have to stand on ceremony." "Oh, it's only ~, ~.")

chēung 窗 N window 窗戶 M go

1303

➔lāaimàaih tīnchēung 拉埋天窗 (lit.) close the high window on the roof 把房頂的天窗關上
(idi.) PH get married 結婚：*Néih nìhngéi ìnsai ge la, néih tùhng néuih pàhngyáuh faaidī ~ lā.* (You are not young, and you'd better hurry up and ~ with your girlfriend.) (*Originally, it is a way to keep the privacy of a married couple by

closing the high window on the roof.)

chìhhei 瓷器 N porcelain, chinaware 瓷器 M gihn

1304

➔chìhhei pung gōngngáh 瓷器碰缸瓦 (lit.) hit earthenware with chinaware 用瓷器砸陶器
(idi.) PH not worth running such a risk/ struggling with people of much lower social status 不值得冒這樣的險／跟社會階級比你低很多的人鬥爭：*Gógo mìhnglàuh sēuiyìhn sīk gūngfū, daahnhaih kéuih béi yàhn dágip gójahnsí, dōu ìngám fáankong, faisih ~ lā.* (Although the well-known man knew Chinese martial arts, he dared not resist when he was robbed by a thief. He thought that it was ~.)

chìhng 罉 N/M an earthenware jar, a jug for wine; measure meaning 'a jar/ jug of' 罈子; 量詞：一罈子 M go

1305 ✓

➔chouchìhng 醋罉 (lit.) N a big jar for vinegar 盛醋的罈子 M go
(idi.) N jealous lover 妒忌心很重的情侶：*Kéuih néuih pàhngyáuh haih ~ làih ge, kéuih jaanháh kèihtā néuihjái dōu ìndāk.* (He has a jealous girlfriend. He cannot praise other girls.)

1306

➔dálaahn (go) chouchìhng 打爛(個)醋罉 (lit.) break the vinegar jar 把醋罈子打翻

211

(idi.) PH (said of lovers) become very jealous (指情侶)忽然充滿醋意 ： *Néih tàuhsīn tùhng gógo leng néui kīnggái, néih néuih pàhngyáuh ~ la. Faaidī heui tamfāan kéuih lā.* (Your girlfriend ~ because you talked to that pretty girl just a moment ago. Hurry up and calm her down.)

chín/chìhn 錢 N money 錢 M dī

1307

➔chānsāangjái bātyùh gahnsān chìhn 親生仔不如近身錢 (lit.) PH one's own child is not as good as the money on hand 親生子(女)不如身邊的錢那樣好 ： *Sēuiyihn wah yéuhngyih fòhng lóuh jē, daahnhaih ~, néih dōu haih jihgéi chóuhfāan dī chín hóu(dī).* (People say, 'Bring up a child and s/he will support you when you are old.' However, ~. You'd better put aside some money for yourself.)

1308✓

➔chéungchín 搶錢 (lit.) rob money 劫財

(idi.) VO (said of commercial traders) ask for too much money like robbers, daylight robbery (指從事商業活動的人)索價太高像強盜 ： ⓐ *Gógo yīsāng ~, jouh go síu sáuseuht jauh yiu gam dō chín.* (That doctor ~ for just performing a minor operation.) ⓑ *Gógāan ngàhnhòhng ~, yiu ngóhdeih béi gam gōu leihsīk.* (That bank ~. It imposes such a high interest rate on us [when borrowing money from it.])

1309

➔chihnchāt 錢七 (lit.) money seven 錢及七

(idi.) N very old car (that you can hear its groans, which sound similar to 'chihn' and 'chāt' when its engine is being started) 很陳舊的汽車,開動時發出像'錢'及'七'的聲音 M ga ： *Sān chē ngóh jauh móuh búnsih máaih la, máaih ga ~ jājāháh lō.* (I can't afford to buy a new car. I can just buy a ~ for daily use.)

1310

➔faat chín hòhn 發錢寒 (lit.) have a fever for money 為錢發熱

(idi.) PH extremely crave for money 非常渴望有錢 ： *Jouh gam dō fahn gīmjīk, ~ mè!* (He has so many part-time jobs. Does he ~?)

1311

➔fongdāi máaih louh chìhn 放低買路錢 (lit.) put down money for buying the road 放下買路錢

(idi.) PH (used to be said by robbers) leave your money before you go (以前賊人打刧時說) 放下錢才可以走 ： *Kéuih góngsiu gám deui ngóh wah, "Néih yihgā jáu àh? ~ sīn lā!"* (He said to me jokingly, "Are you leaving now? ~.")

1312

➔fonglouh kāichìhn→yáhn séi yàhn 放路溪錢→引死人 (lit.) paper money cast on the roadside→to attract the dead 放在路邊的紙錢→是用來吸引死人的

(idi.) HIT deadly attractive 極吸引人 (*'Kāichihn' is a kind of paper offering to ghosts and is used as a kind of currency in the underworld. 'Séi', literally meaning 'to die or be dead', can be used as a BF, or an adverb metaphorically meaning 'extremely'.)： *Gógo singgám néuih sīng ge sānchòih jānhaih leng la, ~ → ~.* (That sexy actress's figure is terrific. It's ~.)

1313
→gaakyeh chìhn 隔夜錢 (lit.) money left over last night 昨晚剩下的錢
(idi.) N money left over for use 剩下來可以用的錢 ： ⓐ *Gó gāan poutáu ge mùhn seuhngbihn tipjó yātjēung jí séiyuh, "Bún dim mòuh ~." Yānwaih lóuhbáan pa yáuh chaahklóu làih tāuchín.* (There is a paper taped on the door of the store. It is written on it, "There is no money put overnight in our store." This is because the shopowner is afraid that thieves will come and steal money.) ⓑ *Kéuihdī chín yahtyaht chīng, bīndouh yáuh ~ (yuhng) ā?* (He uses up all his money every day. How could it be possible for him to have ~?)

1314
→gwaatchín 刮錢 (lit.) scrape off money 把錢刮下
(idi.) VO grab money by unfair means 斂財 ： *Gógo tāam gūn ~ jó yāt daaih bāt ~ sīnji teuiyāu.* (Before he retired, the corrupt official had grabbed a large sum of money.) Adj. like to grab money by unfair means

喜歡財的 ： *Gógāan hohkhaauh hóu ~ ga, sihngyaht yiu hohksāang gāau māt fai gāau maht fai.* (That school ~. The students always have to pay for this or that.)

1315
→hāakchín 黑錢 (lit.) black money 見不得光的錢
(idi.) N (1) money for bribery 行賄的錢 M dī ： *Béi ~ tùhng sāu ~ dōu haih yáuh jeuih ge.* (Giving or taking ~ is a crime.) (2) money of triad gang 黑社會的錢 ： *sái ~* (launder ~)

1316
→sīgéi chín 私己錢 (lit.) private money 私己錢
(idi.) N pin money (that a woman gets from the money given by her husband to pay family expenses) 女子從家庭開支中私自省下及儲蓄的錢 ： *Sēuiyihn go lóuhgūng yáuhchín jē, néih dōu yiu wánfāan dī ~ ji hóu.* (Although your husband is rich, you still need to have some ~.)

1317
→sīn sái meihlòih chìhn 先使未來錢 (lit.) PH spend the money that people haven't earned yet 花還未賺到的錢 ： *Yìhgā ngàhnhòhng sèhngyaht giu yàhn jechín, jīkhaih gúlaih yàhn ~ ge jē.* (Nowadays, the banks always lure people to get a loan from them. They are actually encouraging people to ~.)

1318
→tipchín máaih laahn sauh 貼錢買難受 (lit.) pay money to buy

213

oneself hardship to endure 出錢買苦難來受

(idi.) PH although one has paid for it, one still has to suffer 雖然付了錢,卻還要受苦 : *Góchi chāamgā hòuhwàh léuihhàhngtyùhn, dímjī chēutfaat jīhauh jauh behngjó, gwái gam sānfú, jānhaih ~.* (That time I joined a luxury tour group. However, I fell sick after we set out. I felt very bad. The saying is true that ~.)

1319

➔ yāt fān chìhn, yāt fān fo 一分錢一分貨 (lit.) pay one cent, and you'll get the thing that is worth one cent 一分錢一分貨

(idi.) PH what you buy is worth the money you pay for it, quality is commensurate with price 品質與價錢成正比 : *"Sáimāt yiu jeuk mìhngpàaih sāam a!" "~, maht yáuh só jihk ge."* ("Why do you always wear brand-named clothes?" "~. Although they are expensive, it's still worth buying them.")

1320

➔ yáuh chín (dōu) móuh mehng héung/sái 有錢(都)冇命享/使 (lit.) have a lot of money but no life in which to spend it 有很多錢但沒有生命去享用

(idi.) PH although one has a lot of mone, one cannot spend it because one is going to die/dead 人雖然有錢, 但因為(快要)死了沒有機會用 : *Kéuih jungjó Luhkkhahpchói móuh géi nói jauh faatyihn yáuh kēnsá." "Jānhaih hósīk la, ~."* ("Not long after he won the

Mark Six, he found he had cancer." "What a pity! ~.")

ching 秤 N a Chinese weighing scale 秤 M go

1321 ✓

➔ chingtòh 秤砣 (lit.) N the sliding weight of a steelyard/Chinese scale 秤錘 M go

(idi.) N one who clings to somebody else 常不離身的人 M go : *Ngóhge jái léuhng seui, ngóh chēutyahp dōu yiu chingjyuh kéuih, hóuchíh go ~ gám.* (My son is only two years old. I need to bring him along wherever I go. He is just like ~.)

1322

➔ gūng bāt lèih pòh, ching bāt lèih tòh 公不離婆,秤不離砣 (lit.) a husband should not leave his wife alone just as the sliding weight should not be detached from the scale 公不離婆,秤不離秤錘

(idi.) PH husbands and wives should always go in pairs, just like the sliding weight and the scale 夫婦應出雙入對,就像秤跟秤錘一樣 : *Mhóu béi néihge lóuhgūng jouh taaihūngyàhn a, ~, ~ ā ma.* (Don't let your husband emigrate without you. You should know that ~, ~.)

chòh 鋤 N hoe 鋤頭 M go

1323 ✓

➔ chòh 鋤 (lit.) V dig with a hoe 用鋤頭掘

(idi.) V (1) blame/find fault with a person especially in a meeting or conference : *hōiwúi ge sìhhauh béi*

214

yàhn ~ (be criticized/ condemned by others in the meeting) (2) study (books) very hard 非常用功溫習 : *lēi (màaih) hái tòuhsyūgún ~ syū* (stay in the library and ~)

chòhng 床/牀 N bed 床/牀 M jēung

1324

→chòhnghahdái tekyín → gōugihk yáuhhaahn 床下底踢毽 → 高極有限 (lit.) play shuttlecock under a bed→ it cannot go high 在床底下踢毽子→不可以踢得很高

(idi.) HIT only limited achievement can be expected 成就有限 :
ⓐ *Kéuih gam láahn duhksyū, dī sihngjīk gánghaih ~ → ~ lā.* (He is very lazy in his studies. I'm sure that his grades must be ~ → ~.)
ⓑ *Kéuih sēuiyìhn wah jouh gīngléih jē, daahnhaih gógāan m̀haih daaih gūngsī, sóyíh sānséui dōu haih ~ → ~ jē.* (Although he is a manager, the company where he works in is not a large one. So his salary is actually ~ → ~.)

1325

→chòhngtàuh dágāau chòhngméih wòh 床頭打交床尾和 (lit.) fight at the head of the bed but make up at the foot of the bed 在床頭打架,但在床尾和好

(idi.) PH (said of a married couple) can easily make up after a quarrel (指夫婦)爭吵後很快便和好如

初 : *"Kéuihdeih léuhng gūngpó sèhngyaht ngaaigāau." "Sáimāt dāamsām ā, ~."* ("The couple always quarrels." "You don't need to worry about them, they ~.")

1326

→duhnghéi chòhngbáan 戙起床板 (lit.) put up the wooden frame of the bed 把床上的大木板豎起

(idi.) A. PH (work) until after midnight (工作)至深夜 : *Fahn bougou gāmyaht yiu gāau sóyíh kàhmmáahn ~ jouh.* (I need to hand in the report today, so I worked ~ last night.)

1327

→laamgwo chòhngtàuh dōu haih fuhmóuh 躐過床頭都係父母 (lit.) whoever gets on the head of the bed of your father/ mother is your mother/ father 跨過你父親／母親的床頭的人都是你的母親／父親

(idi.) PH whoever marrys one of your parents is also your parent 跟你父親／母親結婚的人就是你的母親／父親 : *Kéuih sēuiyìhn m̀haih néihge chānsāang màhmā/ bàhbā, daahnhaih ~, néih dōu yiu haauseuhn kéuih ge bo.* (Although s/he is not your own mother/father, ~. You are still supposed to be filial to her/ him.)

daahngūng 彈弓 N spring 彈簧 M go

1328

→jōng daahngūng 裝彈弓 (lit.) install a spring 裝上彈簧

(idi.) VO set up a trap 設一個陷阱 : *Yauh wah bōsí m̀wúih yuhng nīdī yéh, yìhgā kéuih jīkhāak yiu, néih haih m̀haih ~ ngóh ~ a?* (You said that our boss would not use these things, but he wants them right now. Did you ~ for me?) also see 0722

dāng 燈 N lamp, light 燈 M jáan

1329 ✓

➔dihndāng dáam → m̀tūnghei 電燈膽→唔通氣 (lit.) a light bulb→(it does) not ventilate 電燈泡→密不通風 (idi.) HIT said of a person who is not aware that he should stay away from two lovers 不知情識趣,妨礙別人談戀愛的人 : *Kéuihdeih léuhnggo heui táihei, ngóhdeih m̀hóu jouh ~ → ~, jójyuh yàhndeih paaktō.* (The two of them are going to the cinema. We'd better not be ~ → ~ and spoil the atmosphere.)

dang 凳 N chair, stool 椅子, 凳子 M jēung

1330

➔pāi go tàuh béi néih dong dang chóh 批個頭俾你當凳坐 see 0793

1331

➔sāamgeuk dang 三腳凳 (lit.) a three-legged chair (which will collapse) 有三條腿的椅子(會使你倒下) (idi.) N trap 陷阱 M jēung : *béi ~*

ngóh chóh (set a ~ for me) also see 0989

dāngjáan 燈盞 N oil lamp 燈盞 M go

1332

➔chīn gáan maahn gáan, gáanjeuhk go laahn dāngjáan 千揀萬揀,揀著個爛燈盞 (lit.) have tried to pick an oil lamp for tens of thousands of times but end up picking a broken one 千挑萬選,選了一個破的油燈 (idi.) PH a very picky choice is the worst one 最嚴格的選擇卻是最差的選擇 : *Kéuih paakjó hóudō chi tō, sīnji kyutdihng tùhng yìhgā ge lóuhgūng gitfān, dímji yùhnlòih kéuih hóu laahn dóu ge. Nīchi jānhaih ~, ~ lo.* (She had had many boyfriends before she decided to marry her present husband. However, it turned out that he was a gambler. ~, ~. The saying is really right.)

dānglùhng 燈籠 N lantern 燈籠 M go

1333

➔ngàuhpèih dānglùhng → dím gihk dōu m̀mìhng 牛皮燈籠→點極都唔明 see 0349

1334

➔séi yàhn dānglùhng → bou daaih sou 死人燈籠→報大數 (lit.) the lantern for the dead→(people) would add numbers (to the age of the dead on it) 喪禮所掛的燈籠→一定會替死者添加歲數

(idi.) HIT exaggerate the amount 把數目誇大： ⓐ*Máaih nīdī gám ge yéh yiu gam dō chín ge mē, kéuih ~ → ~ jī ma, lóuhbáan yātdihng wúih chàhsou jē.* (He spent so much money to buy such things, he must have ~ → ~ of money. Our boss certainly will check on the money spent.) ⓑ*Góchēut hei bīndouh yáuh gam dō yàhn tái ā, dī heiyún ~ → ~ jī ma.* (That movie was not that popular. The cinemas just ~ → ~ of audience in the box office record.) (*It is a Chinese custom that people would add extra years to the age of the dead and write it on a white lantern at his funeral.)

dāu 兜 N/M bowl, pot; measure meaning 'a bowl/ pot of' 缽; 量詞: 一缽 M go

1335
➔jādāu 揸兜 (lit.) hold in hand an earthenware bowl 手拿著瓦缽
(idi.) VO be a beggar 做乞丐： *Kéuih yíhchìhn haih yáuhchínlóu, sāumēi pocháan, yihgā yiu ~.* (He was once a rich man. Later he went bankrupt, and now he ~.)

dáu 斗 N/M dipper; a Chinese peck, measure for wine 斗; 酒的量詞 M go

1336
➔jengdáu 正斗 (lit.) the right dipper 正確的斗
(idi.) Adj. terrific, very good 很棒： *Ngóh chāamgā gógo léuihhàhng tyùhn hóu ~ ga.* (The tour group I joined is ~.) (*Some people just say 'jeng'.)

1337
➔tēngga m̀tēng dáu 聽價唔聽斗 (lit.) listen to the price but not the dipper (i.e. the weight) 只聽價錢,沒聽多重
(idi.) PH pay attention to the price but not to how many/ much you can buy 只理會價錢而沒有理會可以買到多少： *Néih yíhwàih hóu pèhng là, ~, kèihsaht géi gwai.* (You thought it was cheap. You just ~. In fact, it's quite expensive.)

dēng 釘 V/N nail 釘住; 釘子 M háu/ ngáan

1338
➔dá syū dēng 打書釘 (lit.) nail books 在書本上打釘子
(idi.) VO be a bookworm in a bookshop 整天在書店中看書的人： *Yihgā dī yàhn jihnghaih deuijyuh bouh dihnlóuh, hóu síu yàhn jūngyi ~ ge la.* (Nowadays people only like to use their computers. Very few people like to ~.)

1339 ✓
➔dēng 釘 (lit.) V/ N nail 釘住; 釘子 M háu/ ngáan
(idi.) V (1) die 死： *Kéuih behngjó hóu noih, kàhmyaht ~ jó lo.* (He had been sick for a long time and ~ yesterday.) (2) pick on, treat somebody maliciously 針對別人： *Ngóh móuh dākjeuih kéuih ā, m̀jī dímgáai kéuih sèhngyaht ~ jyuh ngóh.* (I haven't offended him. I don't know why he ~ me all the time.) (3) keep an eye on someone

by going after him 跟蹤並注意別人的行動 : *Ngóh gokdāk kéuih hóu hóyìh, sóyíh kéuih chēutchēut yahpyahp ngóh dōu ~ jyuh kéuih.* (He seemed suspicious, and so I ~ him wherever he went.)

1340

➔ **dēnggoi** 釘蓋 (lit.) nail the lid (of one's coffin) 把棺木的蓋釘好 (idi.) VO die 死 : *Néih yātyaht sihk sahp bāau yīn àh? Néih séung faaidī ~ àh?* (You smoke ten packets of cigarette each day, don't you? Do you want to ~ soon?)

1341

➔ **dēngpàaih** 釘牌 (lit.) nail/peg the license plate 把執照的牌子釘住 (idi.) VO (usually said of professionals) be dropped from the register (and not allowed to practice) (通常指專業人士)吊銷牌照/ 被取消執業資格(不能營業) : *Nīgo yīsāng yānwaih yīséi yàhn, sóyíh ~ jó ~.* (This doctor caused a patient's death by his wrong diagnosis, so he was ~.)

1342

➔ **laahn syùhn dōu yáuh sāam gān dēng** 爛船都有三斤釘 (lit.) even the wreckage of a ship has three catties of nails in it 破爛的船也有三斤重的釘 (idi.) PH even if a person from a wealthy family goes bankrupt, he still has some money to rely on 一個來自富有家庭的人就算潦倒了, 也總還有一點兒錢 : *"Kéuih búnlòih haih mihgmùhn mohngjuhk*

làih ga, hósīk yìhgā pojó cháan." "Óh, gám ~ gé." ("He was born to a prestigious family. What a pity that he is bankrupt now." "Oh, ~.")

1343

➔ **mó mùhndēng** 摸門釘 (lit.) touch the door nail 摸到門上的釘子 (idi.) VO fail to see one's friend when calling on him because he is out 訪友不遇 : *Néih tīngyaht mhóu làih wán ngóh la, ngóh gēng néih ~.* (Don't call on me tomorrow. I don't want you to ~.)

1344

➔ **sāamchyun dēng** 三寸釘 (lit.) a nail that is three inches long 三寸長的釘子 (idi.) N a short man 矮的男子 M go : *Mhóu táisíu kéuih ~, kéuih sān sáu hóu lìhngwuht.* (Don't look down on him because he is ~. He can make agile movement.)

dihn 電 N electricity 電 M dī

1345 ✓

➔ **chūngdihn** 充電 (lit.) VO recharge battery 上電 (idi.) VO refresh oneself (usually by taking a trip and then get ready to work hard again) 鬆弛身心(多指旅遊)之後再投入工作 : *Fongga jauh heui ~, fāanlàih joi boksaat.* (Take a leave to ~ so that you can prepare yourself for harder work when you come back.)

1346 ✓

➔ **dihn** 電 (lit.) N electricity 電 M dī

(idi.) N (1) charm, attraction like an electric shock 迷人的吸引力像觸電的感覺 : *Kéuih sēung ngáahn yáuh ~.* (There is ~ in his/ her eyes.) (2) battery 電池/電芯 M gauh; pàaih : *yahp ~* (put in ~) V give people electric shock 用電擊人 : ⓐ *yuhng dihn páahng ~ yàhn* (~ someone by using an electric rod) ⓑ *(béi dihn) ~ séi* (be killed by ~)

1347
→**fongdihn** 放電 (lit.) discharge electricity 釋放電能
(idi.) VO (said of a person) lures the opposite sex (指人)向異性灌迷湯 : *"Chàhn síujé heung néih ~ wo." "Ngóh ìnwúih gwodihn ge."* ("Miss Chan tries to ~ you." "I won't be lured by her/ she can't make it.")

1348 ✓
→**gwodihn** 過電 (lit.) V get an electric shock 被電擊
(idi.) V (said of a person) be conquered by the lure of the opposite sex (指人)被異性灌迷湯成功了 : see 1347

1349 ✓
→**séuhngdihn** 上電 (lit.) VO recharge battery 上電
(idi.) VO (said of drug addicts) take drugs (指癮君子)吸毒 : *~ jó ~ jīhauh jauh lùhng jīng fú máahng* (become energetic and vigorous like a dragon or a tiger after ~)

díp 碟 N plate, dish 碟子 M go/jek (*When used as a measure, it is 'dihp'.)

1350
→**cheungdíp** 唱碟 (lit.) a singing plate 會唱歌的碟子
(idi.) N musical record, disc 唱片 M jēung/ jek : *Yihgā hóu síu ~ lo. Dōsou haih CD.* (Now there are very few ~. Mostly there are compact discs.)

1351 ✓
→**díp** 碟 (lit.) N plate, dish 碟子 M go/ jek
(idi.) N musical/ compact disc 唱碟,光碟 M jek/ jēung : *chēut ~* (to produce a ~)

1352
→**fāanbáan díp** 翻版碟 (lit.) N pirated CD/record 盜版光/唱碟 M jēung/ jek : ⓐ *Yáuhdī hohksāang waihjó wánchín, gíngyihn bōng yàhn maaih ~.* (Some students even sell ~ for others in order to earn money.) ⓑ *Maaih ~ haih faahnfaat ge, gíngchaat wúih lāai néih.* (It's illegal to sell ~. The police will arrest you.)

1353
→**fēidíp** 飛碟 (lit.) flying disc 會飛的碟
(idi.) N (1) UFO in the shape of a disc 碟形不明飛行物體 M go/ jek : *Búngóng Tīnmàhntòih hái Sāngaai seuhnghūng faatyihn yātjek ~.* (The observatory of Hong Kong spotted a ~ in the sky above the New Territories.) (2) (a kind of snack) toastie (一種小吃)烘麵包,中有餡料 M go : *mòhgū jīsí ~* (~ with mushroom and cheese)

dói 袋 N bag 袋子 M go (*When used as a measure, it is 'doih'.)

1354

➔cheuthei dói 出氣袋 (lit.) a bag for letting out air 用來排出氣體的袋子
(idi.) N a person who serves as a vent to somebody's anger 被其他人發洩怒氣的人 M go : *Daaihyàhn m̀hóu jēung saimānjái dongjouh ~.* (Adults should not see their children as ~.)

1355

➔doihdoih pìhngngōn 袋袋平安 (lit.) every bag is safe 每一個袋都平安
(idi.) PH it's great to have it (usually money) put into one's pocket 能把它(多指錢)放進口袋裏,真是太好了 : *Kéuih béichín néih néih maih ~ lō, dímgáai m̀yiu jēk?* (He gave you money. You could just ~. Why didn't you take it?)

1356

➔gúheidói 鼓氣袋 (lit.) an inflated bag 充了氣的袋
(idi.) N an introvert who always keeps her/ his mouth shut 性格內向,整天不說話的人 M go : *Kéuihdeih léuhng go hóu m̀tùhng, yāt go haih hōilùhng jéuk, yātgo haih ~.* (The two of them are very different. One is talkative like a bird chirping in its open cage, but the other is ~.)

1357

➔gūnghéi faatchòih, laihsih dauhlòih, yāt mān m̀ngoi, sahp mān doihlohk dói 恭喜發財,利是逗來,一蚊唔愛,十蚊袋落袋 (lit.) PH Happy New Year! Please give me lucky money. I don't want one dollar, but I'll put it into my pocket if it is ten dollars 恭喜發財,請給我紅封包,一元的我不要,十元的我才會放進口袋裏(*This is a joke said by naughty children.) : "~, ~, ~, ~." "Saimānjái m̀hóu gam tāamsām." ("~, ~, ~, ~!" "Don't be so greedy, you children.")

1358

➔sáidói 洗袋 (lit.) wash the pocket 把口袋洗乾淨
(idi.) VO lose all the money (in one's pocket[s]) 輸光口袋裏的錢 : *Kàhmyaht kéuih heui Oumún, gitgwó ~ fāanlàih.* (Yesterday he went to Macau. He ended up ~ [in gambling].)

dōu 刀 N knife, sword, chopper 刀子, 大刀 M bá

1359

➔dōujái geu daaih syuh 刀仔鋸大樹 (lit.) saw down a big tree with a small knife 用小刀鋸斷大樹
(idi.) PH win a large sum of money (in gambling) by betting with just a little money 投注小量金錢而贏得很多錢 : *Dóumáh lē, ~ jauh m̀gányiu, chīnkèih m̀hóu dóusaai fu sāngā.* (It will do you no harm if you ~ in horse-racing. But you should by no means spend all your money betting on the horses.)

220

1360

➔faai dōu jáam lyuhn màh 快刀斬亂麻 (lit.) quickly cut up the entangled hemp with a knife 快刀斬亂麻
(idi.) PH quickly tackle a problem 盡快把問題解決 : *Ngóh jouhyéh jūngyi ~, m̀jūngyi tōtō lāailāai gám ge.* (My work attitude is to ~. I don't like to let problems drag on.)

1361

➔hōidōu 開刀 (lit.) cut open with knife 用刀切開
(idi.) VO (1) perform/ undergo an operation 動手術 : ⓐ *Yīsāng tùhng kéuih ~.* (The doctor ~ on him.) ⓑ *Go behngyàhn yiu ~.* (The patient has to ~.) (2) start to take action (which will have a bad influence on others) 開始作出(對別人有壞影響的)行動 : *Gūngsī yiu chòihyùhn, sáusīn heung dāikāp ge jīkyùhn ~.* (Our company wants to lay off some people. It will ~ on low-ranking staff members first.)

1362

➔síhāang gwāandōu → màhn m̀màhndāk, móuh m̀móuhdāk 屎坑關刀→聞唔聞得，武唔武得 (lit.) the sword of Gwāangūng is put in the dung pit, you can neither smell it nor use it for fighting 公廁的關刀,不可以聞也不可以用
(idi.) HIT a person with an imposing appearance turns out to be good for nothing 相貌堂堂的人卻一點也不中用 : *Tái kéuih gam daaih gauh,*

sihngjīk chā, jouh síu síu chōuchúhng yéh jauh wah sānfú, jīngyāt ~ → ~, ~. (He has a strongly built figure. But he doesn't do well in his studies. He'll feel very tired after doing just a little work. He is really ~ → ~.)

1363

➔wūlēi dāandōu 烏厘單刀 (lit.) black sword with one blade 黑色單鋒的刀
(idi.) PH such a mess 亂七八糟 : *Yātlouh jouh gūngfo yātlouh tái dihnsih, dī gūngfo jouhdou ~.* (He watched TV while he was doing his homework. That's why his homework was ~.)

fēilám 菲林 N film (negative) 照相的底片 M jēung; tùhng/gyún

1364 ✓

➔fēilám(gyún) 菲林(卷) (lit.) N film (negative) 照相的底片 M jēung; tùhng/gyún
(idi.) N (black) sesame roll 芝麻卷 M dihp; gauh : *M̀gōi, yāt dihp ~.* (One plate of ~ please.)

fú 釜 N kettle 炊具 (* 'Fú' is rarely used by itself.)

1365

➔dá fútàuh 打釜頭 (lit.) hit the rice cooker 敲打炊具
(idi.) VO (said of a cook) takes away some money for buying food (指廚子)拿走一部分菜錢 : *"Gam síu sung gé, gánghaih go fótáu ~ la," poutáu dī fógei wah.* ("There's so little food [to eat]. The cook must have ~," said the employees of the shop.)

fu 褲 N trousers, pants 褲子 M tiuh

1366
→chèuihfu fongpei 除褲放屁 see 0623

1367
→jāp tiuh futàuhdáai leuih fu sāngā 執條褲頭帶累副身家 (lit.) accidentally pick up a belt and then waste all the money (to buy a new pair of trousers to match it) 拾得一條褲的帶子卻因此而花去所有的錢(去買一條新褲子配它) (idi.) PH penny gain, pound loss 因小失大 ： A-Wóng chāujéung chāudóu yātjēung Bālàih lòihwùih gēipiu. Kéuih séung tùhng taaitáai yātchái heui, sóyíh máaihdō yātjēung. Hái Bālàih, taaitáai yauh bokmehng máaihyéh, sáijó hóudō chín. Góchi jānhaih ~. (Wong won a round trip plane ticket to Paris in a raffle. He wanted to go with his wife, so he bought one more ticket. In Paris, his wife spent much money on a shopping spree. ~. The saying is right.)

1368
→kwàhn lāai fu lāt 裙拉褲甩 (lit.) pull the skirt but the trousers slip down 顧得拉好裙子,褲子卻滑下來 (idi.) PH so hasty in getting dressed that embarrassment may take place 穿著衣物的時間太匆促,難免發生尷尬的事 ： Ngóh dōu meih jeukchàih heifuhk jauh yiu chēutchèuhng, gáaudou ngóh ~ gám. (I was not ready with my costume before I went on the stage. It made me look funny when I ~ while on the stage.)

1369
→lahk/ laahksaht futàuh(dáai) 勒實褲頭(帶) (lit.) tighten the belt 過緊日子 (idi.) PH lead a harder life especially eat less 生活得苦些,尤指少吃東西 ： Nīpáai m̀gau gūng hōi, ngóhdeih yātgā yiu ~ la. (I haven't gotten enough work to do recently [and so I can't earn enough money]. Our whole family has to ~.)

gānléung 斤両 M catty and tael 斤和兩

1370
→bun gān baat léung 半斤八両 (lit.) half a catty and eight taels 半斤八両 (*There are sixteen taels in one Chinese catty.) (idi.) PH (said of two persons) well-matched in capability 兩個人的才能不相上下 ： Néih yáuh Yīnggwok mihng haauh boksih hohkwái, kéuih yáuh Méihgwok mihng haauh boksih hohkwái, daaihgā dōu ~. (You received a doctorate from a famous university in the UK and he from one in the States. Both of you are ~.)

1371 ✓
→gānléung 斤両 (lit.) (Chinese system of measurement of weight) catty and tael 斤和両 (idi.) N capability 才能 ： Kéuih haih ngóh gaaujó ǹghnihn ge

222

hohksāang, kéuih yáuh géidō ~ ngóh jeui chīngchó. (S/he is a student I have taught for five years. I know very well how capable s/he is.)

1372

➔néih yáuh bun gān, ngóh yáuh baat léung 你有半斤，我有八兩 (lit.) you have half a catty and I have eight taels 你有半斤,我有八兩
(idi.) PH You have your own strategy and I have my own 你有甚麼辦法,我也有甚麼辦法 : *Néih chéng leuhtsī, ngóh dōu chéng leuhtsī. ~, ~.* (You got a solicitor [to sue me], and I also got one [to defend myself against your accusation.] ~, ~.)

geng 鏡 N mirror 鏡子 M go/faai

1373

➔méihyàhn jiu geng 美人照鏡 (lit.) a beauty looks at herself in the mirror 美人照鏡子
(idi.) PH eat all the food on the dish (and leave it shining like a mirror) 碟子上的東西吃光後像鏡子般發亮,可以照人 : *Fógei séuhngchoi yātjahnggāan jauh ~ làh!* (It is ~ shortly after the dish was served by the waiter!) (*It is also Chinese courtesy not to finish the last piece of food on the dish.)

1374

➔m̀seun geng 唔信鏡 (lit.) not believe the mirror 不信鏡子
(idi.) PH refuse to recognize the (ugly) truth 不肯承認(不好的)事

實 : *Dōu wah nīgihn sāam m̀chan néih, wúih yíngdāk néih hóu fèih ge lā, yauh ~.* (I've told you that this dress doesn't suit you. It would make you look very fat, but you ~.)

1375

➔sáanggeng 省鏡 (lit.) polish the mirror 擦亮鏡子
(idi.) Adj. beautiful/ handsome (face that will shine in the mirror) 漂亮／英俊（的臉孔在鏡中發亮） : *Kéuihge yéung hóu ~.* (S/he has a ~ face.)

goi 蓋 N lid, cover 蓋子 M go

1376

➔hòhlāan séuigoi 荷蘭水蓋 (lit.) bottle cap of soft drinks 汽水瓶的瓶蓋
(idi.) N medal of honour 勳章 M go : *Yáuh mātyéh daaih chèuhngmín yiu chēutjihk, kéuih jauh wúih daaijyuh go ~ ge la.* (He wears his ~ when attending big events.)

gú 鼓 N drum 鼓 M go

1377 ✓

➔dágú (lit.) VO beat a drum 打鼓
(idi.) VO very hungry 肚子很餓 : *Ngóhge tóuh ~ gán ~.* (My belly is ~ now.)

gūnchòih 棺材 N coffin 棺材 M fu/ go

1378

➔fósíu gūnchòih→daaih taan 火燒棺材→大(炭)嘆 (lit.) fire burns a coffin→ what remains is a big

223

lump of charcoal 用火燒棺木→棺木
變成一塊大炭
(idi.) HIT enjoy life as much as one
can 享受生活：*Lójó gam dō teuiyāu
gām, hóyíh ~ → ~ lo!* (I've gotten so
much money for my pension. Now I
can ~.) (*A pun is made on 炭
[charcoal] and 嘆 [enjoy life]. Both
of them are pronounced 'taan'.)

1379
→màhngin gūnchòih hēung 聞
見棺材香 (lit.) can smell the odor
of a coffin 嗅到棺木的味
(idi.) PH very old and will die soon
年紀很大將會死：~ *dōu juhng gam
hóu fóhei.* (He is ~. Why does he still
get angry with people that easily?)

1380
→ ṁgin gūnchòih dōu ṁlàuh
ngáahnleuih 唔見棺材都唔流
眼淚 (lit.) not shed tears until one
sees the coffin 不見到棺木也不會流
眼淚
(idi.) PH one would dread only when
encountering great difficulties or
realizing that he is in great danger 不
到危急關頭不感到害怕：*"Ngóh giu
kéuih ṁhóu jēung sèhngfu sāngā lóheui
cháau gúpiu, kéuih ṁtēng ngóh hyun."
"Gánghaih lā, ~, kéuih dōu meih sigwo
pochaan ge jīmeih."* ("I had advised
him not to speculate on the stock
market with all his money, but he
didn't listen to me." "Of course, ~. He
has never been in such a difficult
situation as to go bankrupt.")

1381
→tòih gūnchòih lāt fu→
sātláihséi yàhn 抬棺材甩褲→

失禮死人 (lit.) trousers slip when
one is carrying a coffin (on his
shoulder) → (it's) a disgrace to the
dead 抬棺木的時候褲子滑下來,失
禮了棺木中的死人
(idi.) HIT it's too deadly
embarrassing 太失禮人了 (*'Séi
literally means 'to die' or 'be dead'.
It becomes an adverb of degree
meaning 'too deadly' or 'absolutely'
when used metaphorically.)：*Ngóh
léuhnggo jáinéui hái yàhn mihnchihn
jāang yéh sihk, jānhaih (~) → ~ lo.* (My
son and daughter were fighting over
something to eat in front of so many
people. It's really (~) → ~ !)

gūngjái公仔**N doll, figure** 洋
娃娃, 模型人兒 **M go**

1382
→chésin gūngjái 扯線公仔
(lit.) marionette (i.e. puppet moved
by strings) 牽線木偶
(idi.) N one who is controlled by
others 受人控制的傀儡 M go：*Dī
yíhyùhn bātgwo haih júngléih ge ~ jē.*
(The Senators are merely the ~ of
the Prime Minister.)

1383
→gūngjái mihn 公仔麵 (lit.)
doll's noodles 娃娃的麵
(idi.) N instant noodles 即食麵 M
bāau：*Sāam chāan dōu sihk ~, bīn
yáuh yīk ga?* (You eat ~ for your
three meals [every day]. How can
it do you good?) (*The first brand
of instant noodle is
'Gūngjái[mihn]'.)

1384
→gūngjái sēung 公仔箱 (lit.

a box for dolls 放洋娃娃的箱子
(idi.) N TV (screen) 電視(螢幕)：
*Gahnlòih kéuih gīngsèuhng hái ~
chēutyihn bo!* (Recently he's been/
we can see him on ~ so often.)

1385
→mā gūngjái 孖公仔 (lit.)
twin dolls 一對洋娃娃
(idi.) N (said of lovers) always go in
pairs 常出雙入對的情侶 M deui：
*Kéuihdeih léuhnggo sìhsìh
chēutsēung yahpdeui, hóuchíh deui ~
gám.* (The two of them always hang
out together, just like ~.)

gwaitúng 櫃桶 N drawer 抽屜
M go

1386
→chyūn gwaihtúngdái 穿櫃
桶底 (lit.) pierce through the
bottom of the drawer (for money)
把(盛錢的)抽屜底弄穿
(idi.) PH (said of employees) steal the
employer's money (指僱員)偷去僱
主的錢： ⓐ*Dī fógei chan lóuhbáan
m̀háidouh ge sìhhauh jauh ~.* (The
employees ~ while the employer is
away.) ⓑ*Kéuihge jéfū béi kéuih hái
gūngsī bōngsáu, dímjī kéuih ~.* (His
brother-in-law let him help in his
company. However, he ~.)

**gwan 棍 N/M rod, club, stick;
measure for a lashing** 棍子；
量詞：(用棍子)一擊 **M tìuh/ jī**

1387
→gáausí gwan 攪屎棍 (lit.) a
stick used for stirring shit 用來攪
動屎的棍

(idi.) N stirrer, a person who
instigates others to do something
troublesome 鼓動別人做麻煩事
的人 M go： ⓐ*Kéuih jingyāt ~,
sìhngyaht lìhng yàhn bātwòh.* (He is
really like ~. He always causes
quarrels between people.) ⓑ *Dī
gūngyàhn yiu bahgūng, bīngo jouh ~
nē?* (The workers will go on a
strike. Who is the ~?)

1388
→gwōnggwan 光棍 (lit.) naked
rod 光滑的棍子
(idi.) N swindler, conman 騙子 M/
go/ tìuh ： *gwōnggwan yuhjeuhk
móuh pèih chàaih* see 1295, also see
1197

**hàaih 鞋 N shoe 鞋子 M jek;
deui**

1389 ✓
→chaathàaih 擦鞋 (lit.) VO
polish/ shine shoes 把皮鞋擦亮
(idi.) VO shine one's shoes, flatter
others 奉承別人，討人歡心 ：
Saigaaijái, hóu sīk ~. (He is a
smoothie. He knows very well how
to ~.)

1390 ✓
→haàih 鞋 (lit.) N shoe 鞋 M
jek; deui
(idi.) P the sound of a sigh heaved
when doing hard work 工作辛苦的
嘆息聲 ： *"Jīngyuht m̀hóu máaih
hàaih, yùhgwó m̀haih, jauh wúih
sèhng nìhn jouhdou ~ háai sēng ge
la." "Màihseun jē."* ("Don't buy
shoes during the first lunar month.
Otherwise you will have to do hard

work and sigh for the whole year."
"It's just superstition.")

1391 ✓
→hàaihchāu 鞋 揪 (lit.) N
shoe-horn 鞋拔子 M go
(idi.) N a person with a long chin
下巴長的人 ： *"Kéuih go yéung
dím ga?" "Yáuh síusíu ~."* ("What
does s/he look like?" "S/he has quite
a long chin.")

1392
→móuh hàaih wáan kehk jáu
冇鞋挽屐走 (lit.) no shoes, so
one would put on a pair of clogs and
run away 沒有鞋子,就連木屐也要
穿上,以便逃走
(idi.) PH leave/flee as quickly as
possible 盡快離開 / 逃走 ：
ⓐ *Lóuhsai yauh hāakbok, yauh
sihngyaht laauh yàhn, dī gūngyàhn
yāt wándóu daihyih fahn gūng jauh ~
lo.* (The boss is stingy and always
blames his men. They will ~ as
soon as they find a new job.)
ⓑ *Gójoh daaihhah faatyihn yātgo
gaisih jadáan chèuihsih wúih baauja,
dī gēuimàhn yāt jīdou jauh ~.* (A
time bomb was found in that
building, and it might blow up any
time. The residents ~ on knowing
that.)

1393
→tùhng néih wáan hàaih 同你
挽鞋 (lit.) I'll carry the shoes for
you 我替你拿鞋子
(idi.) PH (when making a bet) I'll do
something humble for you if what I
say turns out to be wrong (打賭)要是
我說的話錯了,我就替你做卑微的

事 ： *Kéuih nīsai dōu m̀wúih
faatdaaht ge la, yùhgwó wúih, ngóh
jauh ~.* (He'll never make a fortune
this life. If he had, ~.) (*0793 is a
much more emphatic way of saying
than this one.)

hòhbāau 荷包 N purse, wallet
錢包 M go

1394
→dá hòhbāau 打荷包 (lit.) hit
the purse/ wallet 打錢包
(idi.) VO (said of pickpockets) steal
money/ wallets (from other people's
pockets) (指扒手)偷去別人口袋裏
的 錢 或 錢包 ： ⓐ *béi yàhn ~*
(money is stolen by a pickpocket)
ⓑ *Dī pàhsáu dōsou bīkhái
chēmùhndouh, dáng néih lohkchē
jauh ~.* (The pickpockets often flock
to the bus/ train door. They will ~
when people get off.)

hohkfai 學費 N school fees 學
費 M dī

1395 ✓
→gāau hohkfai 交學費 (lit.)
pay school fees 交學費
(idi.) VO (said of mahjong game
beginners) lose some money [and
pay it as school fees] (初學打麻將的
人)輸錢當繳付學費 ： *Néih
ngāamngāam hohksīk dá màhjeuk,
haih yiu ~ dī ~ sīn ge la.* (You've
just learned how to play mahjong,
of course you need to ~.)

jām 針 N/M needle; stitch 針;
量詞: 一針 M háu/ngáan/jī

1396 ✓

→jām 針 (lit.) N needle 針 M háu/ ngáan/ jī

(idi.) V pick on others 針對別人 : *Ngóh móuh dākjeuih kéuih ā, m̀jī dímgáai kéuih sihngyaht ~ jyuh ngóh gé.* (I haven't offended him. I don't know why he always ~ me.)

jámtàuh 枕頭 N pillow 枕頭 M go

1397

→gou jámtàuh jóng 告枕頭狀 (lit.) accuse someone by means of a pillow 用枕頭告狀

(idi.) PH (said of a woman) accuses someone while she is in bed with her husband (指女人)在床上向丈夫控訴某人 : *Néih wah dímgáai kéuih lóuhgūng laauh néih? Kéuih ~ lō.* (You wonder why her husband scolded you. It's all because she ~.)

1398

→saufā jámtàuh 繡花枕頭 (lit.) embroidered pillow (which is just a wad of cotton inside) 繡花枕頭 (裏面只是一團棉花)

(idi.) N a person with a beautiful appearance but no inner talents 外表美麗但沒有內涵的人 : *Dī māt táai maht táai, jyū gwōng bóu hei, ~ làih ge jīmáh.* (The so-called taitais [i.e. married ladies of the upper class] wear lots of jewellry, but they are actually just ~.)

1399

→sipgōu jámtàuh séunghàh 攝高枕頭想吓 (lit.) put the pillow higher up (under one's head)

and think 把枕頭墊高一點及想一想

(idi.) PH sleep over it, think it over in bed 睡前好好的想一下 : *Gāmmáahn ~, táiháh yáuh mē baahnfaat deuifuh góbāan yàhn.* (~ tonight, and see if there is any way to cope with those people.)

jānjyū 珍珠 N pearl 珍珠 M lāp

1400

→jānjyū dōu móuh gam jān 珍珠都冇咁真 (lit.) even pearls are not so real as this 珍珠也不及它真

(idi.) PH it's very true 絕對是真的 : *"Néih wah gógāan daaih ngàhnhòhng yiu jāplāp, m̀haih ah máh!" "Haih a, ~!"* ("You said that big bank would close down. Are you kidding?" "No, ~!")

1401

→wòhgón kám jānjyū 禾桿冚珍珠 (lit.) a pearl is covered by hay 珍珠被稻草蓋著

(idi.) PH a rich person who behaves like a poor person 表面上窮,其實很有錢 : *Néih tái kéuih sihk hàahmyùh chēngchoi, jeukdāk laahn sān laahn sai gám, kèihsaht kéuih ~ je.* (You see him eat very simple things [salted fish and vegetables] for a meal and wear worn out clothes. [And so you think he is a poor person.] In fact, he is ~.)

jē 遮 N umbrella 傘子 M bá

1402

→lohkyúh dāam jē → séi

dóng 落雨擔遮→死(擋→)黨
(lit.) (people) put up an umbrella in
the rain→ they try their best to
keep out of the rain 在下雨天打傘
→拼命的把雨遮擋
(idi.) HIT buddies, very good
friends 非常要好的朋友 ：
*Kéuihdeih léuhnggo jìngyāt haih ~
→ ~ lèih ge.* (The two of them are
really ~ → ~.)

1403
➔tùhng jē m̀tùhng beng, tùhng
yàhn m̀tùhng mehng 同遮唔
同柄，同人唔同命 (lit.) PH
the same kind of umbrellas have
different handles, the same group/
kind of people have different lot 相
同的傘,有不同的柄,相同的一班
人,可是有不同的際遇 ： *A-Wóng
tùhng ngóh tùhngsih yahp nīgāan
gūngsī ge, daahnhaih kéuih hóu faai
sīngjīk, ngóh jauh yūk dōu m̀yūk,
jānhaih ~, ~ lo.* (Wong and I joined
this company at the same time. He
was promoted to a higher post very
soon. I haven't been yet. The saying
is true that ~, ~.)

**jēun 樽 N/M bottle; measure
meaning 'a bottle of' 瓶子；
量詞: 一瓶 M go**

1404 ✓
➔yahpjēun 入樽 (lit.) VO
pack the beverage into a bottle 把
飲品用瓶子裝好
(idi.) N (a kind of shooting skill in
basketball) slam-dunk 一種投籃技
術,籃球員把球放入籃內 ： *Go
làahmjái wáan ~, dímjī làahmkàuh

gá tiuh chyúh dahtyihn tyúhnjó,
sèhnggo gá ditlohklàih jaahksēung
kéuih.* (The boy was playing ~.
Suddenly the basketball stand broke
and fell on him. He was hurt.)

jí 紙 N paper 紙 M jēung

1405
➔jí gam bohk 紙咁薄 (lit.) PH
as thin as a sheet of paper 像紙那樣
薄 ： ⓐ *Gógo gām pàaih ~.* (The
gold medal is ~.) ⓑ *yàhnchihng ~*
(the ties among people have become
very weak/people have little regard
for human relationship)

1406 ✓
➔sājí 沙紙 (lit.) N sandpaper
沙紙 M jēung
(idi.) N certificate 證書,文憑 M
jēung ： *Kéuih jēung jihgéi ge ~
báaihái haaktēngdouh.* (He put/
displayed all his ~ in his sitting
room.) (*'Sā' is the transliteration
of 'cert'.)

**jīpiu 支票 N check, cheque 支
票 M jēung**

1407✓
➔hūngtàuh jīpiu 空頭支票
(lit.) N bounced cheque 不能兌現
的支票 M jēung
(idi.) N wild promise 不會實踐的
諾言 M jēung ： *Néih yīngsihngjó
ngóh jauh yiu jānhaih jouh sīnji hóu
a, m̀hóu hōi ~ a.* (Since you have
made a promise, you should by all
means do it for me, and don't give
me a ~.)

jīupàaih 招牌 N billboard, signboard 招牌 M go/faai

1408 ✓

➔chaak jīupàaih 拆招牌 (lit.) VO tear down the shop-sign 拆下招牌

(idi.) VO destroy the good reputation of a shop or a business person 破壞店舖或商人所建立的聲譽 : ⓐ*Gógo táiseunglóu yauh wah hóu lēk ge, daahnhaih nīchi góng ge dōu m̀ngāam gé, ngóh yiu ~ kéuih ~.* (That fortune-teller is said to be good at palm reading and face reading. But what he said [about me] this time is wrong. I'm going to ~.) ⓑ*Ngóhdeih poutáu haih lóuh jihhouh, yùhgwó maaih gá yéh, jauh wúih béi yàhn ~ ge la.* (Our shop has been well-known for a long time, but if we sell counterfeit things, our good reputation will be ruined.)

1409 ✓

➔jīupàaih 招牌 (lit.) N billboard/signboard of shops 招牌 N go/ faai

(idi.) ATT things that a shop is famous for 店舖最著名的出品 : ⓐ~ *faahn/ dímsām/ fo* (~ rice/ dimsum/ things [/products]) ⓑ*Móuhdá hei haih nīgāan dihnyíng gūngsī ge ~ hei.* (Kungfu movie is the ~ movie that this company is good at making.)

jōng 莊 N banker (in gambling) 莊家 M go

1410 ✓

➔lahmjōng 冧莊 (lit.) VO (said of the banker in mahjong) be the

banker again after having won a game (打麻將) 贏了再做莊家

(idi.) VO do it again, make a comeback 再來一次 : *Kéuih yihgā jouhgán hohksāang wúi wuihjéung. Kéuih séung chēutnín ~.* (Now he is the president of the student union. He would like to ~ next year.)

jūk 竹 N bamboo 竹子 M jī

1411 ✓

➔jūksīng 竹升 (lit.) N bamboo cane 竹竿 M jī/ tiuh

(idi.) N young Chinese born overseas (*They have no exposure to Chinese culture and so they are like a bamboo pole which is hollow inside.) 海外出生的華僑青年(對中國文化一無所知就像中空的竹竿) M go : *Hóudō ~ làih Hēunggóng hohkfāan dī Jūngmàhn.* (Many ~ come to Hong Kong to learn some Chinese.) also see 0988

1412 ✓

➔màahnggūng jūk 盲公竹 (lit.) N blindman's cane 盲人的手杖 M jī

(idi.) N useful guidance/ thing or people who can show you the way 很有用的指引(人或物均可) M jī : ⓐ *Ngóh ngāamngāam làihdou nīdouh, yàhndeih sāangsō, chyùhnkaau néih nī jī ~ ja.* (I just came here and I know nothing about this place. Luckily, I have you as my ~ [in everything].) ⓑ*Dī yàhn m̀sīk máaih gúpiu, kéuihdeih dong dī sówaih 'Gúpiu Jínàahm' haih ~.* (People who don't know how to buy stocks and shares tend to consider the so-called 'Stocks Guide' a ~.)

1413

➔yāt jūkgōu dá yāt syùhn yàhn 一竹篙打一船人 (lit.) beat all the people on the boat with a single bamboo pole 用一枝竹竿打船上所有的人

(idi.) PH take one for all, have prejudice against certain people for just seeing one instance 以偏概全, 看見一個事例就以爲全部人都是這樣 : *Kéuih wah, "Ngóhge lóuhbáan hóu sēui." A-Chán wah, "Gogo lóuhbáan dōu haih lā." Ngóh wah, "Mhóu ~, yáuhdī lóuhbáan hóu hóu ge."* (He said, "Our boss is bad (to us)." Chan said, "So are all the bosses." I said, "Try not to ~. Some of them are very good bosses.")

jūng 盅 N/M cup, bowl; measure meaning 'a cup of' 盅; 也是量詞 M go

1414

➔kitjūng 揭盅 (lit.) open (the lid of) a cup 把杯子的蓋掀起

(idi.) VO make public/ announce (a result) (把結果)揭曉 : *Bīngo hauhsyúnyàhn wúih jouh Chòihjingsī Sījéung, géiyaht jīhauh jauh wúih ~.* (It will be ~ in a few days who is going to be the Secretary for Finance.)

kehk 屐 N wooden clogs 木屐 M jek; deui/sēung

1415

➔jouhdou (hóuchíh) jek kehk gám 做到(好似)隻屐噉 (lit.) work like a pair of wooden clogs 工作得像木屐

(idi.) PH work like a dog 工作得很辛苦 : *~, juhng béi lóuhbáan laauh.* (I've been ~, but I am still scolded by our boss.)

kwàhn 裙 N skirt, dress 裙子 M tiuh

1416

➔kwàhndaai gwāanhaih 裙帶關係 (lit.) PH apron string relationship or influence 裙帶關係 : *Kéuih jī sóyíh hóyíh hái ngóhdeih gūngsī jouh jyúyahm, haih yānwaih yáuh ~ jī ma. Kéuihgo múi haih lóuhbáan ge taaitáai.* (The reason why he is the section head is because he has ~ in our company. His sister is the wife of our boss.)

1417

➔lāai yàhn kwàhn kám jihgéi geuk 拉人裙冚自己腳 see 0421

laahpsaap 垃圾 N rubbish, garbage 垃圾 M dī

1418 ✓

➔laahpsaap 垃圾 (lit.) N rubbish, garbage 垃圾 M dī

(idi.) N rubbish, things of no importance, 垃圾，一文不值的東西 : ⓐ *Kéuih sé nīpīn yéh, gáanjihk ~!* (This article that he writes is ~!) ⓑ *Nīdeuih bō, ~!* (This ball team is ~!) ⓒ *laahpsaap chùhng* see 0014 ⓓ *gáusí laahpsaap* see 0195

1419 ✓

➜laahpsaap gōng 垃圾缸
(lit.) N rubbish bin 盛廢物的缸 M
go
(idi.) N messy and dirty place 又髒
又亂的地方 M go : *Gāan ngūk
hóuchíh go ~ gám.* (The house is
like a ~.)

lòh/ló 鑼 N gong 鑼 M go

1420 ✓

➜dálòh/ ló 打鑼 (lit.) VO beat
a gong 打鑼
(idi.) VO look for someone urgently
急於找尋一個人 : *Néih heuijó bīn
a? Ngóhdeih ~ gám wán néih.*
(Where have you gone? Everybody
is looking for you like ~.) (*In the
old days, a man would beat a gong to
call the attention of the villagers
when- ever there was something
urgent for them to know.)

1421 ✓

➜hōilòh 開鑼 (lit.) VO (said of
opera troupes) start (the
performance by) beating a gong (指
戲曲劇團)開始(表演時)打鑼
(idi.) VO (said of horse-racing
season or football season) starts (馬
季或球季)開始 : *Máhgwai jauhlàih
~ la, dī máhmàih yauh yáuh gēiwuih
la.* (The horse-racing season will ~
soon, and the punters will have [lots
of] opportunities.)

**lòuh 爐 N cooker, oven, stove,
fireplace, hearth, burner 爐
M go**

1422 ✓

➜chēutlòuh 出爐 (lit.) VO just

come out of oven 剛從焗爐裏出來
(idi.) ATT (1) oven fresh 新鮮熱辣
的 : ~ *mihnbāau/ dímsām* (~ bread/
dimsum) (2) new, just made 新的,剛
產生的 : ~ *góngjé/ yíngdai/ yínghauh*
(the ~ Miss Hong Kong/ best actor/
best actress)

1423 ✓

➜fàhnfalòuh 焚化爐 (lit.) N
incinerator for burning rubbish 焚毀
垃圾的爐 M go
(idi.) N a person who eats too much
很貪吃的人 M go : *Kéuih haih ~
làih ge, daahnhaih sihkgihk dōu
mfèih.* (He is ~. But no matter how
much he eats, he won't get fat.)

1424

➜hēunglòuh dán 香爐躉 (lit.)
incense burner 香爐
(idi.) N the only son/ male heir (of a
family) 獨子／唯一的子嗣 M go :
*Kéuih dāk yātlāp jái, haih kéuihdeih
chyùhngā ge ~, jēunglòih hōijī
saanyihp dōu kaausaai kéuih ge la.*
(He has only one son, who is ~ of
the family. The responsibility of
carrying on the family line is all put
on him.)

**lùhng 籠 N/M steamer, cage;
measure for dimsum 籠子; 點
心的量詞 M go**

1425

➜chēutlùhng 出籠 (lit.) come
out of the cage 走出籠子
(idi.) VO (1) (said of new
commodities) be released for sale ,
be on the market, available, be out
推出新產品 : *Chúngmaht*

saichougēi ~, m̀sái jihgéi tùhng dī chúngmaht chūnglèuhng la. (The [newly invented] pet cleaner is now ~. Pet owners don't need to clean their pets themselves.) (2) (said of new TV programs) be on air 推出新電視節目：*Hingjūk tòihhing ge dihnsihkehk gāmyaht ~ la bo.* (The new TV series marking the anniversary of the TV station/ company will ~ tonight.)

1426 ✓
➔jīnglùhng 蒸籠 (lit.) N steamer for dimsum 蒸點心的籠 M go
(idi.) N low land in summer time 夏天低地的情況 M go：*Nīdouh seibihn dōu haih sāan, sóyíh hahtīn hóuchíh go ~ gám.* (There are hills around this place, so it's like a ~ in summer.)

mahkséui 墨水 N ink 墨水 M dihk; dī

1427
➔dou diu dōu móuh dihk mahkséui 倒吊都冇滴墨水 (lit.) even if you hang a person upside down, there's not a drop of ink (coming out from his body) 把一個人倒懸，也沒有一滴墨水(從他身體內走出來)
(idi.) PH illiterate, uneducated 沒念過書：*Ngóh ~, dím sé sī a?* (I am ~. How can I write poems?)

m̀hnlaahp 棉納 N cotton quilted jacket 棉襖 M gihn

1428
➔laahn m̀hnlaahp 爛棉納

(lit.) worn out cotton quilted jacket (which still can keep you warm) 破爛的棉襖(卻仍能保暖)
(idi.) N cheap old thing that still can support you 殘破的東西卻仍能維持你的生活 M gihn：*Ngóh yáuh yātgāan gauh láu sāujōu, sēuiyihn hóu pèhng, daahnhaih sēuisēuidéi dōu haih gihn ~.* (I have an old flat which I rented to somebody. Although the rent is cheap, I can earn a living from this ~.)

mìhntōi 棉胎 N cotton quilted sheet 棉被 M jēung

1429 ✓
➔kám mìhntōi 冚棉胎 (lit.) VO cover oneself with a cotton quilted sheet (in bed) (睡覺時)蓋棉被
(idi.) VO (1) people say this when they hear others sing awfully 聽到別人唱歌難聽而起疙瘩：*Kéuih cheunggō àh? Ngóh yiu ~ ji dāk la.* (Is he going to sing? I need to ~.) (2) a kind of card game especially designed for children 一種特別為兒童設計的紙牌遊戲：*wáan ~* (play the card game of ~)

móu 帽 N hat, cap 帽子 M déng

1430
➔daai gōumóu 戴高帽 (lit.) put on a top hat 戴上高的帽子
(idi.) VO flatter, give high praise 說討好人的說話／太過稱讚別人：ⓐ *Kéuih sihsih béi gōumóu yàhn daai, hóu sīk tam yàhn.* (He is a flatterer. He is good at pleasing others.) ⓑ *Kéuih m̀jūngyi ~ ge.* (He

232

doesn't like to be ~.) also see 0790 and 0791

1431

➔daai luhkmóu 戴綠帽 (lit.) put on a green hat 戴上綠色的帽子 (idi.) VO (said of a man) be disgraced by his wife having an affair with another man (指男人)妻子與別人有染而蒙羞 : ⓐ *Kéuih ~ jó ~ dōu juhng m̀jī.* (He doesn't even know that he is ~.) ⓑ *béi luhkmóu lóuhgūng daai* ([said of a woman] disgraces her husband for having an affair with another man) (*'Luhkmóu' was a green kerchief worn by the husband of a prostitute in former times. An updated expression of 'daai luhkmóu' is 'fānngoih chìhng', i.e. extra-marital affair.)

1432

➔ daai seifōng móu 戴四方帽 (lit.) put on a square hat 戴上四方的帽子 (idi.) VO graduate from a university (when a graduate can wear mortar-board) 大學畢業(畢業生可戴上方頂帽) : *Yíhchìhn ngóh hóu sihnmouh yàhn ~, yìhgā, jihgéi dōu hóyíh daai la!* (Before, I envied those who could ~. Now, I myself can wear one.)

1433 ✓

➔gōumóu 高帽 (lit.) N top hat 高的帽子 M déng (idi.) N flattery, high praise 恭維的說話 M déng : *Néih m̀sái béi(déng) ~ ngóh daai la, ngóh sauhm̀héi.* (You don't have to give me ~. I don't deserve it.)

ngáahngeng 眼鏡 N eye glasses 眼鏡 M fu/go

1434

➔dit ngáahngeng 跌眼鏡 (lit.) drop eye-glasses 眼鏡掉了下來 (idi.) VO be a little disappointed (when one's expectation of others turns out to be wrong) (對別人的期望過高)有點失望 : *Tái kéuihge yéung, ngóh yíhwàih kéuih duhksyū hóu lēk, dímjī kéuih háau daih mēi, ngóh jānhaih ~ lo.* (He looked as if he would have done very well in his studies. But it turned out that he came last in his class. I was really ~.)

1435

➔yáuhsīk ngáahngeng 有色眼鏡 (lit.) colored spectacles 有色眼鏡 (idi.) N prejudice 偏見 M fu: *daaijó ~* (see something through ~)

páai 牌 N mahjong blocks or poker cards 麻將牌或樸克紙牌 M jek (for mahjong); jēung (for poker)

1436 ✓

➔daaih páai 大牌 (lit.) PH (in playing cards or mahjong) upper hand 強勢的牌 M pōu; fu (idi.) Adj. put on airs 擺架子 : *Ngóhdeih bōsí hóu ~, sihngyaht dēunhéi go fún.* (Our boss likes to ~. He always makes you aware that he is the boss.) ATT famous movie or TV stars or singers 著名的影視明

233

星或歌星 : ~ *mihngsīng, gánghaih chihdou lā.* (~ movie or TV stars will certainly come late.)

pāidohng 批盪 **N/V white wash** 粉飾牆壁

1437

→Yidaaihleih pāidohng 意大利批盪 (lit.) white wash in Italian style 意大利式的粉飾牆壁
(idi.) N very heavy make-up 很濃的化妝 : *Múihchi chēutgāai jīchihn, kéuih dōu jouh yātlèuhn ~.* (Every time before she goes out, she spends a lot of time on ~.)

péih 被 **M bed sheet** 被單子 **M jēung**

1438

→gónglàih góngheui sāam fūk péih 講嚟講去三幅被 (lit.) talk over and over about the bed sheet folded three times 說來說去還是說那三摺的被
(idi.) PH always repeat the same old thing 常重複說一樣的意思 : *Kéuih ~, dōu haih giu néih m̀hóu yihmàhn.* (He ~. All he wants is to stop you from emigrating to a foreign place.)

1439

→tīn ditlohklàih dong péih kám 天跌落嚟當被冚 (lit.) take heaven as a bed sheet if it falls on you 天塌下來便把它當被單子蓋在身子
(idi.) PH this is what an optimist would say or have in mind when encountering difficulties 樂觀的人遇到困難時會這樣說／想 : *Kéuih nīgo yàhn hóu lohkgūn ge, ~.* (He is an optimistic person, ~.)

pùhn 盆 **N/M pot, basin; measure meaning 'a pot/basin of'** 盆子; 量詞: 一盆 **M go**

1440

→dálaahn sāpùhn mahn dou dūk 打爛沙盆問到篤 (lit.) PH break the earthen pot and (the real meaning of the expression is to) keep asking until one gets the answer(s)/ to the bottom of the thing one is doubtful of 打破陶盆(該句真正的意思是)問個究竟 : *Néih m̀hóu ~, sèhngyaht mahn dímgáai lā. Ngóh dōu m̀jī gam dō yéh.* (Don't be ~ and always keep asking why. [Even] I don't know so much about it.)

1441

→pùhnmúhn butmúhn 盆滿缽滿 (lit.) bowl and pot are full (of food/ money) 盆跟缽都盛滿(食物／錢)
(idi.) PH make much money 賺了很多錢 : *jaahndou ~* (earn so much that it is like ~)

sāanngāai 山埃 **N cyanide** 氰化鉀 **M dī**

1442 ✓

→sāanngāai 山埃 (lit.) N cyanide (CKN, a kind of poison) 氰化鉀(一種毒藥) M dī
(idi.) N completely wrong tips 完全錯誤的消息,情報 : ⓐ *Kéuih béi ngóhdeih ge háausi/ choimáh tīpsí haih ~ làih ge.* (The exam/ racing

234

tips that he gave us are ~.) (b) ~ *tīpsí* (the kind of tips that are ~)

sáugān 手巾 **N handkerchief** 手帕 **M tìuh**

1443

→sauchói sáugān→bāau syū 秀才手巾→包(書)輸 (lit.) a scholar's handkerchief→ is used to wrap the books 秀才的手巾→是用來把書包起來的
(idi.) HIT I am sure you will lose/one is bound to lose (你)一定會輸 : *Kéuih dóuchān chín dōu syū, jingyāt haih ~ → ~.* (He always loses in gambling. He is just like ~ → ~.)
(* 'Bāausyū' is a pun made on 'wrap the books' and 'bound to lose.')

séui 水 **N water** 水 **M dihk; dī**

1444

→bohngséui 磅水 (lit.) weigh water 量水的重量
(idi.) VO give money 付錢 : *~ jó ~ sīnji yáuhdāk kīng.* (We won't talk about this until you ~.)

1445✓

→bōuséui 煲水 (lit.) VO boil water 燒水
(idi.) VO make something out of nothing (usually rumors about those in show business) 製造謠言,通常是演藝界人士的新聞 : *Gógo néuih mihngsīng ngāamngāam tùhng go yáuhchínlóu gitfān móuh géi noih jauh wah yiu lèihfān, ~ ji gwa.* (That actress said she was going to divorce her rich husband shortly after they got married. Probably it's ~.)

1446 ✓

→bun túng séui 半桶水 (lit.) PH half a bucket of water 半個桶子的水
(idi.) PH know next to nothing about something; have a limited command of a certain kind of skill or have incomplete knowledge about something 一知半解,對一種知識或技能未完全掌握好 : *Ngóhdī Yīngmán dōu haih ~ ge ja.* (My English is not good enough.)

1447

→chāuséui 抽水 (lit.) draw water 把水抽走
(idi.) VO (1) (usually in mahjong) take away a small portion of money from the winner of each game (to pay for the rent of the mahjong tiles or to use it for enjoyment after the game) 通常指打麻將時)每次從贏家抽取一少部分錢作麻將牌的租錢或打牌之後的聯歡 : *Ngóhdeih dápáai yiu ~, dáyùhn jauh heui sihk yātchāan.* (We play mahjong and we'll ~. Then we can go out for a rich meal.) (2) reap money or get benefits out of the price paid by others 從中賺取利益 : *Séuifo pèhngdī haih yānwaih m̀sái béi doihléihsēung ~.* (Things that are not imported and distributed by retail agents are cheaper because distributors cannot ~.) also see 1459

1448

→dohkséui 度水 (lit.) measure water 量度水(的深度)
(idi.) VO borrow money from others 跟別人借錢 : *Daaihlóu, ~ jyuh yātgauh ~ làih, dāk m̀dāk a?* (Big

235

brother, could I borrow one hundred dollars from you?)

1449 ✓

➔fongséui 放水 (lit.) VO let the water go, turn on the tap (to get water) 放水
(idi.) VO give someone the green light 讓別人通行無阻 ： *Néih béijó hāakchín kéuih kéuih maih ~ béi néih lō.* (You give him a bribe and then he will ~.)

1450 ✓

➔gwoséui 過水 (lit.) VO clear away detergent with water 把洗滌劑用水清洗
(idi.) VO pay/ give money to 付／給錢 ： ~ *jauh fongséui.* (You ~ me and I'll give you water.) (*The example sentence was used in the 1960s to depict the bribe taking of firemen.)

1451

➔jamgwo hàahmséui 浸過鹹水 (lit.) have been soaked in salt water (i.e. sea water) 被鹹水(即海水)浸過
(idi.) PH have studied abroad 曾到外國留學 ： ~ *haih mtùhngdī ge, ngáahngaai dōu futdī lā.* (People who ~ are really a little different/ better. They have wider vision.)

1452

➔lēukséui 掠水 (lit.) rob water 劫水
(idi.) VO see 1308

1453

➔máaihséui 買水 (lit.) buy water 買水
(idi.) VO a ritual performed by the eldest son at his father's funeral 在父親喪禮中一項由長子擔當的儀式 (*However, the full form should be called 'dāamfāan ~'. After one dies, his eldest son goes to a nearby river in which he throws some coins in order to get some water to wipe the face of his dead father.) ： *Yùhgwó néih msāang jái, bīndouh yáuh yàhn bōng néih ~ a?* (If you don't have a son, is there anyone who would perform the ritual for you [at your funeral]?)

1454

➔ngàhnhòhng séuijam 銀行水浸 (lit.) floods in the bank 水淹銀行
(idi.) PH too much deposited money in the bank 銀行有太多存款 ： ~, *sóyíh leihsīk gam dāi.* (There is ~, so the interest rate is that low.)

1455

➔pokséui 撲水 (lit.) rush to get water 趕着尋找水源
(idi.) VO go everywhere to get money which is urgently needed, a rush for money 有急需而要四處張羅金錢 ： ~ *gwonìhn* (~ for the [Chinese] New Year)

1456

➔put láahng séui 潑冷水 (lit.) pour cold water 潑冷水
(idi.) VO discourage somebody 使人覺得沒趣 ： *A-Chán wah, "Ngóh séung máaih gójek ngoihbaih." A-Wóng wah, "Gójek ngoihbaih yātdihng wúih dit." A-Lóh wah, "Néih mhóu ~ lā."* (Chan said, "I want to

236

buy that foreign currency." Wong said, "It will definitely fall." Lo said, "Don't ~ on him.")

1457

➔sāmséui 心水 see 0643 and 0669

1458 ✓

➔séui 水 (lit.) N water 水 M dihk; dī
(idi.) N money 錢 : *Chēutjó lèuhng, sóyíh daaihbá ~.* (Today is my pay day, and so I will get a lot of ~.) (*Water is indispensable to our life, and so is money.)

1459

➔séuifo 水貨 (lit.) water commodities 水做的貨
(idi.) N commodities which are imported and distributed without an agent and so they are cheaper 不經代理商入口及發行的貨品比較便宜 M dī : *Gógāan poutáu jyūn maaih séuifo.* (Things that are sold in that shop are all ~.) (*There's no guarantee of quality or maintenance for 'séuifo'. Also see 1460.)

1460

➔séuihaak 水客 (lit.) water traveller 水上遊客
(idi.) N people who carry things for sale on their trips 在旅途上售賣貨物的旅客 : *Jouh ~ chèuihsih hóyíh jaahn dóu gēipiu.* (If you work as a ~ on your trips, you can easily earn enough money for your plane ticket.) (*Things that a 'séuihaak' sells are 'séuifo', see 1459. Sometimes, selling 'séuifo' may be regarded as smuggling.)

1461 ✓

➔séuipóuh 水泡 (lit.) N lifebuoy 救生圈 M go
(idi.) N the only thing that one can rely on (in making a living) 可以依賴的或賴以為生的唯一的東西 M go : *Nīgāan poutáu sēuiyihn yauh sai yauh gauh, daahnhaih haih ngóhdeih chyùhngā ge ~ làih ge la.* (This shop is small and old, yet it's ~ for our whole family.)

1462

➔séui wàih chòih 水為財 (lit.) PH water is (the symbol of) wealth 水是財富(的象徵) : *"Yùhgwó lohk daaih yúh, nīdouh wúih séuijam." "Mgányiu, ~ ā ma."* ("Heavy rains will cause floods here." "It doesn't matter. ~, isn't it?") (* It is a common saying in Chinese geomancy that water can bring wealth.)

1463

➔síngséui 醒水 (lit.) wake up water 把水弄醒
(idi.) V be quick enough to realize 立即醒悟到 : *Tàuhsīn lóuhsai m̀gōuhing néih góng ge syutwah, ngóh tùhng néih dá ngáahnsīk néih dōu m̀~.* (Our boss was not pleased with what you said just a moment ago. I winked at you but you were not ~.)

1464 ✓

➔sūkséui 縮水 (lit.) VO (said of clothes) shrink after washing 衣物洗後縮小
(idi.) ATT become smaller or lower 變得越來越小 : ⓐ *Dī yéh yuht*

237

làih yuht gwai, dī ngàhnjí jauh yuht làih yuht ~. (Things are getting more and more expensive, but money becomes ~ in value.) ⓑ *Sāuláu (gójahnsí) sīnji faatgok gāan láu haih ~ láu.* (Not until we took over the flat did we find that it was a ~ flat.)

1465
➔syùhntàuh chek→dohkséui 船頭尺→度水 (lit.) ruler put at the bow→(is used) to measure (the depth of the) water 放在船頭的尺→是用來量度水的深度的 (idi.) HIT a person who likes to borrow money from others 喜向人借貸的人 : *Sihngyaht dōu jouh ~ → ~.* (You always act as ~ → ~.) also see 1448

1466
➔wùihséui 回水 (lit.) return the water 退回水 (idi.) VO refund 退還金錢 : *Kéuih sāudōjó ngóhdeih chín, faaidī giu kéuih ~.* (He overcharged us. Be quick and get him to ~.)

1467
➔yātgauh séui 一嚿水 (lit.) a wad of water 一大塊水 (idi.) PH (quite an old way of saying) one hundred Hong Kong dollars 港幣一百塊錢 (舊的說法) : see 1448, also see 0093

1468
➔yātpit séui 一撇水 (lit.) one slide of water 一撇筆劃的水 (idi.) PH (quite an old way of saying) one thousand Hong Kong dollars 港幣一千元 (舊的說法)

(*'Pit' is the sliding stroke on top of the Chinese character for '千', i.e. thousand, and so it's another way of referring to 'thousand'.) also see 0878

1469 ✓
➔yātpùhn séui 一盆水 (lit.) one basin of water 一個盆子的水 (idi.) PH (quite an old way of saying) ten thousand Hong Kong dollars 港幣一萬元 (舊的說法) (*'Pùhn', i.e. basin, is a container of large capacity.)

1470
➔yàuh gōn séui 游乾水 (lit.) swim dry/without water 不在水中游泳 (idi.) PH play mahjong (when one moves his hands as if swimming when shuffling the tiles) 打麻將(洗牌時手的動作像游泳) : *hái sātāan ~* (~ at the beach)

1471 ✓
➔yàuhséui 游水 (lit.) VO swim 游泳 (idi.) ATT (said of seafood) very fresh (and still alive) (海鮮)非常新鮮(還活著) : *~ hóisīn/ yú/ hā* (~ seafood/ fish/ shrimp) also see 0070 and 0992

seunfūng 信封 N envelope 信封 M go

1472 ✓
➔daaih seunfūng 大信封(lit.) N big envelope 大的信封 M go (idi.) N a letter telling you that you have been fired 解僱信 M go : *jipdóu ~* (received ~)

238

sīk 骰 N dice 骰子 **M lāp**

1473 ✓
➔dásīk 打骰 (lit.) VO shake/ throw the dice 擲骰子
(idi.) VO take charge of 負責 : *Nīdouh yàuh kéuih ~ saai ~* (He ~ everything here.)

1474
➔jāsī 揸骰 (lit.) hold the dice 拿 着骰子
(idi.) VO same as 1473

sin 扇 N fan 扇子 **M bá**

1475
➔chāuhauh sin 秋後扇 (lit.) fan (put away) after autumn 秋後扇
(idi.) N one who is no longer needed/ regarded as helpful after having finished doing something for others 爲人出了力後被人冷落 : *Yiu ngóh bōng kéuih gójahnsí, jauh deui ngóh gwái gam hóu, bōngyùhn kéuih (ngóh) jauh ~.* (He was very nice to me when he needed my help, but after that I became like a ~.)

1476
➔jā daaih kwàihsin 揸大葵扇 (lit.) hold in hand a big palm-leaf fan 手拿著大的葵扇
(idi.) PH be a match-maker 做媒 : *tùhng néih ~* (~ for you) (*One can see in Chinese opera that a woman match-maker always has such kind of fan in her hand.)

sin 線 N thread, wire, line
線 M tiuh

1477
➔chésin 扯線 (lit.) pull the thread 拉線
(idi.) VO (1) be a matchmaker 做 媒 : *Néih geiyihn jūngyi Wòhng síujé, yauh m̀gám jēui kéuih, bātyùh ngóh tùhng néih ~ ā.* (You are very fond of Miss Wong but dare not court her, let me ~ for you, OK?) (2) act as/ be a go-between 作中間 人 : ⓐ *Ngóh tùhng A-Chán hahpjok, dōuhaih A-Wóng tùhng ngóhdeih ~ ja.* (I co-operate with Chan all because Wong ~ for us.)
ⓑ *chésin gūngjái* see 1382

1478 ✓
➔chèuhngsin 長線 (lit.) N long thread 長的線 M tiuh
(idi.) ATT long term (planning/ investment) 長遠的(計劃/投資) : ⓐ *~ gaiwaahk* (~ planning) ⓑ *Máaih làahmchàuh gú haih ~ tàuhjī, m̀haih tàuhgēi.* (Buying blue chip stocks is a ~ investment, not a speculation.)

1479 ✓
➔chīsin 黐線 (lit.) VO wires get fused 線黏在一起
(idi.) VO crazy, mad 發瘋 : ⓐ*Kéuih sauhm̀jyuh chigīk, ~ jó ~.* (He was badly struck by the blow and became ~.) ⓑ*Néih ~ mè, jēung go jái dásihng gám.* (Are you ~? You have beaten your son so badly.) PH nonsense, crazy 廢話 : *Ngóh jūngyi kéuih? ~!* ([Do you think] I'm in love with him? [You're] ~!)

1480 ✓

➡️daapcho sin 搭錯線 (lit.) PH get the wrong number on the phone 打電話撥錯了號碼

(idi.) PH misunderstand (the intended meaning of others), get one's wires crossed 誤會了別人說話的含意 : *Ngóh yíhwàih lóuhsai giu ngóh fuhjaak dōdī gūngjok jauh wúih gā ngóh sān, dímjī m̀haih."* "*Néih ~ jē.*" ("I thought my boss would give me a pay raise because he told me to assume more duties. But he didn't." "You just ~.")

1481 ✓

➡️dyúnsin 短線 (lit.) N short thread 短的線 M tiuh

(idi.) ATT short term (investment) 短期的（投資） : *Chèuihjó chèuhngsin tàuhjī jīngoih, ngóh juhng jūngyi jouhháh dī ~ tàuhjī.* (Besides long term investments, I also like ~ investments.)

1482

➡️fong chèuhng sin diu daaih yú 放長線釣大魚 (lit.) let the fishing line go as long as possible in order to catch big fish 把魚絲線放長以釣得大魚

(idi.) PH wait patiently for the benefits one anticipates 耐心等待所期望的好處來臨 : *Ngóhdeih deui kéuih hóudī, kéuih gáng yáuh yātyaht wúih làih ngóhdeih douh bōng ngóhdeih ge. Ngóhdeih ~ lā.* (Let's try to be nicer to him. I'm sure one day he will come and help us. Let's ~.)

1483

➡️gam ngāam sin 咁啱線

(lit.) (in singing Cantonese opera) perfectly in tune with the pitch 與調子的音高很吻合

(idi.) PH what a coincidence, as it happens 真湊巧 : ⓐ *~ a! Néih yauh làih àh!* (~! You are also here.) ⓑ *Kéuih yáuh gāpsih yiu wán A-Chán, ~ A-Chán yauh m̀háidouh.* (He wanted to talk to Chan about something urgent. ~, Chan was not there.)

1484 ✓

➡️sin 線 (lit.) N thread, wire, line 線 M tiuh

(idi.) BF the pitch for Cantonese operatic songs 粵曲中的定絃 : *"Gāmyaht cheung mē ~ a?" "C sharp."* ("What ~ would you like today for singing?" "C sharp [as 'do' in the upper register].")

1485

➡️sinyàhn 線人 (lit.) thread man 做線的人

(idi.) N informer 向警方提供歹徒消息的人 M go : *Gíngfōng gāngeui ~ ge jīlíu sihnggūng jēung dī dáaitòuh kēuibouh.* (Based on the information given by ~, the police successfully arrested the gangsters.)

sō 梳 N comb 梳子 M bá/ go

1486

➡️mahn wòhséung je sō→ saht móuh 問和尚借梳→實冇 (lit.) ask a monk for a comb→ certainly he has none 問和尚借梳子→他一定沒有

(idi.) HIT ask the wrong person (for something) 問人借東西卻問錯了對

240

象：*"Baih la, ngóhdeih yuhngsaai yìhm, bātyùh mahn gaaklèih Chàhn sīnsāang je lā."* *"Kéuih dōu m̀jyúfaahn ge, maih jīkhaih ~ → ~."* ("Oh, too bad! We run out of salt. Let me ask Mr. Chan who lives next door to give/ lend us some." "He doesn't cook. You just ~ → ~.")

1487 ✓

➔sō 梳 (lit.) N/V comb 梳子; 梳理頭髮 M bá/go

(idi.) N the grade of 'E' 拿 E 等成績：*yātbá ~* (see 1488)

1488 ✓

➔yātbá sō 一把梳 (lit.) PH a comb 一個梳子

(idi.) PH all get 'E' 全拿了 E 的成績：*"Háausi sihngjīk dím a?"* *"~ lō!"* ("How are your exam results?" "I ~!")

sósìh 鎖匙 N key 鑰匙 M tìuh; chāu

1489

➔sātsìh gaapmaahn 失匙夾萬 (lit.) a safe with its key lost 掉了鑰匙的夾萬

(idi.) N a rich person who cannot make use of his wealth 一個不能動用財富的有錢人 M go：*Kéuihdeihge gājuhk hóu yáuhchín, daahnhaih kéuih bàhbā m̀jéun kéuih sái gódī chín, kéuih jingyāt ~.* (He is from a very rich family. But his father won't allow him to use their money. He is just like ~.)

1490

➔yāttìuh sósìh m̀héung,

léuhngtìuh sósìh lāanglāang héung 一條鎖匙唔響，兩條鎖匙冷冷響 (lit.) one key would not make noise, but two would 一條鑰匙不會響,兩條鑰匙就會鈴鈴作響

(idi.) PH It's fine to have one wife, but not two (because they would always quarrel) 一個太太家裏很寧靜,兩個就不會寧靜了(因為常有爭吵)：*"Jihchùhng A-Chán ge yihnāai làihjó jīhauh, kéuih ngūkkéi jauh sìhsìh gāchòuh ngūkbai."* *"Gánghaih lā, ~, ~."* ("Since Chan's mistress has come to live with his family, I can hear quarrels in his house all the time." "Of course, ~, ~.")

syunpùhn 算盤 N abacus 算盤 M go

1491

➔mahtdái syunpùhn 密底算盤 (lit.) closed-bottom abacus 封了底的算盤

(idi.) N a person very shrewd with money 很會精打細算的人 M go：*Kéuih nīgo ~, mātyéh dōu syundou chīngchīng chóchó.* (He is ~. He always calculates carefully and budgets strictly.)

tāi 梯 N ladder 梯子 M tòhng/ bá

1492 ✓

➔dāamtāi 擔梯 (lit.) VO carry a ladder 挑梯子

(idi.) VO all get 'H' 全拿了 H 的成績：*háausi ~* (~ in the exam) also see 1495

1493

➔néih yáuh Jēung Lèuhng gai, ngóh yáuh gwochèuhng tāi 你有張良計，我有過牆梯 (lit.) you get the strategy devised by Jēung Lèuhng to trap me, luckily I have a ladder by which I can climb over the wall and get away from your trap 你有張良計,我有過牆梯 (idi.) PH a policy is well-matched by another 一個對策有另一個對策對付它 : *Nīdouh yahttáu báaidong jauh yáuh chāaiyàhn lāai jē, ngóhdeih yehmáahn làih maaihyéh maih dāk lō, ~, ~ ā ma.* (If we put up our stalls here at daytime, we'll be caught by the police. But it'll be fine if we come at night. You know ~, ~.)

1494

➔ngáijái séuhng làuhtāi→ bouhbouh gōusīng 矮仔上樓梯→步步高升 (lit.) a short guy climbing up a ladder→ (he goes up) step by step 矮子爬梯子→一步一步的往上爬 (idi.) HIT climb the job escalator stably 職位步步高升 : *Ngóh jouhjó yihsahp nihn sīnji jouhdou gīngléih/ haauhjéung, jíhaih ~ (→ ~) jē, néih jauh hóu lā, chóh jihksīng géi.* (I had worked for twenty years before I became a manager/ school principal. I'm just like ~ (→ ~). You have been more successful. You are a high flyer.)

1495 ✓

➔tāi 梯 (lit.) N ladder 梯子 M tòhng/ bá

(idi.) N the grade of 'H' 拿 H 等成績 : *dāam* ~ (see 1492)

tói 枱 N table 桌子 M jēung

1496 ✓

➔báaiséuhng tói 擺上枱 (lit.) put on the table 放在桌子上 (idi.) PH (said of people) be used by others as a device for propaganda 被人利用作宣傳的手段 : "*Gūnghéi néih! Néih syúnjó jouh ngóhdeih ge doihbíu.*" "*Ngóh béi yàhn ~ jē!*" ("Congratulations! You have been elected as our representative." "I'm just being ~.")

1497

➔maaih tói 賣枱 (lit.) sell table 賣桌子 (idi.) VO sell a shop and also the facilities inside it 鋪子及裏面的設備一併賣出 : *Gógāan fēifaatpóu yíhgīng ~ jó ~ béi yàhn la.* (That barber shop has been sold.)

1498

➔tóidái gāauyihk 枱底交易 (lit.) under-table transaction 桌子下做買賣 (idi.) PH do a transaction privately and secretly 私下交易 : *Gógāan daaih ngàhnhòhng sāukaujó nīgāan gūngsī, daahnhaih yānwaih haih ~, sóyíh móuh māt yàhn jī.* (That big bank took over this company. However, it is a ~, so few people know about it.)

túng 桶 N/M bucket, pail, barrel; measure meaning 'a

pail/ bucket of' 桶子; 量詞:一桶 **M go**

1499

➔faahntúng 飯桶 (lit.) a container for rice 用來盛飯的桶子 (idi.) N a stupid fool who only knows how to eat 只會吃飯的笨蛋 M go : *Go daaihhah gúnléihyùhn béi dī jyuhhaak laauh, "Yáuh cháak yàuh hauhmún jáuyahplàih tāuyéh dōu m̀jī, jingyāt ~!"* (The caretaker was scolded by the residents, "A burglar broke in by the back door but you didn't know it. You ~!")

1500 ✓

➔séuitúng 水桶 (lit.) N bucket, pail 盛水的桶子 M go (idi.) N (said of people) have a body shape like a bucket 像水桶的身型 : *Kéuih fèihdou hóuchíh go ~ gám.* (S/he is fat and looks like a bucket.)

wái 位 N seat, post 位子, 職位 M go

1501

➔chēutwái 出位 (lit.) out of the (former) place 離開了(原來的)位置/座位 (idi.) VO climb the ladder of success (by questionable means) (用不大好的方法)走上成功的道路 : *Dī néuih mihngsīng jeukdāk gam singgám, bok ~ jī ma.* (The actresses put on very sexy dresses. They just want to ~.) Adj. inappropriate (speech or behaviour in terms of one's social status) (一個人的言行相對於他的身份來說)

不 恰 當 : *Yáuh dī séhwúi mihnglàuh góngyéh hóu ~.* (Some social celebrities would say something very ~.)

1502 ✓

➔fēigēi wái 飛機位 (lit.) N plane seat 飛機上的座位 M go (idi.) N seats high up and far away from stage in a theater 離舞台又遠又高的座位 M go : *Chóh daaihtòhng chihn jauh gánghaih gokdāk hóutái lā, ngóhdeih chóh ~ jauh gokdāk màhmádéi jē.* (People who sat at the front stall found the show exciting. But it's different to us because we sat on those ~.)

1503 ✓

➔jāpwái 執位 (lit.) VO (in mahjong) choose a seat or exchange seats among the players (by picking a tile indicating a direction) (打麻將)選擇或調換座位(要先挑一個指示方向的牌) (idi.) VO (said of high ranking officials in the government) reshuffle, shake-up in posts (政府高級官員)職位大調動 : *Jingfú gōugūn daaih ~ : Mauhyihkchyúh Jéung jouh Fòhngngūkchyúh Jéung, Yīgúngúk Jyújihk jouh Mauhyihkchyúh Jéung. Yihnyahm Fòhngngūkchyúh Jéung jouh Yīgúngúk Jyújihk.* (There will be a ~ among the high officials. The Director of the Trading Authority is going to be the Director of the Housing Authority. The Chairperson of the Hospital Authority is going to be the Director of the Trading Authority, and the present Director of the Housing Authority is going to chair the Hospital Authority.)

1504

➜sāamsaat wái 三煞位 (lit.)
three devils' place 三個凶神的地方
(idi.) N/PW a post that has to deal
with tough situations or difficult
people 要應付難應付的人和事的
職位 M go : *Nīgo ~ móuh yàhn
jūngyi chóh.* (No one likes to fill
this ~.)

1505

➜séuhngwái 上位 (lit.) go up
the seat 走上座位
(idi.) VO climb up/ be promoted to
a much higher position (on one's job
ladder) 攀上/升上更高職位 :
*Ngóhdeih gūngsī yáuh gam dō lēk
yàhn, ngóh bīndouh yáuh gēiwuih
~ ā!* (There are so many capable
people in our company. How would
it be possible for me to ~ ?)

wohk 鑊 N wok/frying pan
煎鍋 M go/jek

1506

➜baau daaih wohk 爆大鑊
(lit.) blast a big frying pan 大鑊爆炸
(idi.) PH make public a big scandal
把秘密 / 醜聞公開 : *Kéuih
námjyuh ~, heung ICAC géuibou
kéuihdeih bouhmùhn ge a-táu tāamwū.*
(He is planning to ~ to the ICAC, i.e.
Independent Commission Against
Corruption, that the head of their
department is involved in bribery.)

1507

➜bóuwohk 補鑊 (lit.) mend
the (cracked) pan 修補(破的)鍋
(idi.) VO remedy (a mishap) 補救
(不幸的事) : *Gódī dyún jōng láu, dī*

*sihngginsēung tàihchēut ~ ge
baahnfaat, jauh haih gā dōdī
jōngchyúh.* (As for the apartment
blocks built with shortened piles,
the contractors suggested that they
could ~ by adding more piles to the
blocks.)

1508 ✓

➜daaih wohk 大鑊 (lit.) N a
big wok 大的鍋 M go/ jek
(idi.) N great trouble 非常糟糕的事
M chi : ⓐ*Nīchi ~ la! Dī haak béi
ngóh sēung ge sáusīk, sihngdoih
mginjó.* (This time I'm in ~. I lost
the bag of jewels that my customers
asked me to set/design for them.) ⓑ
*Nīchi ~ la! Dihnlóuh yahpbihn ge
jīlíu chyùhnbouh móuhsaai.* (This
time we're in ~! The data in the
computer has all gone.) Adj. very
troublesome 很糟糕很麻煩 :
Sihkcho yeuhk wúih hóu ~ ga. (It
would be ~ if one takes wrong
medicine.) ATT government
resources 政府資源 : *sihk ~ faahn*
see 1048.

1509

➜hāakwohk 黑鑊 (lit.) black
Chinese wok/ frying pan 黑色的鍋
(idi.) N misforune (that somebody has
to be held responsible for) 不幸的事
(應有人負責) M jek : *Hēunggóng ge
sān gēichèuhng yáuh hóudō mahntàih,
daahnhaih móuh yàhn yiu mē nījek ~.*
(Hong Kong's new airport had many
blunders, but no one was held
responsible for them.)

1510 ✓

➜jā wohkcháan 揸鑊鏟 (lit.)

VO hold the spatula of a wok 拿著
鍋鏟
(idi.) VO work as a cook in a
restaurant 在飲食店中當廚子 ：
*Kéuih yíhchihn haih dímsām sīfú,
yihgā jouh ~ ge.* (Before, he was a
dimsum maker, and now he ~.)

1511
→me(hāak)wok　揹（黑）鑊
(lit.) carry a (black) wok on one's
back 背(黑)鍋
(idi.) VO be held responsible (for a
mishap) 爲一宗不幸事件負責 ：
*Sēuiyìhn dī gōugūn jouhcho sih,
daahnhaih jingfú wah móuh yàhn
yiu ~.* (Although the high officials
had done things wrong, the
government said that no one was to
be held ~.)

1512
→suhk yàhn máaih po wohk
熟人買破鑊 (lit.) buy a broken
wok from someone you know 從相
識的人那裏買了一個破爛的鍋
(idi.) PH buy from an acquaintance
something which turns out to be
flawed 從相識的人那裏竟買了有
瑕疵的東西 ： *Ngóh máaihjó
A-Wóng góga yihsáu chē, yùhnlòih
yáuh hóudō mahntàih, jānhaih ~.* (I
bought a used car from Wong. Later I
found it had quite a lot of problems. I
certainly have ~.)

1513 ✓
→wohk　鑊 (lit.) N wok/ frying
pan 煎鍋 M go/ jek
(idi.) M a measure for one mishap 不
幸事件的量詞 ： ⓐ*Nī ~ giht la.*
(We're in big trouble this time.) ⓑ

yāt ~ suhk see 0932 N mishap,
misfortune 不幸事件 M go/ jek ：
*Gamdō dyúnjōng láu, bīngo yiu mē
nīgo ~ a?* (There are so many
buildings built with short piles.
Who is to be held responsible for
this?) also see 1511

1514
→wohkwohk giht 鑊鑊杰(lit.)
every time cooking with a wok makes
such a mess 每一次用鍋煮東西都
糟糕
(idi.) PH everything one does is very
troublesome 所做的都糟透了 ：
*Nīgo júngtúng séuhngtòih jīhauh,
sānge fòhngngūk jingchaak gáaudou
làuhsíh lam, sānge gīngjai jingchaak
gáaudou gīngjai sēuiteui, jānhaih
hóyíh wah ~.* (After the president
had been sworn in, his new housing
policy made the property market
plunge, and his new financial policy
caused the recession.　You could
say that ~.)

1515
→yātwohk póuh 一鑊泡(lit.)
a wok of bubbles 滿鍋是泡沫
(idi.) PH (situation) such a mess 情
況糟糕，一塌糊塗 ： *Sān jingfú
séuhngchèuhng yauh gáau nīyeuhng
gáau góyeuhng, gáaudou ~, móuh
yeuhng yéh sihnggūng.* (After the
take-over, the new government
made new policies for this and that.
But all of them were unsuccessful,
all ~, just blunders.)

wún 碗 N/M bowl; measure meaning 'a bowl of' 碗;量詞: 一碗 N go/ jek

1516

➔ **bóujyuh faahnwún** 保住飯碗 (lit.) protect one's rice bowl 保護飯碗

(idi.) PH protect oneself from not being fired 保住工作使自己不會被辭退 : ⓐ *Kéuih gam kàhnlihk jeunsāu, dōu haih séung ~ jē.* (He studies very hard after work in order to ~.) ⓑ *Yìhgā gūngsī yiu chòihyùhn, jeui gányiu haih ~ sīn.* (Now our company is going to lay off some staff. The most urgent thing to do is to ~.)

1517

➔ **dálaahn faahnwún** 打爛飯碗 (lit.) break the rice bowl 打破飯碗

(idi.) PH lose one's job 失業 : *Néih sèhngyaht fáandeui lóuhsai góng ge yéh, yānjyuh ~ a.* (You always oppose/ disagree with our boss. Be careful or you'll ~.)

1518 ✓

➔ **faahnwún** 飯碗 (lit.) N rice bowl 飯碗 M go/ jek

(idi.) N job 工作 M go : *Néih fahn gūng yauh taan yauh dō chín, nīgo ~ heui bīndouh wán ā? Néih m̀hóu gam yùhngyih wah m̀jouh a.* (You have a job that is easy to do and the pay is good. How could you find such ~ elsewhere? So don't say you'll quit so easily.)

1519

➔ **gām faahnwún** 金飯碗(lit.) golden rice bowl 金做的飯碗

(idi.) N very secure job with a high salary (usually in the government)

(政府裏)又穩定又高薪的工作 M go : *Kéuih hái ngoihgwok làuhyùhn hohk fāanlàih jauh wándóu go ~ laak.* (He got a ~ soon after he finished his studies overseas.)

1520

➔ **jāang faahnwún** 爭飯碗 (lit.) scramble for a rice bowl 爭奪飯碗

(idi.) VO compete for jobs 爭奪工作 : ⓐ *Búndeih ge daaih hohksāang wán gūng jouh yíhgīng nàahn ge la, juhng yáuh dī làuhhohksāang fāanlàih tùhng kéuihdeih ~.* (Local university graduates already find it hard to get a job. There are also overseas graduates who ~ with them.) ⓑ *Dī ginjūk gūngyàhn kongyíh dī ngoihlòuh làih tùhng kéuihdeih ~.* (The construction workers protest against the importation of expatriate laborers who ~ with them.)

1521

➔ **jiu báan jyú wún** 照板煮碗 (lit.) follow the sample and cook another bowl of it 照樣板/樣品再煮一個

(idi.) PH (1) do as the given sample 依樣葫蘆,照樣去做 : ⓐ *M̀sái gáau gam dō yéh la, kéuih dím jouh ngóh ~ maih dāk lō.* (Don't bother to make anything new out of it. We just ~ and do it the same way he does.) ⓑ *Néih táiháh kéuih dím jouh, yihnhauh ~ jauh dāk la.* (You watch him do this and then you simply ~.) (2) pay somebody in his own coin, treat someone in the same way he has treated you 以其人之道還治其人之

身：*Yíhchìhn kéuih jouh a-táu, kéuih sìhsìh jāmdeui néih, yìhgā lèuhndou néih jouh a-táu, néih màih ~ jāmdeuifāan kéuih lō.* (When he was in charge, he always picked on you. Now it's your turn to be in charge, you just ~ and pick on him.)

1522

→tit faahnwún 鐵飯碗 (lit.) iron rice bowl 鐵做的飯碗
(idi.) N very secure job (in the government) 政府裏很穩定的工作：*Yíhchìhn dī yàhn sihnmouh dī gūngmouhyùhn yáuh ~.* (Before, people envied civil servants for having ~.) (*Civil servants in the Hong Kong government could not be so easily fired before 1997. That was like an iron rice bowl which cannot be broken.)

1523

→yáuh wún wah wún, yáuh dihp wah dihp 有碗話碗，有碟話碟 (lit.) talk about bowls as there are bowls and talk about plates as there are plates 有碗就說碗,有碟就說碟
(idi.) PH tell all what one knows (about certain thing) 知道甚麼就說甚麼,不必隱藏：*Kéuih jēung gógihn sih, ~, ~, góngsaai béi ngóh tēng.* (He told me about that in a ~ way.)

yī 衣 **N clothes** 衣服 (*'Yī' is rarely used by itself.)

1524

→sīn ging lòhyī hauh ging yàhn 先敬羅衣後敬人 (lit.) PH have respect for one's clothing first and then for him 先敬羅衣後敬人：*Ṁhaih wah tāam leng, bātgwo jeukdāk hóudī yàhndeih deui néih wúih hóudī, ~ ā ma.* (It's not because I like to dress up. However, if one is better dressed, one would get better service. Don't you know that people tend to ~?) also see 1000 and 1140

7. Nature

chàhn 塵 N dust 塵 M dī

1525 ✓

➔chàhn 塵 (lit.) N dust 塵 M dī (idi.) Adj. proud, boastful 驕傲自誇 : *Kéuih gam ~, m̀gwaaidāk hóu síu yàhn jūngyi tùhng kéuih lòihwóhng lā.* (He is so ~. That's why few people like to befriend him.)

1526 ✓

➔sāchàhn 沙塵 (lit.) N sand and dust 沙跟塵 M dī (idi.) Adj. see 1525

chóu 草 N grass 草 M tìuh; dēui/ jah

1527 ✓

➔chóu 草 (lit.) N grass 草 M tìuh; dēui/ jah (idi.) N (messy like) grass (像)草(那樣凌亂) : *dī tàuhfaat hóuchíh jah ~ gám* (the hair is messy like ~) Adj. (said of handwriting) illegible (字跡)潦草 : ⓐ*Kéuih sé ge jih hóu ~.* (His handwriting is ~.) ⓑ~ *jih* (cursive writing)

1528

➔jeukchóu 着草 (lit.) wear grass 穿上草 (idi.) VO (said of a fugitive criminal) escapes, runs away 犯了法的人逃走到別處 : *Kéuih haih hāak séhwúi daaihlóu, dímgáai gáaudou yiu ~ a?* (He is a gang leader. How come he's become a fugitive and ~?)

1529 ✓

➔pōu chóupèih 鋪草皮(lit.) VO lay sod/ turf 鋪上塊草皮 (idi.) VO lose money to the Jockey Club in horse racing 賽馬輸了錢給馬會 : *Dī yàhn dóu máh, kèihsaht dī chín maih béi Máhwúi ~.* (People bet on horses. In fact, their money is given to the Jockey Club for the laying of the turf [in the race course]/ they always ~.)

1530

➔syun séi chóu 算死草 (lit.) calculate dead grass 計算死了的草 (idi.) PH be shrewd-headed (with what is to one's own advantage), be calculating 斤斤計較自己的好處 : *Kéuih nīgo yàhn, jingyāt ~, dím wúih yīk néih ā!* (He really is a ~ person. He won't let you gain any benefits.)

dihn 電 N electricity 電

1531 ✓

➔dihn 電 see 1345–1349

1532✓

➔símdihn 閃電 (lit.) VO/ N there's lightning/ lightning 閃電 (idi.) A rapidly 迅速 : ~ *gitfān* (get married ~)

fā 花 N flower 花 M dó/ déu; jī; jaat; dēui

1533 ✓

➔fā 花 (lit.) N flower 花 M dó/ déu; jī; jaat; dēui

(idi.) Adj. (1) not clear 朦朧不清 : ⓐ *Go dihnsih hóu ~* (The TV's reception is poor/~.) ⓑ *Lāp jyunsehk hóu ~, m̀dāk chīng.* (This diamond's clarity is low.) (2) having scars 有破損痕跡 : *Néih yuhng fongdaaih geng jauh wúih táidóu lāp yúk ge bíumihn hóu ~.* (You can see the scars on the surface of the piece of jade if you look at it with a magnifying glass.) V scar 有損破 : *Jek gām gaaijí ~ jó.* (The gold ring gets ~.) RVE (1) make dirty 弄污了 : *Bīngo gam baakyim waahk~jó buhng chèuhng a?* (Who is so naughty as to make the wall dirty by drawing something on it?) (2) get scarred 弄致有破損痕跡 : *Go bīu jíng~jó.* (The watch gets ~.)

1534
➔**fāfā gūngjí** 花花公子 (lit.) flower rich young man
(idi.) N dandy, playboy 花花公子 M go : *Gógo yáuhchín ~ jēuigán yáigo néuih mìhngsīng.* (That rich ~ is chasing after a movie actress.)

1535
➔**fāfā lūklūk** 花花綠綠 (lit.) flowers and green 花花綠綠
(idi.) Adj. PH colorful, gaudy 很多顏色的 : ⓐ *~ ge ngàhnjí* (~ dollar bills) ⓑ *Géisahp seui yàhn, juhng jeuk ~ ge sāam.* (You are not young but you still put on ~ clothes.)

1536
➔**fāhùhng** 花紅 (lit.) flower red
(idi.) N bonus 紅利 M dī : *Gaausyū*

ge, *nihnméih móuh sēunglèuhng, móuh ~, juhng yiu gāauseui tīm.* (Teachers neither have annual double pay nor ~, yet they still have to pay tax at the end of the year.) (*Bonuses were traditionally the flower-red money wrapped up in red paper.)

1537
➔**fālīlūk** 花厘綠 (lit.) flowers and green 花花綠綠
(idi.) Adj. PH (1) colorful, gaudy 很多顏色的 : ⓐ *Ngóh jūngyi jihngsīk ge sāam, m̀jūngyi ~ ge.* (I like clothes of one colour, not ~ ones.) ⓑ *Fūk wá ~ gám, m̀jī waahk māt.* (The picture is too ~. I don't know what is painted on it.) (2) look messy and not neat 看起來凌亂不整潔 : *Dī jih sédou ~ gám.* (The handwriting is ~ [and so it's illegible].)

1538 ✓
➔**waahkfā** 畫花 (lit.) VO draw flower 畫花兒
(idi.) RV (1) make dirty by drawing something on it 塗污 : ~ *bún syū* (~ the book) also see 1533 RVE(1) (2) give/ be given a bad record/ remark on one's document(s) (such as driving license, passport or working file) 在某人的證明文件例如駕駛執照, 護照或工作檔案上寫上不好的紀錄或評語 : *chēpàaih/ wuhjiu/ gūngjok géiluhk ~ jó* (be ~ on one's driving license/ passport/ working file)

fó 火 N fire 火 M bá; dī
1539
➔**báfó** 把火 (lit.) (a) torch of fire 一個火把

(idi.) Adj. very angry 很生氣 : *Kéuih góilàih góiheui dōu juhng yáuh cho, (ngóh) jānhaih hóu ~.* (He has already corrected many mistakes, but there are still some. I'm really ~.) VO very angry 很生氣 : ~ *géi/ gwái* ~ (~)

1540

➔faatfó 發火 (lit.) start fire 開始有火

(idi.) VO burst into anger 發怒,火了 : ⓐ*Ngóh m̀~ néih dong ngóh séi ge/ behng māau.* (You treat me as if I were dead/ a sick cat if I don't ~.) also see 0255 ⓑ*Ngóh yāt ~ jauh wúih dá yàhn ge la.* (I would beat someone/ you if I ~.)

1541 ✓

➔fó 火 (lit.) N fire 火 M bá; dī

(idi.) N anger 怒氣 M bá; dī : ⓐ *Dánggihk kéuih dōu m̀làih, dángdou ngóh (yāt)bá ~/bá (gwái) ~ .* (I waited and waited, but he still didn't come. I grew very angry with him.) ⓑ*Kéuih yìhgā yāt tóuh ~.* (Now he is filled with ~.) ⓒ *fó jē ngáahn* see 0556 ⓓ *ngáahn fó baau* see 0579 ⓔ*fógéng* 0392

1542

➔fógwán 火滾 (lit.) fire is boiling 火到了沸點

(idi.) Adj. very angry, boiling with rage 非常生氣 : *Néih jouh māt gam ~ a? Bīngo gīknāu néih a?* (Why are you so ~? Who has irritated you?)

1543

➔fóhei 火氣 (lit.) vapor of fire 火的氣體

(idi.) N anger 怒氣 M dī : *"Lóuhyàhnyún yáuh géigo lóuhyàhn dá daaih gāau." "Géi sahp seui yàhn juhng gam hóu ~ àh!"* ("Two or three inmates are fighting in the home for the aged/ old-folk's home." "Oh, people so old are still filled with ~ [like youngsters]!")

1544

➔fó hùhng fó luhk 火紅火綠 (lit.) fire is red and green 紅色和綠色的火

(idi.) PH face is red with rage in a quarrel 吵架時面紅耳赤 : *ngaaigāau ngaaidou ~* (fight as ~) (* 'Fó hùhng fó luhk' is more emphatic than 0529.)

1545

➔fó seuhng gā yàuh 火上加油 (lit.) pour oil on fire 火上加油

(idi.) PH fan the flames (and make things worse) 煽動情緒 (令行動更激烈) : *Kéuih yíhgīng hóu nāu, néih juhng ~, m̀gwaaidāk kéuih yiu dá yàhn lā.* (He was already very angry, yet you still ~. That's why he wanted to beat us.)

1546

➔fó sīu kèihgōn → chèuhng taan 火燒旗杆→長 (炭) 嘆 (lit.) fire burns a flagstaff→what remains is a long stick of charcoal 用火燒旗杆→就會留下長長的炭條

(idi.) HIT can enjoy life forever 以後可以寫意地生活了 : *Jungjó Luhkhahpchói tàuhjéung jauh hóyíh ~ → ~ la.* (If I win the first prize of the Mark Six, then I can ~ → ~.) (*A pun is made on 炭 [charcoal] and 嘆 [enjoy life]. Both of them are pronounced 'taan'.) also see 1378

1547✓

→hing 熨 (lit.) Adj. hot 熱
(idi.) Adj. angry, irritated 生氣 : *Sáimāt gam ~ a?* (You don't have to be so ~!)

1548

→sāmfó sihng 心火盛 (lit.) fire in the heart burns fiercely 心裏的火燃燒旺盛
(idi.) Adj. PH easily get angry (人) 很容易生氣 : *Hauhsāangjái dōsou ~.* (Most young people will ~.)

1549

→sān gūn séuhngchèuhng sāambá fó 新官上場三把火 (lit.) when a new official begins his term of office, he would have three torches 新官上任三把火
(idi.) PH a new broom sweeps clean/ a person newly appointed is eager to make great changes 新官上任多喜作大改革 : *~, kéuih yāt sīngjó haauhjéung jauh gáau nīyeuhng, gói góyeuhng.* (~. He set up this and changed that soon after he became principal of our school.)

1550

→séifó 死火 (lit.) fire dies out 火死了

(idi.) VO (said of a car) engine stops/ cannot be started 汽車的引擎發生故障, 不能開動 : *Ga chē hàahnghàahnghá ~ jó ~.* (The engine of our car stopped while we were still on the way.) PH Oh, no! 糟糕 : *~ la! Ngūkkéi bōugán yéh, ngóh ǹgeidāk sīkfó jauh chēutgāai la.* (~! I forgot to turn off the stove before I went out. Something is still cooking in my house.)

fūng 風 N wind 風 M jahn/ jahm

1551

→dáfūng dōu dáǹlāt 打風都打唔甩 (lit.) cannot be blown off by typhoon 颱風也不能(把他們)吹散
(idi.) PH (said of newly-weds) even typhoon cannot break them up (指新婚夫婦) 颱風也不能把他們拆散 : *"Tūngsing wah gāmyaht haih chyùhn nìhn gitfān ge jeui hóu yahtjí, dímjī gāmyaht gwa baathouh fūngkàuh." "Sáimāt pa jē, jing sówaih ~."* ("According to the Chinese almanac/ calendar [for this year], today is the best day for wedding. However, typhoon signal no. 8 is hoisted today." "Don't worry. As the saying goes, ~.")

1552✓

→fāanfūng lohkyúh 翻風落雨 (lit.) PH wind blows again and it rains 風又起,又下雨
(idi.) PH when the weather changes 天氣有變化 : *Yāt ~, ngóh tiuh yīugwāt jauh wúih tung.* (I'll have backache whenever ~.)

1553

→faat ngāpfūng 發啞風 (lit.) shoot and utter the breeze 嘴裏發出風

(idi.) VO (1) talk nonsense 亂說 : *Kéuih wah kéuih lóuhdauh haih deihcháan daaihwòhng, néih tēng kéuih ~ là!* (He said his father was a real estate tycoon. He just ~ [and don't listen to him].) (2) chat idly, gas about 閒聊瞎扯 : *Pàhngyáuh hàahngmàaih yātchái ~ háh ~ , móuh hoih ā.* (There's no harm for friends to get together to ~.)

1554

→hon fūng sái léih 看風駛舵 (lit.) see how the wind blows before one sets sail 看看風向怎樣才張帆航駛

(idi.) PH be speculative and take advantage of the situation 注意當時情況及把握時機 : *Kéuih nīgo yàhn hóu sīk ~ ge, bōsí táihéi bīngo kéuih jauh tok bīngo.* (He knows very well how to ~. He will do things to favour those appreciated by our boss.)

1555 ✓

→sahphouh fūngkàuh 十號風球 (lit.) PH typhoon signal no. 10 十號風球

(idi.) PH be nine or ten months pregnant 懷孕九至十月 : *Kéuih yìhgā chégán ~, chèuihsìh dōu sāangdāk ge la.* (She is ~ . She will have her baby delivered anytime.)

1556

→seuhn fūng sái léih 順風駛

珧 (lit.) sail (the boat) before the wind 乘著風勢駕駛船隻

(idi.) PH avail oneself of an opportunity 把握機會 : *Ngóh gin lóuhsai jaan ngóhdeih jauh ~ giu kéuih gā yàhngūng.* (Our boss showed appreciation [for our work]. I ~ and asked him to give us a pay raise.)

1557

→yáuh fūng sáijeuhn léih 有風駛盡珧 (lit.) there is wind so set the ship in full sail 有風便把船張滿帆

(idi.) PH (1) avail oneself of an opportunity as much as possible 盡量把握當下的機會 : *Kéuih nīgo yàhn ~, mātyéh fūkleih dōu lódou jeuhn.* (He is a man who likes to ~. He has enjoyed all the benefits entitled to him.) (2) put on airs as much as one can in a favourable situation 氣勢凌人因爲自己的形勢很好 : *Jouh yàhn mhóu ~. Saigaai wúih lèuhnláuh jyún ge.* (Don't treat me in a ~ way. Fortune will not stay with the same person all the time.)

fūngséui 風水 N Chinese geomancy, fungshui 風水 M dī

1558

→fūng lèuhng séui láahng 風涼水冷 (lit.) wind is cool and water is cold 風很涼, 水很冷

(idi.) PH (said of a place) very cool and pleasant 地方非常清涼舒適 : *Nīdouh lèih sāangeuk yáuh géi chīn gūngchek, fuhgahn yauh yáuh yātgo buhkbou, sóyíh hahtīn ~.* (It's just thousands of meters from here to the foot of the mountain and there is a waterfall nearby. So in summer, it's ~ here.)

1559

→fūngséui／saigaai lèuhnlàuh jyún 風水／世界輪 流 轉 (lit.) fungshui/ the world always turns round and round like a wheel 風水/世界不停地運轉如輪 (idi.) PH good fortune will not stick with one person only 好的時勢不會 停留在一個人身上： *Néih m̀sái gam chàhn, ~, jēunglòih kéuih wúih lēkgwo néih dōu m̀díng.* (You don't need to be so proud. ~. He might do better than you in the future. Who knows!)

1560

→fūngséuilóu ngāak néih sahp nìhn baat nìhn 風水佬呃 你 十 年 八 年 (lit.) fungshui master can only/ may cheat you for nine or ten years 風水師傅只能/會 騙你十年八載 (idi.) PH (I don't want to cheat you and) what I now say is true (我不想 騙 你） 我 說 的 都 是 真 話 ： *~, daahnhaih ngóh góng ge geuigeui dōu haih jān ge.* (~, but all I am telling you is true.) also see 1094

gām 金 N gold 金 M gauh; léung; ōnsí; dī

1561

→Gāmsāan 金 山 (lit.) gold mountain 金的山 (idi.) N/ PW (quite an old term for) the States 美國 （的舊稱）： ⓐ ~ *cháang* (oranges imported from ~)ⓑ ~ *a-baak* (Chinese old men from the States) (*More than a hundred years ago, some Chinese people emigrated to the States to do hard labor in gold-mines.)

1562

→Gauh Gāmsāan 舊 金 山 (lit.) old gold mountain 舊的金山 (idi.) N/ PW San Francisco 三藩市 (*The city of Melbourne was named 'Sān Gāmsāan', which literally means 'new gold mountain'.) ： *Kéuih a-yèh géi sahp nìhn chìhn gwojó ~.* (His grandfather went to ~ decades ago.)

gong 鋼 N steel 鋼 M dī

1563

→gongtíu 鋼條 (lit.) steel rod 鋼筋 (idi.) N (said of a person) thin but strong and healthy 瘦而強壯的人 M tiuh ： *Kéuih sēuiyìhn sau, daahnhaih haih ~ làih ga.* (Although he is thin, he is ~.)

gwōng 光 N light 光 M dī

1564 ✓

→jáugwōng 走 光 (lit.) VO expose film negative 底片曝光 (idi.) VO (usually said of a woman) (so carelessly dressed that) her underwear is showing (通常指女性) 穿衣不小心,內衣物露了出來 ： *Néih jeuk gam dyún ge kwàhn, chóh ge sìhhauh yiu síusāmdī a, yānjyuh wúih ~.* (Be careful of ~ when you sit down since you put on such a short skirt.)

hei 氣 N air, breath 空氣, 呼吸
M dī

1565
➔jūnghei 中氣 (lit.) middle air 中間的空氣
(idi.) N lung power 中氣, 肺活量 : *Gógo nàahm gōuyām (cheunggō) hóu gau ~.* (That tenor has good ~ [when singing].)

1566
➔móuh hei 冇氣 (lit.) no air 沒有空氣
(idi.) PH (1) breathless, out of breath 喘不過氣來 : *páau jó yātgo hyūn jē jauh ~ la* (be ~ after running around the [running] track for just one time) (2) die, no breath 沒有氣息, 斷了氣, 死了 : *kéuih yìhgīng ~.* (He is already ~.)

1567
➔seuhnghei m̀jip hahhei 上氣唔接下氣 (lit.) upper air not connect with lower air 上邊的空氣跟下邊的空氣不連接在一起
(idi.) PH breathe hard/ heavily, pant 喘氣 : *jáudou ~* (~ as one runs)

1568
➔sokhei 索氣 (lit.) ask for air 索取空氣
(idi.) VO (1) be exhausted 疲累得透不過氣來: *jouhdou ~* (~ in one's job) also see 0335 (2) breathe in 吸入空氣 : *Xgwōngsī deui go behngyàhn góng, "~, yánjyuh, fūhei."* (The X-ray technician told the patient, "~, hold it, and then breathe out.") Adj. exhausting,

tiring 令人疲累的 : *Jouh nīfahn gūng hóu ~.* (This is a ~ job.)

1569
➔yàhnhei 人氣 (lit.) human breath 人的呼吸
(idi.) N (1) liveliness (有)生氣 : *Léuhng gūngpó jyuh gam daaih gāan ngūk, sóyíh kéuihdeih sìhsìh chéng pàhngyáuh làih wáan, béi gāan ngūk yáuh dōdī ~.* (The [married] couple felt quite lonely living in such a big house. Therefore, they always invited friends to come so as to add ~ to their house.) (2) lots of people (moving around) 熱鬧, 多人來往 : *Hái dūngtīn, ~ dō ge deihfōng móuh gam dung.* (Places with ~ would not be so cold in winter.) (3) popularity 知名度 : *Gógo dihnsih ngaihyùhn nīpáai ~ gápsīng.* (That TV artist has become very popular recently.)

1570
➔yāttiuh hei 一條氣 (lit.) one (beam of) air 一條空氣
(idi.) A. PH in one go 一口氣 (沒有停) : *Néih ~ hàahng sahp chàhng làuhtāi, gánghaih sānfú lā.* (You've climbed ten flights of stairs in ~, of course you're exhausted now.) also see 0489

1571 ✓
➔yihthei 熱氣 (lit.) N vapor of heat 熱的氣體 M dī
(idi.) N heating of body (mostly resulting from eating too many things that are hot, fried or deep fried) 身體內的燥熱, 通常由於吃了太多刺激

或煎炸食物而引起的：*Yāt yáuh ~ jauh yiu yám lèuhngchàh.* (When one has too much ~ inside his body, he should drink some [Chinese] herbal tea.) Adj. causing/ having much body heating 引致/ 有體內燥熱：*Néih sihk gam dō ~ yéh, ìngwaaidāk gam ~ lā.* (You've eaten so much hot food. That's why you're ~.)

lèuhng 涼 Adj. cool 清涼

1572

→lèuhng chàh 涼茶 (lit.) cooling tea 令人清涼的茶

(idi.) N Chinese herbal tea 中國人用草藥煎成的茶：*Nīdī ~ hóu lèuhng ge, yámjó wúih ō.* (This kind of ~ is very strong. You'll have to clear your bowels shortly after drinking it.) also see 1157 ATT ©

1573

→sāmlèuhng 心涼 (lit.) heart feels cool 心裏涼快

(idi.) Adj. feel happy about the misfortune of someone one dislikes 對你不喜歡的人的不幸感到高興：*Néih hóu jāng kéuih ge. Kéuih yìhgā gáaudou yiu fan gāai néih jauh ~ lā.* (You hate him so much that you would feel ~ now because he has become homeless/ a street person.)

lèuih 雷 N thunder 雷 M dī

1574

→gin lèuih héung m̀gin yúh lohk 見雷響唔見雨落 (lit.) (one) can hear the thunder, but can't see the rain 聽見打雷,看不見下雨

(idi.) PH all talk, but no action 只說

不做：*Gáamseui ge yíhngon tūnggwojó gam noih, jingfú dōu meih sahthàhng, ~.* (The bill for the reduction of taxation was passed a long time ago, but the government has not put it into implementation as yet. This is just ~.)

1575

→móuh lèuihgūng gam yúhn 冇雷公咁遠 (lit.) a place so far that even the god of thunder cannot get there 在連雷神也沒有的那樣遠的地方

(idi.) PH a place that is very very far away 在很遠很遠的地方：*Kéuih būnjó heui ~, ngóhdeih dím heui taam kéuih a?* (He has moved to ~ from here. How can we go and call on him?)

màhn 紋 N stripes, lines, veins M tìuh

1576

→náumàhn 扭紋 (lit.) twisted grain of a tree/piece of wood 樹木或木塊上扭曲的木紋

(idi.) Adj. (usually said of children) be peevish (小孩)鬧彆扭：ⓐ*Gwāaigwāaidéi, m̀ hóu gam ~ lā.* (Be a good child and don't ~.) ⓑ *náumàhn chàaih* see 1297

muhk 木 N wood 木 M gauh/lūk; faai

1577 ✓

→daumuhk 鬥木 (lit.) VO/ N do carpentry/ carpentry 木工/做木工

(idi.) VO do a time-consuming job 做一件需時很久的工作 : ⓐ*Ngóh ṁhaih hóu sīk jih, yiu ngóh séseun jauh hóuchíh ~ gám.* (I am semi-illiterate. For me, writing a letter is like ~.) ⓑ *~ gám dau yātpīn leuhnmán chēutlàih* (to produce a thesis is like ~)

1578 ✓

➔muhk 木 (lit.) N wood 木 M gauh/ lūk; faai
(idi.) Adj. expressionless, look dull 木無表情 : ⓐ*Kéuih wah jauh wah haih tīnwòhng geuihsīng, daahnhaih jouhhei ge bíuchihng hóu ~.* (It is so said that he is a superstar, yet he is quite ~ when starring in movies.) ⓑ *muhk háu muhk mihn* see 0536

1579

➔muhkduhk 木獨 (lit.) wood alone 獨是木頭
(idi.) Adj. (said of a person) looks dull and is not sociable 性格內向,不喜言笑的人 : *Kéuih go yàhn hóu ~, chēutlàih wánsihk béigaau sihtdái.* (He is quite ~. It won't be easy for him to be successful in earning money.)

1580

➔muhkmuhk duhkduhk 木木獨獨 (lit.) wood alone 獨是木頭
(idi.) PH look dull and stay alone 表情呆滯,離群獨處 : *Jouh māt A-Chán gāmyaht ~ gám a? Haih maih yáuh dī mē'éh sāmsih a? Pihngsìh kéuih ṁhaih gám ge bo.* (Why is Chan ~ today? Is there anything that is bothering him? Normally he is not like that.)

1581

➔yātgauh muhk gám 一嚿木噉 (lit.) like a log 像一塊木頭
(idi.) PH look dumb and be not active enough, a stick 樣貌呆笨又不善交際的人 : *Néih ~, lóuhsai dím wúih jūngyi néih ā?* (You ~. How would our boss like you?)

ngàhn/ngán 銀 N silver 銀子 M léung; gauh; dī

1582 ✓

➔ngán 銀 (lit.) N silver 銀
(idi.) N money 錢 : ⓐ *wé ~* (be a ~ grabber) ⓑ *Jāusān móuh ~ jauh ṁhóu lám máaih gam dō yéh lā.* (You don't have any ~ with you, so should think of buying so many things.) BF coins (of different denominations) (不同幣值的)錢幣 : ⓐ*yātgo ńgh hòuhjí/ yātmān ~* (a fifty-cent/ one-dollar ~) ⓑ*sáan ~* (small ~)

1583

➔sái tùhngngán gaap daaihsēng 使銅銀夾大聲 (lit.) use copper coins (i.e. fake money) but still talk in loud voice 使用銅幣(即偽幣)仍大聲說話
(idi.) PH cheat people but still be fierce with others 欺騙別人還要兇惡對人 : *Néih maaih gá yéh, juhng gam ngok, ~!* (You sell things that are fake, but you are still so fierce. You are like one who ~!) (*In the past, people used silver coins in mainland China.)

257

sā 沙 N sand 泥沙 M lāp; dī

1584

→dihtlohk deih/déi láfāan jah sā 跌落地捌翻漌沙 (lit.) fall on the ground but pretend to pick up a handful of sand 跌在地上但裝作抓一把泥沙

(idi.) PH commit mistake/ do something wrong but still try to cover it up 做錯了事但仍想掩飾: *"Hohksāang m̀mìhngbaahk kéuih gaausyū." "Kéuih wah kéuihdeih juhng meih jaahpgwaan kéuihge gaaufaat wóh." "~!"* ("The students don't understand what he teaches." "He said they just hadn't gotten used to his way of teaching." "~!")

1585

→saimānjái wáan nàihsā 細蚊仔玩泥沙 (lit.) (like) children playing with sand (像)小孩玩泥沙

(idi.) PH not take something seriously 不認真，兒戲/嬉: *Fānyān/ Gitfān haih jūng sān daaih sih, néih gú ~ mè!* (People should regard marriage as the most important thing in life, and don't take it as ~.)

1586

→sūksā 縮沙 (lit.) shrink the sand 縮小的泥沙

(idi.) V change one's mind (and thus fail to keep one's promise)改變主意(以致不能實踐諾言): *Kéuih wah tùhng ngóhdeih yātchái gin lóuhbáan kīng gā yàhngūng ge sih, ngóh hēimohng kéuih m̀wúih ~.* (He said he would join us to go to see our boss and talk with him about pay raise. I hope he won't ~.)

sāp 濕 Adj. wet, humid 濕, 潮濕

1587

→yāmsāp 陰濕 (lit.) dark and humid 陰暗潮濕

(idi.) Adj. (said of a person) cunning and mean 指人陰險狡猾: *Kéuih nīgo yàhn hóu ~ ga. Kéuih m̀wúih daaihsēng laauh néih, daahnhaih jauh wúih béi sāigwá pèih néih cháai.* (He is ~. He never scolds you in a loud voice, but he would set traps for you.)

sehk 石 N pebble, stone 石子 M lāp; rock 石頭 M gauh

1588 ✓

→daaihsehk 大石 (lit.) N big rock 大石頭 M gauh

(idi.) N see 1589

1589 ✓

→sehk 石 (lit.) N pebble, stone, rock 石子, 石頭 M lāp; gauh; faai

(idi.) N (1) anxiety, weight on one's mind 憂慮 M gauh : ⓐ *sām léuihbihn hóuchíh yáuh gauh ~ (jaakjyuh)* gám (as if there is a ~ weighing on one's mind/ very anxious) ⓑ *Kéuih tùhng go jái wándóu mihng haauh jīhauh, sām léuihbihn hóuchíh fongdāi gauh ~ gám.* (After her son was admitted to a prestigious school, she had a feeling of release.) (2) stones inside human body 人體內的結石 : *sahn/ dáam ~* (kidney/ bladder ~)

séui 水 N water 水 M dī

1590

séui 水 see 1444–1471

sīng 星 N star 星星 M lāp

1591✓

➔soubá sīng 掃把星 (lit.) N shooting star that looks like a broom 像掃帚的流星 M go
(idi.) N one who brings bad luck to others 給別人帶來不幸／壞運氣的人 M go：*Kéuih heuidou bīngāan gūngsī jauh bīngāan gūngsī jáplāp, jingyāt ~ làih ga.* (He is ~ because whichever company he worked in, it closed down.) (*Formerly, 'soubá sīng' was a curse hurled at a woman by her husband's family if her husband was bankrupt or died shortly after their marriage.)

taaihūng 太空 N/PW outer space 太空

1592✓

➔taaihūng yàhn 太空人 (lit.) N spaceman, astronaut 太空人 M go/ wái
(idi.) N a man whose wife is abroad 太太在外國的男人 M go：*Kéuih taaitáai tùhng dī jáinéui làuhhái ngoihgwok, kéuih jihgéi jauh fāanlàih Hēunggóng wéngán, jouh ~ dōu móuh baahnfaat ge la.* (His wife and children are living abroad. He came back to Hong Kong to make money. He doesn't like living without his wife, but he has no choice.)

tīn deih 天地 N heaven and earth, sky and land 天跟地

1593

➔chētīn chēdeih 車天車地 (lit.) car in heaven and on earth 車在天上地上

(idi.) PH talk big 吹牛：*"Kéuih wah jihgéi hái Yīnggwok mihng daaihhohk lóyùhn sehksih hohkwái, joi heui Méihgwok mihng daaihhohk ló boksih hohkwái." "Kéuih háidouh ~ jī ma, kèihsaht kéuih lihn daaihhohk dōu meih duhkgwo."* ("He said that after he had received a Master's degree from a famous university in Britain, he then received a doctorate from a famous university in the States." "He just ~. In fact, he has never studied in any universities before.")

1594 ✓

➔deihjan 地震 (lit.) N/ V earthquake/ have an earthquake, quake 地震 M chi/ chèuhng
(idi.) V/N shake-up in large business enterprise in which resignations or sackings of managerial staff take place 大公司高級職員的人事大 變動：*Ngóhdeih gūngsī daaih ~, júng gīngléih daaimàaih léuhnggo jyúyahm jáujó.* (The general manager quit together with two of the department heads, which shook our company.)

1595

➔deihseuhng jāpdóu bóu, mahn tīn mahn deih lóm̀dóu 地上執到寶，問天問地攞唔倒 (lit.) pick up from the ground a treasure which one can't ask heaven or earth for it 在地上拾到寶物，是你問天或地都不會給你的
(idi.) PH I won't give you the thing I found on/ picked up from the ground 我不會把拾到的東西給

你：*"Néih jāpdóu yāt baak mān àh? Nīngchēutlàih chéng ngóhdeih yámchàh ā!" "Mdāk, ~, ~."* ("So you found $100 on the ground. How about [taking it out and] treating us to tea with it?" "No, ~, ~.")

1596
→hāakmàaih(saai) tīndeih 黑埋(晒)天地 (lit.) heaven and earth become all dark 天地都黑了 (idi.) PH the sky is covered with dark clouds (and a storm is coming) (暴風雨來臨前)天上陰雲密佈： *Yihgā ~, nīdouh yauh móuh ngáh jē tàuh, ngóhdeih faaidī jáu lo.* (Now it's ~, and there's no shelter [from the rain] here. We'd better hurry up and go.)

1597
→mohng tīn dágwa 望天打卦 (lit.) look at the sky and cast horoscope 望着天空求卦 (idi.) PH wait boringly and idly for a chance to come 呆候機會來到： *Sihngyaht chóhhái ngūkkéi ~, gám dím wándóu gūng jouh ga!* (You just sit and ~ at home. How can you find a job by so doing?) (* 'Mohng tīn dágwa' can also be used in a HIT as the matching segment of 'Mōlōchāai baaisàhn→ ~', see 1598.)

1598
→Mōlōchāai baaisàhn→tái tīn 摩囉差拜神→睇天 (lit.) When Indians or Pakistanis worship their gods→they look (up) at the sky 印度人或巴基斯坦人拜神的時候→他們仰望天空 (idi.) HIT at the mercy of God/Heaven 聽天由命： *Gīngjai géisí fuhksōu?!*

Jānhaih ~ → ~. (When will the economy revive?! It's ~ → ~.) (*'Mōlōchāai' was Indian or Pakistani policemen. Later, it was used to stand for men from India or Pakistan.)

1599
→tīn sāu néih/ kéuih 天收你／佢 (lit.) Heaven will take you/him back 上天把你/他收回 (idi.) PH God will damn you/ him 上天懲罰你／他： *Kéuih jouhjó gam dō waaih sih, ~!* (He has done so many evil things, ~!)

1600
→tīnseuhng lèuihgūng, deihhah káuhgūng 天上雷公，地下舅公 (lit.) there's the god of thunder in heaven, and on earth one has the brother(s) of his mother 天上有雷公,地下有舅公 (idi.) PH the brother(s) of one's mother has important status in social interactions 母親的兄弟地位重要： *Sēuiyihn néih kauhfú chóhgwo gāam jē, daahnhaih néih dōu yīnggōi jyūnging kéuih bo, ~, ~ ā ma.* (Even though your uncle has been in jail, you should still respect him. ~, ~, you know.)

1601✓
→tīntái 天體 (lit.)N heavenly bodies 天體 M go (idi.) N naked body, nudism 裸體： *Hái ngoihgwok dī yàhn chāamgā ~ yìhng, Hēunggóng jauh móuh la.* (People can join ~ camps in foreign countries. However, there are no such camps in Hong Kong.)

260

1602

➜ tīn yātbun, deih yātbun 天一半，地一半 (lit.) half up in the sky and half down on earth 一半在天,一半在地
(idi.) PH scatter all over (東西)四散 ： *Tokyihsó léuihbihn ge saimānjái, sēuiyihn léuhng-sāam seui gam sai, dōu yiu jihgéi sihkfaahn, daahnhaih jauh sihkdou ~ gám lō.* (Children at the daycare center have to eat by themselves even though they're just two or three years old. But when they eat, the rice/ food gets ~.)

1603

➜yāt tīn dōu gwōngsaai 一天都光晒 (lit.) the whole sky is brightening up 整個天空都亮起來
(idi.) PH (1) (hard times have gone and) happy sunny days are coming 苦盡甘來 ： *Ngóhdeih ge bouhmùhn jyúgún hóu sēui ge, kéuih yìhgā jáu la, jānhaih ~.* (Our department head is very bad to us. Now he quits. It's really ~!) (2) the truth is out (and the person suffering a wrong is vindicated)真相大白, 沉冤得雪 ： *Gógo yìhfáan wah, "Néihdeih jūkdóu jānjing ge hūngsáu, jānhaih ~ lo!"* (That suspect said, "You found the real murderer. Now it's ~ [and I'll be freed]!")

tit 鐵 N iron 鐵 M gauh; dī

1604

➜jātit 揸鐵 (lit.) hold iron 拿著鐵
(idi.) VO be a policeman 做警察 ： *Ngóhdeih dím gau kéuih ngok a,*

kéuih haih ~ ge. (How can we be fiercer than he? He is ~.) (*'Tit' symbolizes the gun a policeman bears.)

1605

➜laahn tùhng laahn tit 爛銅爛鐵 (lit.) broken bronze/ copper and broken iron 破爛的銅和鐵
(idi.) PH scrap metal (i.e. copper and iron) 廢銅及廢鐵 ： *Nīgo gauh bīu, ngóhdeih dong ~, kéuih jauh donghaih bóu, yānwaih haih kéuih a-yèh làuhdāi béi kéuih ge.* (We think this old watch is nothing but ~. However, he treasures it very much because it was left to him by his grandfather.)

1606

➜mē/tòhtit 揹/駝鐵 (lit.) carry iron on one's back 背着鐵
(idi.) VO see 1604

1607

➜tityàhn 鐵人 (lit.) iron man 鐵做的人
(idi.) N very strong man who can endure hard work 身體強壯又吃得苦的人 M go ： *Yahttáu jouhyéh, yehmáahn duhksyū, fongga yauh heui jouh gīmjīk, néih gú néih haih ~ mè/ tit dá ge mè!* (You work in the daytime and study at night. Even on holidays, you do part-time jobs. Do you think you are an ~ / made of iron?)

wàhn 雲 N cloud 雲 M gauh; dī

1608

➜yāt gauh wàhn gám 一嚿雲 gám

噉 (lit.) like a cloud 好像一片雲
(idi.) PH be muddled and lost 感到
混 沌 茫 然 ： ⓐ *Séuhngtòhng
gwajyuh yàuhfauh, sīnsāang
góngsyū kéuih jauh ~.* (He is always
day-dreaming in class. He is ~ and
does not understand what the
teacher is saying.) ⓑ *Kéuih
gáaisīkjó hóu dō chi, ngóh juhnhaih
hóuchíh ~.* (He had explained it to
me many times, but still I was ~.)

yuhtgwōng 月光 **N moon** 月亮
M go; moonlight 月光 **M dī**

1609
→nìhn sā'ah máahn yáuh
yuhtgwōng 年 卅 晚 有 月 光
(lit.) (unless) there is moonlight on
Chinese New Year's Eve (除非)除夕
晚上有月光
(idi.) PH (something that is)
impossible 事 情 沒 可 能 發 生 ：
*Kéuih wúih gaaidóu? Chèuihfēi ~
lā!* ([You mean] He will kick the habit
of gambling? No, [unless] ~.)
(*According to the Chinese calendar,
one will never see any moonlight at
the end or the beginning of a month or
a year.)

1610
→saai yuhtgwōng 曬 月 光
(lit.) bathe in moonlight 在月光下
流連
(idi.) VO lovers' walk in the
moonlight 情 侶 晚 上 同 遊 ：
*A-Chán tùhng néuih pàhngyáuh
hàahngdāk hóu maht bo, kéuihdeih
máahnmáahn ~.* (Chan and his
girlfriend are going steady. Every-
night, they go out ~.)

8. Numbers

baat 八 NU eight 八

1611 ✓

→baat 八 (lit.) NU eight 八

(idi.) Adj. nosy, curious to know about others' affairs 愛理別人閒事 : ⓐ*Kéuih hóu ~ ga, mē'éh dōu séung jī.* (She is very ~. She wants to know everything [about others].) ⓑ*Jouh nàahmyán m̀hóu gam ~ lā.* (As a man, one shouldn't be so ~.) V be a gossip hound, socialize around in order to kill time or to get special information 跟人閒聊以打發時間或打探消息 : *Ngóh dākhàahn mòuh sih jauh seiwàih heui tùhng yàhn ~ háh.* (When I have free time, I would like to ~ everywhere.) (* 'Baat' is the short form of 'baatgwa', see 1130.)

1612

→baatbaat gáugáu 八八九九

(lit.) double eight and double nine 兩個八跟兩個九

(idi.) PH eighty or ninety per cent, almost all 八九成, 差不多全部 : *Ngóhdī gūngfo joukdāk ~ la.* (My homework is ~ done.)

1613 ✓

→baatjih 八字 (lit.) N the Chinese character for 'eight' 中文的 '八'字

(idi.) N the eight symbols of celestial stems and earth branches of the year, the month, the day, and the hour when one was born 人出生時的年、月、日及時辰的天干地支,一共八個字

M dī : *Dímgáai yàhndeih jouh yáuhchínlóu/ Dímgáai yàhndeih tiuh mehng gam hóu, kéuih dī ~ sāangdāk hóu lō.* (Why are some people so rich/ Why is life so kind to others? It's because they were born at an auspicious time/to succeed.)

1614

→baatjih sōu 八字鬚 (lit.) N moustache like the Chinese character for 'eight' 像'八'字的鬍子 : *làuh ~* (to grow/ have ~)

chāt 七 NU seven 七

1615

→chātchāt baatbaat 七七八八

(lit.) double seven and double eight 兩個七跟兩個八

(idi.) PH seventy or eighty per cent, most 七八成, 大部分 : *Dī hàhngléih jāpdāk ~ la.* (~ of the luggage is packed.)

1616

→chāt gwok gam lyuhn 七國咁亂(lit.) as chaotic as the seven states (during the Epoch of Warring States [in Chinese history], 475–221 B.C.) 像中國戰國時代有七國那麼亂

(idi.) PH messy, chaotic 混亂, 凌亂 : *Ngóhdeih hohkhaauh sahpnìhn yātchi daaih jōngsāu, dī yéh yiu būnlàih būnheui, gáaudou ~.* (Our school is having a big renovation once every ten years. Everything has to be moved here or, there, which makes our school a very ~ place.)

1617

➔chāt lóuh baatsahp 七老八十 (lit.) seven old and eighty 七老及八十

(idi.) PH in one's seventies or eighties, seventy or eighty years old (* Actually it is rarely used to tell the age of people.) 七八十歲 ： *(Ngóh) Meih dou ~, yìhgīng jāusān behngtung.* (Although I am not yet ~, I already have health problems [all over my body].)

1618

➔jouhchāt 做七 (lit.) make/ do seven 做七

(idi.) VO have Buddhist or Taoist ritual services for the dead seven days/ every seven days after his death 人死後第/每七天為他做法事 ： *tùhng kéuih ~* (~ for him/her) (*Nowadays, ritual services are held only on the seventh day and the forty-ninth day after one's death.) also see 1619 and 1620

1619

➔méih chāt 尾七 (lit.) the last seven 最後的七

(idi.) N the forty-ninth day after one's death 人死後第四十九天 ： *Gāmyaht haih kéuih ~, ngóhdeih yiu wán yàhn bōng kéuih dá jāai.* (Today is his/her ~. We are supposed to hold Buddhist or Taoist ritual services for him/her.) (*see 1618)

1620

➔tàuhchāt 頭七 (lit.) the first seven 第一個七

(idi.) N the seventh day after one's death 人死後第七日 ： *Gāmyaht haih kéuih ~, ngóhdeih yiu baaiháh kéuih.* (Today is his/her ~. We are supposed to pay tribute and burn paper offerings to him/her.) (*see 1618)

gáu 九 **NU nine** 九

1621 ✓

➔daihgáu 第九 (lit.) N the ninth 第九

(idi.) PH low standard, sloppy 差勁 ： *Kéuih gaausyū jauh lēk jē, jouh sāangyi jauh ~ lo.* (He can teach very well, but is poor ~ in doing business.)

1622

➔ gáu gáu gáu 九九九 (lit.) nine nine nine 九九九

(idi.) PH emergency telephone number in Hong Kong 香港的求救電話號碼 ： *Yáuh mē'éh sih jauh dá ~ (bouging) lā.* (You can dial ~ in case of an emergency [and report your case to the police].)

1623

➔gáu ṁdaap baat 九唔搭/答八 (lit.) nine does not match/ answer eight 九不對八

(idi.) PH no connection/ relevance between what is said by two persons 答非所問 ： *Tùhng kéuih góngyéh, ~ gám.* (When talking with him, he is like ~.) also see 0352

1624

➔gáusìhng gáu 九成九 (lit.) ninety-nine per cent 百分之九十九

(idi.) A most likely 很可能 ： *Kéuih*

pihngsìh hóuchíh máhlāu gám tiulàih tiuheui, daahnhaih gāmyaht jauh chóhháidouh m̀yūk, ~ haih yáuh behng la. (Normally he is [very naughty] like a monkey jumping here and there. But today he just sits there and is quiet. ~ he is sick.) PH almost all 差不多全部：*"Gódī yéh jouhsìhng dím a?" "~ OK ge la."* ("How is your work going?" "It's ~ done.")

luhk 六 NU six 六

1625✓

→luhk gwok daaih fūngseung 六 國 大 封 相 (lit.) PH a Cantonese opera about a man born in the Warring States period (475–221B.C.) who rose from nothing to become a prime minister of six kingdoms 粵劇'六國大封相'：戰國時代一個平民做到六國的丞相

(idi.) PH killing of people 殺不少人：*Hóuchói gíngchaat hóu faai làihdou, yùhgwó m̀haih, gó gā yàhn jauh wúih séuhngyín ~ ge la.* (Luckily, the police came soon. Otherwise, people would have killed each other in that family.)

1626

→luhk luhk mòuh kùhng 六六無窮 (lit.) double six is endless 兩個六是無窮盡的

(idi.) PH six is a never-ending number 六六無窮：*Kéuih ge chē pàaih haih luhk-luhk-luhk, yānwaih ~ wóh.* (The number on his car plate is 666, because he said ~.) also see 1638

maahn 萬 NU ten thousand 萬

1627

→maahn jūng mòuh yāt 萬中無一 (lit.) there's none out of ten thousand 一萬個之中也沒有一個

(idi.) PH very rare 非常罕有：*Gam hóu ge yàhn, hái yihgā làih góng, jānhaih ~.* (Nowadays, such a good person is ~.)

1628

→maahnyāt 萬一 (lit.) one out of ten thousand 萬分之一

(idi.) A in case (something undesirable happens) 如果(有甚麼不好的事情發生)：ⓐ*Daai bá jē lā, ~ lohkyúh, dōu m̀wúih dahpsāp ā ma.* (Bring an umbrella. You won't get wet ~ it rains.) ⓑ *M̀hóu máaihsaai yātjek ngoihbaih, yiu fānsáan tàuhjī, ~ kèihjūng yātjek dit dōu m̀wúih siht gam dō chín ā ma.* (Don't invest your money in just one foreign currency. You should invest in different ones. You won't lose that much money ~ one of them suddenly falls.)

1629

→m̀pa yātmaahn, ji pa maahnyāt 唔怕一萬，至怕萬一 (lit.) one should not be afraid of ten thousand, but one out of ten thousand 不怕一萬,最怕萬一

(idi.) PH one should not be afraid of commonality, but contingency 最怕／小心有意外：*Nīpáai daaihhah jōngsāu, ngoihbihn daapjó jūkpàahng, néih yehmáahn yiu sāanhóu chēung sīnji fan, ~, ~ ā ma.* (Our apartment block is being renovated, and there's scaffolding all outside. Make sure that you have closed the windows before going to bed. You know, ~.)

sāam 三 NU three 三

1630

➔ jouh yauh sā'ah luhk, m̀jouh yauh sā'ah luhk 做又卅六，唔做又卅六 (lit.) you can get thirty-six (dollars) if you work, and you can still get thirty-six (dollars) even if you don't work 做可以拿到三十六(塊錢),不做也可以拿到三十六(塊錢) (idi.) PH there's no difference in pay between a hardworking employee and a lazy one 勤力或懶惰的僱員都拿到同樣的薪水 ： ~, ~, ngóhdeih sáimāt gam bokmehng wo. (~, ~. So, why do we have to work so hard?) (*At one time in mainland China, people all received a wage of thirty-six dollars.)

1631

➔ m̀léih sāam chāt yihsahp/ yah yāt 唔理三七二十／廿一 (lit.) not care about that 3 multiplied by 7 makes 21 不管三七二十一 (idi.) A. PH regardless of/ damn the consequences 甚麼後果也不管 ： Sēuiyihn yáuh yàhn hyun ngóh yiu lám chīngchó sīnji jouh, daahnhaih ngóh ~, jouhjó sīnji syun. (Although I had been advised to think carefully before doing that, I did it ~.)

1632

➔m̀sāam m̀sei 唔三唔四 (lit.) neither three nor four 不三不四 (idi.) Adj. PH (said of people) not of good background 不正經,背景不好的人 ： Dī ~ ge yàhn dōsou haih

sèhtàuh syú ngáahn ge. (People who are ~ are mostly mean-looking: with a head like that of a snake, and eyes like those of a rat.) PH odd, not appropriate 奇奇怪怪的, 不合適 ： ⓐ Nghdím ji luhkdím hōi chàhwúi, dī sihgaan ~ gám. (5p.m. to 6p.m. is not an appropriate time for a tea party.) ⓑ Néih sihkmàaihsaai dī ~ ge yéh, gánghaih chèuhng waih m̀tóh lā. (You've eaten something ~. That's why you feel sick in your stomach.) ⓒ Néih m̀hóu heui dī ~ ge deihfōng a. (Don't go to those ~ places.)

1633

➔sāam chèuhng léuhng dyún 三長兩短 (lit.) three long ones and two short ones 三個長的, 兩個短的 (idi.) PH misfortune that results in death 不幸而死亡 ： Ngóhdeih yātgā kaau kéuih wánchín sāngwuht, yùhgwó kéuih yáuh mātyéh ~, ngóhdeih jauh m̀jī dím syun. (He is the breadwinner of our family. If he dies, we don't know what to do then.) (* 'Sāam chèuhng léuhng dyún' is the indirect way of saying 'coffin', which is made of three long pieces of wood and two shorter ones when not yet being covered with the lid.) also see 0981

1634

➔sāam jīm baat gok 三尖八角 (lit.) three sharp ones and eight angles 三個尖的和八個角 (idi.) PH triangle or odd shape 三角形或不規則的形狀 ： Yáuhdī yàhn m̀jūngyi jyunsehkyìhng ge ngūk. Kéuihdeih gokdāk haih ~. (Some people don't like diamond-shaped house. They think it's ~.) (*According to Chinese Fung Shui, a house which

266

is square, rectangular or round in shape is much better than one in other shapes.)

1635

→saamkāp 三級 (lit.) N (said of indecent or obscene media) grade III (指不雅及淫褻的傳媒) 三級 : ~ *pín/ hei* (~ movie)

1636

→saamluhk 三六 (lit.) three and six 三六

(idi.) N dog meat 狗肉 : *sihk* ~ (eat ~) (*see 1637)

1637

→saamluhk gwán yāt gwán, sàhnsīn dōu kéihm̀wán 三六滾一滾，神仙都企唔穩 (lit.) PH when dog meat is cooking, even a fairy (would be intoxicated by the aroma and so) cannot stand (firmly) 烹煮狗肉的時候，那香味連神仙嗅到都會站不穩 : " ~, ~. *Néih dōu làih siháh lā!*" *"Hái Hēunggóng sihk gáuyuhk haih faahnfaat ga."* ("~, ~. Come and try some!" "It's illegal to eat dog meat in Hong Kong.") (*A pun is made on the sum of three and six, i.e. nine→gáu, which has the same sound as 'dog' in Cantonese.)

1638

→saam saam bāt jeuhn, luhk luhk mòuh kùhng 三三不盡，六六無窮 (lit.) double three is endless, and so is double six 兩個三及兩個六都是無窮盡的

(idi.) PH three and six are never ending numbers (when going after a decimal point) 三三不盡,六六無窮:

Kéuih hóu jūngyi sāam tùhng luhk nī léuhng go lāmbá, yānwaih ~, ~. (He likes these two numbers, 3 and 6, because ~, ~.)

sahp 十 NU ten 十

1639

→daaihhaam sahp 大喊十 (lit.) the tenth brother who cries very loudly 第十個哭得很大聲的兄弟 (idi.) N usually said of a child who cries very loudly 哭得很大聲的小孩 M go : *Sāusēng lā, ~!* (Stop crying so loudly, hey you ~!) (* 'Daaihhaam Sahp' is a name of a character in a movie in the 1960s. His tears flow like a stream.)

1640

→sahpgo jeuhkjó Nu go 十個著咗 NU 個 (lit.) PH NU out of ten 十個之中佔了若干個 : *Hēunggóng ge hohksāang, sahpgo jeuhkjó chātgo daai ngáahngeng.* (In Hong Kong, seven students out of ten wear glasses.)

1641

→sahp jī baat gáu 十之八九 (lit.) eight or nine out of ten 十之八九

(idi.) PH (1) almost all 差不多全部 : *Hohksāang ~ dōu m̀jūngyi háausi.* (~ students don't like taking exams.) (2) very probably, ten to one 很可能 : *Kéuih gam chìh, ~ haih sākchē lā.* (He is so late. ~ , there's a traffic jam.)

1642

→sahpjūk 十足 (lit.) ten and full 十分充足

(idi.) A exactly (look like) 完全(相似)：*Kéuih ~ (chíh) kéuih màhmā gám yéung.* (He looks ~ like his mother.) N all 全部：ⓐ *Yàhndeih góng ge yéh, kéuih seundou ~.* (He believes ~ what other people say.) ⓑ *Kéuih chíh (dou) ~ kéuih màhmā.* (He looks ~ as his mother.)

1643
→sahpjūk sahp 十足十 (lit.) one hundred per cent and ten 十分再加一分
(idi.) PH the more emphatic way of saying than 1642

1644
→sahpńgh sahpluhk 十五十六 (lit.) fifteen and sixteen 十五和十六
(idi.) PH hesitate to make a decision 遲疑不決：*Kéuih giu ngóh máaih gójek máh, ngóhge sām ~, yānwaih boují ge máhgīng wah gójek máh ge johngtaai màhmádéi, dímjí béi kéuih páauchēut.* (He had told me to bet on that horse, but I ~, because the racing guide in the newspaper said that it was not in good shape. But it won.)

1645
→sahp yáuh gáu 十有九 (lit.) ten has nine 十個有九個
(idi.) PH nine out of ten 十個之中有九個：see 1641

sei 四 NU four 四
1646
→A-sei 阿四(lit.) the fourth one 阿四
(idi.) N maid servant 女佣人 M

go：*Yìhgā jouh baahngūngsāt johléih hóuchíh jouh ~ gám, yauh yiu jāpyéh, yauh yiu bōuséui.* (Now an office assistant is like a ~. She has to tidy up things and boil water.)

1647 ✓
→seimaahn 四萬 (lit.) NU forty thousand 四萬
(idi.) N very sweet smiling face/ huge grin (like the Chinese character for 'four' on a mahjong tile) 很燦爛的笑容(像麻將牌'四萬'上的'四'字)：~ *gám ge mihnháu/ siuyùhng* (a ~ grin)

1648
→sijeng 四正 (lit.) square and right 四方及端正
(idi.) Adj. good for being square in shape 因爲是四方形，所以好：*Gāan ngūk hóu ~, hóu yih báaichit.* (The house is ~, and it will be easy for you to decorate it.)

1649
→sisi jengjeng 四四正正 (lit.) square and right 四方及端正
(idi.) PH good for being square in shape 因爲是四方形，所以好：*Gāan fóng ~, go tēng jauh sāam jīm baat gok.* (The room is ~, but the sitting room is bad for its odd shape.)

sou 數 N number; amount, quantity 數字; 數目, 數量 M go；sum 計算題 M tiuh
1650
→bóusou 補數 (lit.) remedy numbers 補救數字

(idi.) VO do it as a sort of remedy 補情，補回 ： *Kàhmyaht néih sāangyaht, ngóh móuh tùhng néih hingjūk, gāmyaht ~ fāan ~.* (Yesterday was your birthday, but I didn't celebrate it with you. Let me ~ today.)

1651
➔dájó syū sou 打咗輸數(lit.) count the numbers lost 計算輸去的數字
(idi.) PH be prepared for the loss/failure of 有心理準備是會輸/失敗的 ： *Nī dāan gūnsī, ngóh ~ ge la.* (I'm ~ of the case [in court].)

1652
➔dūksou 篤數 (lit.) prick the numbers 刺出數字
(idi.) VO inflate the numbers 誇大數字 ： *sānchíng jījoh ge sìhhauh ~* (~ in the budget when applying for subsidy [from the government]) also see 1334

1653
➔góngsou 講數 (lit.) talk about numbers 談數目
(idi.) VO negotiate (about a difficult situation or problem) 談判(難解決的事) ： *Gūngyàhn tùhng lóuhbáan ~, yùhgwó ṁgāsān yāt sìhng, kéuihdeih jauh gaijuhk bahgūng.* (The workers ~ with their employer. If he refused to give them 10 per cent pay raise, their strike would go on.)

1654
➔hauhsou 後數 (lit.) back number 後面的數字
(idi.) PH someone will pay for it/me

later 稍後有人(替我)付錢 ： *Yātgo síubā sìhnghaak lohkchē gójahnsí deui sīgēi wah, "Ṁgōi, ~!"* (A minibus passenger said to the driver when he got off, "~, please!")

1655
➔jáausou 找數 (lit.) look for a number 找尋數字
(idi.) VO pay a bill (usually for a meal) 結帳 (通常是一頓飯) ： ⓐ *Chàhlàuh fógei deui yātgo chàhhaak wah, "Néih juhng meih ~ bo! Séung sihk bawòhng yéh àh?"* (The restaurant waiter said to a customer, "You haven't ~ yet. You want to have a free meal [without ~] ?) ⓑ *Néih yiu ~ jó dī kāat ~.* (You have to pay the balance of your credit card.) also see 1655(2) ⓐ

1656
➔jáusou 走數 (lit.) gone the number 數字跑了
(idi.) VO run away from one's debts 不付債 (跑了) ： *Dī daaihyíhlūng ṁbéi dī jaaijái ~.* (The loan sharks won't let their debtors ~.)

1657
➔jeuhksou 着數 (lit.) 對的數
(idi.) N benefits, advantages 好處 M dī ： ⓐ *Léuhng gāan daaih gūngsī hahpbing, dī jīkyùhn yáuh mē ~ sīn?* (What ~ will the employees get from the merger of the two big companies?) ⓑ *wán yàhn ~* (take ~ of others) (* For ⓑ , some people will say 'wán yàhn bahn'.)

1658
➔màaihsou 埋數 (lit.) close number 結束數目

269

(idi.) VO settle accounts 結算 : *Gāmyaht poutáu ~ ge sihauh, faatgok dī sou m̀ngāam.* (When we ~ in our shop today, we found there was something wrong with the numbers of the accounts.)

1659
→ méihsou 尾數 (lit.) tail/ ending number 最後的數字
(idi.) N balance, amount (of money) still owed after some payment has been made 餘下尚欠的(金錢)數目 M dī; bāt : *Gógāan gūngsī jāpjó lāp, ngóhdeih sāum̀dóu dī ~.* (That company has closed down, and we can't get the ~ from them.)

1660
→ sāusou 收數 (lit.) collect numbers 收集數字
(idi.) VO collect debts 討債 : ⓐ ~ *lóu* (debt collector) ⓑ ~ *gūngsī* (debt collecting company)

1661✓
→ sou 數 (lit.) N number; amount, quantity; 數字; 數目, 數量 M go; sum 計算題 M tìuh
(idi.) N (1) money 錢 M dī : ⓐ *gūngsī* ~ (~ of the company) ⓑ *gūng* ~ (running expenses/fund) (2) debt 債 M dī : ⓐ *jāang ngàhnhòhng ge kāat* ~ (money owed to a bank credit card) ⓑ *daaihyìhhlūng* ~ (money owed to a loan shark) ⓒ *chīngjó dī* ~ (have cleared the debts)

1662
→ syunsou 算數 (lit.) calculate numbers 計算數字

(idi.) PH (1) forget it 算了吧 : ~ *lā!* (~!) (* Some people would just say 'syun lā'.) (2) count in 計算在內 : *Nīchi m̀~, joi làih yāt chi.* (We won't count it this time. Do it again.)

1663
→ táisou 睇數 (lit.) look at numbers 看數字
(idi.) VO pay a bill (usually in a food shop) 結帳(通常在食店中) : *Ngóhdeih jáu sīn, m̀gōi néih ~ ā.* (We'll go first, and please ~!)

1664
→ yahpsou 入數 (lit.) enter number 放進數字
(idi.) VO (1) deposit money 存錢 : ~ *jí* (deposit slip [of a bank]) (2) pay (money) 付錢 : ~ *ngóh* ~ (be paid by me/ charge it to my account) (3) put the blame on 不好的事算在某人頭上 : *Seuhngchi haih ngóh jouhcho, daahnhaih nīchi haih kéuih jouhcho, yauh ~ màaih ngóh ~.* (Last time I made a mistake. This time he did it wrong, but you ~ as mine.)

1665
→ yáuh fānsou 有分數 (lit.) have (numbers for) grades 有評分
(idi.) PH can manage it 心中有數 : *Kéuih haih yàhnsih gīngléih, dímyéung fānpui gūngjok, kéuih ~ ge la.* (He is the personnel manager. He certainly knows how to assign duties.)

yāt 一 NU one 一

1666

→A-yāt 阿一 (lit.) the number one person 阿一
(idi.) N leader/ boss/ the person in charge 領導人/上司/負責人 : *gíngdéui* ~ (the Police Commissioner)

1667✓

→daihyāt 第一 (lit.) N the first 第一
(idi.) N the leading one, the number one, the best 最好/出色 : *Ngóh yihngjó daihyīh, jauh móuh yàhn gám yihng ~ ge la.* (No one would boast that he can outdo me.)

1668

→fāangwáilóu tái bóng→ dou sóu daih yāt 番鬼佬睇榜→倒數第一 (lit.) a foreigner reads the results of an exam→ he takes the last for the first 洋人看放榜,把最末的當第一
(idi.) HIT an indirect way of saying that one is the last in an exam or a race 考試或比賽之中最落後的一個的間接說法 : *"Kéuih nīchi háausi háau daih géi a?" "~ → ~."* ("What are/is his results/ position in this exam?" "~ → ~.") (* Westerners read from left to right, but in the old days Chinese read from right to left.)

1669

→yāt bāt lèih yih, yih bāt lèih sāam 一不離二 , 二不離三 (lit.) one won't go away from two, and two won't go away from three 一不會離開二, 二不會離開三
(idi.) PH similar things (will) occur one after another 同類事件接二連三的發生 : *"Tàuhsīn dálaahn go būi, yìhgā yauh ditlaahn go wún." "Néih juhng wúih jínglaahn yātyeuhng yéh tīm, ~, ~ ā ma."* ("I just broke a cup, and now I dropped a bowl and broke it." "You'll break one more thing later. You know, ~.")

1670 ✓

→yātchīn lihng yāt 一千零一 (lit.) one thousand and one 一千零一
(idi.) PH the only one 唯一的 : *Sìhng hahp jyūgūlīk, juhng jihngfāan ~ lāp jē.* (There is only one piece of chocolate left in the whole box.)

1671

→yāt jauh yāt, yih jauh yih 一就一 , 二就二 (lit.) one is one, and two is two 一是一,二是二
(idi.) PH said of a person who does not bother to say too much about things and does not like to drag on 做事斬釘截鐵, 不願拖拖拉拉的人 : *Kéuih nīgo yàhn, ~, ~, m̀wúih tùhng néih dō góng.* (He is one who ~, ~. He won't waste your time talking about irrelevant things.)

1672

→yāt ńgh yāt sahp 一五一十 (lit.) one five and one ten 一個五一個十
(idi.) A. PH (tell) in detail 詳詳細細的(講) : *Kéuih jēung gógihn sih ~ góngsaaibéi ngóh jī.* (He told me about that in a ~ way.)

271

yih 二 NU two 二

1673
→A-yí 阿二 (lit.) the number two (wife) 第二名(太太)
(idi.) N mistress 情婦 M go : *heui ~ douh yám tōng* (go to the house of one's ~ to have the soup she prepares)

1674
→sauh yàhn yihfān sei, jouhdou yāttìuh hei 受人二分四，做到一條氣 (lit.) if you receive twenty-four (dollars) from others, you have to work for them until you are exhausted 收了人家廿四(塊錢), 你便要做到筋疲力盡
(idi.) PH an employee has to work very hard before he can earn little money 僱員做到筋疲力盡才賺到一點點錢 : *Hàaih, ~, ~, chèuihfēi haih jihgéi jouh lóuhbáan ge jē.* (Alas, ~, ~, unless he himself becomes an employer.)

1675
→yih dá lúk 二打六 (lit.) two beats six 二打六
(idi.) PH (usually said of operatic troupe musicians) low standard (通常指戲班裏的樂師)水平低 M go : *Kéuih jí bātgwo haih ~ jī ma, bīn jihk gam dō yàhngūng a?* (He is just a ~ musician. He does not deserve so much pay.)

1676
→yihsáu 二手 (lit.) second hand 二手
(idi.) ATT used/ old 用過的／舊

的 : ⓐ *~ chē/ láu/ gongkàhm* (~ car/ flat/ piano) ⓑ *Hóudō yàhn jūngyi máaih mihngsīng ge ~ sāam.* (Many people like to buy the ~ clothes of movie stars.) ⓒ *~ yīn* (~ / passive smoking)

1677
→yih yāt tīm jok ngh 二一添作五 (lit.) two and one make five 二跟一變做五
(idi.) PH to divide something equally 平均的分 : *Nīdī chín, ngóhdeih ~, fānjó kéuih lā.* (We'll get the money shared equally.) (* 'Yih yāt tīm jok ngh' can be put in this way: $1 \div 2 = 0.5$, i.e. one half.)

9. People

A-Tó 阿佗 N humpback, hunchback 佝僂的人 **M go**

1678

➔A-Tó hàahnglouh→jūngjūng déi 阿駝行路→[鐘鐘]中中哋 (lit.) a hunchback walks→ he dodders/ (with his back) bending down 駝子走路→龍鐘 (idi.) HIT medium, so-so, not bad 中等, 馬馬虎虎 : *"Kéuih ge sihngjīk dím a?" "~ → ~ lā."* ("How are his results [in the exam]?" "~ → ~!") (*A pun is made on 鐘 [the walking posture of a hunchback] and 中 [medium]. Both of them are pronounced 'jūng'.)

1679 ✓

➔A-Tó dōu béi kéuih/néih gīk jihk 阿駝都俾佢/你激直 (lit.) even the back of a humpbacked person would become straight on being outraged or angered by him/you 駝子的背都被他/你氣直了 (idi.) PH an exaggeration so said when someone has done something stupid to make you mad 一種誇張的說法, 別人做了令你啼笑皆非的事 : *"Ngóhge gūngyàhn giu kéuih máaih ngàuhyuhk, kéuih máaihjó jyūyuhk, giu kéuih seidím heui jip go jái fonghohk, kéuih nghdím heui, jānhaih ~." "Gám, néih cháaujó kéuih lō."* ("I told my domestic helper to buy beef, but she bought pork. I told her to bring my son home from school at four, but she went at five. I really got mad at her." "You can fire her.")

boksih 博士 N a person having a doctorate 有博士學位的人 **M go/wái**

1680

➔chàh boksih 茶博士 (lit.) a man having a doctorate of tea 茶博士 (idi.) N teahouse waiter (who is expert in pouring tea) 茶樓裏負責倒茶的伙計 M go : *"~ luhkchān go sailóugō! Mhaih ah máh!" "Go sailóugō jáulàih jáuheui ā ma."* ("The ~ hurt the child [when pouring hot tea]! Oh no!" "It's because the child ran around in the teahouse.")

Chòuh Chōu 曹操 N Chou Chou, a man of the Three Kingdoms Period, is regarded as a bad man in Chinese history 曹操, 三國時期的人, 在中國歷史上被視爲奸人

1681

➔Chòuh Chōu dōu yáuh jīsām yáuh, Gwāangūng dōu yáuh deuitàuh yàhn 曹操都有知心友, 關公都有對頭人 (lit.) even Chou Chou, a bad man, has very good friends and Kuan Yu, the Martial God of China, has enemies 連曹操也有知心, 關羽也有敵人 (idi.) PH even a bad person has friends and a good person has enemies 壞人也有好朋友,好人也有敵人：*"Kéuih gam sēui, bīngo wúih tùhng kéuih jouh pàhngyáuh ā."* *"Yáuh dōu ṁdihng ga, ~, ~ ā ma."* ("He is so bad, I wonder who will be friends with him." "He may have friends. You know the saying, ~, ~, don't you?")

1682

→yātgóng Chòuh Chōu, Chòuh Chōu jauh dou 一講曹操,曹操就到 (lit.) Chou Chou arrives as soon as you talk about him 一說曹操,曹操就到

(idi.) PH speak of the devil, the person arrives just when you mention his name 一說起某人,某人就來到：*Ngóhdeih ṁsái dáng la. ~, ~!* (We don't have to wait. ~, ~!)

dóng 黨 N political party 政黨 M go

1683✓

→dóng 黨 (lit.) N political party 黨 M go

(idi.) BF robbers 賊匪：ⓐ *bōktàuh* ~ (head-bashing ~) ⓑ *paak boktàuh* ~ (shoulder-patting ~ who pretend to be your friend and pat your shoulder. They then threaten you to give them money.) ⓒ *séi~* (buddy, very good friend) also see 1402

fuhmóuh 父母 N parents M dī

1684

→joih gā kaau fuhmóuh, chēut ngoih kaau pàhngyáuh 在家靠父母,出外靠朋友 (lit.) PH when at home, you have your parents to rely on/ take care of

you, when going out into society, you need to rely on your friends：*Sīk dōdī pàhngyáuh gánghaih hóu lā, hōigóng yáuh wah ~, ~ ā ma. Bātgwo yiu síusām sīk pàhngyáuh jē.* (It is certainly good to have more friends. As the saying goes, ~, ~. However, you need to be careful in choosing your friends.) also see 1327

gājē 家姐 N elder sister 姊姊 M go

1685 ✓

→daaih gājē 大家姐 (lit.) N one's eldest sister 家中大姐 M go

(idi.) N woman gang leader 黑幫女首領：*Gógo néuih yihfáan haih yātgo hāak séhwúi ge ~.* (That woman suspect is a ~.)

gō 哥哥 BF/N elder brother 哥哥 M go

1686

→daaihgō daaih 大哥大 (lit.) big brother the great 比大哥更大

(idi.) N (1) mobile phone 手提電話 M go：*Chōchō chēut ge ~ haih hóu daaih ge.* (The first ~ were very big.) (2) gang leader 幫會首領 M go：*Hóudō yàhn dōu jī kéuih haih ~.* (Many people know he is a ~.) also see 0279

1687

→yātgō 一哥 (lit.) the number one elder brother 排行第一的哥哥

(idi.) N the leading one, head (of a department) 處於領導地位的人／部門首長：ⓐ*Gíngdéui ~ jauh haih Gíngmouhchyúh Jéung lō.* (The ~ of the police force is the Police

Commissioner.) ⓑ *Gūngmouhyùhn ~, jauh haih Jìngmouhsī Sījéung, dōu m̀gáamsān, dím hóyíh yiu gūngmouhyùhn gáamsān nē?* (The ~ of the civil servants in Hong Kong, i.e. the Secretary for Domestic Affairs, did not cut her/ his salary. How can s/he impose a paycut on civil servants?)

gūn 官 N official 官 M go

1688

→jouhgwaan hātyìh/ yī láahn jouh gūn 做慣乞兒懶做官
(lit.) accustomed to being a beggar and so unwilling to be an official 做慣乞兒就不願做官
(idi.) PH get used to living leisurely 安於悠閒的生活：*Ngóh yihgā ~, néih béi go gīngléih ngóh jouh ngóh dōu m̀yuhn jouh a.* (I ~ now. I would not take it even if you offer me the post of a manager.)

1689

→meih gin gūn sīn dá sāamsahp daaih báan 未見官先打三十大板 (lit.) one is given thirty lashes first before he can see the official 還未見官便要先給打三十下
(idi.) PH suffer loss first before one really starts to achieve something 還沒有正式開始便要先吃虧：*~, chāamgā gógo fanlihn fochihng yiu sīn gāau géichīn mān bouméngfai, tùhng ongām sáujuhkfai.* (~! I have to pay several thousand dollars for enrollment, going through the procedures and the deposit before I can participate in the training course.)

1690

→m̀pa gūn, ji pa gún 唔怕官，至怕管 (lit.) one should not be afraid of an official, but one's supervisor 不怕官，最怕被人管
(idi.) PH one should not be afraid of one's big boss, but one's immediate boss 不怕大老闆，只怕你的直屬上司：~, ~, *néih m̀hóu díngjohng kéuih a, yānjyuh kéuih sé néih bougou.* (~, ~, so don't quarrel with him. Otherwise he may report it to your boss.) also see 0458

gūng 公 BF old man 老公公

1691 ✓

→daaihsēnggūng 大聲公 (lit.) N a man with a loud voice 嗓門大的男人 M go
(idi.) N loud-speaker, megaphone 揚聲器 M go：*Sīnsāang yuhng ~ giu dī hohksāang pàaihdéui.* (The teacher used a ~ to tell the students to line up.)

1692 ✓

→yih sūkgūng 二叔公 (lit.) N the second younger brother of one's grandfather 祖父的二弟 M go
(idi.) N pawn shop 當鋪：*Ngéi yaht dáng chín sái, bātyùh nīng go bīu heui ~ douh dongjyuh sīn lā.* ([We are] in need of money for these few days. Let me go to ~ and pawn this watch.)

1693

→yihsahp/yah sei haau lóuhgūng 二十／廿四孝老公
(lit.) a husband as virtuous as the twenty four filial sons (in Chinese

history) 像二十四個孝子那樣的好
丈夫
(idi.) N a perfect and considerate
husband 非常好又體貼的丈夫 M
go : *Néih gógo jānhaih ~, māt dōu
tēngsaai néih wah.* (You really have a ~.
He listens to everything you say.)

**hātyī 乞兒 N beggar 乞丐 M
go**

1694
➔hái hātyī dāu lá faahn sihk
喺乞兒兜搲飯食 (lit.) grab rice
to eat from a beggar's bowl 在乞丐
的缽裏拿他的飯吃
(idi.) PH take away petty/ the only
benefit(s) from someone inferior to
or poorer than you 連景況比你差的
人,你也要奪取他們的利益 : *Go
gūngchóng lóuhbáan yiu dī gūngyàhn
jēung dī jéunggām béi gūngchóng
jouh fūkleih gēigām, maih jīkhaih ~.*
(The factory boss asked the workers
to contribute their bonus to the
welfare fund of the factory. Isn't
that like ~?)

1695 ✓
➔hātyī 乞兒 (lit.) N beggar 乞
丐 M go
(idi.) N (a term of abuse) you mean
man (罵人語)下賤卑鄙 : ⓐ*Jingfú
yauh wah jīyùhn m̀gau, jauh cháau dī
dāikāp jīkyùhn, gōukāp ge gūn jauh
móuh sih, jing ~!* (The government
says that it lacks resources and should
start laying off minor staff members.
But the high ranking officials are
alright. ~!) ⓑ*jouhgwaan hātyih/ yī
láahn jouhgūn* see 1688

jái 仔 N son 兒子 M go

1696
➔baaihgājái 敗家仔 (lit.) N a
prodigal son who wastes all the
money and properties of his family
耗盡家中財產的兒子 M : *Kéuih
lóuhdauh jihngdāi hóudō chòihcháan
béi kéuih daahnhaih kéuih dóu chín
syūsaai, jingyāt ~.* (His father left a
lot of money and properties to him,
but he lost all of them in gambling.
He really is a ~.)

1697 ✓
➔gúwaahkjái 蠱惑仔 (lit.) N
cunning boy 奸詐男孩 M go, tiuh
(idi.) N teenagers having connections
with triads and so sometimes they
may be mistaken for triad members
與黑社會有來往的青少年,有時被
人當是黑社會 : *Yáuh syū m̀duhk
jouh ~!* (You don't study [hard], but
associate with triads!) (* 'Gúwaahk'
is an adjective meaning 'cunning,
tricky'. Sometimes it can be used as
a noun meaning 'dirty tricks' as in
'chēut ~', to use ~.)

1698
➔hāakjái 黑仔 (lit.) black boy
黑的小孩
(idi.) Adj. unlucky 倒霉 : *Gahnlói
dóuchān chín dōu syū, jānhaih ~.*
(Recently I always lose when
gambling. I am really ~.) also see
0881 and 0882

1699 ✓
➔jái 仔 (lit.) N son 兒子 M go
(idi.) N not a proper term for
'boyfriend' (粗話)男朋友 M tiuh :
kéuihtiuh ~ (her ~) BF (1) small 細

小 : *tói/ syū/ ngūk/ bihbī* ~ (~ table/ book/ house/ baby) (2) young 年 輕 : *làahm/ néui/ lóuhpòh/ lóuhgūng* ~ (~ boy/ girl/ wife/ husband) (3) young guy 年輕男性 : ⓐ *hauhsāang/ fèih/ ngái/ Méihgwok/ gwái* ~ (young/ fat/ short/ American/ foreign ~) ⓑ *boují/ maaihchoi* ~ (~ who sells newspaper/ vegetables) (4) fresh, inexperienced 沒有經驗的 : *yīsāng/ leuhtsī/ sān/ sānpàaih* ~ (doctor/ lawyer/ worker/ driver ~) (5) used as a suffix to surnames to show intimacy to a friend 加在比你年輕 的朋友的姓氏後面,表示親切 : *Chán/ Jēung* ~ (young Chan/ Cheung) (6) things related to babies 與嬰兒 有關的東西 : *sihk jūk/ faahn* ~ (eat [baby food]: rice gruel/ rice ~)

1700
➜*jāpjái* 執仔 (lit.) pick up a boy 拾起男孩
(idi.) VO be a mid-wife 做接生 : *Kéuih hái fēigēi seuhngbihn sāang bihbī, yātgo hūngjūng síujé bōng kéuih ~.* (She is going to deliver a baby on the plane. An air hostess will act as her ~.)

1701
➜*kwàhngeuk jái* 裙腳仔 (lit.) skirt edge son 裙邊的兒子 (idi.) N a son who is much influenced by his mother and finds it hard to be independent 常受母親 影響很難獨立自主的兒子 M go : *Néih béi go jái chēutgwok làuhhohk, siháh yātgo yàhn duhklahp sāngwuht, kéuih maih m̀wúih jouh ~ lō.* (You should let your son study abroad

and live alone. Then he can be more independent and won't be ~.)

1702
➜*lihng sāang baaihgājái, mohk sāang chéundeuhn yìh* 寧生敗家仔,莫生蠢鈍兒 (lit.) PH one would rather have a prodigal son than a stupid son 寧願生耗盡家 中錢財的不肖兒子,也不要生蠢的 兒子 : ~, ~. *Ngóhge jái sēuiyìhn laahndóu, daahnhaih dōu hóugwo néih sāangjó go baahkchī jái.* (~, ~. Although I have a son who gambles, it's better than having a mentally handicapped son as you do.)

1703
➜*lóuhdauh yéuhng jái jái yéuhng jái* 老豆養仔仔養仔 (lit.) a father raises his son, and the son raises his own son 父親養兒子, 兒子又養自己的兒子 (idi.) PH it is very rare for a son to support his parents when they are old 很少有兒子反哺父母 : ~, m̀hóu jíyi jáinéui yéuhngfāan néih a. *Kéuih m̀chī néih maih tāusiu lō.* (~ . So don't expect your sons and daughters to take care of you [when you are old]. You should be happy if they do not ask you for money.)

1704
➜*lóuhyàhn sìhng lyuhnjái* 老 人成嫩仔 (lit.) psychologically, old people become/ are like children 老人 在心理上變成小童 (idi.) PH better treat the elderly as young children 最好把老人當作小童 看待 : "*Yáuhdī lóuh yàhngā hóu yúhngyih faat pèihhei, yiu yàhn tam*

kéuih." "~ ā ma." ("Some of the elderly get outraged very easily, and they like others to please them." "That's what people say ~.")

1705
➔yih ngh jái 二五仔 (lit.) two five boy 二五小伙子
(idi.) N spy in a triad society 黑社會裏的間諜 M go : *Néih (hái ngóhdeihdouh) jouh ~! Séi là!* (You are the ~ [in our place]! Go to Hell!) (*'Yih ngh' [two five] can be taken as two halves [i.e. 0.5x2], which symbolize the split allegiance of a triad member to two triad groups.)

1706
➔yihsai jóu 二 世 祖 (lit.) ancestor of the second generation 二世祖先
(idi.) N good-for-nothing son of a rich man 有錢人的不肖兒子 M go : ~ *jihnghaih sīk taan saigaai, bīn sīk wánchín ā.* (A ~ only knows how to enjoy life. He is not good at making money.)

jēunggwān 將軍 N general 將軍 M go/ wái

1707
➔dāudūk jēunggwān 兜篤將軍 (lit.) (in Chinese game of chess) go behind the 'general' and take it (下中國棋用)走到'將軍'後面把它吃掉
(idi.) PH not attack the enemy at the front, but at the back 不在正面而在背後攻擊敵人：*Dī féitòuh yihgā lèihái ngūk yahpbihn, ngóhdeih ~, yàuh hauhmún gūnggīk kéuihdeih.* (The bandits are inside the house.

We can ~, waiting for them by the back door.)

1708
➔fótáu (daaih) jēunggwān 伙頭(大)將軍(lit.) N a cook 廚子 M go (*'Fótáu' [a cook] is given an epithet 'Daaih Jēunggwān' [the Great General] because a man in the Tang dynasty [618–907A.D.] worked as a cook in the army before he became a general.) : *Yíhchìhn kéuih hái yāt gāan gūngchóng jouh ~, sāumēi heuijó yāt gāan chàhlàuh jouh dímsām sīfú.* (He used to be a ~ in a factory, and later on he worked as a dimsum master in a restaurant.)

1709 ✓
➔jēunggwān 將 軍 (lit.) N general 將軍 M go
(idi.) VO (in Chinese game of chess) check! (下中國棋用語)取你的將軍! : *Yùhgwó néih gám hàahng, ngóh jauh ~ néih ~ ge la.* (If you make that move, I'll ~.)

johngyùhn 狀元 N the top successful candidate in the imperial examination 狀元，君主時代全國考試第一名 M go/wái

1710
➔hòhnghòhng chēut johngyùhn 行行出狀元 (lit.) PH every trade has very best and successful person 每個行業都有成功人士 : ~, *jeui pa néih ìnháng ngàaih jē .* (~. The only thing is whether you are willing to work hard or not.)

1711

→wuihháau johngyùhn 會考
狀元 (lit.) N top scorers in
HKCEE 香港中學會考成績最好的
考生 M go ： *Gāmnìhn yáuh gáu
go sahp yāu ~.* (There are nine
candidates who have gotten 10 As in
HKCEE this year.) (*HKCEE, see
0506)

jyú 主 **BF master, lord** 主人

1712

→gwojyú 過主 (lit.) pass on to
the next host 到另一個主人那裏
(*Originally, people say this to a
beggar when they want him to go
away to beg from other people.)
(idi.) PH (1) go away, get out of
here 走吧, 快滾 ： *Néih dōu m̀haih
làih máaihyéh ge, gáaugáaujan, ~ lā.*
(You don't come to buy our things.
You just fool around here. ~.) (2) pass
on to the next person 傳給下一個
人 ： *Néih lahmjó gamdō chi jōng,
faaidī ~ lā.* (You've been the banker
for so many [mahjong] games. [I
hope you'll lose this game and] Let
the next one be the banker.) (*In
mahjong, if the banker wins a game,
he will be banker again. Also see
1410)

1713

→haakgā jim deihjyú 客家
佔地主 (lit.) visitor occupies the
place of the landlord (and would not
retreat) 客人佔了主人的地方
(idi.) PH make use of the place the
owner has rented to you and act as if
you were the owner 把別人租給你
的地方像業主般使用 ： *Néih
jyuhhái chānchīk ngūkkéi, daahnhaih*

*sihsih chéng pàhngyáuh fāanheui
wáan, jánhaih ~.* (You live in your
relative's house, but you always invite
friends to have fun there. Your act is
~.)

**Jyū Yih-síng 朱義盛 N
formerly a native in Canton
who specialized in making
jewelry plated with gold** 從前
在廣州專門製造鍍金首飾的人

1714

→Jyū Yih-síng 朱義盛 (lit.)
see above
(idi.) N fake jewelry 假的首飾 M
dī ： *Kéuih daai ge haih jān ge
sáusīk, ngóh daai ge haih ~ jē.* (The
jewelry she is wearing is genuine.
What I wear is just ~.)

kyùhnsī 拳師 N boxer 拳師
M go

1715

→hauhbeih kyùhnsī→ting dá
後備拳師 → 聽打 (lit.) a
stand-by boxer→waits for the fight
後備拳師→等候比賽打鬥
(idi.) HIT (said of a man) will soon
be given a good beating 將會被人
打 ： *Kéuih jāang daaih yíhlūng dī
chín móuh dāk wàahn àh? Gám,
kéuih yiu jouh ~ → ~ sīn dāk la.* (He
can't pay his debts to the loan shark.
Then he needs to be ~ → ~.)

lá 嫲 BF female, woman 女
性的

1716

→lá/ ná 嫲 (lit.) female 雌性的
(idi.) Adj. (said of a man) womanish

(指男人)女性化 ： *Kéuih góngyéh yāmsēng sai hei, hóu ~.* (He speaks in a low and soft voice. He is very ~.)

1717
➔láládéi 嫲嫲哋 (lit.) PH (said of a man) a little womanlike 有點女性化 ： *Kéuih sāangdāk gōu daaih wāimáahng, daahnhaih góngyéh yáuhdī ~.* (He is tall and has a well built figure. But he talks in a ~ way.)

1718
➔láyìhng 嫲型 (lit.) the style of being a woman 女性的性格
(idi.) N a man who behaves like a woman 女性化的男人 M go: *Néih hái bīndouh sīkdóu nīgo ~ a?* (Where did you meet this ~?) Adj. see 1716

Làuh Béi 劉備 N a king of the Three Kingdoms Period 劉備 (三國時代的一個君主)

1719
➔Làuh Béi je Gīngjāu→yāt je móuh wùihtàuh 劉備借荊州→一借冇回頭) (lit.) Làuh Béi borrowed the land of Gīngjāu→he never returned it 劉備借荊州→之後一直沒有歸還
(idi.) HIT never return the money/thing borrowed from others 借了別人的錢／東西不歸還 ： *Kéuih mahn ngóh jechín, wah jeuhn faai wàahnfāanbéi ngóh, dímjī ~ → ~.* (He asked me to lend him money and said he would return it to me as soon as possible. But he ~ → ~.)

lóu 佬 BF guy, man of lower social status 身份地位比較低下的男人

1720
➔bóuhàaihlóu→yāt ché dou háu 補鞋佬→一扯到口 (lit.) a shoe-cobbler→as soon as he pulls the thread for mending shoes, it reaches his mouth 補鞋匠→一拉修補鞋子的線,線便拉到他的口
(idi.) HIT impatient (especially when waiting for a meal) 沒有耐性 (尤其在等吃的時候) ： *"Yáuh faahn sihk meih a?" "Ngāamngāam sīnji hōichí jyú jī ma, ~, ~."* ("Is the meal ready yet?" "I've just started to cook it. How come you are so ~, ~?")

1721
➔daaihlāplóu 大粒佬 (lit.) big piece guy 大顆的男人
(idi.) N VIP 大人物 M go: *Yáuh ~ làih fóngmahn Hēunggóng, sóyíh gēichèuhng bóuōn yìhmmaht.* (There's a ~ coming to visit Hong Kong. Therefore, the airport is on high alert.)

1722 ✓
➔daaihlóu 大佬 (lit.) N one's eldest brother 大哥 M go
(idi.) N big brother, leader of a triad gang 黑幫首領 M go: *Hāakbōng pùhnmahn yātgo yàhn, "Bīngo haih néih ~?"* (A man would be questioned by a triad member, "Who is your ~?") PN (when addressing someone who looks like a triad member) you (對貌似黑社會的人的稱呼)你 ： *~ yáuh mē mjūngyi, chéng chèuihbín góng.* (Please feel free to tell us if there is anything that ~ doesn't like.)

➔gwōnggwanlóu gaau jái, pìhnyìh mohktāam 光棍佬教仔，便宜莫貪 (lit.) PH a swindler admonishes/warns his son not to be covetous of any petty benefits 騙徒教兒子不要貪任何小便宜 : "*Wa! Hái gógāan sīyàhn chòihmouh gūngsī chyùhnchín yáuh sahpngh lèih leihsīk bo!*" "*~, ~. Néih dōu haih jēung dī chín chyùhnhái daaih ngàhnhòhng hóudī.*" ("Wow! One can get an interest rate at 15 per cent from that private financial company." "~, ~. It would still be best for you to put your money in a big bank.")

1724

➔màahnglóu tip fùh➔dou tip 盲佬貼符➔倒貼 (lit.) a blind man tapes a Taoist charm (on the wall) → he puts it upside down 盲人貼符咒→他把它倒過來貼 (idi.) HIT not only cannot earn any money, but also have to give money 不但拿不到錢，還要賠錢 : *Ngóhdeih hōi nījúng fanlihn bāan, jíhaih jeuhngjīngsīk sāu síu síu hohkfai, kèihsaht haih ~ → ~ ge.* (We run this kind of training course and we just charge students a token amount of money. In fact, we ~ → ~.) (*~ → ~ is a tailless pun. 'Dou tip' sounds like 'to tape upside down' or 'on the contrary pay money.')

1725 ✓

➔sailóu 細佬 (lit.) N younger brother 弟弟 M go (idi.) N an unfriendly way of addressing other men by triad members 黑幫對別(的男)人不客氣

的稱呼 : *Wai ~, néih haih bīndouh ga?* (Hey, ~, which [secret] society are you from?) PN (said of a man) an old and humble way of saying 'I/me' 舊時男人謙虛的自稱 : *Dōjeh daaihgā deui ~ gam hóu.* (Thank you for having been so nice to ~.)

lóuhdauh 老豆 N father 父親 M go

1726

➔gīkséi lóuhdauh wán sāan baai 激死老豆搵山拜 (lit.) PH (said to an unfilial child) kill the father by doing something unfilial, but then pay tribute to him at his tomb 把父親氣死後到他墳前拜他 : *Néih jēung lóuhdauh ge chín syūsaai, yauh jēung kéuih gāan poutáu jáplàp, néih haih maih séung ~ ā!* (You lost all your father's money in gambling, and closed down his shop. Do you want to ~ ?)

1727

➔lóuhdauh daaihbá 老豆大把(lit.) plenty of fathers 父親有很多 (idi.) PH father has a lot of money 父親有很多錢 : *"Ngóhge tùhnghohk yauh yiu máaih chē, yauh wah yiu heui ngoihgwok làuhhohk." "Ṁhóu hahn gam dō la, yàhndeih ~ ā ma."* ("My schoolmate is going to buy a car and will study abroad." "You don't have to envy him. His ~.") also see 0322

1728

➔ṁjī lóuhdauh sing māt 唔知老豆姓乜 (lit.) not know/

281

forget even the surname of one's own father 連自己父親姓甚麼也不知道 (idi.) PH immerse oneself in something (usually bad) 太沉溺於某事上 ： *Kéuih hái gāan sīkchihng kālāōukēi yauh chēunggō yauh yámjáu, wáandou ~.* (He sang and drank at the vice karaoke bar. He was having such a good time that he did ~.)

mā 媽 N mother 媽媽

1729 ✓

➜mā媽 (lit.) N mother 媽 (idi.) V be scolded by/ to scold somebody else with foul language 被人用粗言穢語罵／用粗言穢語罵人 ： *béi yàhn ~/ ~ yàhn* (be ~ / ~ other)

mùihyán 媒 人 N matchmaker 媒人 M go

1730

➜jouh mùihyán juhng yiu bāau sāangjái mè 做媒人仲要包生仔咩 (lit.) be a match-maker and still have to guarantee that you will have a son? 替你做媒人還要擔保你生兒子麼? (idi.) PH how could you demand such an impossible/ a harsh guarantee from me? 你怎可以要求我保證你那麼多事情呢? ： *Ngóh gaaisiuh kéuih tùhng néih bóujaahp, néih mahn ngóh haih mhaih yātdihng wúih ló A. ~!* (I introduced him to you to be your private tutor. You asked me if you would certainly get an A for your grade. ~!)

1731

➜mjouh mùihyàhn sāamdoih

hóu 唔做媒人三代好 (lit.) PH your next three generations will be good if you don't try to be a matchmaker 要是你不做媒人,那你的後代便會好 ： *"Ngóh séung tùhng A-Chán jouh mùihyán." "Jouh mē'éh ā. ~ a!"* ("I want to be a matchmaker for Chan." "Cut it out. ~!") also see 0124

nàahmyán 男人 N man 男人 M go

1732

➜daaih nàahmyán 大男人 (lit.) big man 大男人 (idi.) Adj. PH chauvinist, chauvinist pig (i.e. a man, a man who likes to dominate woman) 男性主義的 ： *Kéuih hóu ~ ge, hái ngūkkéi māt dōu mjouh, jihnghaih yiu taaitáai fuhksih.* (He is a ~. He doesn't do any housework at home. He just wants to be served by his wife.)

1733

➜jyuhgā nàahmyán 住家男人 (lit.) home living man 住在家裏的男人 (idi.) N family man, a man who enjoys family life 喜歡家庭生活的男人 M go ： *Kéuih hóu jūngyi jouh gāmouh, sèhnggo ~ gám. Kéuih taaitáai jauh hóu lā.* (He likes to do housework. He is a ~. I envy his wife.)

1734

➜nàahmyàhn lóuh gáu 男人老九 (lit.) man old nine 男人老九 (idi.) PH a real man 真正的男人 ： ⓐ ~, mhóu gam jīsih lā. (You, ~,

282

don't be so nosy.) (b) *làahmyán kaaudākjyuh, jyūlá wúih séuhng syuh* see 0231

1735

→nàahmyàhnpòh 男人婆 (lit.) N mannish lady, tomboy 男性化的女人 M go : *Kéuih sèhnggo ~ gám.* (She is such a ~.)

nāai 奶 BF middle-aged married woman 結了婚的中年女性

1736 ✓

→sīnāai 師奶 (lit.) N Mrs./ an address to middle-aged married women; housewife 太太, 對結了婚的中年女性的稱呼; 主婦 M go/wái (idi.) Adj. (said of fashion) fit for women but not for young girls (服裝)適合成熟女性不適合少女 : *Màhmā deui go néui wah, "Jeuk nīgihn sāam lā." Go néui wah, "M̀jai, gam ~."* (The mother said to her daughter, "Put on this dress." "No, it is too ~ -like," said the daughter.) N housewives 家庭主婦 M go : *~ saatsáu* (a male TV artist who has ~ as his fans, or a [handsome] man who attracts ~)

1737

→yihnāai 二奶 (lit.) N the number two wife, mistress 二房太太,情婦 M go : *Gahnlòih hóudō làahmyán heui daaihluhk bāau ~, jouhsihng yātgo séhwúi mahntàih.* (In recent years, many men have gone to mainland China and have got a ~

there, which is causing social problems [in Hong Kong].)

néui 女 N daughter 女兒 M go

1738

→hóu néui léuhng tàuh mùhn 好女兩頭瞞 (lit.) a good daughter would hide the truth from her husband and her parents 好的女兒會把事情瞞着丈夫和父母 (idi.) PH a peace-maker would not tell the ugly truth to the two parties involved 好人會隱瞞不好的事情, 免大家傷和氣 : *"Bàhbā yáuh kēnsá. Ngóh m̀gám wahbéi kéuih jī, yauh m̀gám wahbéi màhmā jī." "Néih maih ~ lō."* ("My father has cancer. I dare not tell him. I dare not tell my mother, either." "~! That's what you are supposed to do.")

1739 ✓

→néui 女 (lit.) N daughter 女 M go (idi.) N (1) not a proper term for 'girlfriend' (粗話) 女朋友 M tiuh : *kéuih tiuh ~* (his ~) (2) young girl 年輕女孩子 M tiuh : *gótiuh ~* (that ~) (3) club girl 在男性娛樂場所做事的少女 : *hái club jouh ~* (work as a ~)

1740

→wòhngdai néui → m̀yāu ga 皇帝女→唔憂嫁 (lit.) the king's daughter→ (she) need not worry about her marriage at all 皇帝的女兒→一點也不用擔心嫁不出去 (idi.) HIT quality thing/ capable person is so highly sought after that one need not worry about its/ his/ her future 品質高的人或物不愁沒有

283

出路的 ： *Kéuih yáuh Méihgwok mihnghaauh ge MBA, hóudō daaih gūngsī jāangjyuh chéng kéuih, jing sówaih* ~ → ~. (He's gotten an MBA from a prestigious university in the States. Many big companies want to employ him. Just as the saying goes, ~ → ~. He needn't worry [about his job] at all.)

pàhngyáuh 朋友 **N friend M go**

1741
→faatsīu yáu 發燒友 (lit.) friend has fever 發燒的朋友
(idi.) N a person who has a fever/ mania for doing something 對某種嗜好狂熱的人 M go ： *Kéuih haih sipyíng/ dihnyíng/ gīngkehk/ hāaifāai* ~. (He is a photography/ movies/ Peking opera/ Hi-Fi ~.)

1742
→jihgéi yáu 自己友 (lit.) one's own friend 自己的朋友
(idi.) N people of/ from the same group 自己人 ： *(Daaihgā dōu haih)* ~, *m̀sái gam yihm lā.* (We are ~. Don't be so strict [on me/ us].)

1743
→yáu 友 (lit.) friend 朋友
(idi.) N not a proper term for 'man', 'guy' (粗俗說法) 男人 M tiuh ： *Yāttiuh* ~, *jihng gāigāi.* (I'm alone and lonely.) BF companion 伴 ：
ⓐ *màhjeuk* ~ (playmate in mahjong)
ⓑ *bō* ~ (team member in ball games)
ⓒ *syū* ~ (schoolmate, classmate)
ⓓ *màhfàahn* ~ (trouble maker)

pòh 婆 **BF old woman** 老婆婆

1744
→wòhngmihnpòh 黃面婆 (lit.) yellow-faced woman 黃色臉孔的女人
(idi.) N a woman who does not care about her beauty after her marriage, go/ run to seed 婚後不顧儀容的女人 M go ： *M̀gwaaidāk néih lóuhgūng bāau yihlāai lā, néih táiháh néih, sèhnggo* ~ *gám.* (You should not blame your husband for having a mistress. Look! You are totally a ~.)

sauchói 秀才 **N young scholar** 秀才 **M go/wái**

1745
→sauchói yàhnchìhng jí yātjēung 秀才人情紙一張(lit.) a scholar's gift for others is just a sheet of paper 秀才人情紙一張
(idi.) PH it's only a very small token of appreciation 很微薄的禮物 ： *Nījēung sāangyaht/ gitfān kāat haih ngóhdeih sungbéi néih ge,* ~ *ja.* (This birthday/ wedding card is our gift for you. ~.)

1746
→sauchói yuhdóu/ jeuhk bīng, yáuh léih syut bāt chīng 秀才遇倒/着兵，有理說不清
(lit.) a scholar encounters a soldier→although he has good reasons, he is unable to reason with the soldier 秀才遇到兵,有理說不清
(idi.) PH no matter how one tries, one fails to reason with/ convince somebody else 縱然有道理,也難令人覺得自己清白 ： *"Go haak yāt*

lohkchē jauh wàhndāi, go baahkja jauh wah ngóh johngchān kéuih, góchi jānhaih ~, ~ lo," go dīksí sīgēi wah. ("The customer fainted and fell on the ground when he got off the taxi, but the police warden said I had knocked him down. That time ~, ~," said the taxi driver.) also see 0259

síujé 小姐 N miss, lady 小姐 M wái

1747 ✓

➜síujé 小姐 (lit.) N Miss, Lady 小姐 M wái
(idi.) N club girl, hostess in entertainment centres for men 在男性娛樂場所工作的女性 M go : Kéuih hái yehjúngwúi jouh ~. (She works as a ~ in a nightclub for men.)

taaijí 太子 N the crown prince 太子 M go

1748

➜jeukhéi lùhngpòuh dōu ṁchíh taaijí 着起龍袍都唔似太子(lit.) you won't look like a crown prince even if you put on the imperial dress embroidered with dragons 就算穿起龍袍也不像太子
(idi.) PH the gorgeous clothes don't suit you/ make you look great 就算穿起華麗衣服也不像樣 : Kéuih yéung sēui, ~! (He doesn't have good look, even ~.)

tùhngji 同志 N comrade 同志 M go/wái

1749 ✓

➜néuih tùhngji 女同志 (lit.) N a woman comrade 女同志 M go/wái
(idi.) N lesbian, gay woman 女同性戀者 M go : Gógo jihsaat ge néuihjái yùhnlòih haih ~. (It turns out that the girl who killed herself was a ~.)

1750 ✓

➜tùhngji 同志 (lit.) N comrade 同志 M go/wái
(idi.) N (said of a man) homosexual, gay man 同性戀者 M go : ~ jáubā. (a pub for ~)

wòhng 王 BF king 國王

1751

➜bawòhng 霸王 (lit.) hegemony, supreme leader 霸王
(idi.) ATT someone who intends not to pay (money) 故意不付錢的人 : ⓐ sihk ~ yéh (have ~ meal in a restaurant) ⓑ chóh ~ chē (~ his fare) Adj. (usually said of very young children) be aggressive and like to bully others 小童喜侵佔別人的東西或欺負別人 : Nīgo saimānjái hóu ~ ge, sihngyaht yiu ló yàhndeih ge yéh wáan. (This child is ~. He likes to take things from other children and play with them.)

1752 ✓

➜saatyàhn wòhng 殺人王 (lit.) N a relentless killer 殺人王 M go
(idi.) N teacher who likes to make students fail an exam by setting very difficult questions 喜用難的試題讓學生考試不及格的老師 M go : Chàhn sīnsāang yáuh méng haih ~ làih ge la, hóudō hohksāang dōu pa

kéuih. (Mr. Chan is a ~. Many students are afraid of him.)

wòhngdai 皇帝 N emperor 皇帝 M go/wái

1753

→dágūng wòhngdai 打工皇帝 (lit.) employed king 受僱的皇帝

(idi.) N highest salary earner, top tax payer 最高薪僱員 M go : *Gó géigo ~, múih nihn gāauseui dōu yiu gāau géi baakmaahn.* (These ~ have to pay millions of dollars of taxes each year.)

1754

→wòhngdai m̀gāp taaigaam gāp 皇帝唔急太監急 (lit.) the king is at leisure but the eunuch is impatient 皇帝不急太監急

(idi.) PH other people are more anxious than you 當事人不急,別人反而替他著急 : *"Ngóh séung faaidī yám sānpóuh chàh, daahnhaih ngóhge jái wah maahnmáan dōu m̀ chìh."* *"Nīdī giujouh ~ ā ma."* ("I want my son to get married soon, but he believes that it is never too late to get married." "This is what we say ~, isn't it?")

wòhséung 和尚 N Buddhist monk 和尚 M go/wái

1755

→dáyùhn jāai m̀yiu wòhséung 打完齋唔要和尚 (lit.) when the Buddhist service (in which sutras are cited) is over, the monk is not needed any more 法事舉行之後,人們再不需要和尚

(idi.) PH when the goal is achieved, the person who has made an effort to accomplish it is discarded 達到目的之後,再不需要曾出力的人 : *"Gaiwaahk yùhnsihng jīhauh, ngóhdeih nīgo síujóu jauh wúih gáaisaan ge la."* *"Gám maih jīkhaih ~."* ("When the project is completed, our team/task force will be dismissed." "That is just as what people say, ~.")

1756

→sāamgo wòhséung móuh séui sihk 三個和尚冇水食 (lit.) three monks, and there is no water for them to drink 三個和尚就沒有水喝

(idi.) PH rely too much on each other and as a result achieve nothing 太互相倚賴,結果做不成事 : *"Ngóh lámjyuh néih wúih jouh, néih lámjyuh kéuih wúih jouh, gitgwó daaihgā dōu móuh jouh."* *"~ ā ma!"* ("I thought you would do it, and you thought he would. As a result, nobody did it." "Just as the saying goes, ~.") (*The expression is the third part of: yātgo wòhséung dāam séui sihk, léuhnggo wòhséung tòih séui sihk, ~. It means a monk brings water home by himself. When there are two monks, they do it together. But if there are three, they get no water to drink.)

yàhn 人 N man, person, people 人 M go

1757

→gwāanyàhn 關人 (lit.) have something to do with people 與人有關

(idi.) PH none of one's business 與

人無關：*Yāt gāaujó fo, sāujó chín jīhauh jauh ~ lo.* (As soon as I gave them the ordered goods and got my money, I felt I had nothing to do with this any more.)

1758

➡hóu yàhn yáuhhaahn 好人有限 (lit.) good people are limited 好的人有限

(idi.) PH not be considered a good person 不會是好人 : *Bunyé sāamseidím juhng hái kālā ōukēi, m̀faan ngūkkéi, ~ lā.* (One is ~ if one is still at a karaoke bar and has not yet gone home at three or four in the morning.)

1759

➡sūngyàhn 鬆人 (lit.) loosen a person 把人解鬆

(idi.) VO go/ sneak away 溜走 : *yāt gaujūng jauh ~* (~ as soon as time's up)

1760

➡yàhnjā 人渣 (lit.) man trash 人作渣滓

(idi.) N worthless evil people, scum 卑賤無用的人 M go : ⓐ *Dī duhkfáan maaih baahkfán wàih hoih chīngsiunihn, jingyāt ~!* (The drug traffickers ruin teenagers by selling drugs to them. They are ~.) ⓑ *Néih haih làahmyán, gíngyihn hā lóuhyàhn tùhng saimānjái, jingyāt ~!* (You are a man, but you bully the elderly and the children. You are really ~!)

yīsāng 醫生 N doctor 醫生
M go/wái

1761

➡hàahngwahn yīsāng yī behng méih 行運醫生醫病尾 (lit.) a lucky doctor cure the end of an illness 走運的醫生醫治病的結尾

(idi.) PH a doctor is lucky enough to succeed in curing a patient who has almost been cured by another doctor 走運的醫生醫治差不多康復了的病人 : *"Ngóh táijó géigo yīsāng, sihkjó hóudō yeuhk, juhng meih hóufāan, daahnhaih tái kéuih yātléuhng chi jauh hóufāan la." "~ jì gwa!"* ("I had seen many doctors and had taken different kinds of medication, and yet I didn't recover. Later, I went to see him only once or twice, and now I am alright." "Perhaps it's just ~.")

1762

➡wòhngluhk yīsāng 黃綠醫生 (lit.) yellow-green doctor 青黃不接的醫生

(idi.) N a quack, charlatan, sham doctor 庸醫,江湖醫生,沒受過正式及嚴格訓練的醫生 M go : *Yáuh behng jauh jingjing sīksīk wán go jyuchaak yīsāng tái, m̀hóu tāam pèhng tái dī ~.* (When you are sick, you'd better take it seriously and go see a registered doctor. Don't go to a ~ simply because they are cheaper.)

10. Miscellaneous

I. Yīyeuhk kahp Sāngséi (ailments and medicine, life and death)

behng 病 **V/N be sick, be ill; illness; disease** 生病; 疾病 **M go; júng**

1763

➜chan néih behng, ló néih mehng 趁你病，攞你命 (lit.) while you are ill, it kills (you) 趁你生病就奪你命
(idi.) PH when a person is sick, someone does something to make the situation worse for him 趁你有病還加害於你／落井下石 : *Ngóh yauh sātyihp yauh yáuh behng, yihpjyú juhng giu ngóh būn tīm, jānhaih ~, ~.* (I have lost my job and now I'm sick, but the landlord still asks me to move out. He really ~, ~.)

1764

➜dākhàahn séi, m̀dākhàahn behng 得閒死，唔得閒病 (lit.) one has time to die but no time to fall sick 有時間去死,可是沒有時間生病
(idi.) PH extremely busy 忙得不可開交 : *"Néih gam mòhng, dímgáai m̀táuháh a?" "Ngóh jingyāt ~, ~ a, juhng góng táu."* ("You are so busy. Why don't you take a break?" "I'm really ~. It's impossible for me to take a break.")

bintaai 變態 **N (said of insects or in zoology) metamorphosis** 動物或昆蟲變態

1765 ✓

➜bintaai 變態 (lit.) N (said of insects or in zoology) metamorphosis 動物或昆蟲變態
(idi.) N (said of a person) has a sick mind 指人心理不正常,變態 : *Kéuih nīgo yàhn (sāmléih) ~ ge.* (He is a person who is [psychologically] ~.) ATT having a sick mind, psychotic 變態的 : ~ *sīkmō* (a ~ serial rapist) Adj. abnormal (state of mind) (心理)不正常 : *Kéuih hóu ~ ge.* (He is a very ~ person.)

chāugān 抽筋 **VO have (muscle) cramp** 痙攣

1766 ✓

➜chāugān 抽筋 (lit.) VO have (muscle) cramp 痙攣
(idi.) VO feel very uncomfortable in certain parts of the body 身體某些部分很不舒服 : ⓐ*Ngóh (go waih) ngohdou ~.* (I'm so hungry that I have ~ [in my stomach].) ⓑ*jouhdou ~ saai ~* (work so hard that one is likely to have ~) ⓒ*sédou ngóhge sáu ~* (my hand gets ~ after having written for such a long time)

dájām 打針 **VO have/give an injection** 打針, 注射

1767

➜faaigwo dájām 快過打針 (lit.) (even) quicker than having an injection (功效)比打針還快

(idi.) PH very good remedy 功效非
常快：*Kéuih ham, néih béi jyūgūlīk
kéuih sihk, kéuih jauh jíkhāak
sāusēng, ~.* (Give him chocolate
when he cries. He'll stop crying
immediately. ~.)

**diu yìhmséui 吊鹽水 VO
(medical) I.V. 鹽水注射**

1768✓
➔diu yìhmséui 吊鹽水
See 1027

**faatsīu 發燒 VO have a fever
發熱**

1769 ✓
➔tàuhtung faatsīu 頭痛發燒
(lit.) PH headache and fever 頭痛及
發燒
(idi.) PH minor diseases 小病痛：~,
*jihgéi máaih dī yeuhk sihk maih dāk
lō, daaih behng sīnji yiu tái yīsāng jé.*
([I] can buy medicine for a ~. [I] go to
the doctor's only when [I] am
seriously ill.)

gau 救 V save 救

1770 ✓
➔móuhdāk gau 冇得救 (lit.)
PH no way to save (a person) 沒法子
救(他)
(idi.) PH can't do anything about, no
remedy 沒法子補救：ⓐ*Kéuih dī
sihngjīk gam chā, ~ ge la, làuhbāan
lā.* (His grades are so bad that he is ~.
He'd better repeat the course.)
ⓑ*Kéuih gam laahndóu, ~ ge la.* (He
indulges himself in gambling so much
that he is ~.)

jāp 執 V pick up 拾起

1771
➔jāpsāang 執生 (lit.) catch the
newly born (baby, which is the job of
a midwife, also see 1700) 替初生嬰
兒接生
(idi.) V flexible in handling things 靈
活的處理事情：*Jouh yàhnsih
gīngléih chèuihjó yiu yáuh yàhnsih
gúnléih ge jīsīk jīngoih, juhng yiu
sīkdāk ~ sīnji dāk.* (Being a personnel
manager, one is supposed to be
knowledgeable about personnel
management as well as ~.)

**lùhng ngá 聾啞 N deaf and
mute 又聾又啞**

1772 ✓
➔yauh lùhng yauh ngá又聾又
啞 (lit.) PH deaf and mute 又聾又
啞
(idi.) PH cannot understand or speak
the native language when in a foreign
place 在外地不會聽又不會說當地
的語言：ⓐ *Heuidou ngoih gwok,
m̀sīk tēng yauh m̀sīk góng, binsihng
~.* (One will become ~ in a foreign
country because one can't
understand the language.) ⓑ ~
yauh màahng (~ and blind.)

**mehng命 N life, fate 性命, 命
運 M tiuh**

1773 ✓
➔gáauchēut yàhnmehng 攪出
人命 (lit.) PH there's killing of
people 弄出人命來了
(idi.) PH (said of lovers) have a baby

290

unexpectedly (情侶)意外地有了孩子 : *Paaktō m̀gányiu, daahnhaih chīnkèih m̀hóu ~.* (Dating won't do you any harm. But you should by no means ~.)

1774

➔saaimehng 晒命 (lit.) show off life 展示命運
(idi.) VO boast of one's success in life 向人炫耀自己好的命運際遇 : *Néih m̀sái háidouh ~ la. Ngóhdeih jī néih hóu hahngfūk, lóuhgūng sek léih, jáinéui yauh gwāai.* (You don't have to ~. We know that you are blessed with a happy family. Your husband loves you, and your children are good, too.)

ngáu 嘔 V vomit 嘔吐

1775 ✓

➔jokngáu 作嘔 (lit.) V feel sick/ is about to vomit 想嘔吐
(idi.) V (it) makes me sick 令人噁心✓/ 厭惡 : *Géisahp seui ge néuihyán juhng baahnsihng lēngmūijái gám, jānhaih (lihngyàhn) ~.* (That middle-aged woman still dresses herself up like a teenage girl. She really ~.)

1776

➔ngáudihn 嘔電 (lit.) spit electricity 吐電
(idi.) PH see 1777

1777 ✓

➔ngáuhyut 嘔血 (lit.) VO spit blood 吐血
(idi.) PH extremely exhausted 令人極度疲累 : *gaaudou ~* (teach [students/children] so hard that one is ~)

séi 死 V die 死

1778

➔séigwo fāansāang 死過翻生 (lit.) come to life again after death 死了又復活
(idi.) PH a narrow escape from death 死裏逃生, 僥倖生還 : ⓐ *Nīchi fēigēi sātsih jíhaih sauhsēung jānhaih hóyíh wah ~.* (He only got injured in the plane accident. We can say that he had ~.) ⓑ *Kéuih ge kēnsá yīhóujó, jānhaih ~.* (His cancer was cured. He really had ~.)

1779

➔séijó tiuh sām 死咗條心 (lit.) heart died 心死了
(idi.) PH give up (because of frustration) (因受挫折想)放棄 : ⓐ*Ngóh chāamgā gógo béichoi chichi dōu syū, ngóh yíhgīng ~.* (I've taken part in that contest for many times, but I've never won. I've already ~.) ⓑ *Néih jēuijó Wòhng síujé gam noih kéuih dōu m̀jūngyi néih, néih ~ bá lā.* (You've been chasing after Miss Wong for such a long time, and yet she hasn't fallen in love with you. You'd better ~.) (*Some people would say 'sāmsīk' 心息, which literally means 'heart at rest', for 'séijó tiuh sām'.)

tung 痛 V/Adj. ache, hurt; painful 疼痛

1780

➔chèuhng tung bātyùh dyún tung 長痛不如短痛(lit.) to suffer for a long time is worse than to suffer for a short time 長痛不如短痛

291

(idi.) PH stop doing something that makes you suffer 不再做令你痛苦 的事 : *Kéuih tùhng jeuhngfū gámchìhng mhóu, ~, sóyíh kéuih kyutdihng lèihfān.* (She couldn't get along well with her husband. So, ~, she made up her mind to divorce him in order not to suffer any more.) also see 0433 and 0801

wàhn 暈 V/Adj. faint; dizzy 昏,暈眩

1781 ✓

➔ wàhnlohng 暈浪 (lit.) VO/Adj. seasick 暈船

(idi.) VO (said of a man) be entranced at the sight/ by the flattery of a beautiful woman 男人見了美麗女性或被女人灌迷湯而神魂顛倒 : *Kéuih yāt gindóu leng néui jauh ~ (saai daaih) ~ ge la.* (He'll ~ when bumping into good-looking females.)

wānyihk 瘟疫 N plague 瘟疫 M júng

1782 ✓

➔faatwān 發瘟 (lit.) VO have plague 得了瘟疫

(idi.) VO what a plague 真是不幸了 : *Kéuih gam sēui, ngóh jūngyi kéuih àh, ~ lo.* (He is good-for-nothing. Do you mean that I'm falling in love with him? ~ !)

1783 ✓

➔míhnyihk 免疫 (lit.) V immunize 免疫

(idi.) V free from an obligation/ duty 已經做了，所以不用再做 : *"Gāmyaht maaihkèih bo!" "Ngóh*

máaihjó la, sóyíh ~." ("Today is a flag day." "I've already bought one, so I'm ~.") (*In Hong Kong, charities will raise money by selling 'kèih' [lit. 'flag'], which in fact are small stickers.)

1784

➔yūnwóng làih, wānyihk heui 冤枉嚟，瘟疫去 (lit.) come with a wrong and then go with a plague 來得冤枉, 走像瘟疫

(idi.) PH ill/easy gotten money just comes and goes 不義之財來得易去得快 : ⓐ *Kéuih maaih baahkfán jaahnfāanlàih ge chín béi gíngfōng muhtsāujó, jingyāt ~, ~.* (The money he made from trafficking drugs are seized by the police. That is really ~, ~.) ⓑ *Kéuih jung Luhkhahpchói ge chín syūsaai la. ~, ~.* (He gambled away the money he won from the Mark Six. That is ~.)

yī 醫 V heal, cure 醫治

1785 ✓

➔móuh yeuhk yī 冇藥醫 (lit.) PH (said of disease) no medicine to heal 沒有藥可以醫治(的病)

(idi.) PH (said of a person) no remedy for his behaviour (指人的行爲)無可救藥 : *Láahn haih ~ ge.* (There's ~ laziness.)

1786

➔yàhn chéun móuh yeuhk yī 人蠢冇藥醫 (lit.) PH there's no remedy for a person being stupid 蠢笨的人真是沒辦法救治 : ~. *Faaidī hohkfāan jēngdī lā.* (~. Hurry up and learn to be smarter.)

292

1787

➔yàhn haak yàhn, móuh
yeuhk yī 人嚇人，冇藥醫 (lit.)
PH a man horrified by others cannot
be cured by any remedy (and will
probably die) 人嚇人,沒有藥可以
醫好他(或會被嚇死)：*Néih mhóu
baahn gwái baahn máh lā, ~, ~ ga.*
(Don't disguise yourself as a ghost or
other strange beings. You know, ~, ~.)

II. Gwānsih (military)

baau 爆 V explode, blast 爆炸

1788
→baaugaak 爆格(lit.) blast the square frame 爆炸格子
(idi.) VO (said of thieves) break in 入屋爆竊 : *Sēuiyìhn bóuōn hóu yìhm, daahnhaih dōu yáuh chàak ~.* (Although the security is tight, the thieves can still manage to ~.)

1789
→baauláahng 爆冷 (lit.) blast the cold 爆冷
(idi.) VO (1) (in horse-racing) the dark horse wins (賽馬中)冷馬勝出 : *Nī chèuhng ~ daaih ~.* (~ this race, and the dividend is terrific.) (2) unexpected result of a contest that the least likely contestant wins 意料不到的賽事, 形勢最弱的參賽者勝出 : *Nīchi béichoi ~.* (In this race, we have ~.)

1790
→baaupàahng 爆棚 (lit.) blast the bamboo scaffolding for Chinese opera 戲棚爆了
(idi.) VO (1) (said of cinema/ theatre) a full house 戲院滿座 : *Nītou hei hóu sāudāk, yahtyaht dōu ~.* (This movie is very popular. It's ~ every day.) (2) extremely crowded 非常擠迫 : *Sānnìhn hóudō yàhn fāan daaihluhk, heui Lòhwùh ge fóchē ~ saai ~.* (Many people go to mainland China at the New Year, and the trains for Lo Wu are ~.) (3) reach the highest level 達至最高點 : *IQ ~ (~ in one's*

intelligence quotient) (4) be overwhelmed with 充滿了 : *jihseunsām/ oisām ~* (~ self-confidence/ love) Adj. very crowded 很擠擁 : *dī chē/ chàhlàuh/ heiyún hóu ~* (the public transport/ restaurants/ cinemas are ~) N (in mahjong) grand slam (打麻將) 吃大滿貫 : *"Néih sihk mééh wú a?" "Chīngyātsīk, (sihk) ~."* ("What was your winning hand?" "Purity hand, a ~.")

chēung 槍 N gun 槍 M jī/bá

1791
→chéngchēung 請槍 (lit.) ask for a gun 要槍
(idi.) VO ask someone to do the homework/exam for you 請別人代你做功課或考試 : *"Dī gūngfo gam nàahnjouh." "Néih hóyíh ~ gā ma."* ("My homework is so difficult to do." "Oh, you can ~.")

1792 ✓
→chēungsáu 槍手 (lit.) N gunman 持槍的人 M go
(idi.) N one who does homework/ exam or writes article for someone else 代人做功課/考試或寫文章的人 M go : *Yáuhdī jyūnlàahn jokgā dōu wán ngóh jouh ~.* (Even some columnists ask me to ~.)

1793
→diuhjyun chēungtàuh 調轉槍頭 (lit.) turn the gun around (trying to shoot one's comrades)把槍口轉向(想射向戰友)

(idi.) PH turn on/criticize or blame one's group member(s)批評或責怪自己所屬團體的人，倒戈相向： *Hōiwúi ge sihhauh, Chàhn yíhyùhn gíngyìhn ~, laauh jihgéi ge dóngyùhn.* (In the council, Councillor Chan suddenly ~ and unexpectedly condemned a member of his own party.)

1794 ✓

➔gēigwāan chēung 機關槍 (lit.) N machine gun 機關槍 M jī
(idi.) N words one fires at somebody 滔滔不絕的説話 M lèuhn： *Ngóh dōu juhng meih góngyùhn kéuih jauh yātlèuhn ~ gám sougwolàih la.* (He fired words at me [like a machine gun] before I could finish saying.)

deihlèuih 地雷 N land mine
地雷 **M go**

1795 ✓

➔deihlèuih 地雷 (lit.) N land mine 地雷 M go
(idi.) N animal shit on the road 路上動物的糞便 M dī： *Dī móuh gūngdāksām ge yàhn béi dī gáu hái gāaidouh ōsí, néih ìnsíu sām jauh wúih yáaidóu ~ ge la.* (Some people are inconsiderate. They let their dogs shit on the street. Be careful or you'll tread on ~.)

fójin 火箭 N rocket 火箭 M jī

1796 ✓

➔fójin 火箭 (lit.) N rocket 火箭 M jī/ go
(idi.) N the grade of A A 等成績 M jī： *Sihngjīk bíu seuhngbihn yáuh géijī ~.* (There are several ~s on the report card.)

fóyeuhk 火藥 N gunpowder
火藥 **M dī**

1797 ✓

➔fóyeuhk 火 藥 (lit.) N gunpowder 火藥 M dī
(idi.) N things that anger you 令你發怒的東西： *Kéuih sihkjó ~ àh, gam nogk laauh yàhn gé?* (Has he eaten ~? Why did he scold me so furiously?) also see 1058

gim 劍 N sword 劍 M bá

1798

➔fong fēigim 放 飛 劍 (lit.) shoot a sword 放飛劍
(idi.) VO spit 吐痰： *Hàahnggāai ge sihhauh, síusām dī yàhn ~ a.* (When you walk on the street, be careful because people will ~.)

jadáan 炸彈 N bomb 炸彈 M go

1799

➔dihnggwo tòih jadáan 定過抬炸彈 (lit.) stay calm even when carrying a bomb 就算抬炸彈也不用怕
(idi.) PH extremely calm and confident 胸有成竹,從容不迫： *Háausi ge tàihmuhk kéuih dōu sīk daapsaai, gánghaih ~ lā, ìnsái pa ìnkahpgaak.* (He could answer all the questions on the exam paper. He is bound to ~. He need not be afraid of failing the exam.)

1800

➔hùhngsīk jadáan 紅色炸彈 (lit.) red bomb 紅色炸彈
(idi.) N wedding invitation card 結婚

請帖 M go : *Nīgo yuht jipdóu géigo ~, jihgéi yiu hāandī sīnji dāk la.* (I received several ~ this month. I have to be more thrifty in my daily expenses.) (*A traditional Chinese invitation card for a wedding is red in color. However, people don't always like to receive one because they will have to spend money buying wedding gifts.)

jēut 卒 N/BF soldier ; a pawn in Chinese game of chess 兵卒; 中國象棋的卒 M jek

1801 ✓

➔gwohòhjēut 過河卒 (lit.) N the 'pawn' moved across the river on the chessboard (is not allowed to go backward according to the rules of Chinese game of chess. It can only go forward.) 根據中國象棋的規則, 過了河的 '卒' 不可以退後, 只能前進 M jek

(idi.) N a person having no way to quit (once something has started)沒法退縮的人 M jek : *Nīgo gaiwaahk yíhgīng hōichíjó, ngóhdeih hóuchíh ~ gám, yiu gaijuhk jouhyùhn kéuih.* (The project has been started. We're like ~. We can't give up. We have to see it through.)

1802

➔jēutjái 卒仔 (lit.) soldier 兵卒
(idi.) N (staff) members of the lowest rank/ post 最低(職)級的工作人員 M jek : *Ngóhdeih haih ~ làih ge jī ma, yauh m̀haih a-táu.* (We're just ~, not the head.)

1803

➔laahntàuhjēut 爛頭卒 (lit.)

broken head soldier 摔破了頭的兵卒
(idi.) N a person who works extremely hard for his boss but is not appreciated by him 爲老闆賣命工作卻得不到甚麼好處的人 M jek : *Ngóhdeih jí bātgwo haih ~ làih jē, jouhdou séi dōu haih waih lóuhbáan jaahnchín jē.* (We're just like a ~. We work so hard to make money for our boss.)

paau 炮 N cannon 炮 M jī

1804

➔chē daaihpaau 車大炮 (lit.) vehicles and big cannons 車跟大炮
(idi.) VO talk big 吹牛, 說大話 : *Kéuih wah kéuih nihn sān yātbaak maahn, kéuih ~ jī ma.* (He said he had a salary of one million dollars a year. He just ~.)

1805

➔pekpaau 劈砲 (lit.) chop the cannon 劈開大砲
(idi.) VO quit one's job 辭職不幹 : *Lóuhbáan laauh kéuih, kéuih jauh ~ (m̀lōu).* (His boss scolded him, and so he ~.) (* 'Paau' is slang for the gun carried by a policeman. Originally, 'pekpaau' is said of a policeman who unhappily quit his job as he dropped or threw down (i.e. pek) his gun when returning it to the police.)

1806

➔séuipaau 水炮 (lit.) N water-cannon 水炮 : *Sihwāi yínbinsihng gíngmàhn chūngdaht, gíngchaat yūsih faatseh ~ kēuisaan yàhnkwàhn.* (The protest erupted into clashes between the police and the demonstrators. So the police fired ~ to break up the crowd.)

III. Deihfōng (place and direction)

dái 底 PW/BF bottom; background 底下; 背景

1807 ✓

➔bāaudái 包底 (lit.) wrap bottom 包着底部
(idi.) PH willing to balance the budget/ pay money until it is enough 願意補足預算/付不足的金額 : *Yáuh dī fochìhng sāu m̀gau hohksāang, daahnhaih daaihhohk wúih ~.* (Student enrolment in some courses isn't that satisfactory. However, the university is ~.)

1808 ✓

➔dái 底 (lit.) PW botton 底部
(idi.) N (1) background 背景 : ⓐ *Jī m̀jī kéuih mēéh ~ a?* (Do you know his ~?) ⓑ*hāak dái* see 0884 ⓒ*hùhng dái* see 0893 (2) the inside of clothing 衣物的裏面 : *Nī gihn sāam, néih fáanjyun jeuk la, nīdouh haih ~ làih ga.* (You wear this shirt inside out. This is ~.) also see 0525 N (1)

1809

➔gahm deih yàuhséui→ wánjahn gwo dái 拎地游水 → 穩陣過底 (lit.) swim with hands touching the ground→cross over the bottom (of the sea/river) safely 摸着地游泳,很安全的過河
(idi.) HIT a person who does things in a very secure/ safe way 做事非常保險穩妥 : *Kéuih nīgo yàhn ~ → ~, sóyíh kéuih m̀wúih tàuhjī gōu fūnghím ge yéh.* (He is ~. Therefore,

he won't invest his money in high-risk projects/ items.)

1810

➔héidái 起底 (lit.) lift up the bottom 揭起底部
(idi.) VO find out the background of a person 查找一個人的出身背景 : *Kéuih jouh yihnġhjái, dím jī béi yàhn ~.* (He is a spy. However, he has been found out.)

1811

➔hóu maht chàhm gwāi dái 好物沉歸底 (lit.) good things sink to the bottom (of water) 好的東西沉到(水)底
(idi.) PH the best comes last 好的東西到最後才出現 : *"Dímgáai chāujéung juhng meih chāudóu ngóh gé?" "~. Waahkjé tàuh jéung haih néih lē."* ("Why is it still not my turn to win in the lucky draw?" "~. Maybe you are the first prize winner.")

1812

➔lātdái 甩底 (lit.) off the bottom 底部脫了
(idi.) VO fail to turn up 沒有應約 (出現) : *Ngóhdeih yeukhóu heui cheung K, daahnhaih kéuih ~.* (We agreed to go to karaoke bar, but he ~.)

1813

➔módái 摸底 (lit.) touch the bottom 撫摸底部
(idi.) VO (said of prices) reach the

lowest level (物價、股票等) 跌到最低水平：*Làuhga tùhng gúpiu haih gám dit, m̀jī géisí ~.* (Flat prices and share prices just keep falling. I don't know when they will ~.)

1814
→ngohdái 臥底 (lit.) underlie, lie at the bottom 躺在底下
(idi.) N spy 間諜 M go：*Yùhnlòih kéuih haih gíngfōng paaihlàih jouh ~ ge.* (It turns out that he was sent by the police and acted as a ~ in our place.) ATT undercover 秘密（作間諜）：~ gíngyùhn (~ policeman) ~ taamyùhn (~ detective/ agent from the police)

1815
→ngondái 案底 (lit.) legal case background 案件背景
(idi.) N (previous) criminal record 前科/ 犯罪記錄 M chi：ⓐ*yáuh ~* (have a ~) ⓑ*móuh ~* (have a clear record)

1816
→sáidái 洗底 (lit.) clean the background 把背景洗乾淨
(idi.) VO give up the identity as a triad member by surrendering oneself to the police 黑社會成員向警方自首以洗脫及放棄其身份：*Kéuih ~ jīhauh jouhfāan jìng hòhng.* (After he ~, he engaged himself in proper professions.)

1817
→sihtdái 蝕低 (lit.) bottom wear away 底部磨損
(idi.) V suffer loss 吃虧：*Néuihyán tùhng nàahmyán dágāau,*

gánghaih ~ lā. (A woman will certainly ~ when fighting with a man.) Adj. be likely to suffer loss 會吃虧：*Néih gám ge hohklihk, tùhng yàhn gihngjāng, wúih hóu ~ ge bo.* (You are very ~ when competing with others if/because you have such low academic qualifications.)

deihpùhn 地盤 N/PW construction work site 建築地盤 M go

1818 ✓
→deihpùhn 地盤 (lit.) N/ PW construction work site (建築)地盤 M go
(idi.) N/ PW site/ place under control of triads 黑幫控制的地方 M go：*Néih hái kéuihge ~ wánsihk gánghaih yiu béi bóuwuhfai kéuih lā.* (You make money at a ~, of course you have to pay them protection fee.)

gāai 街 N/PW street 街道 M tìuh

1819 ✓
→chēutgāai 出街 (lit.) VO go out (from home) 上街去
(idi.) VO (1) (said of TV show) be on air/ broadcast 電視節目的播映：*Gó géigo jyúchìh góng gódī chōuháu haih m̀~ dāk ~ ge.* (The foul language that the hosts said in this show should be cut.) (2) (said of publications) be put on the market (for sale) 刊物在市場上推出發售：*Bún syū gam dō cho, dím hóyíh ~ a?* (How can the book be ~ since there are so many mistakes in it?)

299

1820 ✓

➔ **hàahnggāai** 行街 (lit.) VO walk/ stroll on the street 逛街 (idi.) VO (1) be a broker 做經紀： *Kéuih jouh ~ ge, sihsih yiu kaau bá háu wánsihk.* (He ~. He makes a living by talking all the time.) (2) (in a fast food shop) take away 拿走 (快餐)： *Faaichāan dim ge lóuhbáan deui chyùhfóng góng, "Cháau faahn, ~."* (The shopkeeper told [the cook in] the kitchen, "Fried rice, ~.")

gāam 監 BF jail, prison 監牢

1821 ✓

➔ **chóh gāam** 坐監 (lit.)VO be in jail 坐牢 (idi.) VO waiting to cross the efficiency bar on the pay scale 呆悶地等待越過薪級表上的關限： *Ngóh yihgā ~ gán ~, táipa dōu haih móuh māt gēiwuih ge la.* (I'm now ~. I'm afraid I have not much chance.) (*Hong Kong government employees are paid according to a fixed pay scale. Every year they have pre-determined increase in pay. There are bars on the pay scale that correspond to the number of years worked. If one can "cross the efficiency bar", it means one can get an extra raise in salary.)

1822

➔ **chóh yìhmàhn gāam** 坐移民監 (lit.) be in a jail for immigrants 移民坐牢 (idi.) PH (said of an immigrant who must) stay in the country for a fixed number of years as a requirement for immigration 在一國家裏逗留一段所需的時間才可完成移民手續： *Lóuhpòh tùhng jáinéui hái*

Gānàhdaaih ~, kéuih jihgéi jauh fāanlàih Hēunggóng jouhyéh. (He came back to Hong Kong for a job, while his wife and children were in Canada where they must ~.)

1823

➔ **māugāam** 跍監 (lit.) squat in jail 蹲在牢裏 (idi.) VO be in jail 坐牢 (*'Māu', i.e. squat, is the posture symbolizing the inability of a person to stand upright or be free to do anything.)： *Jouh faahnfaat sìh haih yiu ~ ga.* (One is liable to ~ for having done something against the law.)

gōu dāi 高低 PW high and/ or low 高和/或低

1824

➔ **gingōu (jauh) baai, gin dāi (jauh) cháai** 見高(就)拜，見低(就)踩 (lit.) show respect for those of higher rank and tread upon those of lower rank 尊敬高級的人卻欺負低級的人 (idi.) PH snobbish 勢利： *Kéuih nīgo yàhn ~, ~ sóyíh kéuihdī hahsuhk m̀jūngyi kéuih.* (He tends to ~, ~, so the people who work under him don't like him.)

hòh 河 N/PW river 河 M **tiuh**

1825

➔ **yàuh chē hó** 遊車河 (lit.) car riding across river 車在河上行走 (idi.) VO go for a ride in a car 乘車兜風： ⓐ *chóh bāsí ~* (go on a bus trip) ⓑ *yàuh syùhn hó* (go on a boat/ ferry trip) also see 0929

jaahm 站 N station 站 M go

1826 ✓

➜bāsíjaahm 巴士站 (lit.) N bus-stop 巴士站 M go

(idi.) N (in mahjong) too slow in discarding a tile whenever it is one's turn 打麻將時出牌很慢的人 : *Faaidī lā, ~! Māt néih jaahmjaahm tihng ga?* (Hurry up, you are ~! The flow of the game always gets stuck when it is your turn.)

1827

➜fēijaahm 飛站 (lit.) fly over the (bus) stop 飛越車站

(idi.) VO (said of bus or train drivers) just drive on to the next stop or station(公共汽車或火車司機)沒有在車站停車一直駛到下一站 : *Sīgēi ~, sìhnghaak lohk m̀dóu chē.* (The bus driver ~, so the passengers could not get off.)

jáudim 酒店 N/PW hotel 酒店 M gāan

1828✓

➜daaih jáudim 大酒店 (lit.)N/PW big hotel 大酒店 M gāan

(idi.) N/ PW (euphemism for) funeral parlour 殯儀館(的委婉語) M gāan : *Kéuih hái bīngāan ~ chēutban a?* (In which ~ was his funeral held?)

1829 ✓

➜jáudim 酒店 (lit.)N/ PW hotel 酒店 M gāan

(idi.) N/PW (euphemism for) hospital 醫院(的委婉語) M gāan : *yahp/jyuh/bōngchan ~ (be hospitalized)*

jó yauh 左右 PW left and right 左右

1830

➜jó yauh jouh yàhn nàahn 左右做人難 (lit.) not know whether to take sides on the left or the right 不知站在左邊或是右邊好

(idi.) PH be in a dilemma, be a friend with a saint and a devil 順得哥情失嫂意 : *Ngóh a mā yiu tùhng ngóh jyuh, daahnhaih ngóh taaitáai m̀jūngyi tùhng ngóh a mā jyuh, ngóh jānhaih ~ la.* (My mother wants to live with me but my wife doesn't like to live with her. This time I am really ~.)

kēui 區 N/PW area, district 地區 M go

1831 ✓

➜hùhngfāan kēui 紅蕃區 (lit.) red Indian region 紅蕃區

(idi.) N/PW the outlaw territory 不法之徒聚居的地方 M go : *Nīdouh haih ~, hóudō m̀sāam m̀sei ge yàhn hái nīdouh chēutyahp.* (It is ~ here where many bad guys come and go.)

la 罅 N slit, chink 縫隙 M tiuh

1832

➜jáu faatleuht la 走法律罅 (lit.) go in and out through the slit of law 鑽法律的縫隙

(idi.) PH find loopholes in law and do things by means of them 利用法律的漏洞做事 : *Ngóhdeih gūngsī yījūk faatleuht jouhyéh, m̀ ~ ge.* (Our company strictly comply with the law. We don't ~.)

Làuh 樓 BF building 樓房

1833 ✓

➜làuhhah 樓下 (lit.) PW downstairs, ground floor (not for an address) 樓下

(idi.) A (for prices) below, within (用於價錢)以下，以內：*Nī jek gúpiu, yāt baak mān ~ jauh hóyíh yahpfo.* (You can buy this stock when/if it is ~ $100.) (*The opposite of 'làuhhah' is 'làuhseuhng'.)

louh 路 N road 道路 M tìuh

1834 ✓

➜sahpjih louhháu 十字路口 (lit.) N/PW crossroads 十字路口 M go

(idi.) N a situation in which one finds it hard to make a decision 難於抉擇的情況 M go：*Ngóh yihgā hái go ~ douh, m̀jī yìhmàhn hóu yīkwaahk làuhhái Hēunggóng hóu.* (I'm now at the ~. I don't know whether it is better for me to emigrate or stay in Hong Kong.)

1835

➜séilouh yāttìuh 死路一條 (lit.) the road of death 是一條死路

(idi.) PH no way out, no remedy (for a situation) 沒有出路：*Gūngsī yùhgwó gaijuhk sihtlohkheui, jauh jíyáuh ~ ge la, jīkhaih jāplāp lō.* (If our company goes on losing money, it will have ~. That means it will be closed down.)

1836

➜yáuh louh 有路 (lit.) there is a road 有一條路

(idi.) VO have an affair with 有染 (指男女有不正當關係)：*Kéuihdeih/ Kéuih tùhng kéuih ~.* (They ~ each other./ He ~ her.)

mùhn 門 N door 門 M douh; jek

1837

➜jáu hauhmún 走後門 (lit.) go by the back door 從後門走進去

(idi.) PH (do something) by unfair means such as to make use of personal connections 用不正當手段例如人事關係去做事：*Yùhgwó jiu jing sáujuhk, néih yáuh pàaih dōu meih dāk a, bātyùh ~ lā, táiháh sīkdāk mēéh yàhn bōng néih lā.* (According to the regular procedure, you have to wait for a long time. You'd better do it ~. See if you know anyone who can help you.)

nàahm 南 PW south 南

1838

➜chīngām nàahn máaih heung nàahm làuh 千金難買向南樓 (lit.) PH a thousand taels of gold cannot buy a flat that faces south 千金難買向南樓

(idi.) PH a flat with the main door or windows facing south is most desirable 向南的房子最受歡迎 (*The Fung Shui of such houses is considered to be very good.)：*Nīgo dāanwái yáuh hóudō heung nàahm ge chēung, sóyíh gwaidī, ~ ā ma.* (There are a lot of windows facing south in this flat, so it is more expensive. As you know, ~.)

seuhng 上 **PW up, above** 上

1839

→seuhngtàuh 上頭 (lit.) up, above 上頭, 上面
(idi.) N superior 上司 : *Ngóhdeih fongga, yiu* ~ *pāijéun sīnji dāk.* (We need the approval of our ~ before we can take leave.)

taap 塔 **N tower** 塔 **M go**

1840 ✓

→jeuhngngàh taap 象牙塔 (lit.) N ivory tower 象牙塔 M go
(idi.) N/ PW university campus 大學校園 M go : *Daaihhohksāang yīnggōi jáuchēut* ~, *dōdī jipjūk séhwúi sīnji dāk.* (University students should get out of the ~, and get in touch with the people of the community.) (* 'Jeuhngngàh taap' is said with a negative implication because it refers to a place of elegance but no connection with the outside world.)

tīnmàhntòih 天文台 **N/PW observatory** 氣象局 **M go**

1841 ✓

→tīnmàhntòih 天文台 (lit.) N/PW observatory 氣象局 M go
(idi.) N a look-out (who keeps watch) 通風報訊的人 : *Ngóhdeih hái nīdouh hōi dóudong, néih jouh* ~, *hāujyuh yáuh chāaiyàhn làih jauh tūngjī ngóhdeih.* (We set up a gambling den here, and you work as the ~. You keep watch and tell us if there is any policeman coming.)

waihji 位置 **N/PW position, location** 位置 **M go**

1842 ✓

→waihji 位置 (lit.) N/ PW position, location 位置
(idi.) N (in horse-racing in Hong Kong) finish first, second or third, be placed (賽馬中)得第一, 第二或第三名: *Nījek haih láahng máh, yùhgwó jungjó / páaudóu* ~ *dōu géi hóu fān.* (It is a dark horse. You can get a lot of dividend if it ~.)

IV. Sìhgaan (time)

chōyāt sahpngh 初一十五 PH the first and the fifteenth day of a lunar month 陰曆每月的第一及第十五天

1843
→néih jouh chōyāt, ngóh jouh sahpngh 你做初一，我做十五 (lit.) you do it on the first day of the (lunar) month, and I will do it on the fifteenth 你做初一,我做十五
(idi.) PH tit for tat 以牙還牙：*Néih deui ngóh hóu, ngóh deui néih hóu, yùhgwó m̀haih jauh ~, ~.* (I'll be nice to you if you are nice to me. Otherwise, it'll be ~, ~.)

1844
→nghsìh fā, luhksìh bin 五時花，六時變 (lit.) change at five and six o'clock 五時六時都有變化
(idi.) PH change one's mind easily 很容易改變主意：*"Kéuih wah gāmnihn heui Ngāujāu léuihhàhng." "Kéuih (nīgo yàhn) ~, ~, chìhdī yauh m̀jī wah heui bīndouh lo."* ("He said he would take a trip to Europe." "He ~, ~. Later he would say he'll go somewhere else.")

dím 點 TW o'clock 點(鐘)

1845 ✓
→sahpsāam dím 十三點 (lit.) TW (Greenwich time) 13:00 標準時間十三時
(idi.) Adj. (said of a girl) not ladylike 女子不端莊嫻淑：*Néih m̀hóu gam ~*

lā, yùhgwó m̀haih dī naàhmjái m̀wúih jēui néih ge la. (Try to behave like a lady. Otherwise, boys will not court you.) N a girl who is not ladylike 不端莊嫻淑的女子 M go：*Kéuih nīgo jìngyāt haih ~ làih ge.* (She is really ~.)

gāang 更 M watch of the night 更

1846
→sāamgāang kùhng, nghgāang fu 三更窮，五更富(lit.) be poor at midnight and rich at dawn 三更窮,五更富 (*Sāamgāang is the third watch of the night, i.e. 11:00p.m.–1:00a.m. Nghgāang is the fifth, i.e. 3:00–5:00a.m.)
(idi.) PH (said of a person) financial situation is unstable 指人經濟狀況不穩定：*Jouh ngóhdeih gīnggéi nīhòhng, ~, ~, yáuh haak jauh dōdī sāuyahp, móuh haak jauh móuh sāuyahp.* (As brokers, our ~. We'll earn more money if we have clients. We won't have any income if there is none.) also see 0734

jīu máahn 朝晚 TW morning and evening/night 早上跟晚上

1847
→jīu gin háu, máahn gin mihn 朝見口，晚見面 (lit.) can see each other's mouth and face in the morning and at night 早上晚上都會見面
(idi.) PH can see each other very often 經常都會見面：*Gaaklèih lèuhnse, ~,*

~, *sóyíh yiu wòhhāp sēungchyú.* (Neighbors ~, so they should try to get along well together.)

1848

→jīu hòhng máahn chaak 朝行晚拆 (lit.) make up a bed in the morning and tear it down/put it back at night 早上把床弄好睡覺,晚上拆掉它

(idi.) PH house is so small that there is even not enough space for a bed 房子小得連床也不夠地方放 : *Ngóhdeih yātgā géi háu jyuh gam sai ge dāanwái, yáuh yàhn yiu fan jipchòhng, ~ lō.* (We are a family of five or six, and we live in such a small flat. Some of us have to sleep in folding beds at night and put them back in the morning.) (*Note that there is an interesting displacement of time words in this idiom. Readers may find it more logical if 'Jīu' and 'máahn' exchange with each other.) also see 0264

1849

→jīu jung syuh, máahn gaai báan 朝種樹,晚剝板(lit.) start to grow a tree in the morning and saw its wood in the evening 早上植樹,晚上把樹木鋸成木塊

(idi.) PH one's income is so low that it is spent soon after it is received, live from hand to mouth 收入微薄,不足溫飽 : *Ngóhdeih nīdī chóugān gāaichàhng, jing sówaih ~, ~, juhng bīndouh yáuh chín jihng ā!* (We people from the grassroot class live the way as the saying goes, ~. How could it be possible for us to have money left over?)

1850

→wán jīu m̀dāk máahn 搵朝唔得晚 (lit.) although one can earn money in the morning, one is still penniless in the evening 早上雖然賺到錢,可是晚上仍然沒錢用

(idi.) PH one's income is so small that one has to lead a hard life, live from hand to mouth 收入太微薄,生活困難 : *Kéuih béi gūngsī cháaujó jīhauh, yihgā jíhaih jouh gīmjīk, ~.* (After he was fired by his company, he just did part-time job. His situation is like ~.)

nìhn 年 N/M year 年

1851

→dūng daaihgwo nìhn 冬大過年(lit.) winter is bigger than year 冬比年大

(idi.) PH the winter solstice is more important than the (Chinese) New Year 冬至比新年更重要 : *Gāmmáahn jouh dūng, geidāk fāanlàih sihkfaahn a, ~ ā ma.* (We'll have rich dinner for the winter solstice tonight. Remember to come home to eat, because ~.) also see 0967 and 0998

sìh 時 TW hour, o'clock 時辰

1852 ✓

→hoihsìh chēutsai 亥時出世 (lit.) PH born at 9–11p.m. 在亥時出生

(idi.) PH/ N (the time) a spoiler/ trouble-maker (is born) 製造麻煩的人(出生的時間) : *Kéuih sìhngyaht cháhwóh ngóhdeih ge gaiwaahk, jingyāt ~.* (He spoils our plans all the

305

time. He is really a ~.) (* "Hoihsìh" is one of the twelve two-hour periods in each day used by the Chinese to tell the time before the invention of clocks.) also see 1853

1853

➔sàhnsìh máauh/ máuhsìh 辰時卯時 (lit.) 7–9 a.m. and 5–7 a.m. 辰時和卯時

(idi.) TW at any time (used in a negative sense) 任何時間(意思比較是負面的)：*Kéuih haih maih jānhaih gam dō yéh jouh a? ~ dōu wah m̀dākhàahn.* (Does he really have so many things to do? He said he was busy every time I asked him.) (*Like 'hoihsìh', 'sàhnsìh' and 'máuhsìh' are among the two-hour periods of the day.)

1854

➔sìhsàhn baatjih 時辰八字 (lit.) time and the eight symbols 時辰及八字
(idi.) PH see 1613

yaht 日 N/M day 天

1855 ✓

➔daih(yih)yaht 第(二)日 (lit.) TW the next day 翌日

(idi.) TW (1) some other day 改天：*Ngóh yihgā yiu jáu la, ~ joi kīng lā.* (I have to go now. Let's talk ~.) (2) in the future 將來：*Néih yihgā m̀gáaudihm kéuih, ~ jauh màhfàahn ge la.* (If you don't get it worked out now, you'll have trouble ~.)

1856 ✓

➔yātyaht 一日 (lit.)TW one day 一天

(idi.) A (1) all the time 整天：~ háidouh dágēi, m̀jouh gūngfo. (He plays TV games ~ and doesn't do his homework.) (2) all in one word 總之：~ dōu haih néih m̀hóu, gaau kéuih sihkyīn, gáaudou kéuih yihgā hohkm̀aaih kāpduhk. (~, it's all your fault. You taught him to smoke and now he even has begun to take drugs.) (3) as long as 只要：Néih ~ hái kéuih sáuhah jouhyéh jauh ~ dōu yiu tēng kéuih wah, chèuihfēi néih m̀lōu jē. (You have to follow his instructions ~ you work under him, unless you quit.)

yuht 月 N month 月, 月份 M go

1857 ✓

➔baatyuht sahpngh 八月十五 (lit.) TW the fifteenth day of the eighth lunar month (i.e. Mid-Autumn Festival) 中秋節

(idi.) N (said of human body) bottom, buttocks 臀部, 屁股 M go：ditchān go ~ (fall on one's ~ and get hurt)

V. Gāautūng (traffic)

bouh 步 **M step** 步

1858

→daaih bouh laamgwo 大步
躝過 (lit.) make a big cross over
(with one's legs) 大步跨過
(idi.) PH escape/ stay away from
misfortune 僥倖逃過厄運 ： *Nīchi
gūngsī chòihyùhn móuh ngóh fán, hó
syunhaih ~.* (I was almost laid off by
our company. I consider it an ~.)

1859

→gin bouh hàahng bouh 見步
行步 (lit.) see a step, walk one step
見一步走一步
(idi.) PH play it by ear, improvise 根
據實際情況而採取行動 ： *Ngóh
lámlàih lámheui dōu lám m̀dóu
baahnfaat gáaikyut nīgihn sih,
wàihyáuh ~ hái lā.* (I thought about it
over and over, and yet I don't know
what to do. All I can do is ~.)

1860

→yāt yàhn hàahng yāt bouh
一人行一步 (lit.) each one walks
a step 每個人走一步
(idi.) PH reach a compromise, give
way 大家讓步, 妥協, 找折衷的辦
法 ： *Lèihfān ge fūfúh jāang léuhng
go jáinéui ge fúyéuhngkyùhn. Sāumēi,
~, múih yàhn fuhjaak yātgo.* (The
divorced couple battled over the
custody of their two children. Later,
they ~. Each of them has custody of
one child.)

chē 車 **N car, vehicle; traffic**
車子, 車輛; 交通 **M ga**

1861

→cháauchē 炒車 (lit.) fry a car
把車子炒
(idi.) VO (1) have car accident,
usually not very serious 汽車發生意
外,通常不太嚴重 ： *Kéuih hōichē taai
faai sóyíh ~.* (He drove too fast and so
he ~.) (2) (said of a racing car) turn
over or run off the track 賽車時車子
翻側或滑出跑道 ： *Kéuih ga chē
yātlouh líhng sīn daahnhaih hái go gáp
wāandouh ~.* (His car was leading all
the way but it ~ at a sharp turn.)

1862

→chēsāangsaai 車生晒 (lit.)
car full of life 車充滿生氣
(idi.) PH same as 1593 and 1804

1863

→chóh seuhnfūng chē 坐順風
車 (lit.) ride in a favorable wind
car 坐順風而行的車子
(idi.) VO get free rides in other
people's cars 坐其他人的順路的車:
Ngóh hó m̀hóyíh ~ néih ~ a? (Can
you give me a ride?)

1864 ✓

→séuhngchē 上車 (lit.) VO get
on vehicles 登上車輛
(idi.) VO (the first time to) be a flat
buyer/owner （第一次）置業 ：
*Hēunggóng jingfú hóu séung bōng
gódī jyuhhái gūngguhng ngūkchyūn
ge yàhn ~.* (The Hong Kong

government would try their best to help those living in the public housing estates to buy a flat.)

chēutyahp 出入 **V go in and out, come and go** 出入

1865 ✓

→chēutyahp 出入 (lit.) V come/ go in and out, come and go 出入

(idi.) N difference 不同之處 M dī : *Néih góng ge tùhng bún syū só góng ge yáuh dī ~.* (There is a little ~ between what you say and what the book says.)

dīksí 的士 **N taxi** 計程車 **M ga/bouh**

1866

→dīklàih dīkheui 的嚟的去 (*Here 'dīk' [from 'dīksí'] has become a verb.) (lit.) PH come and go by taxi 來去都坐計程車 : *"Ngóh chóh dīksí heui yauh chóh dīksí fāan."* *"~ dōu géi haih chín ge bo."* ("I went by taxi and came back by taxi, too." "You ~. It's quite expensive.") also see 0079 and 0080

fēigēi 飛機 **N airplane** 飛機 **M ga**

1867 ✓

→chóh jihksīnggēi 坐直升機 (lit.)VO ride on a helicopter 坐直升機

(idi.) VO be a high flyer 升職很快 : *"Kéuih làihjó ngóhdeih gūngsī móuh géi nói jauh sīngjouh gīngléih la."* *"Wa! ~."* ("He was promoted to manager shortly after he joined our company." "Wow! He ~.") also see 1494

1868

→fong fēigēi 放飛機 (lit.) fly an airplane 放飛機

(idi.) VO fail to show up for an appointment 沒有赴約 : *A-Chán yeukjó ngóhdeih, daahnhaih kéuih jihgéi móuh làih, ~ ngóhdeih ~/ ngóhdeih béi kéuih ~.* (Chan made an appointment with us, but he didn't come. He ~.)

gāautūng dāng 交通燈 **N traffic light** 交通燈號 **M jáan**

1869

→gāautūng dāng→dím hùhng dím luhk 交通燈→點紅點綠 (lit.) traffic light→with red and green on and off 交通燈→有時紅色,有時綠色

(idi.) HIT a person who fools others into doing this or that 愚弄別人做這做那的人 : *"Kéuih yauh giu ngóh máaih nījek gúpiu, yātjahngāan yauh giu ngóh máaih daihyih jek."* *"Néih mhóu tēng kéuih góng a, kéuih jingyāt haih ~ → ~."* ("He told me to buy this stock, and then he told me to buy another one." "Don't listen to him. He just ~ → ~.")

gwái 軌 **BF railtrack** 車軌

1870 ✓

→dihnchē gwái 電車軌 (lit.) N tram tracks 電車的路軌 M tiuh (idi.) N wrinkles on the forehead 額上皺紋 M tiuh : *Ngaahktàuh seuhngbihn yáuh léuhngtiuh ~, séung myihng lóuh dōu mdāk la.* (There are two ~. I have to admit that I am old even though I don't want to.)

hàahng/hàahnglouh 行/行路 V/VO walk 走路

1871

→hàahngbīt 行咇 (lit.) walk on 'beat' 依着拍子走路

(idi.) VO (said of a policeman) out on his beat, on patrol (警察)執行 巡邏任務 : *Kéuih gāmyaht ~ gójahnsìh, táigin yáuh cháak dágip ngàhnhòhng.* (Today when he was ~, he saw some thieves robbing a bank.) (* 'Bīt' is the transliteration of 'beat'.)

1872

→hàahnglouh dá doutan 行路 打倒褪 (lit.) walk but find oneself going backwards 走路竟向後退

(idi.) PH fail to progress or even worse, retrogress 事情不但沒有進展, 還倒退 : *Nīpáai wahnhei yíngjān chā, ~. Yíhwàih bōsí wúih gāsān, dímjī gáamsān; táibaahk hahgo yuht hóyíh gūngyùhn chàhng láu, dímjī ngàhnhòhng ngāamngāam gāsīk, yiu gūngdō géi kèih tūm.* (I'm having bad luck these few days, ~. I was expecting a pay raise, but my boss gave me a paycut. I would have finished paying all the instalments on my flat next month, but the interest rate has just increased, and I now have to pay a few more instalments.)

laahm 纜 N cable, thick rope 纜 M tiuh

1873

→daaih laahm dōu gáaumàaih 大纜都攪唔埋 (lit.) even a big cable cannot tie them together 連大的纜繩都沒法把它們連結在一起

(idi.) PH there's absolutely no link between 事情之間一點關連也沒有: *Gógāan daaihhohk ge haauhjéung cháau yàuhyú tùhng kéuihge jái sīngdāk gam faai, nī léuhnggihn sih ~, dímgáai néih yiu gaapngáang jēung kéuihdeih lāaimàaih yātchái góng jē?* (~ the dismissal of the president of that university and his son's being a high flyer [at the same university]. Why do you insist on putting these two things together?)

lauhhei 漏氣 VO puncture, leak out air 洩氣, 漏氣

1874 ✓

→lauhhei 漏氣 (lit.) VO puncture, leak out air 洩氣, 漏氣

(idi.) Adj. (said of a person) slow in doing things, fail to do things immediately 指人做事慢吞吞, 不立即做 : *Kéuih jouhyéh hou ~ ga. Néih yiu chēuiháh kéuih sīnji dāk.* (He is ~. You really need to rush him.)

ngohn 岸 PW river bank, seashore 岸邊

1875 ✓

→léuhngtàuh m̀dou ngohn 兩頭唔到岸 (lit.) PH cannot reach either side of the river bank 兩邊岸都去不到

(idi.) PH get stuck midway, achieve neither one 中途給卡住了, 東不成西不就 : *Hohkhaauh búnlòih haih yuhng Yīngmán gaausyū ge, yihgā dahtyihn yiu gói yuhng móuhyúh gaauhohk, gáaudou dī hohksāang ~.* (English was the medium of instruction in this school. However, it suddenly switched to [our] mother language [i.e. Chinese]. Now the students are competent in neither one of the language.)

1876 ✓

➔séuhngngohn 上岸 (lit.) VO get on shore 上岸

(idi.) VO attain one's goal 達到目的 : *"Ngóh ngāamngāam gūngyùhn chàhng láu." "Néih jauh hóu lā, ~ jó ~. Ngóh juhng ngàaihgán."* ("I've just finished paying off all the instalments on my flat." "It's great that you can ~. I'm still suffering [from paying the instalments on my flat].")

syùhn 船 N boat, ship 船 M jek

1877

➔daap chàhmsyùhn 搭沉船 (lit.) board a ship and thus cause it to sink 登上一艘船卻因此令它沉沒

(idi.) PH (in gambling) bet together with another person or ask him to place a bet for you, and thus ruining his good luck, and causing him to lose money (賭錢時) 與他人一起下注, 或叫他替你下注, 卻因此破壞他的運氣令他輸錢 : *Néih yèhnggán chín, m̀hóu bōng kéuih máaih máh, gēng kéuih ~.* (You are winning money so far, so don't bet on any horses for him. I'm afraid he won't bring you good luck and will make you lose money.)

1878

➔syùhn dou kiuhtàuh jihyìhn jihk 船到橋頭自然直(lit.) PH when the ship reaches the head of the bridge, it will go straight naturally 船到橋頭自然直

(idi.) PH leave it to chance/ let things slide 順其自然,不必著急 : *"Ngóh geijó géibaak fūng kàuhjīk seun dōu meih yáuh wùihyām." "Óh, ~. Yáuhdī yéh haih m̀sāmgāpdāklàih ga."* ("I've sent hundreds of letters applying for jobs, yet I haven't gotten any reply." "You'd better ~. Sometimes you shouldn't worry so much.") also see 0437 and 1342

tāai 呔 N tyre 輪胎 M go

1879✓

➔baautāai 爆呔 (lit.) VO tyre punctures 輪胎洩氣

(idi.) VO (trousers) rip 衣服爆裂 : *Kéuih jeuk gótiuh fu taai jaak, yāt wāandāi sān jauh ~ jó ~.* (The trousers that he wore were so tight that they ~ when he bent down.)

táaih 軚 N steering wheel 軚盤, 方向盤 M go

1880 ✓

➔jyun/ jyúntáaih 轉軚 (lit.) VO turn the steering-wheel (of a car or a ship) 把(汽車或船的)方向舵輪轉動/轉向

(idi.) VO (said of people) shift one's ground, change attitude 改變立場或態度 : ⓐ *Yíhchìhn kéuih tùhng ngóhdeih yātchàih wah bōsí sēui ge, yìhgā kéuih sīngjó kāp, ngóh pa kéuih ~ jó ~ dōu m̀dihng lo.* (He used to join us in criticizing our boss. Now he has been promoted. I'm afraid he probably has ~.) ⓑ *Gógo jingdóng búnlòih fáandeui jingfú syūyahp ngoihdeih jyūnchòih ge, daahnhaih*

gahnlòih hóuchíh ~ jó ~ gám bo!
(That political party was against the government's policy of importing foreign experts into the territory. But recently, it seems that it has ~.)

yáu 油 N gasoline 汽油 M gūngsīng; gāléun

1881 ✓

→ gāyáu 加油 (lit.) VO refill a car with petrol/ gasoline (汽車)加油
(idi.) VO (1) (hailed by cheering teams) Go! Go! Go! 比賽時啦啦隊的吶喊 (2) work harder, put more effort into 努力些, 加把勁 : *Néih nīpáai hóuchíh teuibouhjó bo. Néih yiu ~ sīnji dāk la.* (It seems that your performance is not as good as it was before. You need to ~.)

Romanization Index

diu yìhmséui 吊鹽水 1027;
1768

diuyú 釣魚 0088

dō go hēunglòuh dō jek gwái 多個 1143
香爐多隻鬼

dohksān dehngjouh 度身定做 0694

dohkséui 度水 1448

doihdoih pìhngngōn 袋袋平安 1355

dóng 薰 1683

dōnghāak 當黑 0881

dōsām 多心 0637

dō sáu 多手 0723

dō sáu dō geuk 多手多腳 0407;
0724

dou diu dōu móuh dihk mahkséui 1427
倒吊都冇滴墨水

dou hàuh ṁdou fai 到喉唔到肺 0388;
0492

douh gōu yāt chek, mō gōu yāt 1188
jeuhng 道高一尺，魔高一丈

dōujái geu daaih syuh 刀仔鋸大 1359
樹

dóumáih 倒米 1006

dóumáih sauhsīng 倒米壽星 1007

dóusé lòh háaih 倒瀉籮蟹 0075

duhk séi syū, séi duhksyū, duhksyū 1089
séi 讀死書，死讀書，讀書死

duhk sípín 讀屎片 1090

duhkwaaih sīsyū 讀壞詩書 1091

duhnghéi chòhngbáan 戙起床 1326
板

dūk buijek 篤背脊 0376

dūk ngáahn dūk beih 篤眼篤鼻 0369;
0554

dūksou 篤數 1652

dūng daaihgwo nihn 冬大過年 1851

dūnggā ṁdá dá sāigā 東家唔打 1250
打西家

dūnggwā dauhfuh 冬瓜豆腐 0981

dyúnsin 短線 1481

fā 花 1533

faahntúng 飯桶 1499

faahnwún 飯碗 1518

faai dōu jáam lyuhn màh 快刀斬 1360
亂麻

faaigwo dájām 快過打針 1767

fāanbáan díp 翻版碟 1352

fāanfūng lohkyúh 翻風落雨 1552

fāangwái(lóu) 番鬼(佬) 1144

fāangwáilóu tái bóng→ dou sóu daih 1668
yāt 番鬼佬睇榜→倒數第一

fáangwāt 反骨 0441

fáan háu fūk siht 反口覆舌 0455

fáanjyun jyūtóuh yātmihn sí 反轉 0216
豬肚一面屎

fáanmín 反面 0520

faat chín hòhn 發錢寒 1310

faatchòih laahpbán 發財立品 1237

faatfó 發火 1540

faat gāi màahng mè 發雞盲咩 0113

faat ngāpfūng 發茄風 1553

faatsīu yáu 發燒友 1741

faatwān 發瘟 1782

fā dō ngáahn lyuhn 花多眼亂 0555

fāfā gūngjí 花花公子 1534

fāfā lūklūk 花花綠綠 1535

fagwātlùhng 化骨龍 0271

fàhnfalòuh 焚化爐 1423

fahohk 化學 1096

faht dōu yáuh fó 佛都有火 1134

faht háu sèh sām 佛口蛇心 0031;
0456

319

321

gōumóu 高帽 1433

gúheidói 鼓氣袋 1356

guhk 焗 0926

gūhòhn gwái 孤寒鬼 1147

gúlóuh dong sihhīng 古老當時興 1259

gūng bāt lèih pòh, ching bāt lèih 1322
tòh 公不離婆，秤不離砣

gūnghéi faatchòih, laihsih dauhlòih, 1357
yāt mān ṁngoi, sahp mān
doihlohk dói 恭喜發財，利是
逗來，一蚊唔愛，十蚊袋落袋

gūngjái mihn 公仔麵 1383

gūngjái sēung 公仔箱 1384

gūnjái gwātgwāt 官仔骨骨 0442

gūnjih léuhnggo háu 官字兩個口 0458

gútùhngsīk 古銅色 0880

gúwaahkjái 蠱惑仔 1697

gwā 瓜 0983

gwāanyàhn 關人 1757

gwaatchín 刮錢 1314

gwahtméih lúng→gáau fūng gáau 0272
yúh 掘尾龍→攪風攪雨

gwái 鬼 1148

gwāidáan 龜蛋 0062

gwái dá gam 鬼打咁 1149

gwái dá gwái 鬼打鬼 1150

gwái fó gam leng 鬼火咁靚 1151

gwái gam 鬼咁 1152

gwāigūng 龜公 0063

gwáigwáidéi 鬼鬼哋 1153

gwáigwái máhmáh 鬼鬼馬馬 0302

gwáigwái syúsyú 鬼鬼祟祟 1154

gwaihdeih wai jyūná/ lá 跪地餵豬 0219
乸

gwáijái 鬼仔 1155

gwái jē ngáahn 鬼遮眼 1156

gwáilóu 鬼佬 1157

gwái máh 鬼馬 0303

gwáimūi 鬼妹 1158

gwái ńgh máh luhk 鬼五馬六 0304

gwái paak hauhméih jám 鬼拍後尾 1159
枕

gwāipó 龜婆 0064

gwáipòh 鬼婆 1160

gwái sēng gwái hei 鬼聲鬼氣 1161

gwái séuhngsān 鬼上身 1162

gwái sihk làih gám sēng 鬼食泥噉 1163
聲

gwáisyú 鬼祟 1164

gwáitàuhjái 鬼頭仔 1165

gwái waahk fùh 鬼劃符 1166

gwa laahpngáap 掛臘鴨 0166

gwán 滾 0927

gwánséui luhk geuk 滾水淥腳 0413

gwánséui luhk jyūchéung 滾水淥 0220
豬腸

gwāt 骨 0443

gwātbei 骨痺 0444

gwāttùh dágú 骨頭打鼓 0445

gwātyuhk 骨肉 0446;
0839

gwa yèuhngtàuh maaih gáuyuhk 0197;
掛羊頭賣狗肉 0362

gwodihn 過電 1348

gwogāai lóuhsyú, yàhnyàhn haam 0263
dá 過街老鼠，人人喊打

gwogwāt 過骨 0447

gwohòhjēut 過河卒 1801

gwojó hói jauh sàhnsīn 過咗海就 1213
神仙

gwojyú 過主 1712

gwo láahnghòh 過冷河 0929

323

329

330

mòuhsīnggáu ngáauhséi yàhn 無聲狗咬死人	0205	
móuh yeuhk yī 冇藥醫	1785	
móuh yíhsing 冇耳性	0828	
móuh yím gāilùhng→jihchēut jihyahp 冇掩雞籠→自出自入	0144	
móuh yīugwāt 冇腰骨	0834	
m̀pa gūn, ji pa gún 唔怕官，至怕 管	1690	
m̀pa máih gwai, ji pa wahn jaih 唔怕米貴，至怕運滯	1011	
m̀pa sihn chòih nàahn sé, ji pa pòuhsaat m̀lèhng 唔怕善財難 捨，至怕菩薩唔靈	1189	
m̀pa yātmaahn, ji pa maahnyāt 唔怕一萬，至怕萬一	1629	
m̀sāam m̀sei 唔三唔四	1632	
m̀seun geng 唔信鏡	1374	
m̀sihk yèuhngyuhk yātsān sōu 唔食羊肉一身臊	0364	
m̀sīk tái yàhn mèih tàuh ngáahn ngaahk 唔識睇人眉頭眼額	0545; 0571	
m̀tái jāng mihn dōu tái faht mihn 唔睇僧面都睇佛面	1136	
m̀tēng kéuih jī dék 唔聽佢枝笛	1114	
m̀tōng m̀séui 唔湯唔水	1021	
muhk 木	1578	
muhkduhk 木獨	1579	
muhkháu muhkmihn 木口木面	0536	
muhkmuhk duhkduhk 木木獨獨	1580	
mùhnháugáu 門口狗	0206	
múhn tīn sàhn faht 滿天神佛	1137	
mùihgwaihùhng(sīk) 玫瑰紅(色)	0897	
m̀yiu mín 唔要面	0537	
nàahmyàhn lóuh gáu 男人老九	1734	
nàahmyàhnpòh 男人婆	1735	

náumàhn 扭紋	1576	
náumàhn chàaih 扭紋柴	1298	
néih ging ngóh yāt chek, ngóh ging néih yāt jeuhng 你敬我一尺，我 敬你一丈	1302	
néih jouh chōyāt, ngóh jouh sahpng̀h 你做初一，我做十五	1843	
néih yáuh bun gān, ngóh yáuh baat léung 你有半斤，我有八両	1372	
néih yáuh Jēung Lèuhng gai, ngóh yáuh gwochèuhng tāi 你有張良 計，我有過牆梯	1493	
néui 女	1739	
néuih tùhngji 女同志	1749	
néuihyán tōngyún 女人湯丸	1023	
ngaahktàuh seuhngbihn séjyuh 額頭上便寫住	0546	
ngáahn 眼	0572	
ngáahnbaahk 眼白	0573	
ngáahn baahkbaahk 眼白白	0574	
ngáahn bātgin wàih jihng 眼不見 爲淨	0575	
ngáahn daaih tái gwolùhng 眼大睇 過籠	0576	
ngáahnfā 眼花	0577	
ngáahnfāfā 眼花花	0578	
ngáahnfó baau 眼火爆	0579	
ngáahn fut tóuh jaak 眼闊肚窄	0580; 0819	
ngáahn gāmgām 眼甘甘	0581	
ngaahnggéng 硬頸	0398	
ngáahngok gōu 眼角高	0582	
ngáahn gwahtgwaht 眼掘掘	0583	
ngáahn hùhng 眼紅	0584	
ngáahn jáamjáam 眼斬斬/眨眨	0585	
ngáahnjái lūklūk 眼仔碌碌	0586	

335

sāmgōnding 心肝蒂		0688
sāmhòhn 心寒		0666
sāmjūk 心足		0667
sāmlèuhng 心涼		1573
sāmngāp 心嗌		0668
sāmséui 心水		0669;
		1457
sām sīsī 心思思		0670
sāmsyūn 心酸		0671
sāmtáahm 心淡		0672
sāmtàuh gōu 心頭高		0673
sāmtàuh hou 心頭好		0674
sāmyúhn 心軟		0675
sām yūkyūk 心郁郁		0676
sān 身		0708
sānfú wánlàih jihjoih sihk 辛苦搵		1043
嚟自在食		
sān gūn séuhngchèuhng sāambá fó		1549
新官上場三把火		
sān gwōng géng leng 身光頸靚		0402;
		0709
sānhàhn 身痕		0710
sān joih fūk jūng bāt jī fūk 身在福		0711
中不知福		
sānsáu 新手		0742
sān síhāang 新屎坑		0773
sān síhāang dōu yáuh sāamyaht		0774
hēung 新屎坑都有三日香		
sān yáuh sí 身有屎		0712
sá taaigihk 耍太極		1126
sātāan lóuhsyú 沙灘老鼠		0270
sātsih gaapmaahn 失匙夾萬		1489
sāttàuh daaihgwo béi 膝頭大過		0714
脾		
sāttàuh gíu ngáahnleuih 膝頭搩眼		0715
淚		

sātwàhn 失魂		1225
sātwàhn lohkpaak		1226
失魂落魄		
sātwàhnyú 失魂魚		0097
sáu 手		0743
sáubáan haih yuhk, sáubui dōu haih		0744;
yuhk 手板係肉，手背都係肉		0843
sauchòih/chói yuh lóuhfú, yàhmsī		0259
dōu yàhm m̀lāt 秀才遇老虎，吟		
詩都吟唔甩		
sauchói sáugān→bāau syū 秀才		1443
手巾→包(書)輸		
sauchói yàhnchìhng jí yātjēung		1745
秀才人情紙一張		
sauchói yuhdóu/ jeuhk bīng, yáuh		1746
léih syut bāt chīng 秀才遇倒/着		
兵，有理說不清		
sáudō 手多		0745
sáu dōdō 手多多		0746
sáu dō geuk dō 手多腳多		0428;
		0747
saudou hóuchíh tiuh chàaih gám		1300
瘦到好似條柴噉		
saufā jámtàuh 繡花枕頭		1398
sáugán 手緊		0748
sáugeuk m̀hóu 手腳唔好		0429;
		0749
sáugwā héi jín 手瓜起膜		0750
sáuhah 手下		0751
sáuhei 手氣		0752
sauhsīng 壽星		1218
sauhsīnggūng diugéng→yìhm		0403
mehng chèuhng 壽星公吊頸→		
嫌命長		
sauh yàhn chìhnchòih, tai yàhn		1239
sīujōi 受人錢財，替人消災		

344

yáuh chín (dōu) móuh mehng héung/sái 有錢(都)冇命享/使	1320	yàuh tàuh dou méih 由頭到尾	0514; 0806
yáuh chín sáidāk gwái tēui mòh 有錢使得鬼推磨	1183	yáuh tàuhfaat bīngo séung jouh laatlēi ā 有頭髮邊個想做癩痢吖	0808
yáuh(fāan) géiháh sáansáu 有(番)幾吓散手	0764	yáuh tàuh yáuh mihn/ mín 有頭有面	0542; 0807
yáuh fānsou 有分數	1665	yáuh wún wah wún, yáuh dihp wah dihp 有碗話碗，有碟話碟	1523
yáuh fūng sáijeuhn léih 有風駛盡球	1557	yáuh (yāt) leih bīt yáuh (yāt) hoih 有(一)利必有(一)害	1270
yáuh gāijái m̀gún gún màh/ ngàh yīng 有雞仔唔管管麻／牙鷹	0152	yèhchoifā 椰菜花	0942
yàuh gōn séui 游乾水	1470	yèhchoitàuh 椰菜頭	0943
yáuh gwāt lohk deih/ déi 有骨落地	0449	yeh gwái 夜鬼	1184
yáuh jaan móuh tàahn 有讚冇彈	1123	yeuhk yiu yàhn bāt jī, chèuihfēi géi mohk wàih 若要人不知，除非己莫為	1267
yáuh jih m̀joih, ló fú làih sān 有自唔在，攞苦嚟辛	1274	yèuhnggú 羊牯	0366
yáuh laaht yáuh m̀laaht 有辣有唔辣	1083	yèuhngmòuh chēutjoih yèuhng sānseuhng 羊毛出在羊身上	0367
yáuh louh 有路	1836	Yidaaihleih pāidohng 意大利批盪	1437
yauh lùhng yauh ngá 又聾又啞	1772	yíh 耳	0830
yáuh mòuh yáuh yihk 有毛有翼	0174	yíhbīn fūng 耳邊風	0831
yáuh ngáahn bātsīk Taaisāan 有眼不識泰山	0600	yih dá lúk 二打六	1675
yáuh ngáahn mòuh jyū 有眼無珠	0601	yíhjái yúhn 耳仔軟	0832
yáuhsām 有心	0680	yíhjyū 耳珠	0833
yáuh sām m̀pa chìh, sahpyuht dōu haih baaimihn sìh 有心唔怕遲，十月都係拜年時	0681	yihmchōng tóudeih/ déi→ hàahmsāp baakfú 鹽倉土地→鹹濕伯父	1223
yàuhséui 游水	1471	yìhnāai 二奶	1737
yàuhséui hā 游水蝦	0070	yih ńgh jái 二五仔	1705
yàuhséui hóisīn 游水海鮮	0992	yih/sāam háu luhk mihn 二／三口六面	0490
yàuhséui yú 游水魚	0102		
yáuhsīk ngáahngeng 有色眼鏡	1435	yihsahp/yah sei haau lóuhgūng 二十／廿四孝老公	1693
yáuh tàahn móuh jaan 有彈冇讚	1124		
yáuh tàahn yáuh jaan 有彈有讚	1125		